Lecture Notes in Com

Edited by G. Goos, J. Hartman

Advisory Board: W. Brauer   D. C

DATE DUE FOR RETURN		

Springer

Berlin
Heidelberg
New York
Barcelona
Budapest
Hong Kong
London
Milan
Paris
Tokyo

Hubert Comon Jean-Pierre Jouannaud (Eds.)

Term Rewriting

French Spring School of Theoretical Computer Science
Font Romeux, France, May 17-21, 1993
Advanced Course

Springer

Series Editors

Gerhard Goos
Universität Karlsruhe
Vincenz-Priessnitz-Straße 3, D-76128 Karlsruhe, Germany

Juris Hartmanis
Department of Computer Science, Cornell University
4130 Upson Hall, Ithaca, NY 14853, USA

Jan van Leeuwen
Department of Computer Science, Utrecht University
Padualaan 14, 3584 CH Utrecht, The Netherlands

Volume Editors

Hubert Comon
Jean-Pierre Jouannaud
Laboratoire de Recherche en Informatique, Université de Paris Sud
Bat. 490, F-91405 Orsay, France

CR Subject Classification (1991): F.4.2

ISBN 3-540-59340-3 Springer-Verlag Berlin Heidelberg New York

CIP data applied for

© Springer-Verlag Berlin Heidelberg 1995
Printed in Germany

Typesetting: Camera-ready by author
SPIN: 10485595   06/3142-543210 - Printed on acid-free paper

Preface

This volume contains the proceedings of the French Spring School of Theoretical Computer Science held in Font Romeu in May 1993.

The 1993 school was devoted to rewriting in a broad sense. Rewriting is now an important subfield of computer science, relating to many other areas such as formal languages, models of concurrency, tree automata, functional programming languages, constraints, symbolic computations and automated deduction. All these trends were represented at Font Romeu, and invited to contribute to this volume.

The school was organized by Hubert Comon, Jean-Pierre Jouannaud, Jacques Sakarovitch, and Géraud Senizergues for scientific matters, with the help of Patrick Sallé and Colette Ravinet for the local arrangements. There were 19 presentations at the school, among which two were already published, and two others were not submitted in time. Most papers survey a particular area of term or string rewriting, but some contributions contain new technical material. The first two lectures, by Jean-Pierre Jouannaud and Nachum Dershowitz, are introductory surveys on term rewriting. The next two, by Gerard Lallement and Yuri Matiyasevich, are dedicated to word problems for Thue systems. The papers by Hélène Kirchner and Bruno Courcelle survey various extensions of rewriting to congruence classes of terms, graphs, etc. Géraud Senizergues and Max Dauchet explore the relationships between rewriting, grammars, and tree automata. Michael Bertold and Volker Diekert study rewriting techniques for trace languages. Robert Gilman and Philippe Le Chenadec investigate two different approaches to the use of rewriting techniques in group theory. Claude Marché relates rewriting techniques to Gröbner bases computations. Yves Lafont describes a very novel view of rewriting where the tree structure of terms is replaced by two-dimensional diagrams. Philippe Balbiani and Luis Fariñas del Cerro apply rewriting techniques to affine geometry. Finally, Jean-François Rey contributes to the resolution of an old conjecture for Burnside monoids.

We thank Maurice Nivat for inviting us to organize this school and suggesting that it should bring together term rewriting and string rewriting people at least. Although both communities are usually not attending the same events, they have a lot in common, and these days revealed many potential collaborations between them.

The school was sponsored by CNRS, PRC de Programmation, PRC Mathématiques et Informatique, Université de Paris-Sud, and Université Paris 6. We also thank the referees for their work.

Orsay, March 1995   Hubert Comon and Jean-Pierre Jouannaud

Table of Contents

Introduction to Rewriting 1
 Jean-Pierre Jouannaud (Université de Paris Sud)

33 Examples of Termination 16
 Nachum Dershowitz (University of Illinois at Urbana-Champaign)

The Word Problem for Thue Rewriting Systems 27
 Gerard Lallement (Pennsylvania State University)

Word Problem for Thue Systems with a Few Relations 39
 Yuri Matiyasevich (Steklov Institute of Mathematics)

Some Extensions of Rewriting 54
 Hélène Kirchner (CRIN-CNRS and INRIA-Lorraine)

Graph Rewriting: A Bibliographical Guide 74
 Bruno Courcelle (Université de Bordeaux I)

Formal Languages and Word-Rewriting 75
 Géraud Sénizergues (Université de Bordeaux I)

Rewriting and Tree Automata 95
 Max Dauchet (Université de Lille I)

**On Efficient Reduction Algorithms for Some Trace Rewriting
Systems** 114
 Michael Bertol and Volker Diekert (Universität Stuttgart)

Automatic Groups and String Rewriting 127
 Robert H. Gilman (Stevens Institute of Technology)

A Survey of Symmetrized and Complete Group Presentations 135
 Philippe Le Chenadec (INRIA-Rocquencourt)

**Normalized Rewriting - Application to Ground Completion
and Standard Bases** 154
 Claude Marché (Université de Paris Sud)

Equationnal Reasoning with Two-Dimensional Diagrams 170
 Yves Lafont (Laboratoire de Mathématiques Discrètes, Marseille)

**Affine Geometry of Collinearity and Conditional Term
Rewriting** 196
    Philippe Balbiani and Luis Fariñas del Cerro
    (CNRS et Université Paul Sabatier)

**Burnside Monoids, Word Problem and the Conjecture
of Brzozowski** 214
    Jean-François Rey (Université de Paris 6)

Introduction to Rewriting

Jean-Pierre Jouannaud[1]

Laboratoire de Recherche en Informatique, Bat. 490, Université de Paris Sud,
91405 Orsay, France. Email: `jouannaud@lri.fr`

1 Introduction

The use of equations is traditional in mathematics. Its use in computer science
has culminated with the success of algebraic specifications. It is also used for the
axiomatic description of various calculi used in computer science and logic.

Equations can be used for reasoning, by using Leibnitz's law of replacing equals
by equals, a highly non-deterministic way of using equations. In contrast, rewriting
uses the equations in one way, hence eliminating one source of non-determinism.
This one way use is achieved by rewriting according to a well-founded ordering on
terms, hence it is called a reduction. The other sources of non-determinism, choice of
an equation, and of a subterm at which to rewrite can be eliminated as well if every
expression has a unique irreducible form. In this case, rewriting defines a functional
computation.

The theory of rewriting which originates from algebra, theorem proving and
computability theory centers therefore around the notion of normal form, an
expression that cannot be reduced any further. For example, groups are usually
defined by a set of three equations:

$$(x \cdot y) \cdot z \; = \; x \cdot (y \cdot z) \qquad x \cdot x^- \; = \; 1 \qquad x \cdot 1 \; = \; x$$

or, better, by a set of ten rewrite rules defining normal forms:

$$
\begin{aligned}
(x \cdot y) \cdot z &\to x \cdot (y \cdot z) & (x \cdot y)^- &\to y^- \cdot x^- \\
x \cdot x^{-1} &\to 1 & x^- \cdot x &\to 1 \\
x \cdot 1 &\to x & 1 \cdot x &\to x \\
x^- &\to x & 1^- &\to 1 \\
x \cdot (x^- \cdot y) &\to y & x^- \cdot (x \cdot y) &\to y
\end{aligned}
$$

This set of rules is both uniformly *terminating* and *confluent*, which allows to
compute a unique normal form for any expression, and to compare two expressions by
checking their respective normal forms for equality (hence deciding the word problem
for free groups). This procedure is clearly effective, in contrast with replacing equals
by equals which is not.

Obtaining the set of rules automatically from the set of equations is called
completion. The algorithm is due to Knuth and Bendix as well as the above set
of rules for groups [20].

---

[*] This work was parly supported by the PRC "Prrogrammation", and the ESPRIT working
group COMPASS.

This paper surveys the core of rewriting theory. There are many other results worth knowing, such as the relationships between rewriting and automata (see M. Dauchet's paper in this volume), the use of rewriting as a programming language (see [26, 11, 15]), string rewriting (well represented in this volume), other forms of rewriting (see the contributions by H. Kirchner and C. Marché in this volume).

2 Equations and Rewrite Rules

We recall here standard notions about rewrite relations, equations and rewrite rules. Substitutions use greek letters in postfix notation, with Σ standing for the set of substitutions. $\mathcal{T}$ (resp. $\mathcal{G}$) denotes the set of (resp. ground) terms. $\mathcal{P}os(t)$ denotes the set of positions in the term t, $s|_p$ denotes the subterm of s at position p, and $s[t]_p$ the replacement of $s|_p$ by t in s. See [7] for missing notations and definitions.

2.1 Rewrite relations

A binary relation $\rightarrow$ over a set of terms $\mathcal{T}$ is a *rewrite relation* if it is closed both under context application and instantiation, that is

$$\forall s, t, u \in \mathcal{T}, \forall p \in \mathcal{P}os(t), \forall \sigma \in \Sigma, s \rightarrow t \Rightarrow u[s\sigma]_p \rightarrow u[t\sigma]_p.$$

The inverse, symmetric closure, reflexive closure, and transitive closure of any rewrite relation are also rewrite relations. An ordering on terms which satisfies the above property will be called a *rewrite ordering*. An equivalence on terms which satisfies the above property is a *congruence*.

Rewrite relations on terms can be generated by equations, that is unordered pairs of terms, if they are symmetric or else by rewrite rules, that is ordered pairs of terms. So, rewrite rules really differ from equations in their use.

2.2 Equations

Equation are pairs of terms written $l \simeq r$. Let E be a set of equations.

A term s *rewrites* to a term t at position p using an equation $l \simeq r \in E$, if there exist a substitution σ such that $s|_p = l\sigma$, and $t = s[r\sigma]_p$, or $s|_p = r\sigma$, and $t = s[l\sigma]_p$. The *equational proof step* between s and t is written $s \xrightarrow[l \simeq r]{p} t$ in the first case, and $s \xrightarrow[r \simeq l]{p} t$ in the second. We may drop the subscripts or superscripts, use E as a subscript if the actual equation is not important, as well as describe a position by a predicate if necessary (such as $=$ for 0 or 1 step). The sequence $s \xleftrightarrow[E]{*} t$ of equational proof steps between s and t is called a proof, and $\xleftrightarrow[E]{*}$ is the congruence relation generated by E.

The semantics of equations is a particular case of the semantics of first-order predicate logic in which the only predicate symbol is interpreted as the equality. As a consequence, models are algebras rather than first-order structures.

2.3 Rules

Rewrite rule are pairs of terms written $l \to r$. Let R be a set of rewrite rules.

A term s *rewrites* to a term t at position p using a rule $l \to r$ if there exist a substitution σ such that $s|_p$ is the *redex* $l\sigma$, and $t = s[r\sigma]_p$. We write $s \xrightarrow[l \to r]{p} t$ or $t \xleftarrow[l \to r]{p} s$. We may also write $s \underset{R}{\longleftrightarrow} t$ for $s \underset{R}{\longrightarrow} \cup \underset{R}{\longleftarrow} t$, hence using rules as equations. The *derivation relation* $\underset{R}{\xrightarrow{*}}$ is the reflexive transitive closure of the above rewrite relation, while $\underset{R}{\xleftrightarrow{*}}$ is the congruence relation generated by R. The sequence of rewrite steps $s \underset{R}{\xleftrightarrow{*}} t$ is called a *proof*.

For example, given the signature $0, S, +$ for specifying the natural numbers with addition, and the usual rules for defining the addition of two natural numbers, we have the proof:

$$S(x) + 0 \xrightarrow[x+0 \to x]{\Lambda} S(x) \xleftarrow[x+0 \to x]{1} S(x+0) \xleftarrow[x+S(y) \to S(x+y)]{\Lambda} x + S(0)$$

Definition 1. We say that s and t are *convertible* when there is a proof $s \underset{R}{\xleftrightarrow{*}} t$. Proof shapes are depicted by appropriate names: $s \underset{R}{\xrightarrow{*}} u \underset{R}{\xleftarrow{*}} t$ is called a *valley* or *rewrite proof*, in which case we say that s and t are *joinable*, $s \underset{R}{\xrightarrow{=}} u \underset{R}{\xleftarrow{=}} t$ is a *flat* or *diamond proof*, $u \underset{R}{\longleftarrow} s \underset{R}{\longrightarrow} v$ is a *peak*, and $u \underset{R}{\xleftarrow{*}} s \underset{R}{\xrightarrow{*}} v$ is a *mountain*.

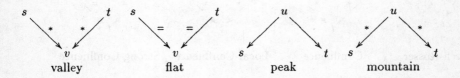

valley　　　　　flat　　　　　peak　　　　　mountain

Fig. 1. Proof Shapes.

Note that a rewrite proof is simply a proof with no peak. The proof in the previous example is a rewrite proof.

We say that a term s is reducible if it contains a redex, and *irreducible* (in *normal form*) otherwise. We denote by $s\downarrow$ a normal form for s, that is an irreducible term t such that $s \underset{R}{\xrightarrow{*}} t$, and we say that R is *functional* (*normalizing*) if every term has a unique computable R-normal form.

3 Confluence Properties

Functionalityis crucial. Unfortunately, it is undecidable and indeed very difficult to obtain. We will therefore approximate it, either from above by strengthening it, or from below, by relaxing it. In both cases, it is useful to study first abstract properties of relations.

3.1 Abstract confluence properties

The uniqueness of normal forms, whether they exist or not, is related to a confluence property of some kind depicted on figure 2:

Definition 2. A relation $\rightarrow$ is said to be:

Church-Rosser if every proof enjoys a rewrite proof:
$\forall u, v \; s.t. \; u \overset{*}{\longleftrightarrow} v, \; \exists t \; s.t. \; u \overset{*}{\longrightarrow} t \overset{*}{\longleftarrow} v,$

confluent if every mountain enjoys a rewrite proof:
$\forall u, s, v \; s.t. \; u \overset{*}{\longleftarrow} s \overset{*}{\longrightarrow} v, \; \exists t \; s.t. \; u \overset{*}{\longrightarrow} t \overset{*}{\longleftarrow} v,$

locally confluent if every peak enjoys a rewrite proof:
$\forall u, s, v \; s.t. \; u \overset{*}{\longleftarrow} s \overset{}{\longrightarrow} v, \; \exists t \; s.t. \; u \overset{*}{\longrightarrow} t \overset{*}{\longleftarrow} v,$

strongly confluent if every peak enjoys a diamond proof:
$\forall u, s, v \; s.t. \; u \longleftarrow s \longrightarrow v, \; \exists t \; s.t. \; u \overset{=}{\longrightarrow} t \overset{=}{\longleftarrow} v,$

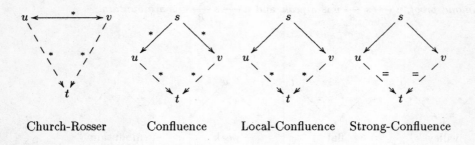

| Church-Rosser | Confluence | Local-Confluence | Strong-Confluence |

Fig. 2. Confluence Properties.

These properties are intimately related. First of all, the Church-Rosser property and confluence are equivalent as can be easily shown by induction on the length of an arbitrary proof (or better on $\longleftrightarrow_{mul}$ which allows a single use of the induction argument). Confluence and local confluence are not equivalent in general, as shown on the picture 3. They are equivalent when the relation $\rightarrow$ is terminating, a result known as Newmann's lemma [24], whose proof by induction on $\rightarrow$ is pictured below.

Definition 3. A relation $\rightarrow$ is said to be *terminating* (*strongly normalizing*) if there exists no infinite sequence of related elements $t_1 \rightarrow t_2 \rightarrow \ldots \rightarrow t_i \rightarrow \ldots$.

Theorem 4. *Assume* $\rightarrow$ *is terminating. Then* $\rightarrow$ *is confluent iff it is locally confluent.*

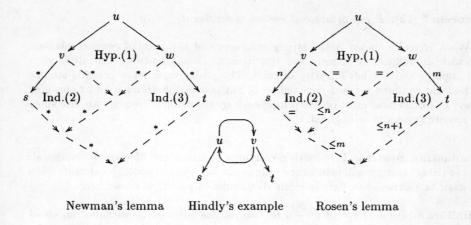

Newman's lemma   Hindly's example   Rosen's lemma

Fig. 3. Newman's and Rosen's Lemmas.

The alternative to termination is the use of strong confluence, a result due to Rosen [27] which can be proved by using a tiling argument as shown on picture 3.

Theorem 5. *A relation → is confluent if it is strongly confluent.*

Although strong confluence appears to be very special, it is often used to prove the confluence of a relation → by applying it to another relation ⇒ having the same transitive closure as →. This applies in particular to the pure lambda-calculus, and more generally to combinatory reduction systems in the sense of Klop [19].

3.2 Confluence properties of rewrite relations

In practice, what really matters is to have functionality for ground terms. We therefore will distinguish two kinds of confluence properties of a rewrite relation, on $\mathcal{T}$ called *Church-Rosser* and *confluence*, and on $\mathcal{G}$ called *ground Church-Rosser* and *ground confluence*. Ground confluence, however, is undecidable even for terminating relations. In contrast, confluence can be more easily grasped, and we will see that it is indeed decidable for terminating rewrite relations.

Orthogonal Systems

Definition 6. A rewrite system R is *linear* if the left-hand side of each rule in R is linear, *overlapping* if a left-hand side unifies with a renamed non-variable subterm of any other left-hand side or with a renamed proper subterm of itself, and *orthogonal* if it is both left-linear and non-overlapping.

The importance of orthogonal systems lies in the following result:

Theorem 7 [12]. *Every orthogonal system is confluent.*

What is really shown is the strong confluence of the parallel rewrite relation, in which all redexes in a term are rewritten at once thanks to the absence of overlappings and the left-linearity of rules. The strong confluence proof is similar to the local confluence proof depicted on 5, but convertible terms s and t can now always be joined in at most one step from each by rewriting all redexes at once since the rewrite system is orthogonal.

Terminating Systems Terminating confluent systems are of course functional: any rewriting strategy will lead to the unique normal form. Besides, local confluence can itself be restricted to finitely many distinguished peaks, as shown now:

Definition 8. Let $l \to r$ and $g \to d$ be two rewrite rules (with variables renamed apart) and σ a most general unifier of g and a nonvariable subterm $l|_p$ of l. Then the peak $r\sigma \xleftarrow[l \to r]{\Lambda} l\sigma \xrightarrow[g \to d]{p} l\sigma[d\sigma]_p$ is said *critical*, and the equation $r\sigma \simeq l\sigma[d\sigma]_p$ is called a *critical pair*. We use $cp(R)$ for the set of all critical pairs between rules in R.

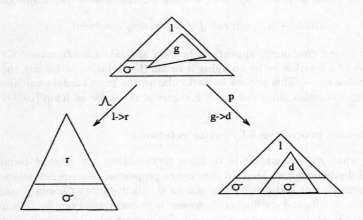

Fig. 4. Critical Pair.

Note that a finite rewrite system R has a finite set $cp(R)$ of critical pairs, and that there are "trivial" critical pairs in the above definition, when overlapping a rule with itself at the root.

Theorem 9 [20]. *A rewrite system is locally confluent if and only if all its critical pairs are joinable.*

The proof is depicted on figure 5

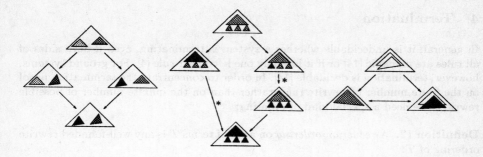

Fig. 5. Critical Pair Lemma.

Therefore, a terminating system is confluent if and only if all its critical pairs are joinable, a decidable property.

For the group theory obtained by orienting the three afore mentionned equations from left to right, there are four critical pairs of which two are confluent and the other two are not. Check how associativity overlaps itself yielding one of the two joinable critical pairs.

Canonical systems Rewrite systems which are both terminating and confluent are called *convergent*. We now consider an additional property in order to characterize a rewrite system under a given order.

Definition 10. A system R is *reduced* if the following terms are irreducible:
the right-hand side r of each rule $l \to r \in R$, and
any term s properly encompassed into a left-hand side l of a rule $l \to r \in R$.
A confluent, terminating, and reduced rewrite system is called *canonical*.

In particular, a strict subterm of a left-hand side must be irreducible in a reduced system. Note also that a reduced system may contain two rules $l \to r$ and $l' \to s$ such that l' is a renaming of l. In contrast, this is not possible in a canonical system due to confluence. Canonical systems have an interesting uniqueness property, an observation first made by Lankford:

Theorem 11 [22]. *Suppose R and S are two canonical (not necessarily finite) rewrite systems having the same equational theory. Suppose further that the combined system $R \cup S$ is terminating. Then R and S must be the same (up to renaming of variables).*

This result has important consequences (see section 5). Its proof is routinely obtained by expressing that each rule in R has a rewrite proof in S and vice versa.

4 Termination

In general, it is undecidable whether a system is terminating, even if both sides of all rules are monadic [14] or if it has only one left-linear rule [4]. For ground systems, however, termination is decidable [14]. In order to concentrate the termination proof on the finite number of rewrite rules rather than on the infinite number of possible rewrites, we need a special kind of ordering:

Definition 12. A *reduction ordering* on a set of terms T is any well-founded rewrite ordering of T.

Termination is assured if each of the rules in R is contained in a reduction ordering; conversely, if R is terminating, then the relation $\xleftrightarrow[R]{+}$ itself is a reduction ordering.

Rewrite ordering are necessary for proving termination of rules which may apply at subterms. Rules applying always at the top, of which PROLOG is a particular case do not require well-founded orderings closed under replacement. Similarly, ground rules do not require well-founded orderings closed under instantiation.

We therefore need to provide with powerful enough reduction orderings that will enable us to solve the practical cases we may face with. A popular method for designing reduction orderings is by interpreting terms in some well-founded set, the set of terms being a particular case. We will insist here in *divide and conquer* methods for building term orderings, based on the use of functionals that preserve well-founded orderings. There are three major ones.

Lexicographic extension The *lexicographic extension* transforms n well-founded orderings $>_1, \ldots, >_n$ on n sets $S_1, \ldots, S_n$ into a well-founded ordering $(>_1, \ldots, >_n)_{lex}$ on the product $S_1 \times \ldots \times S_n$, by letting:

$$(a_1, \ldots, a_n)(>_1, \ldots, >_n)_{lex}(b_1, \ldots, b_n) \text{ if}$$

$$a_1 >_1 b_1 \text{ or } a_1 = b_1 \text{ and } (a_2, \ldots, a_n)(>_2, \ldots, >_n)_{lex}(b_2, \ldots, b_n)$$

We use to write $>_{lex}$ when all orderings $>_1, \ldots, >_n$ are the same ordering $>$. This definition extends to quasi-orderings, by using the equivalences associated to the quasi-orderings instead of the syntactic equality.

For example, $>$ (strict subterm) and $\triangleright$ (encompassment, defined as $t \triangleright s$ if a subterm of t is an instance of s and not vice-versa) are well-founded orderings on terms. To prove the claim, we interpret a term t by the pair $\langle |s|, |\{p \in \mathcal{P}os(t) : t|_p \in \mathcal{X}\} - \{\mathcal{V}ar(t)|\}\rangle$, and compare pairs in the lexicographic extension $(>_N)_{lex}$.

Multiset Extension The *multiset extension* transforms any well-founded ordering $>$ on a set S into a well-founded ordering $\geq_{mul}$ on multisets on S. It is defined as the reflexive transitive closure of the relation between two multisets, say M_1 and M_2 such that M_2 is obtained from M_1 by replacing any element x by a finite number (possibly zero) of elements strictly smaller than x in the ordering on S.

Term Extension The *term extension*, also called *recursive path ordering* transforms any well-founded ordering $\succ$ (called a *precedence*) on an alphabet $\mathcal{F}$ of function symbols into a rewrite-ordering $\succ_{rpo}$ on terms in $\mathcal{T}(\mathcal{F})$. To define it, we must first assign a status, lexicographic or multiset to all function symbols in $\mathcal{F}$, therefore split into two subsets *Lex* and *Mul*. The induced ordering is as follows:

$$s = f(s_1, \ldots, s_m) \succeq_{rpo} g(t_1, \ldots, t_n) = t$$

if either of the following (1 or 2 or 3) hold:

(1) $s_i \succeq_{rpo} t$ for some s_i, $i \in [1..m]$
(2) $f = g$ and

case a: $f \in Lex$, and $\begin{cases} s \succ_{rpo} t_1, \ldots, s \succ_{rpo} t_n \\ (s_1, \ldots, s_n)(\succeq_{rpo})_{lex}(t_1, \ldots, t_n) \end{cases}$

case b: $f \in Mul$, and $(s_1, \ldots, s_n)(\succeq_{rpo})_{mul}(t_1, \ldots, t_n)$.
(3) $f \succ g$ and $s \succ_{rpo} t_i$ for all $i \in [1..n]$;

where $s \succ t$ if $s \succeq t$, but $s \not\preceq t$. When the precedence on function symbols is total, then the recursive path ordering is total. The ordering is strict if there are no multiset symbols, and its equivalence is generated by Malcev's permutative axioms for the multiset symbols otherwise. See [6] for a more general version of this ordering mixing syntactic and semantic considerations.

There are two ways to extend the recursive path ordering to a rewrite ordering on terms with variables. The finest extension ($s \succeq_{rpo} t$ iff $s\gamma \succeq_{rpo} t\gamma$ for all ground substitutions γ) turns out to be decidable [3, 17] but NP-hard. The other (polynomial) one is obtained by considering the variables as new constants which do not compare with other function symbols nor between themselves in the precedence.

For example, we can prove the termination of the Ackerman's function by using the lexicographic version of the recursive path ordering:

$$ack(0, y) \to succ(y)$$
$$ack(succ(x), 0) \to ack(x, succ(0))$$
$$ack(succ(x), succ(y)) \to ack(x, ack(succ(x), y))$$

For example, the third rule is contained in $>_{lpo}$ since x occurs in $succ(x)$ and $ack(succ(x), succ(y))$ is lexicographically greater than $ack(succ(x), y)$.

5 Completion of a set of rules

When a terminating set of rules is not locally confluent, non-joinable critical pairs may be simplified, then oriented and added as new rules. Rules may be simplified as well in order to obtain a canonical set. This process is called Knuth-Bendix completion [20]. In completion, the axioms used are therefore in a constant state of flux; these changes are expressed as inference rules, which add a dynamic character to establishing the existence of rewrite proofs. This view of completion, then, has two main components: an inference system, used in the completion process to generate new rewrite rules, and a rewrite relation on proofs, that shows how any proof can be normalized to a rewrite proof, as long as the appropriate rules have been generated.

So, adding new rules by computing critical pairs is simply a tool used to achieve our goal: to transform every proof into a rewrite proof using interreduced rules by rewriting (minimal) subproofs which do not obey the above property. According to [8], we will break the tradition by displaying the proof transformations first, and the inference rules second. Let $\succ$ be our reduction ordering used to orient rules, and $\gg$ the well-founded ordering on rules defined as follows: $s \to t \gg l \to r$ if (i) $s \rhd l$ under the encompassment ordering, or else (ii) $s \doteq l$ and $t \succ r$.

5.1 Completion Proof Rewrite Rules

$$u \longleftarrow s \longrightarrow v \quad \Rightarrow \quad u \xrightarrow{\;*\;} \xleftarrow{\;*\;} v$$
$$if \ u \longleftarrow s \longrightarrow v \ is \ not \ a \ critical \ peak$$

$$u \underset{l \to r}{\overset{q}{\longleftarrow}} s \underset{g \to d}{\overset{q \cdot p}{\longrightarrow}} v \quad \Rightarrow \quad u \underset{r\sigma \simeq l\sigma[d\sigma]_p}{\longleftrightarrow} v$$
$$if \ u \longleftarrow s \longrightarrow v \ is \ a \ critical \ peak$$

$$u \underset{l \simeq r}{\overset{p}{\longleftrightarrow}} v \quad \Rightarrow \quad u \underset{l \to r}{\overset{p}{\longrightarrow}} v$$
$$if \ l \succ r$$

$$u[l\sigma]_p \underset{l \simeq r}{\overset{p}{\longleftrightarrow}} u[r\sigma]_p \quad \Rightarrow \quad u[l\sigma]_p \underset{g \to d}{\overset{p \cdot q}{\longrightarrow}} u[l'\sigma]_p \underset{l' \simeq r}{\overset{p}{\longleftrightarrow}} u[r\sigma]_p$$
$$if \ l \underset{g \to d}{\overset{q}{\longrightarrow}} l'$$

$$u \underset{s \simeq s}{\longleftrightarrow} u \quad \Rightarrow \quad u$$

$$u[l\sigma]_p \underset{l \to r}{\overset{p}{\longrightarrow}} u[r\sigma]_p \quad \Rightarrow \quad u[l\sigma]_p \underset{l \to r'}{\overset{p}{\longrightarrow}} u[r'\sigma]_p \underset{g \to d}{\overset{p \cdot q}{\longrightarrow}} u[r\sigma]_p$$
$$if \ r \underset{g \to d}{\overset{q}{\longrightarrow}} r'$$

$$u[l\sigma]_p \underset{l \to r}{\overset{p}{\longrightarrow}} u[r\sigma]_p \quad \Rightarrow \quad u[l\sigma]_p \underset{g \to d}{\overset{p \cdot q}{\longrightarrow}} u[l'\sigma]_p \underset{l' \simeq r}{\overset{p}{\longleftrightarrow}} u[r\sigma]_p$$
$$if \ l \underset{g \to d}{\overset{q}{\longrightarrow}} l' \ and \ l \to r \gg g \to d$$

In the sequel, we will use $\Rightarrow_{KB}$ for the rewrite relation on proofs generated by the above rules. These proof rewrite rules are built up in a very natural way. The first two express the critical pair lemma. The third is the orientation of an equation into a rule. Note that the critical pair may not yet be an axiom, so it will have to be *generated*. The fourth is the simplification of equations, which again *produces* a new equation while it eliminates an old one making the underlying process of equation and rule generation non-monotonic. The fifth eliminates equations that have become trivial after some simplifications. The sixth reduces rules on the right, in order to achieve canonicity. The last reduces rules on the left, yielding new equations that must be again checked for orientation. The extra condition for the application of this rule is required for proving termination of these proof rewrite rules. So, all proof rewrite rules except the first two change the set of axioms, hence give rise to appropriate inference rules.

5.2 Completion Inference Rules

An *inference rule* (for our purposes) is a binary relation between pairs $(E; R)$, where E is a set of equations and R is a set of rewrite rules. We define the following set KB of six inference rules:

Deduce:	$(E; R) \vdash (E \cup \{s \simeq t\}; R)$	if $s = t \in \mathbf{cp}(R)$
Orient:	$(E \cup \{s \simeq t\}; R) \vdash (E; R \cup \{s \to t\})$	if $s \succ t$
Simplify:	$(E \cup \{s \simeq t\}; R) \vdash (E \cup \{s \simeq u\}; R)$	if $t \to_R u$
Delete:	$(E \cup \{s \simeq s\}; R) \vdash (E; R)$	
Compose:	$(E; R \cup \{s \to t\}) \vdash (E; R \cup \{s \to u\})$	if $t \to_R u$
Collapse:	$(E; R \cup \{s \to t\}) \vdash (E \cup \{u \simeq t\}; R)$	

$$\text{if } s \xrightarrow[l \to r]{p} u \text{ with } s \to t \gg l \to r$$

The role of these inference rules is to make sure that if a left-hand side of a proof rewrite rule matches a particular proof, then that proof can be rewritten. This may not be the case unless E and R contain the additional rules and equations which are needed in the right-hand side of the proof rewrite rule. Adding these equations and rules is the role of the inference rules.

We write $(E; R) \vdash_{KB} (E'; R')$ if the latter may be obtained from the former by one application of a rule in KB.

5.3 Termination

Given a starting set E of equations, let us call $R*$ and $E*$ the smallest set of equations and rules which is closed under the above inference rules. To this set, we can associate the corresponding infinite set of proof rewrite rules defined in section 5.1. The role of these rules is to normalize proofs. Hence, their termination is a crucial property. To this end, let us define an ordering on proofs in which a proof is interpreted as a multiset of elementary proof steps, and a proof step is in turn interpreted by a pair of a multiset and a term as follows:

the equational proof step $s \longleftrightarrow t$ is interpreted by the pair $\langle \{s, t\}, \perp \rangle$;

the rewrite proof step $s \xrightarrow[l \to r]{} t$ is interpreted by the pair $\langle \{s\}, l \to r \rangle$.

Pairs are compared lexicographically, using the multiset ordering $\succ_{mul}$ induced by the given reduction ordering $\succ$ for the first component, and the ordering $\gg$ on rules for the second. Multisets of pairs, measuring the complexity of proofs, are compared by the multiset extension of the ordering on pairs. The ordering on proofs is therefore

$$((\succ_{mul}, \gg)_{lex})_{mul}.$$

Note how this ordering considers the justification of proofs, and not just the terms in it. Since the ordering is built up from well-founded orderings by means of extension that preserve well-founded orderings, the obtained ordering is well-founded. Checking the rules is a usefull exercise.

5.4 Completion Sequences

In practice, the completion rules are usually applied in some order, yielding a *completion sequence* $(E_0; \emptyset) \vdash_{KB} (E_1; R_1) \vdash_{KB} \cdots \vdash_{KB} (E_n; R_n) \cdots$ which may be infinite (completion *diverges*) or finite in case there are no possible non-redundant inferences after some finite step n. In the latter case, completion *succeeds* if $E_n = \emptyset$, and *fails* otherwise.

Completion succeeds when given the following fragment of group theory:

$$x \cdot 1 \simeq x, 1 \cdot x \simeq x, x^- \cdot (x \cdot y) \simeq y,$$

by generating the eight-rule canonical system

$$
\begin{array}{ll}
1 \cdot x \to x & x \cdot 1 \to x \\
x^- \cdot x \to 1 & x \cdot x^- \to 1 \\
1^- \to 1 & (x^-)^- \to x \\
x^- \cdot (x \cdot y) \to y & x \cdot (x^- \cdot y) \to y
\end{array}
$$

using size as the reduction ordering. A completion sequence, in which *Simplification*, *Compose* and *Collapse* are applied eagerly will always succeed for this example. In contrast, completion diverges when given the single following equation $fgfx \simeq gfx$, where f and g are both unary (prefix) operator symbols, by generating rules of the form $fg^n fx \longrightarrow g^n fx$.

Divergence is undecidable [18]. Note that no trick can circumvent divergence except changing the completion ordering, since by canonicity of the obtained set of rules, there cannot exist both a finite and an infinite set of rules defining the same congruence and included in the same well-founded ordering on terms.

5.5 Fairness

The role of the rewrite rules on proofs is to show that every proof is eventually normalized, this is why termination of these rules is crucial, and that normal form proofs are indeed rewrite proofs. For this latter property to hold, an hypothesis is needed, called *fairness*. Let us call *persisting* a rule which is never reduced on the left nor on the right once it has been generated:

$$E_\infty = \bigcup_{i \geq 0} \bigcap_{j \geq i} E_j \qquad R_\infty = \bigcup_{i \geq 0} \bigcap_{j \geq i} R_j$$

A completion sequence is *fair* if the critical peaks formed with the persisting rules are all reducible with respect to the rewrite rules on proofs. This is so, if the corresponding critical pairs have been computed, but this may not be always necessary. If success occurs after a finite number n of steps, then the resulting system is a decision procedure for E_0. In case of divergence, a semi-decision procedure can be obtained if the completion sequence is *fair*:

Theorem 13 [13]. *Given two terms s and t such that $s \stackrel{*}{\underset{E_0}{\longleftrightarrow}} t$, and a fair completion sequence $(E_0; \emptyset) \vdash_{KB} \cdots \vdash_{KB} (E_n; R_n) \cdots$ s.t. E_∞ is empty, there exists an integer i such that s and t have the same normal form with respect to R_j for all $j \geq i$.*

The strategy described below by a regular expression is fair:

$$((\textbf{Collapse}^*; \textbf{Compose}^*; \textbf{Simplify}^*; \textbf{Delete}^*; \textbf{Orient}^*)^*; \textbf{Deduce})^*$$

Efficiency of completion is strongly related to the possibility of eliminating redundant critical pair computations, especially in the context of completion modulo. See [1, 28] for various critical pair criteria and [2, 25, 21] for completion strategies which eliminate redundancy.

6 Solving queries

A convergent set R of rewrite rules for some equational theory E allows one to solve various kinds of queries. A query will be a logical formula built over the equality predicate, to be interpreted in some (possibly quotient of) term algebra ($\mathcal{T}(\mathcal{F})$ or $\mathcal{T}(\mathcal{F},\mathcal{X})$) by the congruence generated by the set E (equivalently R) of axioms. Accordingly, the query will be solved in the quotient under consideration (we may simply say in $\mathcal{T}(\mathcal{F})$ or $\mathcal{T}(\mathcal{F},\mathcal{X})$ in the following, leaving the quotient implicit). We will distinguish queries after their logical complexity. Since conjunctions and disjunctions do not cause particular problems, we will simplify our notations by forgetting about these two connectives, hence consider quantified atomic formulae.

6.1 Word problems and universal queries

Query: $s = t$, where s and t are ground.

This query is solved by computing the normal forms of s and t and comparing them. Such a query is usually called a word problem. Since the convergence property of the set R of rules yields a decision procedure for equality, we can also answer to negated such queries:

Query: $s \neq t$, where s and t are ground.

Word problems generalize to universal queries by considering the variables as new constants thanks to skolemization:

Query: $\forall Var(s,t)\ \ s = t$ or its negation $\exists Var(s,t)\ \ s \neq t$

Note that the equality predicate is implicitly interpreted here in $\mathcal{T}(\mathcal{F},\mathcal{X})$, an algebra with infinitely many free constants. Adding new constants in an arbitrary algebra may not be sound: there are indeed pathological algebras with a decidable word problem for which universal queries are undecidable.

6.2 Existential queries

These queries may have free variables as well as existentially quantified ones:

Query: $\exists X\ \ s = t$, where $X \subseteq Var(s,t)$

The goal here is to find (ground) values for the free variables that make the formula true in the quotient of the Herbrand universe by the congruence generated by a convergent set of rules R. Variables in X are auxiliary variables (*parameters*) whole value is useless. The values of the free variables are supposed to be enumerated by the resolution process. This will be achieved by means of a set of non-deterministic transformation rules (see [7]).

The above technique extends to negative queries, by making use of ground reducibility tests [9].

6.3 Inductive queries

These queries have all their variables universally quantified over ground terms. Inductive queries do not differ from universal queries at the syntactic level, but the equality predicate is interpreted in the quotient of the ground term algebra. Answering to an inductive query normally requires an induction scheme (over the term algebra). This induction scheme can actually be hidden in a completion process.

Query: $\forall X \in \mathcal{T}(\mathcal{F})$ $s = t$, where $X \subseteq Var(s, t)$

For convergent systems R_0, any equation between distinct ground-normal forms is considered to be inconsistent with R_0. The observation that an equation $s = t$ is valid in the initial algebra associated with R_0 iff no inconsistency follows from $R_0 \cup \{s \simeq t\}$ is the basis of the method of inductive theorem proving pioneered by Musser [23]: if there exists a ground-convergent system with the same ground normal forms as R_0, and which presents the same equational theory as $R_0 \cup \{s \simeq t\}$, then inconsistency is precluded.

Solving these queries will therefore be done by adding the equation $s = t$ to the algebra, and completing the set $R_0, \{s \simeq t\}$. To ensure that normal forms are not changed during completion, it will be enough to check the left hand sides of the added rules for ground-reducibility [5, 16]: A term s is *ground reducible* by R at a set of *covering positions* S iff all its ground instances by irreducible substitutions are reducible by R at a position in S. For example, $s(s(x))$ is ground reducible by $s(s(0)) \rightarrow 0$ at the set $\{A, 1\}$ of positions.

Since we are only interested in ground-normal forms, ground-convergence will be enough. As a consequence, not all critical pairs are actually needed. Only those obtained by overlapping with R_0 at a set of covering positions of the generated rules are necessary. This modified completion process may terminate with sucess or diverge, in which two cases the starting equation was an inductive theorem, or fail, or stop with a non-ground-reducible left-hand side, in which case the starting equation was not an inductive theorem [5, 16, 10].

References

1. Leo Bachmair and Nachum Dershowitz. Critical pair criteria for completion. *Journal of Symbolic Computation*, 6(1):1–18, 1988.

2. Leo Bachmair, Harald Ganzinger, Christopher Lynch, and Wayne Snyder. Basic paramodulation and superposition. In Deepak Kapur, editor, *Proc. 11th Int. Conf. on Automated Deduction, Saratoga Springs, NY, LNCS 607*. Springer-Verlag, June 1992.

3. Hubert Comon. Solving symbolic ordering constraints. *International Journal of Foundations of Computer Science*, 1(4):387–411, 1990.

4. Max Dauchet. Simulation of a turing machine by a left-linear rewrite rule. In *Proc. 3rd Rewriting Techniques and Applications, Chapel Hill, LNCS 355*, 1989.

5. Nachum Dershowitz. Applications of the Knuth-Bendix completion procedure. In *Proceedings of the Seminaire d'Informatique Theorique*, pages 95–111, Paris, France, December 1982.

6. Nachum Dershowitz and Charles Hoot. Topics in termination. In *Proc. 5th Rewriting Techniques and Applications, Montréal, LNCS 690*, 1993.

7. Nachum Dershowitz and Jean-Pierre Jouannaud. Rewrite systems. In J. van Leeuwen, editor, *Handbook of Theoretical Computer Science*, volume B, pages 243–309. North-Holland, 1990.

8. Hervé Devie. Une approche algébrique de la réécriture de preuves équationnelles et son application à la dérivation de procédures de complétion. Thèse de Doctorat, Université de Paris-Sud, France, Octobre 1991.

9. Maribel Fernández. Narrowing based procedures for equational disunification. *Applicable Algebra in Engineering Communication and Computing*, 3:1–26, 1992.

10. Laurent Fribourg. A strong restriction of the inductive completion procedure. *Journal of Symbolic Computation*, 8:253–276, 1989.

11. Kokichi Futatsugi, Joseph Goguen, Jean-Pierre Jouannaud, and Jose Meseguer. Principles of OBJ2. In *Proc. 12th ACM Symp. Principles of Programming Languages, New Orleans*, 1985.

12. Gérard Huet. Confluent reductions: abstract properties and applications to term rewriting systems. *Journal of the ACM*, 27(4):797–821, October 1980.

13. Gérard Huet. A complete proof of correctness of the Knuth-Bendix completion algorithm. *Journal of Computer and System Sciences*, 23:11–21, 1981.

14. Gérard Huet and Dallas S. Lankford. On the uniform halting problem for term rewriting systems. Research Report 283, INRIA, March 1978.

15. Gérard Huet and Jean-Jacques Lévy. Computations in orthogonal term rewriting systems. In Gordon Plotkin and Jean-Louis Lassez, editors, *Computational Logic: essays in Honour of Alan Robinson*. MIT Press, 1990.

16. Jean-Pierre Jouannaud and Emmanuel Kounalis. Automatic proofs by induction in theories without constructors. *Information and Computation*, 82(1), July 1989.

17. Jean-Pierre Jouannaud and Mitsuhiro Okada. Satisfiability of systems of ordinal notations with the subterm property is decidable. In *Proc. 18th Int. Coll. on Automata, Languages and Programming, Madrid, LNCS 510*, 1991.

18. Hélène Kirchner and M. Hermann. Meta-rule inference from crossed rewrite systems. Draft version, presented at CTRS, Montreal, 1990.

19. Jan Willem Klop. Term Rewriting Systems. In S. Abramsky, Dov.M. Gabbay, and T.S.E. Maibaum, editors, *Handbook of Logic in Computer Science*, volume 2, pages 1–116. Clarendon Press, 1992.

20. Donald E. Knuth and Peter B. Bendix. Simple word problems in universal algebras. In J. Leech, editor, *Computational Problems in Abstract Algebra*, pages 263–297. Pergamon Press, 1970.

21. Claude Marché. Réécriture modulo une théorie présentée par un système convergent et décidabilité des problèmes du mot dans certains classes de théories équationnelles. Thèse de Doctorat, Université de Paris-Sud, France, 1993.

22. Y. Métivier. About the rewriting systems produced by the knuth-bendix completion algorithm. *Information Processing Letters*, 16(1):31–34, 1983.

23. D. Musser. Proving inductive properties of abstract data types. In *Proc. 7th ACM Symp. Principles of Programming Languages, Las Vegas*, 1980.

24. M. H. A. Newman. On theories with a combinatorial definition of 'equivalence'. *Ann. Math.*, 43(2):223–243, 1942.

25. Robert Nieuwenhuis and Albert Rubio. Basic superposition is complete. In B. Krieg-Bruckner, editor, *Proc. European Symp. on Programming, LNCS 582*, pages 371–389, Rennes, 1992. Springer-Verlag.

26. M. J. O'Donnell. *Equational Logic as a Programming Language*. MIT Press, 1986.

27. Barry K. Rosen. Tree-manipulating systems and church-rosser theorems. *J. of the Association for Computing Machinery*, 20(1):160–187, January 1973.

28. H. Zhang. Automated proof of ring commutativity problems by algebraic methods. *Journal of Symbolic Computation*, 9:423–427, 1990.

33 Examples of Termination[*]

Nachum Dershowitz

Department of Computer Science, University of Illinois, Urbana, IL 61801, USA

Abstract. A graded sequence of examples—presented in a uniform framework—spotlights stages in the development of methods for proving termination of rewrite systems.

Let T be the set of all terms over some vocabulary. A *rewrite system* over T is a (finite or infinite) set of *rules*, each of the form $l \rightarrow r$, where l and r are terms containing variables ranging over T. A rule $l \rightarrow r$ applies to a term t in T if a subterm s of t matches the left-hand side l with some substitution σ of terms in T for variables appearing in l. The rule is applied by replacing the *redex s* in t with the corresponding right-hand side $r\sigma$ of the rule, to which the same substitution σ of terms for variables has been applied. We write $t \rightarrow u$ to indicate that the term t in T *rewrites* in this way to the term u in T by a single application of some rule. Note that more than one rule can apply to t and rules can apply at more than one subterm s. Rewrite systems have long been used as decision procedures for validity in equational theories, that is, for truth of an equation in all models of the theory. They are also used as a specification and programming language. See [Dershowitz and Jouannaud, 1990; Klop, 1992; Plaisted, 1993] for recent surveys of term-rewriting and some of its applications.

A rewrite system is *terminating* if there are no infinite derivations $t_1 \rightarrow t_2 \rightarrow t_3 \cdots$. Termination is undecidable. A proof of termination must take into consideration the many different possible rewrite sequences permitted by the *nondeterministic* choice of rules and subterms. We present a series of examples culled from the literature to illustrate the progression of techniques used to prove termination of vanilla-flavored rewriting.[1] We describe these techniques in a manner designed to highlight similarities and follow a logical sequence that is not perfectly chronological. Not covered here are methods based on transformations of the given system, including those for more intricate forms of rewriting (notably, when permutation of operands of associative-commutative operators is permitted prior to rewriting). A survey of termination methods for rewriting may be found in [Dershowitz, 1987].

Example 1 (Loops). T. Evans [1951] gave the first rewrite-based decision procedure,

---

[*] Research supported in part by the U. S. National Science Foundation under Grants CCR-90-07195 and CCR-90-24271.

[1] I apologize for not providing the provenance of many of the examples.

using these dozen rules to compute normal forms:

$$
\begin{aligned}
x\backslash x &\rightarrow e & x\cdot(x\backslash y) &\rightarrow y \\
x/x &\rightarrow e & (y/x)\cdot x &\rightarrow y \\
e\cdot x &\rightarrow x & x\backslash(x\cdot y) &\rightarrow y \\
x\cdot e &\rightarrow x & (y\cdot x)\backslash x &\rightarrow y \\
e\backslash x &\rightarrow x & x/(y\backslash x) &\rightarrow y \\
x/e &\rightarrow x & (x/y)\backslash x &\rightarrow y \;.
\end{aligned}
$$

This system obviously terminates, since application of any rule to any redex in t decreases the size (number of symbols) $|t|$ of t. To quote Evans, "[T]he effect of an elementary reduction is to reduce the length of a word by at least 1." □

Example 2 (Fragment of Group Theory). Similarly,

$$
\begin{aligned}
1\cdot x &\rightarrow x & x\cdot 1 &\rightarrow x \\
x^-\cdot x &\rightarrow 1 & x\cdot x^- &\rightarrow 1 \\
1^- &\rightarrow 1 & (x^-)^- &\rightarrow x \\
x^-\cdot(x\cdot y) &\rightarrow y & x\cdot(x^-\cdot y) &\rightarrow y
\end{aligned}
$$

terminates, since

$$
s\rightarrow t \Rightarrow |s| > |t| \;.
$$

Note that it is not enough for every rule's left-hand side to be longer than its right-hand side. If the right-hand side has more occurrences of some variable than does the left, as in a rule like $(x^-)\cdot y \rightarrow y\cdot y$, then an application like $a^-\cdot(a\cdot a) \rightarrow (a\cdot a)\cdot(a\cdot a)$ causes an increase in size.

The size (length) ordering has been particularly popular in work on semigroups, for which $|l| > |r|$, for each rule $l\rightarrow r$, suffices to ensure termination. □

Example 3. Clearly, measures other than size can be used. For example,

$$
f(f(x)) \rightarrow g(f(x))
$$

terminates, since the number of f's decreases. □

Example 4. The lexicographic combination of well-founded orderings is well-founded, so one can show termination of

$$
\begin{aligned}
f(f(x)) &\rightarrow g(f(x)) \\
g(g(x)) &\rightarrow f(x)
\end{aligned}
$$

by considering the pair $\langle \text{size}, \textbf{number of } f\text{s}\rangle$. □

Example 5. In general, one can use any measure $[\![\cdot]\!] : \mathcal{T} \rightarrow W$ such that

$$
s\rightarrow t \Rightarrow [\![s]\!] \succ [\![t]\!] \;,
$$

where $\succ$ is a well-founded ordering on W. For example,

$$
f(f(x)) \rightarrow f(g(f(x)))
$$

terminates, since the number of adjacent f's decreases, regardless of what is substituted for x, or what context surrounds $f(f(x))$. □

Example 6. To show termination of

$$f(g(x)) \rightarrow g(g(f(x)))$$
$$f(g(x)) \rightarrow g(g(g(x))) ,$$

we can use the suggestion of S. Gorn [1973] and consider the tuple of heights (distance from constants in the tree representation of the term) of the fs. Moving an f right decreases the height of that f while increasing the height of fs to its left, so we compare the heights lexicographically: $\langle$**number of fs, height of rightmost f, . . . , height of leftmost f**$\rangle$. □

Example 7 (Dutch National Flag). Consider the rules:

$$w(r(x)) \rightarrow r(w(x))$$
$$b(r(x)) \rightarrow r(b(x))$$
$$b(w(x)) \rightarrow w(b(x)) .$$

The term can be viewed as an integer in base 3, with "blue" $b = 2$, "white" $w = 1$, and "red" r and any other symbol appearing in a term as 0. □

Example 8 (Differentiation). One of the problems on a qualifying exam given by R. Floyd at Carnegie-Mellon University in 1967 was to prove termination of

$$Dt \rightarrow 1$$
$$D(\text{constant}) \rightarrow 0$$
$$D(x + y) \rightarrow Dx + Dy$$
$$D(x \times y) \rightarrow (y \times Dx) + (x \times Dy)$$
$$D(x - y) \rightarrow Dx - Dy .$$

He had in mind a proof using ordinals, such as

$$[\![Dx]\!] = \omega^{[x]} \qquad [\![x + y]\!] = [\![x]\!] + [\![y]\!]$$
$$[\![t]\!] = 1 \qquad [\![x - y]\!] = [\![x]\!] + [\![y]\!]$$
$$[\![\text{constant}]\!] = 1 \qquad [\![x \times y]\!] = [\![x]\!] + [\![y]\!] ,$$

where the sums and products are commutative. □

Example 9 (Semigroups). Z. Manna (who took Floyd's exam) and S. Ness (Manna's student) [1970] suggested a general method based on interpretations $[\![\cdot]\!]$: assign an n-ary function $[\![f]\!] : W^n \rightarrow W$, for some well-founded set W, to each n-ary symbol f, and let $[\![\cdot]\!]$ interpret terms accordingly. With the added *replacement property* (true of the above ordinal notations),

$$x > y \quad \Rightarrow \quad [\![f]\!](. , . x \ldots) > [\![f]\!](\ldots y \ldots) ,$$

for each symbol f, one need only show

$$\forall \bar{x} \ [\![l]\!] > [\![r]\!] ,$$

where $\bar{x}$ are the variables appearing in l and r. For

$$(x \cdot y) \cdot z \rightarrow x \cdot (y \cdot z) ,$$

take

$$[x \cdot y] = 2[x] + [y] \qquad [\text{constant}] = 2 \ .$$

It can be shown that termination of a system for one vocabulary (as here for $\cdot$ and constants) implies termination over any larger vocabulary (which adds symbols not appearing in the system's rules). □

Example 10. Another student taking that test, R. Iturriaga, went on to produce a dissertation on symbolic computation [Iturriaga, 1967] in which a class of systems, including differentiation, were proved terminating. The idea was to use exponential interpretations; the following is somewhat simplified:

$$\begin{aligned}
[x + y] &= [x] + [y] & [Dx] &= 3^{[x]} \\
[x - y] &= [x] + [y] & [t] &= 3 \\
[x \times y] &= [x] + [y] & [\text{constant}] &= 3
\end{aligned}$$

□

Example 11. D. Lankford [1979] championed the use of polynomial interpretations, which suffice even for an expanded differentiation program:

$$\begin{aligned}
Dt &\rightarrow 1 \\
D(\text{constant}) &\rightarrow 0 \\
D(x + y) &\rightarrow Dx + Dy \\
D(x \times y) &\rightarrow (y \times Dx) + (x \times Dy) \\
D(x - y) &\rightarrow Dx - Dy \\
D(-x) &\rightarrow -Dx \\
D(x/y) &\rightarrow (Dx/y) - (x \times Dy/y^2) \\
D(\ln x) &\rightarrow Dx/x \\
D(x^y) &\rightarrow (y \times x^{y-1} \times Dx) + (x^y \times (\ln x) \times Dy) \ .
\end{aligned}$$

Let

$$\begin{aligned}
[x + y] &= [x] + [y] & [x \times y] &= [x] + [y] \\
[x - y] &= [x] + [y] & [x/y] &= [x] + [y] \\
[x^y] &= [x] + [y] & [Dx] &= [x]^2 \\
[-x] &= [x] + 1 & [\ln x] &= [x] + 1 \\
[\text{constant}] &= 2 & [t] &= 2 \ .
\end{aligned}$$

□

Example 12 (Disjunctive Normal Form). For

$$\begin{aligned}
\neg\neg x &\rightarrow x \\
\neg(x \vee y) &\rightarrow (\neg x) \wedge (\neg y) \\
\neg(x \wedge y) &\rightarrow (\neg x) \vee (\neg y) \\
x \wedge (y \vee z) &\rightarrow (x \wedge y) \vee (x \wedge z) \\
(y \vee z) \wedge x &\rightarrow (x \wedge y) \vee (x \wedge z) \ ,
\end{aligned}$$

exponentials are, however, required:

$$\begin{aligned}
[x \vee y] &= [x] + [y] + 1 & [\neg x] &= 2^{[x]} \\
[x \wedge y] &= [x][y] & [\text{constant}] &= 2 \ .
\end{aligned}$$

Primitive recursive interpretations cannot prove termination of all terminating systems, so resort to ordinals or their equivalents is inevitable. □

Example 13. Sometimes, pairs of interpretations come in handy: For

$$
\begin{aligned}
x \times (y + z) &\rightarrow (x \times y) + (x \times z) \\
(y + z) \times x &\rightarrow (x \times y) + (x \times z) \\
(x \times y) \times z &\rightarrow x \times (y \times z) \\
(x + y) + z &\rightarrow x + (y + z) \,,
\end{aligned}
$$

we can use $\langle [\![\text{term}]\!], [\![\text{term}]\!]' \rangle$, where

$$
\begin{aligned}
[\![x \times y]\!] &= [\![x]\!][\![y]\!] & [\![x \times y]\!]' &= 2[\![x]\!]' + [\![y]\!]' \\
[\![x + y]\!] &= [\![x]\!] + [\![y]\!] + 1 & [\![x + y]\!]' &= 2[\![x]\!]' + [\![y]\!]' \\
[\![\text{constant}]\!] &= 2 & [\![\text{constant}]\!]' &= 2 \,.
\end{aligned}
$$

The first two rules decrease the first interpretation; the last two decrease the second, without changing the first. So, a lexicographic comparison of pairs is in order. □

Example 14. Other times, it pays to map terms to pairs [Zantema, 1991]. Looking again at

$$
f(f(x)) \rightarrow f(g(f(x))) \,,
$$

we can let $[\![\cdot]\!] : \mathcal{T} \rightarrow N \times N$ as follows: $[\![f]\!]\langle x, y \rangle = \langle x + y, x \rangle$, $[\![g]\!]\langle x, y \rangle = \langle y, x \rangle$, and $[\![\text{constants}]\!] = \langle 1, 1 \rangle$. Since the interpretation of the term being rewritten decreases in its second component, while the first remains intact, the whole term's value can also be shown decreasing. □

Example 15. Another way to show termination of

$$
\begin{aligned}
f(g(x)) &\rightarrow g(g(f(x))) \\
f(g(x)) &\rightarrow g(g(g(x)))
\end{aligned}
$$

is to look at the pair $\langle \textbf{top}, \textbf{argument} \rangle$, where the top (leftmost) symbols are compared in a precedence (ordering of function symbols), with $f > g$. Both rules decrease the top symbol, and the second component ensures that the decrease carries over recursively to the whole term. For such recursive comparisons to yield a well-founded ordering, the second component must be bounded. That is, one must show that the recursive component (the suffix of the right-hand side) is smaller than the whole left-hand side. For this to in fact be the case, we need to include the proper subterm relation in the ordering, that is, we must have $f(x), g(x) \succ x$. This is the simplest example of a "path ordering" [Plaisted, 1978a; Dershowitz, 1982].

Example 16. Consider, again,

$$
(x \cdot y) \cdot z \rightarrow x \cdot (y \cdot z)
$$

and the triple $\langle \textbf{size}, \textbf{first multiplicand}, \textbf{second multiplicand} \rangle$, where the multiplicands are compared recursively in this lexicographic ordering (for a constant term, minimal elements can be used instead). As before, we need to check that the left-hand side is strictly greater than all the subterms of the right-hand side. □

Example 17 (Group Theory). The first decision procedure obtained by D. Knuth and P. Bendix's [1970] completion program was the following system:

$$
\begin{aligned}
1 \cdot x &\rightarrow x & x \cdot 1 &\rightarrow x \\
x^- \cdot x &\rightarrow 1 & x \cdot x^- &\rightarrow 1 \\
1^- &\rightarrow 1 & x^{--} &\rightarrow x \\
y^- \cdot (y \cdot z) &\rightarrow z & y \cdot (y^- \cdot z) &\rightarrow z \\
(x \cdot y) \cdot z &\rightarrow x \cdot (y \cdot z) & (x \cdot y)^- &\rightarrow y^- \cdot x^- .
\end{aligned}
$$

To prove its termination, Knuth devised a recursive ordering that combined the notion of precedence with a simple linear weight: ⟨**weight, top, first argument, ..., last argument**⟩. (The arguments can be listed in any other permutation just as well.) The weight is the sum of the weights of all the symbols, which are non-negative integers. Symbols are compared in the precedence order; arguments are compared recursively. Constants must have positive weight and a unary symbol may have zero weight only if it is maximal in the precedence. This ensures that terms are greater than their subterms, and, hence, that the arguments are bounded. For the group example, give constants weight 1, other operators weight 0, and let inverse have the greatest precedence. Weight is needed for the simple rules; the precedence is what makes the rule for distributing inverse work; the lexicographic comparison of subterms is all that is needed for associativity. □

Example 18 (Distributivity). For

$$
x \times (y + z) \rightarrow (x \times y) + (x \times z) ,
$$

R. Lipton and L. Snyder [1977] suggested the pair ⟨**natural interpretation, maximum - size**⟩. The "natural" interpretation,

$$
\begin{aligned}
[\![x \times y]\!] &= [\![x]\!][\![y]\!] \\
[\![x + y]\!] &= [\![x]\!] + [\![y]\!] \qquad [\![\text{constant}]\!] = 1 ,
\end{aligned}
$$

is unchanged by rewriting, hence imposes a maximum size (and height) on equal terms, which is then used in the second component to show a decrease. □

Example 19. As Knuth and Bendix pointed out, their method needs to be extended to handle "duplicating" systems (one that has more occurrences of a variable on the right than on the left), such as:

$$
\begin{aligned}
x \times (y + z) &\rightarrow (x \times y) + (x \times z) \\
(y + z) \times x &\rightarrow (x \times y) + (x \times z) \\
(x \times y) \times z &\rightarrow x \times (y \times z) \\
(x + y) + z &\rightarrow x + (y + z) .
\end{aligned}
$$

D. Lankford [1979] suggested extending the method of Knuth and Bendix by using integer polynomial weights (with positive coefficients to guarantee that terms are greater than subterms): ⟨[[**term**]], **top, left argument, right argument**⟩. A natural interpretation, with precedence $\times > +$ does the trick. □

Example 20. To prove termination of

$$\neg\neg x \;\rightarrow\; x$$
$$\neg(x \vee y) \;\rightarrow\; (\neg\neg\neg x) \wedge (\neg\neg\neg y)$$
$$\neg(x \wedge y) \;\rightarrow\; (\neg\neg\neg x) \vee (\neg\neg\neg y) \,,$$

use the multiset {number of and's and or's in $x | \neg x$ in term}. Finite multisets are compared using the well-founded multiset ordering [Dershowitz and Manna, 1979] in which replacing an element with any number of smaller elements decreases the multiset. Since applying a rule does not change the total number of and's and or's, the contribution of superterms of the redex is unchanged thereby. □

Example 21 (Factorial). Oftentimes, one would like to consider the top symbol before the interpretation. That way, one can ignore less significant functions. For

$$p(s(x)) \;\rightarrow\; x$$
$$fact(0) \;\rightarrow\; s(0)$$
$$fact(s(x)) \;\rightarrow\; s(x) \times fact(p(s(x)))$$
$$0 \times y \;\rightarrow\; 0$$
$$s(x) \times y \;\rightarrow\; (x \times y) + y$$
$$x + 0 \;\rightarrow\; x$$
$$x + s(y) \;\rightarrow\; s(x + y) \,,$$

we would use a precedence $fact > \times > + > s > 0$. Then we compare two calls to *fact* by their natural interpretation:

$$[\![fact(x)]\!] = [\![x]\!]! \qquad [\![x \times y]\!] = [\![x]\!][\![y]\!]$$
$$[\![s(x)]\!] = [\![x]\!] + 1 \qquad [\![x + y]\!] = [\![x]\!] + [\![y]\!]$$
$$[\![p(x)]\!] = [\![x]\!] - 1 \qquad [\![0]\!] = 0 \,.$$

To compare terms, we consider $\langle \mathbf{top}, [\![\mathbf{term}]\!] \rangle$, and also let terms be greater than subterms. Instead of the replacement property, one need only ensure that rewriting a subterm does not increase the whole term:

$$s \succ t \text{ and } s \rightarrow t \;\;\Rightarrow\;\; g(\ldots, s, \ldots) \succeq g(\ldots, t, \ldots) \,,$$

for all symbols g, which is not a problem since the interpretation is "value-preserving."

It is enough to show that superterms (as opposed to the redex) do not increase (rather than actually decrease), since this implies that the multiset of pairs for all subterms shows a strict decrease, on account of the fact that terms are taken to be larger than subterms [Dershowitz, 1982]. □

Example 22. Another approach, based on multisets, for proving termination of differentiation is D. Plaisted's [1978a] *simple path ordering*. Terms are mapped into multisets of sequences of function symbols:

$$[\![t]\!] \;=\; \{\text{paths in } t\} \,,$$

where a *path* is a sequence of function symbols, starting with the root symbol, and taking subterms until a constant is reached. Sequences are compared as in Example 15, with the differentiation operator maximal in the precedence. □

Example 23. Nested multiset structures can also be used to prove termination of the differentiation example [Dershowitz and Manna, 1979]:

$$[Dx] = \{[x]\} \qquad\qquad [x+y] = [x] \cup [y]$$
$$[-x] = [x] \cup \{\emptyset\} \qquad [x-y] = [x] \cup [y]$$
$$[\ln x] = [x] \cup \{\emptyset\} \qquad [x \times y] = [x] \cup [y]$$
$$[x/y] = [x] \cup [y] \qquad [\text{constant}] = \{\emptyset\}$$
$$[x^y] = [x] \cup [y] \qquad\qquad [t] = \{\emptyset\} .$$

This is really just an encoding of Floyd's ordinal-based solution. □

Example 24. Consider, once again,

$$(x \cdot y) \cdot z \;\rightarrow\; x \cdot (y \cdot z) .$$

All we really want to consider is the size of the first multiplicand. There could, however, be a product in z with a multiplicand larger than $x \cdot y$, so one needs to add another factor: ⟨size, **size of first multiplicand**⟩, which is simpler than a Knuth-Bendix ordering. Since rewriting does not affect the size of superterms, the whole term does not increase.

Better yet, one can use ⟨**size of first multiplicand**⟩, and say that $s \succ t$ if t is a proper subterm of s or if they're both products, but s's first multiplicand is longer. The ordering is, thus, the transitive closure of the proper subterm relation and the ordering based on the size of the first multiplicand. □

Example 25. For the factorial system, one can imitate a structural-induction proof of termination of the corresponding recursive definitions using ⟨**top**, [**argument**]⟩, where the precedence is as before, $fact > \times > + > s > 0$, simplifying the interpretation to

$$[fact(x)] = 0 \qquad\qquad [x \times y] = [x][y]$$
$$[s(x)] = [x] + 1 \qquad [x + y] = [x] + [y]$$
$$[p(x)] = [x] - 1 \qquad\qquad [0] = 0 ,$$

and taking the first argument of factorial and times, and the second for plus. Again, this is combined with the subterm relation. The value-preserving nature of the interpretation guarantees that superterms do not increase. □

Example 26. The disjunctive normal form example served as motivation for the development of the *recursive path ordering* in [Dershowitz, 1982], in parallel with related ideas in [Plaisted, 1978b]:

$$\neg\neg x \;\rightarrow\; x$$
$$\neg(x \vee y) \;\rightarrow\; (\neg x) \wedge (\neg y)$$
$$\neg(x \wedge y) \;\rightarrow\; (\neg x) \vee (\neg y)$$
$$x \wedge (y \vee z) \;\rightarrow\; (x \wedge y) \vee (x \wedge z)$$
$$(y \vee z) \wedge x \;\rightarrow\; (x \wedge y) \vee (x \wedge z) .$$

Intuitively, the precedence should be $\neg > \wedge > \vee$, and terms should be greater than subterms. Adding the subterms as a second component: ⟨**top**, {**arguments**}⟩, we need to ascertain that the left-hand sides are greater in this ordering than all subterms of the corresponding right-hand sides. We use multisets in this path ordering, so that $(y \vee z) \wedge x \succ (x \wedge y)$. □

Example 27. As with previous methods, sometimes two orderings are better than one. For example, the first rule of

$$h(f(x), y) \;\to\; f(g(x, y))$$
$$g(x, y) \;\to\; h(x, y)$$

suggests the precedence $h \approx g > f$; the second rule, on the other hand, requires $g > h$. So we prove termination with $\langle\textbf{term}, \textbf{number of } g\textbf{'s}\rangle$, using a multiset path ordering based on $h \approx g > f$ for the first component (under which two terms are equivalent when symbols are replaced with equivalents and/or arguments are permuted). □

Example 28 (Conditional Normalization). To prove termination of

$$if(if(x, y, z), u, v) \;\to\; if(x, if(y, u, v), if(z, u, v)) \,,$$

one can treat the first argument of *if* as the top symbol in a recursive path ordering [Dershowitz, 1982]: $\langle\textbf{first argument}, \{\textbf{other arguments}\}\rangle$. Rather than an ordinary precedence, one compares first arguments recursively. □

Example 29 (Ackermann's Function). S. Kamin and J.-J. Levy [1980] suggested a lexicographic version of the recursive path ordering, which is like Knuth-Bendix, but with all terms having the same weight: $\langle\textbf{top}, \textbf{first argument}, \dots, \textbf{last argument}\rangle$, and terms greater than subterms. This works beautifully with examples like:

$$ack(0, y) \;\to\; succ(y)$$
$$ack(succ(x), 0) \;\to\; ack(x, succ(0))$$
$$ack(succ(x), succ(y)) \;\to\; ack(x, ack(succ(x), y)) \,,$$

where the precedence $ack > succ$ is used for the first rule, and the lexicographic aspect for the others. To establish that $s \succ f(t_1, \dots, t_n)$ in this ordering, one must also check (recursively) that $s \succ t_1, \dots, t_n$, i.e. that $ack(succ(x), succ(y)) \succ ack(succ(x), y)$. □

Example 30 (Combinator C). With this lexicographic path ordering, the following can be shown to terminate with no precedence:

$$(((C \cdot x) \cdot y) \cdot z) \cdot u \;\to\; (x \cdot z) \cdot (((x \cdot y) \cdot z) \cdot u) \,.$$

□

Example 31. The lexicographic path ordering cannot directly handle the following system:

$$(x \cdot y) \cdot z \;\to\; x \cdot (y \cdot z)$$
$$(x + y) \cdot z \;\to\; (x \cdot z) + (y \cdot z)$$
$$z \cdot (x + f(y)) \;\to\; g(z, y) \cdot (x + a) \,.$$

But termination can be proved using a *semantic path ordering* [Kamin and Lévy, 1980] with any term of the form $z \cdot (x + f(y))$ greater than any other product, any product greater than any other term, and term greater than its subterms, and products treated lexicographically (left-to-right). Note that no rule application changes the value of the redex. □

Example 32 (Insertion Sort).

$$
\begin{aligned}
sort(nil) &\rightarrow nil \\
sort(cons(x, y)) &\rightarrow insert(x, sort(y)) \\
insert(x, nil) &\rightarrow cons(x, nil) \\
insert(x, cons(v, w)) &\rightarrow choose(x, cons(v, w), x, v) \\
choose(x, cons(v, w), y, 0) &\rightarrow cons(x, cons(v, w)) \\
choose(x, cons(v, w), 0, s(z)) &\rightarrow cons(v, insert(x, w)) \\
choose(x, cons(v, w), s(y), s(z)) &\rightarrow choose(x, cons(v, w), y, z) \ .
\end{aligned}
$$

Termination can be shown using subterm and the quadruple $\langle$**top, argument, top, argument**$\rangle$ to show that the left side is greater than the right and its subterms. The first precedence is $sort > insert \approx choose > cons$; the second, $insert > choose$. For the second component, we take the first argument of *sort*, second argument of *choose* and *insert*, and any constant for the others; for the last component, we take the third argument of *choose*. For details of this *general path ordering*, see [Dershowitz and Hoot, to appear]. □

Example 33 (Battle of Hydra and Hercules). The following system, is terminating, but not provably so in Peano Arithmetic:

$$
\begin{aligned}
h(z, e(x)) &\rightarrow h(c(z), d(z, x)) \\
d(z, g(0, 0)) &\rightarrow e(0) \\
d(z, g(x, y)) &\rightarrow g(e(x), d(z, y)) \\
d(c(z), g(g(x, y), 0)) &\rightarrow g(d(c(z), g(x, y)), d(z, g(x, y))) \\
g(e(x), e(y)) &\rightarrow e(g(x, y)) \ .
\end{aligned}
$$

Use a general path ordering, with semantic component

$$
\begin{aligned}
[\![g(x, y)]\!] &= \omega^{[\![x]\!]} + [\![y]\!] & [\![h(z, x)]\!] &= [\![z]\!] + [\![x]\!] \\
[\![d(z, x)]\!] &= pred_{[\![z]\!]}([\![x]\!]) & [\![e(x)]\!] &= [\![x]\!] \\
[\![c(x)]\!] &= [\![x]\!] + 1 & [\![0]\!] &= = 1 \ ,
\end{aligned}
$$

and compare $\langle[\![$term$]\!]$, **top, second argument of** d **and** $g\rangle$, with precedence $d > g > e$. □

References

[Dershowitz and Hoot, to appear] Nachum Dershowitz and Charles Hoot. Natural termination. *Theoretical Computer Science*, to appear.

[Dershowitz and Jouannaud, 1990] Nachum Dershowitz and Jean-Pierre Jouannaud. Rewrite systems. In J. van Leeuwen, editor, *Handbook of Theoretical Computer Science*, volume B: Formal Methods and Semantics, chapter 6, pages 243–320. North-Holland, Amsterdam, 1990.

[Dershowitz and Manna, 1979] Nachum Dershowitz and Zohar Manna. Proving termination with multiset orderings. *Communications of the ACM*, 22(8):465–476, August 1979.

[Dershowitz, 1982] Nachum Dershowitz. Orderings for term-rewriting systems. *Theoretical Computer Science*, 17(3):279–301, March 1982.

[Dershowitz, 1987] Nachum Dershowitz. Termination of rewriting. *J. Symbolic Computation*, 3(1&2):69–115, February/April 1987. Corrigendum: *4*, 3 (December 1987), 409–410; reprinted in *Rewriting Techniques and Applications*, J.-P. Jouannaud, ed., pp. 69—115, Academic Press, 1987.

[Evans, 1951] Trevor Evans. On multiplicative systems defined by generators and relations, I. *Proceedings of the Cambridge Philosophical Society*, 47:637–649, 1951.

[Gorn, 1973] Saul Gorn. On the conclusive validation of symbol manipulation processes (how do you know it has to work?). *J. of the Franklin Institute*, 296(6):499–518, December 1973.

[Iturriaga, 1967] R. Iturriaga. Contributions to mechanical mathematics. Ph.D. Thesis, Department of Computer Science, Carnegie-Mellon University, Pittsburgh, PA, 1967.

[Kamin and Lévy, 1980] Sam Kamin and Jean-Jacques Lévy. Two generalizations of the recursive path ordering. Unpublished note, Department of Computer Science, University of Illinois, Urbana, IL, February 1980.

[Klop, 1992] Jan Willem Klop. Term rewriting systems. In S. Abramsky, D. M. Gabbay, and T. S. E. Maibaum, editors, *Handbook of Logic in Computer Science*, volume 2, chapter 1, pages 1–117. Oxford University Press, Oxford, 1992.

[Knuth and Bendix, 1970] Donald E. Knuth and P. B. Bendix. Simple word problems in universal algebras. In J. Leech, editor, *Computational Problems in Abstract Algebra*, pages 263–297. Pergamon Press, Oxford, U. K., 1970. Reprinted in *Automation of Reasoning 2*, Springer-Verlag, Berlin, pp. 342–376 (1983).

[Lankford, 1979] Dallas S. Lankford. On proving term rewriting systems are Noetherian. Memo MTP-3, Mathematics Department, Louisiana Tech. University, Ruston, LA, May 1979. Revised October 1979.

[Lipton and Snyder, 1977] R. Lipton and L. Snyder. On the halting of tree replacement systems. In *Proceedings of the Conference on Theoretical Computer Science*, pages 43–46, Waterloo, Canada, August 1977.

[Manna and Ness, 1970] Zohar Manna and Steven Ness. On the termination of Markov algorithms. In *Proceedings of the Third Hawaii International Conference on System Science*, pages 789–792, Honolulu, HI, January 1970.

[Plaisted, 1978a] David A. Plaisted. Well-founded orderings for proving termination of systems of rewrite rules. Report R-78-932, Department of Computer Science, University of Illinois, Urbana, IL, July 1978.

[Plaisted, 1978b] David A. Plaisted. A recursively defined ordering for proving termination of term rewriting systems. Report R-78-943, Department of Computer Science, University of Illinois, Urbana, IL, September 1978.

[Plaisted, 1993] David A. Plaisted. Term rewriting systems. In D. M. Gabbay, C. J. Hogger, and J. A. Robinson, editors, *Handbook of Logic in Artificial Intelligence and Logic Programming*, volume 4, chapter 2. Oxford University Press, Oxford, 1993. To appear.

[Zantema, 1991] Hans Zantema. Classifying termination of term rewriting. Technical Report RUU-CS-91-42, Utrecht University, The Netherlands, November 1991.

The Word Problem for Thue Rewriting Systems

Gerard Lallement

Department of Mathematics, Pennsylvania State University, University Park, Pa 16802, USA.

Abstract. This paper is divided into two parts that can be read independently. Part I is devoted to examples of undecidable Thue rewriting systems. Part II presents the results obtained so far on the conjecture that one-relation Thue systems are decidable.

1 Undecidable examples

1.1 Definitions and examples

Let A be an alphabet and let A^* be the free monoid on A, i.e. the set of all words on A, with concatenation as an operation. We denote by $u \equiv v$ the graphical coincidence of two words $u, v \in A^*$; the empty word of A^* is denoted by 1, and $|w|$ denotes the length of $w \in A^*$. For undefined terminology see [5] or [7].

Given any subset R of $A^* \times A^*$ there is a smallest congruence γ_R on A^* containing the relation R. The quotient monoid A^*/γ_R is said to admit the <u>presentation</u> $T = <A ; R>$. It is customary to assume implicitly that R is a symmetric relation, and thus to write $u = v$ whenever $(u, v) \in R$. The presentation T is in fact a rewriting system, often called a Thue system, from the Norwegian mathematician Axel Thue [15]. The reason why $< A ; R >$ is a rewriting system is the following:

A word $w_2 \in A^*$ is said to be <u>directly derivable</u> from $w_1 \in A^*$ in $< A ; R >$ if $w_1 \equiv xuy$, $w_2 \equiv xvy$ for some $x, y, u, v \in A^*$ and either $u \equiv v$ or $(u, v) \in R$ or $(v, u) \in R$. The word w' is said to be <u>derivable</u> from w in $< A ; R >$ if $w \equiv w_1$, $w' \equiv w_n$ $(n > 1)$ and there are words $w_2, \ldots, w_{n-1}$ such that w_{i+1} is directly derivable from w_i $(1 \le i < n)$ in $< A ; R >$. We shall also say that w can be transformed into (or rewritten as) w' in the system T, and indicate this by writing "$w = w'$ in T" or simply "$w = w'$ " when there is no ambiguity about T. Then we have:

Proposition 1. : *Two words $w, w' \in A^*$ are equivalent modulo γ_R, the smallest congru- ence on A^* containing R, if and only if w' is derivable from w in the Thue system $< A ; R >$.*

Examples 2. : a) $< a, b ; ab = 1 >$. This is a Thue system presenting the bicyclic monoid (see [7], p.14). Each word in A^* can be transformed into a word of the form $b^m a^n$ $(m \ge 0, n \ge 0)$.

b) $< a, b ; baaababa = a >$. It can be shown that $aaabababab a$ is derivable from $baaaa$, but unlike the example in $a)$ this is not obvious. See section 2.5.

The <u>word problem</u> for a Thue system $< A ; R >$ is the following question: Given any two words $w, w' \in A^*$ is it possible to <u>decide</u> whether w' is derivable from w or not?

We leave the notion of decidability undefined. Let us simply say here that a question is decidable if there is an <u>algorithm</u> allowing to solve it. In Example 2 a) the word problem is decidable, essentially because each word $b^m a^n$ is the unique word of shortest length in its equivalence class.

Theorem 3. : *There is a finite Thue system $< A \ ; R >$ (i.e. A and R are finite) with an undecidable word problem.*

This result, going back to 1947, is due to A.A. Markov [9] and E. Post [14]. The proofs of this theorem were non-constructive in the following sense:

1) One proves that there exists a language $L \subseteq A^*$ which is recursively enumerable (this means recognizable by a Turing machine) but not recursive (i.e. such that the problem $w \in L$ is undecidable).

2) One creates a Thue system related to the Turing machine recognizing L, having L as one of its equivalence classes.

The proof of 1) above uses a "universal" partial recursive word function whose existence can be proved without an explicit construction of it, although there are no difficulties in giving a constuctive proof.

The purpose of section 1 is to show how concrete Thue systems with undecidable word problems have been constructed from Theorem 3 or other general undecidability results. The first of these systems has 33 relations and is due to A.A. Markov [10], 1956; the second, due to G.C. Tzeitin [16], 1958, has 7 relations. The undecidable Thue system with the smallest number of relations that I know of is that of J. Matiyacevitch [11], 1967. It looks as follows: $< a, b \ ; aabab = baa, aabb = baa, u = v >$ where u, v are very long words. For further details on this, we refer the reader to Matiyacevitch's presentation at this Spring School.

1.2 The undecidable Thue system of A.A. Markov

The following lemma shows that the equivalence problem to a word w_0 in a Thue system can be reduced to the equivalence problem to the empty word in another one.

Lemma 4. : *Let $T = < A \ ; R >$ and $\overline{T} = < A \cup \{\alpha, \beta\}; R \cup \{\alpha w_0 \beta = 1\} >$ be Thue systems, where α, β are distinct letters not in A. Then $w = w_0$ in T if and only if $\alpha w \beta = 1$ in $\overline{T}$.*

The "only if" part of the proof is obvious, and the "if" part follows from an induction on the length of derivations.

The scheme followed by Markov to construct his undecidable system is as follows:

1) Transform a Thue system where $w = 1$ is undecidable (such a system exists by Theorem 3 and Lemma 4) into an undecidable invertible Post system .

2) Encode invertible Post systems into what we call here a Markov rewriting system.

3) Create a Thue system of 33 relations which will reflect some of the computations of the Markov rewriting system.

In each of these steps of the scheme, undecidability carries over.

An <u>invertible Post system</u> on an alphabet A is a rewriting system $P(A \; ; R)$ where $R \subseteq A^* \times A^*$ and where a direct derivation is defined as $uw \to wv$ or $wv \to uw$ with $(u, v) \in R$. A derivation is either the identity or a finite succession of direct derivations.

Example 5. : $P(a, b \; ; a \to bba, \; b \to aba)$. In this invertible Post system the following is an invertible derivation:

$$a \to bba \to baaba \to aabaaba$$

To each Thue system $< A \; ; R >$ we associate an invertible Post system $P(A \cup \{\alpha\}; \overline{R})$ where α is a letter not in A and $\overline{R} = R \cup R^{-1} \cup (A \times A)$.

For example the invertible Post system associated to $< a, b \; ; ab = 1 >$ is $P(a, b, \alpha; ab \leftrightarrow 1, \; a \leftrightarrow a, \; b \leftrightarrow b)$, where $u \leftrightarrow v$ means $u \to v$ and $v \to u$.

Proposition 6. : *For every $w, w' \in A^*$ we have $w = w'$ in $T = < A \; ; R >$ if and only if $w\alpha = w'\alpha$ in the invertible Post system $P(A \cup \{\alpha\}; \overline{R})$ with $\overline{R}$ defined above.*

For example, if $w \equiv xuy$, $w' = xvy$ and $(u, v) \in R$ then

$$w\alpha \equiv xuy\alpha \to \ldots \to uy\alpha x \quad \text{(using repeatedly } az \leftrightarrow za, \; bz \leftrightarrow zb\text{)}$$
$$uy\alpha x \to y\alpha xv \quad \text{(using } uz \leftrightarrow zv\text{)}$$
$$y\alpha xv \to \ldots \to xvy\alpha \equiv w'\alpha \quad \text{(again, } az \leftrightarrow za, \; bz \leftrightarrow zb\text{)}$$

This shows $w\alpha = w'\alpha$ in $P(A \cup \{\alpha\}; \overline{R})$. The converse is left as an exercise.

As a consequence of Theorem 3, Lemma 4, and Proposition 6 there exists a finitely presented invertible Post system $P(A \cup \{\alpha\}; \overline{R})$ for which the problem $w\alpha = 1\alpha$ is undecidable. If we encode $A \cup \{\alpha\}$ on the alphabet $\{a, b\}$ by $\alpha \to a$ and $a_i \to ab^i a$ for each $a_i \in A$, then we obtain:

Corollary 7. : *There is an invertible Post system on $\{a, b\}$ with a finite number of relations for which the problem $w = a$ is undecidable.*

Any invertible Post system P on $\{a, b\}$ with relations $k_i \to \ell_i$ $(1 \le i \le s)$ can be encoded on $\{a, b, c, d\}$, using c, d as markers, by creating the following word $r(P)$:

$$r(P) \equiv dk_1 c\ell_1 dk_2 c\ell_2 \ldots dk_s c\ell_s d$$

If we also wish to encode the Post derivation $k_i \to \ell_i$, then it suffices to introduce another marker e and to declare that we allow derivations $r(P)ek_i w \leftrightarrow r(P)ew\ell_i$ on the alphabet $\{a, b, c, d, e\}$ with $w \in \{a, b\}^*$. Now if we single out the factors k_i and ℓ_i and call them u and v respectively then $r(P) \equiv xducvdy$. Hence:

$$r(P)ek_i w \equiv xducvdyeuw, \quad r(P)ew\ell_i \equiv xducvdyewv.$$

These considerations lead us naturally to the following definition:

Definition 8. : The Markov rewriting system on $\{a, b, c, d, e\}$ is the system defined by the invertible direct derivations

$$xducvdyeuw \leftrightarrow xducvdyewv$$

for all $x, y \in \{a, b, c, d\}^*$ and all $u, v, w \in \{a, b\}^*$.

A key step in Malcev's proof is:

Theorem 9. : *For any invertible Post system P on $\{a, b\}$ we have $w_1 = w_2$ in P if and only if $r(P)ew_1 = r(P)ew_2$ in the Markov system on $\{a, b, c, d, e\}$. In particular, in the Markov system the equality $uew = uea$ with $w \in \{a, b\}^*$ and u is of the type $r(P)$ above, is undecidable.*

We call words of the form uew where u is of the type $r(P)$ and $w \in \{a, b\}^*$ <u>special</u> words.

Definition 10. : (Markov's undecidable Thue system) The alphabet is

$$A = \{a, b, c, d, e, f, g, h, \overline{a}, \overline{b}, \hat{a}, \hat{b}, m\}.$$

There are 33 relations; 20 relations express the commutations of the letter in $\{a, b, c, d\}$ with those in $\{f, \overline{a}, \overline{b}, \hat{a}, \hat{b}\}$; the other 13 relations are:

$$
\begin{array}{llll}
e\hat{a} = \hat{a}e & e\hat{b} = \hat{b}e & ea = \overline{a}e & eb = \overline{b}e \\
am = \hat{a}m & bm = \hat{b}m & & \\
ha\overline{a} = ah & hb\overline{b} = bh & & \\
ag\hat{a} = ga & bg\hat{b} = gb & & \\
df = dh & fd = gd & & \\
hc = cg & & &
\end{array}
$$

Theorem 11. : *Let z_1, z_2 be two special words in $\{a, b, c, d, e\}^*$. Then $fz_1m = fz_2m$ in Markov's rewriting system. In particular, Markov's Thue system above has an undecidable word problem.*

The easy half of the proof consists in showing that $z_1 = z_2$ in Markov's rewriting system implies $fz_1m = fz_2m$ in the presentation above; we take $z_1 \equiv xducvdyeuw$, and $z_2 \equiv xducvdyewv$. In the following computation, some of the transformations effected on consecutive words have been underlined for clarity:

$$
\begin{array}{ll}
f\underline{xd}ucvdyeuwm = \underline{xdf}ucvdyeuwm & \text{(commutations)} \\
\quad = xdhucvdyeuwm & (df = dh) \\
\quad = xdhucvdy\overline{u}ewm & (eu = \overline{u}e) \\
\quad = xdhu\overline{u}cvdyewm & \text{(commutations)} \\
\quad = xduhcvdyewm & (hu\overline{u} = uh) \\
\quad = xducgvdyewm & (hc = cg) \\
\quad = xducvg\hat{v}dyewm & (gv = vg\hat{v}) \\
\quad = xducvg\underline{dyew}\hat{v}m & \text{(commutation of } \hat{v}) \\
\quad = xducvgdyewvm & (\hat{v}m = vm) \\
\quad = xduc\underline{vf}dyewvm & (gd = fd) \\
\quad = \underline{fxduc}vdyewvm & \text{(commutations)}
\end{array}
$$

(Note: $\overline{u}$ is obtained by barring the letters of u, while $\hat{v}$ is obtained by hatting all letters of the mirror of v)

1.3 The undecidable Thue system of G.C. Tzeitin

Example 12. : Let $A_0 = \{a, b\}$. On the alphabet $A_1 = \{a, b, \overline{a}, \overline{b}, e\}$ consider the Thue system defined by the relations

$$\xi\overline{\eta} = \overline{\eta}\xi, \ e\overline{\xi}\xi = \overline{\xi}e \quad \text{for all} \ \ \xi, \eta \in A_0$$
$$\overline{a}\,\overline{a}a = \overline{a}\,\overline{a}ae \quad \text{(7 relations)}$$

This is Tzeitin's Thue system.

Theorem 13. : *The word problem for Tzeitin's Thue system is undecidable.*

Here is a short sketch of the proof of this theorem:

Given any finite alphabet $A = \{a_1, a_2, \ldots, a_n\}$ define two encodings of A into A_0^* as follows $\overrightarrow{a_i} = b^i a$ and $\overleftarrow{a_i} = ab^i$. Define now w^0 as $w^0 = a\,\overrightarrow{w} = \overleftarrow{w}\,a$ for every $w \in A^*$; in particular $1^0 = a$.

To every Thue system $T = < A\ ; R >$ we can associate the system $T^0 = < A_0; R^0 >$ where $(x, y) \in R^0$ if and only if $x = u^0$, $y = v^0$ and $(u, v) \in R$.

For example if $T = < a_1, a_2, a_3; a_1a_2a_3 = 1, a_3a_2a_3 = a_3 >$ then

$$T^0 = < a, b\ ; abab^2ab^3a = a, \ ab^3ab^2ab^3a = ab^3a > .$$

Let us begin now with a special Thue system

$$\mathcal{A} = < A\ ; w_1 = 1, \ w_2 = 1, \ldots, w_m = 1 > .$$

Construct $\mathcal{B} = < A \cup \{\alpha\}; \alpha = 1, w_1\alpha = 1, w_2\alpha = 1, \ldots, w_m\alpha = 1 >$ and $\mathcal{B}^0$ as indicated above, choosing $\alpha^0 = aa$ (thereby making the mapping $z \to z^0$ from $A \cup \{\alpha\}$ to A_0^* again an encoding). Then $u = v$ in $\mathcal{A}$ if and only if $u = v$ in $\mathcal{B}$ (hardly surprising) if and only if $u^0 = v^0$ in $\mathcal{B}^0$.

Taking $s = (\alpha 1 \alpha w_1 \alpha w_2 \ldots \alpha w_m \alpha)^0$, which encodes $\mathcal{B}$, it can be shown that for every $x, y \in A_0^*$, $x = y$ in $\mathcal{B}^0$ if and only if $\overline{s}x = \overline{s}y$ in Tzeitin's system. Thus if $\mathcal{A}$ is any Thue system with an undecidable word problem, for example such a system presenting a group, we obtain that Tzeitin's system has an undecidable word problem. (P.S. Novikov was the first to prove the existence of an undecidable group presentation in 1955.)

The following simple example shows essentially how Tzeitin's system work

$$\mathcal{A} = < a_1, a_2, a_3;\ a_1a_2a_3 = 1 >$$
$$\mathcal{B} = < a_1, a_2, a_3, \alpha\ ;\ \alpha = 1, a_1a_2a_3\alpha = 1 >$$
$$\mathcal{B}^0 = < a, b\ ;\ aa = a, \ abab^2ab^3aa = a >$$
$$s = (\alpha 1 \alpha a_1a_2a_3\alpha)^0 = aaabab^2ab^3aa$$
$$\overline{s} = \overline{a}\,\overline{a}\,\overline{a}\,\overline{b}\,\overline{a}\,\overline{b}^2\,\overline{a}\,\overline{b}^3\,\overline{a}\,\overline{a}$$

We show why $x = y$ in $\mathcal{B}^0$ implies $\overline{s}x = \overline{s}y$ in Tzeitin's system by showing

$$\begin{cases} 1) \ \overline{s}ua^2v = \overline{s}uav \\ 2) \ \overline{s}uabab^2ab^3aav = \overline{s}uav \end{cases} \text{for all } u, v \in A_0^*$$

1) $\quad \bar{a}\,\bar{a}\,\bar{a}\,\bar{b}\,\bar{a}\,\bar{b}^2\,\bar{a}\,\bar{b}^3\,\bar{a}\,\bar{a}uav = u\bar{a}\,\bar{a}\,\bar{a}\,a\,\bar{b}\,a\,\bar{b}^2\,\bar{a}\,\bar{b}^3\,\bar{a}\,\bar{a}v \qquad$ (by $\xi\bar{\eta} = \bar{\eta}\xi$)

$\qquad\qquad\qquad = u\bar{a}\,\bar{a}\,\bar{a}\,ae\,\bar{b}\,a\,\bar{b}^2\,\bar{a}\,\bar{b}^3\,\bar{a}\,\bar{a}v \qquad$ (by $\bar{a}\,\bar{a}\,a = \bar{a}\,\bar{a}ae$)

$\qquad\qquad\qquad = u\bar{a}\,\bar{a}\,a\,\bar{a}\,e\,\bar{b}\,a\,\bar{b}^2\,\bar{a}\,\bar{b}^3\,\bar{a}\,\bar{a}v \qquad$ (by $\bar{a}\,a = a\,\bar{a}$)

$\qquad\qquad\qquad = u\bar{a}\,\bar{a}\,ae\,\bar{a}\,a\,\bar{b}\,a\,\bar{b}^2\,\bar{a}\,\bar{b}^3\,\bar{a}\,\bar{a}v \qquad$ (by $e\bar{\xi}\xi = \bar{\xi}e$)

$\qquad\qquad\qquad = u\bar{a}\,\bar{a}\,a\,\bar{a}\,a\,\bar{b}\,a\,\bar{b}^2\,\bar{a}\,\bar{b}^3\,\bar{a}\,\bar{a}v \qquad$ (by $\bar{a}\,\bar{a}\,a = \bar{a}\,\bar{a}ae$)

$\qquad\qquad\qquad = \bar{a}\,\bar{a}\,\bar{a}\,\bar{b}\,\bar{a}b\,a\,\bar{b}^2\,\bar{a}\,\bar{b}^3\,\bar{a}\,\bar{a}ua^2v \qquad$ (by $\xi\bar{\eta} = \bar{\eta}\xi$)

2) With similar justifications we have:

$\bar{a}\,\bar{a}\,\bar{b}\,\bar{a}\,\bar{b}^2\,\bar{a}\,\bar{b}^3\,\bar{a}\,\bar{a}uabab^2ab^3aav = u\bar{a}\,\bar{a}\,\bar{a}\,a\,\bar{b}\,b\,\bar{a}\,a\,\bar{b}\,\bar{b}\,\bar{b}\,b\,\bar{a}\,a\,\bar{b}\,\bar{b}\bar{b}\,b\,\bar{b}\,\bar{b}a\,a\,\bar{a}\,av$

$\qquad\qquad = u\bar{a}\,\bar{a}\,\bar{a}\,ae\,\bar{b}\,b\,\bar{a}\,a\,\bar{b}\,\bar{b}\bar{b}\,b\,\bar{a}\,a\,\bar{b}\,\bar{b}\bar{b}\,b\,\bar{b}\,\bar{b}a\,\bar{a}\,av$

$\qquad\qquad = u\bar{a}\,\bar{a}\,\bar{a}\,a\,\bar{b}\,e\,b\,\bar{a}\,a\,\bar{b}\,\bar{b}\bar{b}\,\bar{a}\,a\,\bar{b}\,\bar{b}\bar{b}\,b\,\bar{b}\,\bar{b}a\,\bar{a}\,av$

$\qquad\qquad \cdots\cdots\cdots\cdots\cdots\cdots\cdots$

$\qquad\qquad = u\bar{a}\,\bar{a}\,\bar{a}\,a\,\bar{b}\,\bar{a}\,\bar{b}\bar{b}\,\bar{a}\,\bar{b}\,\bar{b}\bar{b}\,\bar{a}\,\bar{a}ev$

$\qquad\qquad = u\bar{a}\,\bar{a}\,\bar{a}\,\bar{b}\,\bar{a}\,\bar{b}\bar{b}\,\bar{a}\,\bar{b}\,\bar{b}\bar{b}\,\bar{a}\,\bar{a}\,aev$

$\qquad\qquad = u\bar{a}\,\bar{a}\,\bar{a}\,\bar{b}\,\bar{a}\,\bar{b}\bar{b}\,\bar{a}\,\bar{b}\,\bar{b}\bar{b}\,\bar{a}\,\bar{a}\,av$

$\qquad\qquad = \bar{a}\,\bar{a}\,\bar{a}\,\bar{b}\,\bar{a}\,\bar{b}\bar{b}\,\bar{a}\,\bar{b}\,\bar{b}\bar{b}\,\bar{a}\,\bar{a}uav$

2 One-relation Thue systems

2.1 Introduction

In spite of the fact that the word problem for one-relation groups has been shown to be decidable by W. Magnus in 1932 [8], it is still not known if this problem is decidable for Thue systems of the form $< A \; ; u = v >$.

The object of this part is to give an outline of the current state of affairs on one-relation Thue systems, including

(1) S. Adyan's 1966 results on the decidability of the word problem for special systems $< A \; ; w = 1 >$, and for systems $< A \; ; u = v >$ where u, v have distinct initial letters and distinct terminal letters [1].

(2) The 1978 results of S. Adyan and G. Oganesyan [3] showing that the decidability problem can be reduced to the cases $< A \; ; bua = a >$ and $< A \; ; bua = ava >$ where $a, b \in A$, $a \not\equiv b$.

(3) The 1976 results of S. Adyan [2] on the cases in (2); these results allow to show that decidability holds in many cases.

In 1982 (see [12]) Oganesyan gave a rather involved proof of the decidability in the case $< A \; ; bua = a >$, but his proof is unlikely to extend to the case $< A \; ; bua = ava >$. On this case see also [4].

As in Part I we say "the system $< A \; ; u = v >$ is decidable" to mean that the word problem is decidable. If $\varphi : A^* \to B^*$ is a mapping we say that the two systems $T_1 = < A \; ; u = v >$ and $T_2 = < B \; ; \varphi(u) = \varphi(v) >$ are d-equivalent if T_1 and T_2 are both decidable or undecidable.

2.2 Special Thue systems

Theorem 14. *:[1] The Thue systems $< A \; ; w = 1 >$ are decidable.*

The most important step in the proof of this theorem is the construction, from the word w, of a presentation of the group of units of the monoid $M = < A ; w = 1 >$. This construction proceeds as follows:

Let U be the set of all words in A^* representing invertible elements in M. A simple exercise shows that U is a submonoid of A^* such that $xy \in U$ and $zx \in U$ imply $x, y, z \in U$ for all $x, y, z \in A^*$. The base C of U, i.e. its smallest set of generators, has the following characteristic property:

$$xy \in C \text{ and } zx \in C \text{ imply } x \equiv 1 \text{ for all } x, y, z \in A^*.$$

This property allows to show that every word in U can be written uniquely as a product of words in C. Thus U is a free submonoid of A^* with base C, and C is a code (in fact C is a special biprefix code, see [5] p.140). C can be constructed as follows:

Letting $C_0 = \{w\}$ and $C_i = [C_{i-1} - \{xy, zx\}] \cup \{x, y, z\}$ where $xy, zx \in C_{i-1}$ and $yz \not\equiv 1$, $x \not\equiv 1$. The code C is the last of the sets C_i.

Example 15. : $< a, b, c ; abcababc = 1 >$.
$C_0 = \{ab\underline{c}ab\underline{abc}\}$
$C_1 = \{\underline{abc}, \underline{ab}abc, abc\underline{ab}\}$
$C_2 = \{\underline{ab}, c, \underline{abc}\}$
$C_3 = \{ab, c\} = C$

Let Γ be an alphabet in bijection with C via $\varphi : C \rightarrow \Gamma$. This bijection φ extends to a morphism, also denoted by φ, $\varphi : U \rightarrow \Gamma^*$. Hence the Thue system $< A ; w = 1 >$ can be translated by φ into the system $< \Gamma; \varphi(w) = 1 >$ which turns out to be a presentation of the group of units of M. If in Example 5 we take $\varphi(ab) = \alpha, \varphi(c) = \beta$ then the group of units of the example has $< \alpha, \beta; \alpha\beta\alpha\alpha\beta = 1 >$ as a presentation.

Adyan's solution to the word problem proceeds then as follows: For each $z \in A^*$ define the set $\delta(z)$ of direct descendants of z by
$\delta(z) = \{v \in A^* : z = xuy, v = xu'y \text{ for some } u, u' \in U,$
with $|u'| \leq |u|$ and $\varphi(u) = \varphi(u')$ in $< \Gamma; \varphi(w) = 1 > \}$.

By the decidability of one-relation groups [8], $\delta(z)$ is effectively computable as well as the set $\Delta(z)$ of all descendants of z ($\Delta(z)$ is the transitive closure of $\delta(z)$). To conclude, one shows that $z_1 = z_2$ in $< A ; w = 1 >$ if and only if $\Delta(z_1) \cap \Delta(z_2) \neq \phi$.

A recent proof of Theorem 4 due to L. Zhang [17] goes along the same lines but uses an order relation on A which is extended to the usual lexicographic ordering $\leq_\ell$ of words in A^*. In the definition of $\delta(z)$ above, the condition $|u'| \leq |u|$ is replaced by $u' \leq_\ell u$. Standard results on terminating confluent rewriting systems allowed Zhang to shorten quite substantially Adyan's proof.

2.3 Cancellative one-relation Thue systems

The following results answer the questions as to when $< A ; u = v >$ yields a [left, right] cancellative semigroup.

Theorem 16. *:[1] The semigroup presented by $< A ; u = v >$ is left [resp. right] cancellative if and only if the initial [resp. terminal] letters of u and v are distinct.*

In particular $< A \; ; u = v >$ is cancellative if and only if $i(u) \not\equiv i(v)$ and $t(u) \not\equiv t(v)$ where $i(u)$ [resp. $t(u)$] is the initial [resp. terminal] letter of u. For this kind of Thue system we have the following stronger result:

Theorem 17. :*[1] The semigroup presented by $< A \; ; u = v >$ with $i(u) \not\equiv i(v)$ and $t(u) \not\equiv t(v)$ is embeddable in the one-relation group having the same (group) presentation. In particular such a Thue system is decidable.*

Again the last part of this theorem follows from Magnus' result on one-relation groups.

The results in sections 2.2 and 2.3 reduce the decidability of one-relation Thue systems to the case of non special presentations $< A \; ; u = v >$ with $i(u) \equiv i(v)$ or $t(u) \equiv t(v)$. In the next section we show how to reduce the case $i(u) \equiv i(v)$ and $t(u) \equiv t(v)$ to a case $< B; \theta(u) = \theta(v) >$ which is either left or right cancellative.

2.4 Reduction algorithms

These algorithms are due to S. Adyan and G. Oganesyan [3]. They are based on the idea of compressing the presentation relation.

Definitions 18. : a) A bifactor of a word w is a word u such that $w \equiv ux \equiv yu$, for some words x, y.

b) A relation $u = v$ is said to be compressible if u and v have a common bifactor which is not the empty word.

The following are examples of compressible relations:

$$\underline{abaab} = \underline{ab}\,\underline{ab}, \quad \underline{ababa} = \underline{a}, \quad ababa = aba$$

In the last example aba is a common bifactor, but a is a shorter one. The shortest bifactor of a word is a primary (or non self-overlapping) word in the following sense:

Definition 19. : A word $s \in A^*$ is called a primary word if $s \equiv uvu$ implies $u \equiv 1$.

If s is a primary word then any word w either does not have s as a factor or can be written uniquely as $u_1 s u_2 s \ldots u_{k-1} s u_k$.

Theorem 20. : *Let $S = < A \; ; u = v >$ be a Thue system with a compressible relation. There exists a d-equivalent Thue system $S' = < B; \varphi(u) = \varphi(v) >$ with $|\varphi(u)\varphi(v)| < |uv|$, effectively constructible from S.*

Sketch of proof : Let s be the primary common bifactor of u and v. Let B be a denumerable alphabet, $B = \{b_0, b_1, \ldots, b_i, \ldots\}$ in bijection with the denumerable list L of all words that do not have s as a factor, so that the i-th word (for example in lexicographic order) r_i corresponds to b_i. Define a mapping $\varphi : sA^*s \cup \{s\} \to B^*$ by $\varphi(s) = 1$ and $\varphi(szsr_n s) = \varphi(szs)b_n$. Then, as it turns out, φ is a bijection preserving direct derivations from the system $S = < A \; ; u = v >$ to the system $S' = < B; \varphi(u) = \varphi(v) >$ and conversely. We can even reduce the infinite alphabet B to a finite one by suppressing the letters not in $\varphi(u)\varphi(v)$. The mapping φ is called the compression of $u = v$ by s.

Examples 21. : a) $S =< a, b \; ; ababa = aba >$. Here $s \equiv a$, $L = \{b^0, b^1, \ldots, b^n, \ldots\}$; we let $B = \{b_0, b_1, \ldots, b_n, \ldots\}$. Then $\varphi(aba) = b_1$ and $\varphi(ababa) = b_1 b_1$. Thus we obtain $S' =< b_1; b_1^2 = b_1 >$. Since S' is decidable, so is S.

b) $S =< a, b \; ; ababaabbab = ab >$. Here $s \equiv ab$

$$L = \{1, a, b, a^2, ba, b^2, \ldots\}$$
$$B = \{b_0, b_1, b_2, b_3, b_4, b_5, \ldots\}$$
$$\varphi(ab) = 1 \text{ and } \varphi(\underline{ab}\,\underline{abaabbab}) = b_0 b_1 b_2$$

Thus we get $S' =< b_0, b_1, b_2; b_0 b_1 b_2 = 1 >$. Since S' is decidable by Theorem 4, so is S.

Corollary 22. : *For every Thue system $S =< A \; ; u = v >$ with a compressible relation, there exists a d-equivalent Thue system $S' =< B; \psi(u) = \psi(v) >$ with an incompressible relation, and S' is effectively constructible from S.*

This corollary leads us to the study of Thue systems $< A \; ; u = v >$ with $u \not\equiv 1$, $v \not\equiv 1$, and $u = v$ is an incompressible relation.

Let s be the primary bifactor of u and t the primary bifactor of v. Define a word s_0 as follows:

a) s_0 is a left factor of one of s or t and a right factor of the other if such a word exists;

b) s_0 is the shortest of s and t if a word s_0 as in $a)$ does not exist.

Then, using the properties of s and t, one can show that s_0 satisfies:

$$(P) \quad \begin{cases} \text{No right factor of } s_0 \text{ is a left factor of } u \text{ or } v. \\ \text{No left factor of } s_0 \text{ is a right factor of } u \text{ or } v. \end{cases}$$

Note that, in particular, s_0 is a primary word.

Let $A_1 = A \cup \{x\}$ where $x \notin A$. Define $\theta : A^* \to A_1^*$ by

$$\theta(w) = \begin{cases} w & \text{if } s_0 \text{ is not a factor of } w, \\ u_1 x u_2 x \ldots u_{k-1} x u_k & \text{if } w \equiv u_1 s_0 u_2 s_0 \ldots u_{k-1} s_0 u_k. \end{cases}$$

Theorem 23. : *Let $S =< A \; ; u = v >$ be a Thue system with $u \not\equiv 1$, $v \not\equiv 1$, and an incompressible relation. Then $S_1 =< A_1; \theta(u) = \theta(v) >$ with A_1 and θ as above is d-equivalent to S. Furthermore we have $i[\theta(u)] \not\equiv i[\theta(v)]$ or $t[\theta(u)] \not\equiv t[\theta(v)]$.*

Examples 24. : a) $S =< a, b \; ; aababaab = abbabb >$. In this example $s = a\underline{ab}$, $t = \underline{ab}b$. Take $s_0 = ab$.

$$\theta(a\underline{ab}\,\underline{ab}aab) = axxax, \; \theta(\underline{ab}b\,\underline{ab}b) = xbxb$$
$$S_1 =< a, b, x \; ; axxax = xbxb >$$

S_1 is decidable by Theorem 13, and so is S.

b) $S =< a, b \; ; bbaabaabbaa = baa >$. Here $s = bbaa$, $t = baa$. We take $s_0 = baa$.

$$\theta(bbaabaabbaa) = bxxbx, \; \theta(baa) = x$$
$$S_1 =< a, b, x; bxxbx = x >$$

S_1 is decidable (see Section 2.5), and so is S.

c) $S =< a, b \; ; abbababab = aabb >$ gives $s = ab$, $t = aabb$. With $s_0 = ab$ we obtain $S_1 =< a, b, x \; ; xbxxx = axb >$ which is again decidable.

The proof of Theorem 23 consists in showing that a direct derivation in S, say $\alpha u\beta \to \alpha v\beta$, translates into $\theta(\alpha u\beta) \equiv \theta(\alpha)\theta(u)\theta(\beta) \to \theta(\alpha)\theta(v)\theta(\beta) \equiv \theta(\alpha v\beta)$ and conversely. The properties (P) of s_0 are used in analyzing the positions of s_0 in $\alpha u\beta$ and $\alpha v\beta$.

Corollary 25. : *One-relation Thue systems are decidable if the systems $< A \; ; u = v >$ with $i(u) \not\equiv i(v)$ and $t(u) \equiv t(v)$ are decidable.*

2.5   One-relation Thue systems $< A \; ; u = v >$ with $i(u) \not\equiv i(v)$

Lemma 26. : *Let $i(u) \equiv a$, $i(v) \equiv b$. If for any word w we can decide the divisibility on the left of w by a or b, then the system $< A \; ; u = v >$ is decidable.*

Proof Assume we want to decide if $w = w'$ or not. Then we test if w' is divisible on the left by $i(w)$ or not. By the hypothesis this is decidable in case $i(w) \equiv a$ or $i(w) \equiv b$. Otherwise w' is divisible on the left by $i(w)$ if and only if $i(w') \equiv i(w)$. If w' is left divisible by $i(w)$ then $w \equiv i(w)w_1$, $w' = i(w)w_1'$ and by Theorem 12, $w = w'$ if and only if $w_1 = w_1'$ and the decidability problem is reduced to shorter words.

In 1977 S. Adyan created a word transformation procedure allowing in some cases to detect whether or not a word w is left divisible by a or b. This procedure consisting of successions of decompositions and rewritings of words is explained on the following example:

Example 27. : $< a, b \; ; aba = baababaa >$. Is the word $w \equiv bbaaabab$ left divisible by a? This word begins by b, hence it has a left factor in common with $baababaa$. In fact the longest common left factor is b which becomes the first term in the decomposition of w. We repeat this procedure decomposing w from left to right by marking the longest common left factors of the successive suffixes of w with either $baababaa$ or aba:

$$w \equiv bbaaabab \text{ decomposes as } b|baa|abab$$

The word aba (left-hand side of the relation) has appeared in the decomposition. We say that the decomposition of w contains aba as a <u>head</u> (the word "tail" would be more appropriate, because after the head the decomposition stops). Proceed as follows:

(a) If a decomposition has no head then stop.

(b) If a decomposition has a head which is the left [resp. right] side of the relation then transform the word by replacing the head by the right [resp. left] side of the relation, and repeat the decomposition on the new word obtained.

$$w \equiv bbaaabab$$
$$dec(w) = b|baa|\underline{abab}$$
$$w_1 \equiv t(w) \equiv bbaabaababaab$$
$$dec(w_1) = b|baaba|\underline{abab}aab$$
$$w_2 \equiv t(w_1) \equiv bbaababaababaabaab$$
$$dec(w_2) = b|\underline{baababaa}babaabaab$$
$$w_3 \equiv t(w_2) \equiv babababaabaab$$
$$dec(w_3) = ba|ba|ba|baaba|ab$$

According to (a) above we stop. By the next theorem w is not left divisible by a.

Theorem 28. :[2] *The possible outcomes of Adyan's word transformations applied to a word w with $i(w) \equiv a$ [resp. b] are*

(1) After finitely many steps a decomposition without a head is obtained.

(2) After finitely many steps the word w has been transformed into a word w' such that $i(w) \equiv b$ [resp. a].

(3) The transformations go on indefinitely.

Then in case (2) w is left divisible by b [resp. a], and it is not in the two other cases.

The next example shows a very simple instance of (3) above.

Example 29. : $< a, b \, ; a = baabbaa >$. Consider $w \equiv bbaaa$. The successive transformations are:

$$b|baa|\underline{a} \longrightarrow bbaabaabbaa$$
$$b|baab|\underline{a}abbaa \longrightarrow bbaabbaabbaaabbaa$$
$$b|\underline{baabba}abbaaabbaa \longrightarrow babbaaabbaa$$
$$ba|b|baa|\underline{a}bbaa \longrightarrow \ldots$$

After three transformations, the original decomposition $b|baa|\underline{a}$ became $ba|b|baa|\underline{a}bbaa$, creating a <u>loop</u> going on indefinitely.

In order to show that a given one-relation system of the type studied in the present section is decidable, it suffices to show that all loops (if any) can be detected in a finite number of steps. This question is related to the study of the following kind of rewriting systems:

Let Σ, A be two alphabets and let $f : \Sigma \times A \to \Sigma^* \cup A^*$ be a mapping (eventually partially defined). The mapping f (called the alphabet connector) defines rewriting rules of the form $\alpha a \to f(\alpha, a)$ for each $\alpha \in \Sigma$, $a \in A$. For each $\sigma \equiv \alpha_1 \alpha_2 \ldots \alpha_m \in \Sigma^*$ and $w \equiv a_1 a_2 \ldots a_n \in A^*$ we define a one-step rewriting as :
$\sigma w \to \alpha_1 \alpha_2 \ldots \alpha_{m-1} f(\alpha_m, a_1) a_2 \ldots a_n$. A complete rewriting is a succession, possibly infinite, of one-step rewritings. Is it possible, for certain types of mappings f, to determine all infinite complete rewritings?

To one-relation Thue systems of the form $< A \, ; u = a >$ with $i(u) \equiv b$, $b, a \in A$, one can associate one-sided rewriting rules that can be used to detect loops in the following manner:

Write $u \equiv c_i d_i$ where d_i is the left factor of u of length i and c_i the corresponding right factors ($c_i \not\equiv 1$, $d_i \not\equiv 1$). We use Example 29 where $u \equiv baabbaa$ to show how the single two-sided rule yields, in a canonical way, a number of one-sided rules. First we have:

$$c_3 a \equiv baab\underline{a} \longrightarrow baab\underline{baabbaa} \to ad_4$$
$$c_4 a \equiv baa\underline{a} \longrightarrow baa\underline{baabbaa} \to \ldots \to ad_4 d_5$$

These give the following two one-sided rules $c_3 a \to ad_4$ and $c_4 a \to ad_4 d_5$. Further rules are given by the following table, similar to the alphabet connector described above (except for the letter a which can be viewed as a marker).

	ad_4	ad_5
c_6	$c_5 c_6 c_4$	a
c_5	a	$ad_4 d_5 d_4$
c_2	$c_1 c_6 c_4$	ad_4
c_1	ad_4	ad_5

For example the loop shown in Example 29 translates as follows using the one-sided rules above:

$$c_6 c_4 a \longrightarrow c_6 a d_4 d_5 \longrightarrow c_5 c_6 c_4 d_5 \equiv c_5 c_6 c_4 a d_4$$

Defining the language produced by the one-sided rewriting rules as

$$L = \{w : c_{i_1} c_{i_2} \ldots c_{i_k} a \to \ldots \to aw, \; w \in \{d_1, d_2, \ldots\}^*\}$$

one can show that for Example 29 this language is $L = (1 + d_5 + d_5 d_4) d_4^*$. Loops can be detected by computing $c_i a L$ for each left factor c_i. For further details on this approach, see [6].

The case $< A \; ; bua = a >$ has been solved using different methods in [12], [3] but the case $< A \; ; bua = ava >$ remains open.

References

1. S.I. Adyan *Defining relations and algorithmic problems for groups and semigroups,* Tr. Mat. Inst. Steklov Akad. Nauk SSSR, 85 (1966), pp. 1-90 (Russian).
2. S.I. Adyan *Transformations of words in a semigroup presented by a system of defining relations* Algebra i Logika, 15 $n°6$ (1976), pp. 611-621 (Russian)
3. S.I. Adjan and G.U. Oganesyan *On the word and divisibility problems in semigroups with a single defining relation* Izv. Akad. Nauk SSSR, Ser. Mat., 42 $n°2$ (1978), pp. 219-225 (Russian)
4. S.I. Adjan and G.U. Oganesyan *On the word and divisibility relation problems for semigroups with one relation* Mat. Zametki, 41 $n°3$ (1987), pp. 412-421 (Russian)
5. J. Berstel and D. Perrin Theory of codes, Academic Press, (1985)
6. J.B.Bouwsma Semigroups presented by a single relation, Doctoral Dissertation, The Pennsylvania State University, May 1993
7. G. Lallement Semigroups and Combinatorial Applications, Interscience, J. Wiley & Sons, (1979)
8. W. Magnus *Das Identitätsproblem für Gruppen mit einer definierenden Relation* Math. Ann., 106 (1932), pp. 295-307
9. A.A. Markov *On the impossibility of certain algorithms in the theory of associative systems* Dokl. Akad. Nauk SSSR, 55 (1947), pp. 587-590 and 58 (1947) pp.353-356 (Russian)
10. A.A. Markov Theory of algorithms, Tr. Mat. Inst. Akad. Nauk SSSR 42 (1956) (Russian)
11. Yu. V. Matiyasevich *Simple examples of unsolvable associative calculi* Dokl. Akad. Nauk SSSR, 173 $n°6$ (1967), pp. 1264–1266 also Tr. Mat. Inst. Steklov, Akad. Nauk SSSR, 93, pp. 50-88 (Russian)
12. G.U. Oganesyan *On the problems of equality and divisibility of words in a semigroup with a defining relation of the form $a = bA$* Izv. Akad.Nauk SSSR, Ser. Mat., 42 $n°3$, (1978), pp. 602-612 (Russian)
13. G.U. Oganesyan *On semigroups with one relation and semigroups without cycles* Izv. Akad. Nauk SSSR, Ser. Mat., 46 $n°1$ (1982), pp. 84-94 (Russian)
14. E.L. Post 1947 *Recursive unsolvability of a problem of Thue* J. Symb. Logic, 12 (1947), pp. 1-11
15. A. Thue *Probleme über Veränderungen von Zeichenreihen nach gegebenen Regeln* Skr. Vid. Kristiania, I Mat. Naturv. Klasse, $n°10$, (1914), pp. 1-34
16. G.C. Tzeitin *Associative calculus with an unsolvable equivalence problem* Tr. Mat. Inst. Steklov Akad. Nauk SSSR, 52, (1958), pp. 172-189 (Russian)
17. L. Zhang *A short proof of a theorem of Adjan* Proc. Amer. Math. Soc., 116 (1) (1992), pp. 1-3

Word Problem for Thue Systems
with a Few Relations

Yuri Matiyasevich

Steklov Institute of Mathematics
of Russian Academy of Sciences
Saint-Petersburg Branch (POMI RAN)
27 Fontanka
Saint-Petersburg
191011, Russia

Abstract. The history of investigations on the word problem for Thue systems is presented with the emphasis on undecidable systems with a few relations. The best known result, a Thue system with only three relations and undecidable word problem, is presented with details. Bibl. 43 items.

1 Historical Introduction

The *general* theory of rewriting systems is a relatively new area. However, *particular* kinds of rewriting systems were known and studied in mathematics for a long time, in particular, in the theory of semigroups.

Let $S = \langle M, \circ \rangle$ be a *semigroup*, i.e., a set M and a binary operation on it satisfying the associative law

$$(m_1 \circ m_2) \circ m_3 = m_1 \circ (m_2 \circ m_3)$$

for any m_1, m_2, m_3 from M. This law allows one to omit parentheses and write

$$m_1 \circ m_2 \circ m_3$$

or simply

$$m_1 m_2 m_3$$

without ambiguity.

For a semigroup $S = \langle M, \circ \rangle$ there may exist a finite subset

$$A = \{a_1, \ldots, a_n\} \subseteq M$$

such that any element of M can be constructed from $a_1, \ldots, a_n$ with the aid of the operation $\circ$, i.e., every element m from M has a *representation*

$$m = a_{i_1} \circ \ldots \circ a_{i_k} \tag{1}$$

where $1 \leq i_j \leq n$. In such a case we say that S is *finitely generated* and A is a *set of generators*. If each m from M has only one representation (1), then the semigroup is called *free* and, treating A as an alphabet, we can identify M with A^*, the set of all words in A, and identify $\circ$ with concatenation.

More interesting is the case when some elements have more than one representation and hence we have non-trivial *relations*

$$a_{i_1} \ldots a_{i_l} = a_{j_1} \ldots a_{j_l} \tag{2}$$

among the generators.

As soon as we have a single relation, we have countably many of them because (2) implies that

$$m a_{i_1} \ldots a_{i_l} = m a_{j_1} \ldots a_{j_l},$$
$$a_{i_1} \ldots a_{i_l} m = a_{j_1} \ldots a_{j_l} m$$

for any m from M. Also if we have two relations

$$P = Q$$

and

$$Q = R$$

then we have relations

$$Q = P$$

and

$$P = R$$

as well.

It may happen that there is a finite set

$$P_1 = Q_1,$$
$$\vdots \tag{3}$$
$$P_t = Q_t$$

of relations such that any other relation $P = Q$ is implied by relations (3) in the above described way. In such a case the semigroup is called *finitely presented*. A *presentation*, consisting of the alphabet and the set of relations, is also called a *Thue system* and can be viewed as a special kind of rewriting system.

Relation are often written as

$$P_1 \longleftrightarrow Q_1,$$
$$\vdots \tag{4}$$
$$P_t \longleftrightarrow Q_t.$$

Two words, G and H, from A^* are said to be *immediately equivalent* in a given Thue system T, written $G \underset{T}{\longleftrightarrow} H$, if

- either they are graphically equal, written $G \equiv H$ (i.e., equal as words in A^*)
- or there are number i and words X and Y such that $1 \leq i \leq t$ and
  - either $G \equiv X P_i Y$ and $H \equiv X Q_i Y$
  - or $G \equiv X Q_i Y$ and $H \equiv X P_i Y$.

(To make the further exposition a bit smoother the author has deviated from the traditional definition of immediate equivalence; usually this relation is not required be reflexive.)

The transitive closure of $\underset{T}{\longleftrightarrow}$ is denoted by $\underset{T}{\overset{*}{\longleftrightarrow}}$: two words G and H are *equivalent* in T, written $G \underset{T}{\overset{*}{\longleftrightarrow}} H$, if there are words $W_0, \ldots, W_k$ which provide a *derivation*

$$G \equiv W_0 \underset{T}{\longleftrightarrow} W_1 \underset{T}{\longleftrightarrow} \ldots \underset{T}{\longleftrightarrow} W_k \equiv H$$

of word H from word G.

The choice of generators is not unique so a finitely presented semigroup has in general many presentation. On the other hand, given Thue system determines corresponding semigroup up to isomorphism. Namely, one can identify M, the set of elements, with the set of classes of equivalent words; if $\mathcal{G}$ and $\mathcal{H}$ are two such classes and $G_1, G_2 \in \mathcal{G}$, $H_1, H_2 \in \mathcal{H}$, then words $G_1 H_1$ and $G_2 H_2$ are also equivalent and $\mathcal{G} \circ \mathcal{H}$ can be defined as the unique class containing these words.

The name "Thue system" was given after Axel Thue who in 1914 posed in [37] the following problem:

> *Given a finite presentation of a semigroup and two words in the alphabet of generators, determine whether the words are equivalent.*

This problem is known as *Thue's problem* or *word problem for finitely presented semigroups*. One can equally speak about finitely pesented monoid because the empty word, denoted by Λ, evidently plays the role of unit under concatenation. In the Russian literature Thue systems are also known under the name *associative systems* or *associative calculi* and the word problem is also called *the equivalence problem*.

Similar problem was posed a few years earlier by Dehn [12, 13] about groups. A *finitely presented group* can be defined as a finitely presented semigroup in which for every generator a there is another generator, denoted by a^{-1}, and two relations

$$\begin{aligned} aa^{-1} &= \Lambda, \\ a^{-1}a &= \Lambda. \end{aligned} \tag{5}$$

When counting the number of generators, a and a^{-1} are counted for one, and *trivial* relations (5) are not included into the count of relations in a presentation of a group. Corresponding problem for groups is known as *Dehn's problem* or *word problem for finitely presented groups*.

Dehn's problem for groups with single defining relation was solved in 1932 by Magnus [20]. The reader should realize that even at that time (to say nothing about the beginning of the century when the problems were posed) there were neither Turing machines no partial recursive functions, Church's Thesis was not stated yet and the mankind lived in happy ignorance of algorithmically unsolvable problems. Dehn and Thue posed their problems in positive sense: *find* a method which would allow to determing whether the words are equivalent or not.

The situation changed in the middle of 30's with the development of rigorous *general* notion of algorithm and Church's Thesis. These achievements, together with the first examples of algorithmically undecidable problems, formed a basis for tackling Dehn's and Thue's problems in the negative direction.

With respect to semigroups the success was achieved in 1947 by Markoff [23] and by Post [33]. The algorithmical undecidability of Thue's problem was established (see [24]) in the following strong sense:

> *there is a Thue system T and a word G such that there is no algorithm to decide, given a word H, whether it is equivalent to G or not.*

Thue's problem was the first decision problem which arose in mathematics proper (i.e., not in logic or calculability theory) and which was shown algorithmically undecidable.

The above cited result by Magnus indicated that a semigroup with undecidable word problem should have sufficiently many defining relations and one could hope to find partial positive solution of Thue's problem for semigroups defined by a small number of relations. It was natural to seek for the boundary between decidable and undecidable in terms of the number of defining relations, and several researchers devoted their investigations to constructing examples of semigroups with undecidable word problem and a small number of defining relation.

Markoff constructed such a semigroup with 13 generators and 33 relations. It was published at first in short note [24] and later detailed proof was supplied in [25]; see also Lallement's exposition [18] in this volume.

Markoff's result was improved several years later by Scott [35] and by Tseitin to 7 relations. This drastic cutting of the number of relations became possible thanks to Dehn's problem being at that time proved undecidable (both Scott and Tseitin based their constructions on Novikov's result [29, 30]; today examples of finitely presented groups with undecidable word problem can be found in [3, 16, 7, 6, 42, 40, 11, 10]). Tseitin's example was published at first in short note [38] and detailed proof was given in [39]; see also Lallement's exposition [18] in this volume.

Tseitin's semigroup is undecidable in the above mentioned strong sence: *there is a particular word G such that there is no algorithm to decide, given a word H, whether it is equivalent to G or not.* While this semigroup has only 7 relations containing 33 occurences of 5 generators, the length of such a word G known today is measured in thousands of letters. That is why Tseitin has also constructed another Thue system with 9 relations

$$
\begin{aligned}
ac &\longleftrightarrow ca, \\
ad &\longleftrightarrow da, \\
bc &\longleftrightarrow cb, \\
bd &\longleftrightarrow db, \\
eca &\longleftrightarrow ce, \\
edb &\longleftrightarrow de, \\
cdca &\longleftrightarrow cdcae, \\
caaa &\longleftrightarrow aaa, \\
daaa &\longleftrightarrow aaa
\end{aligned}
$$

and proved that *is no algorithm to decide, given a word H, whether it is equivalent to word aaa or not.*

Further progress to undecidable Thue systems with 5 relations was achieved by Makanin [21] and by Matiyasevich [26, 27] as modification of Tseitin's example with 7 relations.

In 1967 the author [26] constructed a Thue system

$$
\begin{aligned}
\alpha\alpha\sigma\alpha\sigma &\longleftrightarrow \sigma\alpha\alpha, \\
\alpha\alpha\sigma\sigma &\longleftrightarrow \sigma\alpha\alpha, \\
L &\longleftrightarrow M
\end{aligned}
\tag{6}
$$

in two letter alphabet $\{\alpha, \sigma\}$ for which the word problem is undecidable. The number of relations, 3, still remains the record one. The cost paid for this reduction of the number of relations was the length of relations, namely word L had 304 letters and word M had 608 letters, so Tseitin's example with 7 relations remains the shortest one, i.e., the one with the least total number of letters in the presentation.

Surprisingly, we still do not have a counterpart of Magnus's result for semigroups with one defining relation. Only partial progress for single relation of special forms was achieved (see surveys by Adian and Makanin [2] and by Lallement [18] in this volume; also see [43]).

Parallel to reduction of the number of defining relations in undecidable semigroups there was reduction of the number of relations in undecidable groups. Here there were two sources of progress. On one hand, there were new ideas specific for the case of groups. On the other hand, constructions of undecidable groups were based on undecidable semigroups, so a reduction for semigroups immediately caused corresponding reduction for groups. Today the smallest number, 12, is achieved in the group constructed by Borisov [6] on the base of authour's semigroup (6) with 3 relations.

Besides groups, semigroup (6) was used for constructing "simple" examples of other undecidable problem. A Thue system (4) with t relations can be rewritten as *semiThue system*

$$
\begin{aligned}
P_1 &\longrightarrow Q_1, \\
Q_1 &\longrightarrow P_1, \\
&\;\;\vdots \\
P_t &\longrightarrow Q_t, \\
Q_t &\longrightarrow P_t
\end{aligned}
\tag{7}
$$

with $2t$ *rules* (relations $\xrightarrow[T]{}$ and $\xrightarrow[T]{*}$ are defined similar to the above definitions

of $\xleftrightarrow[T]{}$ and $\xleftrightarrow[T]{*}$ with the last possibility, $G \equiv XQ_iY$ and $H \equiv XP_iY$, being omitted). Claus [8, 9] (see also [14]) proved that a semiThue system with undecidable word problem and k rules enable one to prove undecidability of *Post correspondence problem* introduced in [33] for $k + 4$ pairs of words. Using (6), Claus established undecidability of Post correspondence problem for 10 pairs of words. Pansiot noticed in [31] that the first two relations in (6) had equal right-hand side parts and hence could be replaced by 3 semiThue rules

$$
\sigma\alpha\alpha \longrightarrow \alpha\alpha\sigma\alpha\sigma,
$$

$$\alpha\alpha\sigma\alpha\sigma \longrightarrow \alpha\alpha\sigma\sigma,$$
$$\alpha\alpha\sigma\sigma \longrightarrow \sigma\alpha\alpha,$$

which together with two rules $L \longrightarrow M$ and $M \longrightarrow L$ form an undecidable semiThue system with 5 rules and, according to Claus's result, imply the undecidability of Post correspondence problem for 9 pairs of words.

The undecidability of the word problem for a semiThue system with 5 rules and the undecidability of Post correspondence problem for 9 pairs of words remained the best results until recently. In December 1993, Sénizergues and the author were able to construct a semiThue system with 4 rules only and with undecidable word problem, which respectively implied the undecidability of Post correspondence problem for 8 pairs of words. Besides the old main idea used for construction of Thue system (6), this new result required a number of new ideas specific to semiThue systems.

The undecidable Thue system (6) has got wide citation (see [1–2, 4–6, 8–11, 14, 17–19, 22, 28, 31, 34, 36, 40–43]) in spite of the fact that the author had never made his proof of undecidability available to broad readership. The only place where the detailed proof had been given by the author was his thesis existing in a few copies. One excuse for this was prompt appearence of Collins's paper [11] containing a detailed proof. However, this proof was rather different from author's original one. An idea of this original proof can be obtained from a joint publication of Boone, Collins and Matiyasevich [4] where this technique was used for obtaining similar but a bit different result; however, this publication is not easily available.

It gives a pleasure to the author to take the opportunity providied by this *Ecole de Printemps* and publish his original proof. The particular Thue system (6) presented in [26] was based on Tseitin's example and hence eventually depended on the deep and difficult result about the unsolvability of Dehn's problem for groups. Below the technique is introduced in a general setting which enables one to construct a Thue system with 3 relation and undecicable word problem starting from any Thue system for which this problem is undecidable.

The author expresses his gratitude to Géraud Sénizergues who read carefully the manuscript and revealed numerous bugs.

2   Construction

2.1   Plan

Let T_0 be an arbitrary Thue system

$$R_1 \longleftrightarrow S_1,$$
$$\vdots \tag{8}$$
$$R_{t_0} \longleftrightarrow S_{t_0}$$

in some alphabet $A_0 = \{a_1, \ldots, a_n\}$. We shall construct another Thue system T_3 defined by 3 relation in a two letter alphabet A_3, and a mapping

$$\sigma : A_0^* \to A_3^*$$

such that two words G_0 and H_0 from A_0^* are equivalent in T_0 if and only if their images, $\sigma(G_0)$ and $\sigma(H_0)$, are equivalent in T_3, i.e.,

$$G_0 \xleftrightarrow[T_0]{*} H_0 \iff \sigma(G_0) \xleftrightarrow[T_3]{*} \sigma(H_0). \tag{9}$$

This mapping σ will be effective, so it will provide a reduction of the word problem for T_0 to the word problem for T_3. Taking for T_0 any Thue system with undecidable word problem we shall obtain a Thue system T_3 with 3 relation and undecidable word problem. If for the system T_0 there is no algorithm to decide, given a word H, whether it is equivalent to some *fixed* word G, then the problem of the equivalence to word $\sigma(G)$ is undecidable for system T_3.

In order to reach our ultimate goal, Thue system T_3, we shall construct two auxiliary Thue systems T_1 and T_2 in some alphabets A_1 and A_2 and for $i = 0, 1, 2$ define mappings

$$\tau_i : A_i^* \to A_{i+1}^*$$

such that for any two words G_0 and H_0 from A_0^*

$$G_i \xleftrightarrow[T_i]{*} H_i \iff \tau_i(G_i) \xleftrightarrow[T_{i+1}]{*} \tau_i(H_i) \tag{10}$$

where

$$G_{i+1} \equiv \tau_i(G_i)$$

and

$$H_{i+1} \equiv \tau_i(H_i).$$

It is clear that we can define

$$\sigma(G_0) \equiv G_3$$

and obtain (9).

Each mapping τ_i will be defined via a word Z_{i+1} from A_{i+1}^* and an *encoding*

$$\rho_i : A_i \to A_{i+1}^*.$$

Such an encoding can be extended in a natural way to a mapping

$$\rho_i : A_j^* \to A_{i+1}^*,$$

namely, if

$$G_i \equiv g_1 \dots g_k$$

then

$$\rho_i(G_i) \equiv \rho_i(g_1) \dots \rho_i(g_k).$$

Mapping τ_i will be defined by

$$\tau_i(G_i) \equiv \rho_i(G_i) Z_{i+1}. \tag{11}$$

It is clear that to prove part $\Longrightarrow$ of the equivalence (10) it will be sufficient to prove that

$$G_i \underset{T_i}{\longleftrightarrow} H_i \implies \tau_i(G_i) \underset{T_{i+1}}{\overset{*}{\longleftrightarrow}} \tau_i(H_i). \tag{12}$$

The proof of the inverse implications $\Longleftarrow$ in (10) will be based on defining mappings

$$\phi_i : A_{i+1}^* \to A_i^*$$

which will be semiinverse to τ_i in the sense that

$$\phi_i(\tau_i(G_i)) \equiv G_i.$$

These mappings ϕ_i will also provide mappings of derivations in T_{i+1} into derivations in T_i in the following sense: as soon as

$$\tau_i(G_i) \equiv W_0 \underset{T_{i+1}}{\longleftrightarrow} W_1 \underset{T_{i+1}}{\longleftrightarrow} \cdots \underset{T_{i+1}}{\longleftrightarrow} W_k \tag{13}$$

is a derivation in T_{i+1},

$$G_i \equiv \phi_i(W_0) \underset{T_i}{\longleftrightarrow} \phi_i(W_1) \underset{T_i}{\longleftrightarrow} \cdots \underset{T_i}{\longleftrightarrow} \phi_i(W_k) \tag{14}$$

will be a derivation in T_i.

2.2 System T_1

Our first goal is the reduction of the word problem for T_0 to the word problem for a Thue system T_1 with defining relations

$$\begin{aligned} P_1 &\longleftrightarrow Q_1 \\ &\vdots \\ P_{t_1} &\longleftrightarrow Q_{t_1} \end{aligned} \tag{15}$$

such that words $P_1, \ldots, P_{t_1}$, and words $Q_1, \ldots, Q_{t_1}$ have equal and non-zero lengths, i.e.,

$$|P_1| = \ldots = |P_{t_1}| = p \neq 0$$

and

$$|Q_1| = \ldots = |Q_{t_1}| = q \neq 0.$$

To this end we extend alphabet A_0 by a new genetator, namely, we define

$$A_1 = \{a_1, \ldots, a_n, a_{n+1}\}.$$

Let

$$p = \max\{|R_1|, \ldots, |R_{t_0}|, |S_1|, \ldots, |S_{t_0}|\} + 1,$$
$$q = p + 1.$$

For each relation $R_i \longleftrightarrow Q_i$ of system T_0 we will include into (15) the relation

$$R_i a_{n+1}^{p-|R_i|} \longleftrightarrow S_i a_{n+1}^{q-|S_i|}. \tag{16}$$

Also for each generator a_j from A_1 we include into (15) the relation

$$a_j a_{n+1}^{p-1} \longleftrightarrow a_{n+1} a_j a_{n+1}^{q-2} \tag{17}$$

Thanks to the latter relations, for every j we have

$$a_j a_{n+1}^q \underset{T_1}{\overset{*}{\longleftrightarrow}} a_{n+1}^q a_j a_{n+1}^q$$

and by induction on the length of an arbitrary word G

$$G a_{n+1}^q \underset{T_1}{\overset{*}{\longleftrightarrow}} a_{n+1}^q G' a_{n+1}^q$$

for some word G'.

Encoding ρ_0 is the identity $\rho_0(a_j) \equiv a_j$, and mapping τ_0 is defined by (11) with $Z_1 \equiv a_{n+1}^q$.

Let us check (12) for $i = 0$. Case $G_0 \equiv H_0$ is trivial. Let now $G_0 \equiv X R_i Y$, $H_0 \equiv X S_i Y$. We have:

$$
\begin{aligned}
\tau_0(G_0) &\equiv X R_i Y a_{n+1}^q \\
&\underset{T_1}{\overset{*}{\longleftrightarrow}} X R_i a_{n+1}^q Y' a_{n+1}^q \\
&\underset{T_1}{\longleftrightarrow} X S_i a_{n+1}^q Y' a_{n+1}^q \\
&\underset{T_1}{\overset{*}{\longleftrightarrow}} X S_i Y a_{n+1}^q \\
&\equiv \tau_0(H_0).
\end{aligned}
$$

Case $G_0 \equiv X S_i Y$, $H_0 \equiv X R_i Y$ follows by the symmetry of relation $\underset{T_1}{\overset{*}{\longleftrightarrow}}$.

The inverse mapping ϕ_0 is nothing more than the projection of alphabet A_1 onto alphabet A_0, i.e., $\phi_0(G_1)$ is the result of deleting all occurences of letter a_{n+1}. To check that ϕ_0 does transform a derivation (13) in T_1 into a derivation (14) in T_0, it suffies to note that

$$\phi_0(X P_i Y) \equiv \phi_0(X)\phi_0(P_i)\phi_0(Y)$$

and,

$$\phi_0(X Q_i Y) \equiv \phi_0(X)\phi_0(Q_i)\phi_0(Y),$$

and either $\phi_0(P_i) \longleftrightarrow \phi_0(Q_i)$ is a defining relation of T_0 or $\phi_0(P_i) \equiv \phi_0(Q_i)$, depending on whether $P_i \longleftrightarrow Q_i$ is a relation of type (16) or (17).

2.3 System T_2'

Let $A_2' = \{a, b\}$ and ρ_1 be the encoding such that

$$\rho_1 : a_j \mapsto aab^j ab^{n+2-j}. \tag{18}$$

Let t be the smallest power of 2 which is not less than t_1,

$$t = 2^u.$$

Let P_i and Q_i denote words P_{t_1} and Q_{t_1} whenever $i \geq t_1$. Let for $i = 1, \ldots, t$

$$L_i \equiv \rho_1(P_i),$$
$$M_i \equiv \rho_1(Q_i).$$

We first consider system T_2' with t relations

$$L_1 \longleftrightarrow M_1,$$
$$\vdots \tag{19}$$
$$L_t \longleftrightarrow M_t.$$

It is evident

$$G_1 \overset{*}{\underset{T_1}{\longleftrightarrow}} H_1 \iff \rho_1(G_1) \overset{*}{\underset{T_2'}{\longleftrightarrow}} \rho_1(H_1)$$

thanks to the fact that the P's and Q's are non-empty words. The role of our choice of t as a power of 2 will become clear later.

A reduction of the word problem for arbitrary Thue system to the word problem for a Thue system in a two letter alphabet was done by Hall [15] using an encoding different from (18). Our special choice of ρ_1 pursued several goals. First, similar to system T_1 the lengths of left-hand sides and the right-hand sides of all relation in (19) are equal, respectively, to some numbers l and m. Second, we shall use later the fact that a word of the form $\rho_1(G_1)$ does not contain more than two consecutive a's, and all couples of consecutive a's originate from the first two a's in encoding (18).

2.4 System T_2

Our new system T_1 has more relations than the original system T_0. The next system T_2 will have only 5 relation independent of the number of relation in T_0. The idea is to compress all relation (19) into a single one. Let

$$L_i \equiv l_{i1} \ldots l_{il},$$
$$M_i \equiv m_{i1} \ldots m_{im},$$

$$L \equiv l_{11} l_{21} \ldots l_{t1} \ldots l_{1l} l_{2l} \ldots l_{tl},$$
$$M \equiv m_{11} m_{21} \ldots m_{t1} \ldots m_{1m} m_{2m} \ldots m_{tm},$$

and let T_2 be the Thue system in alphabet

$$A_2 = \{a, b, e\}$$

with relations

$$eaa \leftrightarrow ae, \qquad\qquad (20)$$

$$eab \leftrightarrow be, \qquad\qquad (21)$$

$$eba \leftrightarrow ae, \qquad\qquad (22)$$

$$ebb \leftrightarrow be, \qquad\qquad (23)$$

$$L \leftrightarrow M. \qquad\qquad (24)$$

Thanks to relations (20)–(23)

$$e^u X x \xleftrightarrow[T_2]{*} x e^u$$

for any x from A_2' and any word X from $A_2'^*$ having length $t-1$. By induction on the length of an arbitrary word G we have

$$G e^u \xleftrightarrow[T_2]{*} e^u G'$$

for some word G', in particular, for any i

$$L_i a e^u \xleftrightarrow[T_2]{*} e^u a^{t-i} L a^i.$$

Let τ_1 be defined by (11) and (18) with $Z_2 \equiv a e^u$. Let us check (12) for $i = 1$. For the nontrivial case $G_1 \equiv X P_i Y$, $H_1 \equiv X Q_i Y$ we have:

$$\tau_1(G_1) \equiv \rho_1(X) L_i \rho_1(Y) a e^u$$

$$\xleftrightarrow[T_2]{*} \rho_1(X) L_i a e^u Y'$$

$$\xleftrightarrow[T_2]{*} \rho_1(X) e^u a^{t-i} L a^i Y'$$

$$\xleftrightarrow[T_2]{} \rho_1(X) e^u a^{t-i} M a^i Y'$$

$$\xleftrightarrow[T_2]{*} \rho_1(X) M_i a e^u Y'$$

$$\xleftrightarrow[T_2]{*} \rho_1(X) M_i \rho_1(Y) a e^u$$

$$\equiv \tau_1(H_1).$$

The definition of ϕ_1 is the most tricky part of the whole construction. This mapping is defined by *semiThue system with priorities* having three blocks of rules:

$$eaa \longrightarrow ae,$$

$$eab \longrightarrow be,$$

$$eba \longrightarrow ae,$$

$$ebb \longrightarrow be;$$

$$aab^1ab^{n+1} \longrightarrow a_1,$$

$$\vdots$$

$$aab^{n+1}ab \longrightarrow a_{n+1};$$

$$e \longrightarrow \Lambda,$$

$$a \longrightarrow \Lambda,$$

$$b \longrightarrow \Lambda.$$

The rules of the first block correspond to relations (20)–(23); the rules of the second block correspond to the encoding (18). To calculate $\phi_1(G)$ one has at first apply the rules from the first block until reaching a word G' to which none of the rules from the first block can be applied any longer; after that rules of the second block should be applied as long as possible producing a word G''; finally, the rules from the third block should finish transforming G into a word G''' from A_1^*. It is not difficult to understand that each of these three blocks of rules constitutes a *confluent, strictly length-decreasing* semi Thue system so these words G', G'' and G''' are completely determined by word G and do not depend on the particular way in which the rules were applied; these words will be denoted respectively by $\phi'(G)$, $\phi''(G)$ and $\phi_1(G)$.

Suppose that we have a derivation (13) with $i = 1$. Let us prove by induction on k that in such a case

$$\rho_1(G_1)ae^u \equiv \phi'(W_0) \underset{T_2'}{\longleftrightarrow} \phi'(W_1) \underset{T_2'}{\longleftrightarrow} \cdots \underset{T_2'}{\longleftrightarrow} \phi'(W_k) \tag{25}$$

is a derivation in T_2' (we consider now T_2' as a system in alphabet A_2 rather than in A_2').

The base $k = 0$ is evident. Suppose now that (25) is a derivation, $W_k \equiv XUY$ and $U \longleftrightarrow V$ or $V \longleftrightarrow U$ is a relation of system T_2. If it is one of the four relations (20)–(23), then clearly $\phi'(XVY) \equiv \phi'(W_k)$. Without loss of generality it remains to consider only the case $U \equiv L$, $V \equiv M$. Being equivalent in T_2' to $\rho_1(G_1)ae^u$, the word $\phi'(W_k)$ does not contain more than two consecutive a's. On the other hand, word L begins with $2t = 2^{u+1}$ a's and hence word X should contain at least u occurences of letter e. It cannot contain more than u occurences because word $W_k \equiv XUV$ is equivalent to $\tau_1(G_1)$ in T_2. The difference of the lengths of words L and M is divisible by t, so it is easy to understand that, for some words X', Y' and number i,

$$\phi'(W_k) \equiv \phi'(XLY) \equiv X'L_iY'e^u$$

and

$$\phi'(XMY) \equiv X'M_iY'e^u$$

so these two words are equivalent in T_2'. The induction is completed.

Now that we know that (25) is a derivation in T_2', we see that (14) is a derivation in T_1.

2.5 System T_3

Let $A_3 = \{c, d\}$ and let ρ_2 be the following encoding:

$$\begin{aligned}
\rho_2(a) &\equiv c, \\
\rho_2(b) &\equiv cd, \\
\rho_2(e) &\equiv dd.
\end{aligned} \tag{26}$$

We define τ_2 by (11) with Z_3 being the empty word. Let T_3 be the system

$$\begin{aligned}
ddcc &\longleftrightarrow cdd, \\
ddcdc &\longleftrightarrow cdd, \\
\rho_2(L) &\longleftrightarrow \rho_2(M).
\end{aligned}$$

To check (12) for $i = 2$ it suffies to observe that

$$\rho_2(eaa) \xleftrightarrow[T_3]{} \rho_2(ae),$$

$$\rho_2(eab) \xleftrightarrow[T_3]{} \rho_2(be),$$

$$\rho_2(eba) \xleftrightarrow[T_3]{} \rho_2(ae),$$

$$\rho_2(ebb) \xleftrightarrow[T_3]{} \rho_2(be).$$

The inverse mapping ϕ_2 can be defined as follows:

$$\begin{aligned}
\phi_2(\Lambda) &\equiv \Lambda, \\
\phi_2(d) &\equiv \Lambda, \\
\phi_2(Gc) &\equiv \phi_2(G)a, \\
\phi_2(Gcd) &\equiv \phi_2(G)b, \\
\phi_2(Gdd) &\equiv \phi_2(G)e.
\end{aligned}$$

Besides the required identity

$$\phi_2(\tau_2(G_2)) \equiv G_2$$

for every word G from A_3^* we have either

$$\tau_2(\phi_2(G)) \equiv G$$

or

$$d\tau_2(\phi_2(G)) \equiv G.$$

Suppose that we have a derivation (13) with $i = 2$. Let us prove by induction on k that in such a case (14) is a derivation in T_2. The base of induction, $k = 0$, is trivial. Let $W_k \equiv XUY$ where either $U \longleftrightarrow V$ or $V \longleftrightarrow U$ is a defining relation of T_3. Let

$$y\tau_2(\phi_2(Y)) \equiv Y$$

where either $y \equiv \Lambda$ or $y \equiv d$. We have:

$$\phi_2(W_k) \equiv \phi_2(XUY) \equiv \phi_2(X)\phi_2(Uy)\phi_2(Y)$$

and

$$\phi_2(XVY) \equiv \phi_2(X)\phi_2(Vy)\phi_2(Y),$$

and either $\phi_2(Uy) \longleftrightarrow \phi(Vy)$ or $\phi_2(Vy) \longleftrightarrow \phi(Uy)$ is a defining relation of T_2 with the exception of the case when $y \equiv d$ and $U \longleftrightarrow V$ or $V \longleftrightarrow U$ is the "long" relations $\rho_2(L) \longleftrightarrow \rho_2(M)$. But this case is impossible because, as it was shown above, the word $\phi_2(X)$ should contain all u occurences of letter e while the word $\phi_2(Uy)$ ends with e.

References

1. S. I. Adian. On P. S. Novikov's and his disciple's investigations on algorithmical problems in algebra (in Russian). *Trudy Mat. Inst. Steklov.*, 133:23–32, 1973.

2. S. I. Adian and G. S. Makanin. Investigations on algorithmical problems in algebra (in Russian). *Trudy Mat. Inst. Steklov.*, 168:197–217, 1984.

3. W. W. Boone. The word problem. *Ann. Math.*, 70(2):207–265, 1959.

4. W. W. Boone, D. Collins, and Ju. V. Matijasevič. Embedding into semigroups with only a few defining relations. In J. E. Fenstad, editor, *Proceedings of the Second Scandinavian Logic Symposium*, volume 63 of *Studies in Logic and the Foundations of Mathematics*, pages 27–40, Amsterdam, 1971. North-Holland.

5. W. W. Boone and D. J. Collins. Embeddings into groups with only a few defining relations. *J. Austral. Math. Soc.*, 18(1):1–7, 1974.

6. V. V. Borisov. Simple examples of groups with undecidable word problem (in Russian). *Mat. Zametki*, 6(5):521–532, 1969.

7. J. L. Britton. The word problem. *Ann. Math.*, 77(1):16–32, 1963.

8. V. Claus. Die Grenze zwischen Entscheidbarkeit und Nichtentscheidbarkeit. *Fernstndeinkurs für die Fernuniversität Hagen*, Open University, Hagen, 1979.

9. V. Claus. Some remarks on PCP(k) and related problems. *Bull. EATCS*, 12:54–61, 1980.

10. D. J. Collins. A simple presentation of a group with unsolvable word problem. *Illinois J. Math.*, 30(2):230–234, 1986.

11. D. J. Collins. Word and conjugacy problems in groups with only a few defining relations. *Z. Math. Logik Grundlag. Math.*, 15(4):305–323, 1969.

12. M. Dehn. Über die Topologie des dreidimensionalen Raumes. *Math. Ann.*, 69:137–168, 1910.

13. M. Dehn. Über unendliche diskontinuierliche Gruppen. *Math. Ann.*, 71:116–144, 1912.

14. A. Ehrenfeucht and G. Rozenberg. On the (generalized) Post correspondence problem with lists of length 2. *Lect. Notes Comput. Sci.*, 115:408–416, 1981.

15. M. J. Hall. The word problem for semigroups with two generators. *J. Symbolic Logic*, 14:115–118, 1949.

16. G. Higman. Subgroups of finitely presented groups. *Proc. Roy. Soc.*, 262(1311):455–475, 1961.

17. G. Lallement. Presentations de monoides et problems algorithmiques. *Lecture Notes in Mathematics*, 586:136–144, 1977.

18. G. Lallement. The word problem for Thue rewriting systems. *This volume*, 1994.

19. J. Lockhart. Triviality problem for semigroups of deficiency 1. *J. Symbolic Logic*, 42(3):457–458, 1977.

20. W. Magnus. Das Identitäts problem für Gruppen mit einer definierenden Relation. *Math. Ann.*, 106:295–307, 1932.

21. G. S. Makanin. On the word problem for finitely presented semigroups. *Soviet Math. Doklady*, 7:1478–1480, 1966.

22. C. Marché. On ground AC-completion. *Lect. Notes Comput. Sci.*, 488:411–422, 1991.

23. A. A. Markoff. Impossibility of certain algorithms in the theory of associative systems (in Russian). *Dokl. Akad. Nauk SSSR*, 55(7):587–590, 1947.

24. A. A. Markoff. Impossibility of certain algoroths in the theory of associative systems (in Russian). *Dokl. Akad. Nauk SSSR*, 58(3):353–356, 1947.

25. A. A. Markoff. Theory of algorithms (in Russian). *Trudy Mat. Inst. Steklov.*, 42, 1954. Translated in Israel Program of scientific Translations. Jerusalem, 1961. MR 17, 1038, MR 24, A2527.

26. Yu. Matiyasevich. Simple examples of undecidable associative calculi (in Russian). *Dokl. Akad. Nauk SSSR*, 173:1264–1266, 1967. English translation in: *Soviet Math. Dokl.*, 8;555–557, 1967.

27. Yu. Matiyasevich. Simple examples of undecidable canonical calculi (in Russian). *Trudy Mat. Inst. Steklov.*, 93:50–88, 1967. English translation in: *Proc Steklov Inst. Math.*, 93:227–252, 1968.

28. V. L. Murskii. Unrecognizable properties of finite systems of identity relations (in Russian). *Dokl. Akad. Nauk SSSR*, 196(3):520–522, 1971.

29. P. S. Novikov. On algorithmical undecidability of the word problem in the theory of groups (in Russian). *Dokl. Akad. Nauk SSSR*, 85(4):709–712, 1952.

30. P. S. Novikov. On algorithmical undecidability of the word problem in the theory of groups (in Russian). *Trudy Mat. Inst. Steklov.*, 44, 1955.

31. J. J. Pansiot. A note on Post's correspondence problem. 12(5):233, 1981.

32. E. L. Post. A variant of recursively unsolvable problem. *Bull. Amer. Math. Soc.*, 52:264–268, 1946.

33. E. L. Post. Recursive unsolvability of a problem of Thue. *J. Symbolic Logic*, 12:1–11, 1947.

34. L. Priese. Über ein 2-dimensionales Thue-System mit zwei Regeln und unentscheidbaren Wortproblem. *Z. Math. Logik Grundlag. Math.*, 25(2):179–192, 1979.

35. D. Scott. A short recursively unsolvable problem. *J. Symbolic Logic*, 21:111–112, 1956.

36. G. Sénizergues. Some undecidable termination problem for semi-Thue systems. To appear in *Lect. Notes Comput. Sci.*, 1994

37. A. Thue. Probleme über Veränderungen von Zeichenreihen nach gegebenen Regeln. *Skrifter utgit av Videnskapsselskapet i Kristiania*, I. Matematisk-naturvidenskabelig klasse, 10, 34pp., 1914. Reprinted in: A. Thue. Selected Mathematical Papers. Oslo, 1977, 493–524.

38. G. S. Tseitin. An associative calculus with undecidable problem of equivalence (in Russian). *Dokl. Akad. Nauk SSSR*, 107(3):370–371, 1956.

39. G. S. Tseitin. An associative calculus with undecidable problem of equivalence (in Russian). *Trudy Mat. Inst. Steklov.*, 52:172–189, 1958.

40. M. K. Valiev. Universal group with twenty-one defining relation. *Discrete Math.*, 17:207–213, 1977.

41. M. K. Valiev. Examples of universal finitely-presented groups (in Russian). *Dokl. Akad. Nauk SSSR*, 211(2):265–268, 1973.

42. M. K. Valiev. On polynomial reducibility of word problem under embedding of recursively presented groups in finitely presented groups. In J. Bečvář, editor, *Mathematical Foundations of Computer Science 1975*, volume 32 of *Lect. Notes Comput. Sci.*, pages 432–438. Springer-Verlag, 1975.

43. A. Yasuhara. The solvability of the word problem for certain semigroups. *Proc. Amer. Math. Soc.*, 26(4):645–650, 1970.

Some Extensions of Rewriting

Hélène Kirchner

CRIN-CNRS & INRIA-Lorraine
BP 239
54506 Vandœuvre-lès-Nancy Cedex
E-mail: Helene.Kirchner@loria.fr

Abstract. Automated deduction motivates the introduction of several extensions of rewriting, especially ordered rewriting, class rewriting and rewriting with constraints. This paper is a survey of these three notions, shows the evolution between them and their increasing power of expressivity.

1   Introduction

Term rewriting techniques have a wide range of applications in mainly two domains: the first one is the operational semantics of logico-functional programming languages. This area led to various extensions of the rewriting concept, like order-sorted rewriting [29], conditional rewriting [16], priority rewriting [38], concurrent rewriting [18], or graph rewriting [11] .... The second domain is automated theorem proving where rewriting techniques are of primarily use in provers using demodulation or simplification inference rules to prune the search space. In this context, it appears that most of interesting proofs in mathematical structures, set and graph theory, or geometry, involve in their axiomatization some equalities which cannot be immediately used as rewrite rules. This motivates the introduction of several extensions, especially ordered rewriting, class rewriting and rewriting with constraints. This paper is a survey of these three notions, shows the evolution between them and their increasing power of expressivity. Although these three extensions are better motivated by theorem proving purposes, they also have promising applications in programming languages.

The termination property of a rewrite system is crucial to compute normal forms of terms and reduction orderings ensure termination as soon as, in the rewrite system, every left-hand side is greater than the corresponding right-hand side. This is the key point to choose an orientation for an equality and to use it as a rewrite rule. Two kinds of equalities may cause failure of orientation: the first one, like $f(x) = g(y)$, does not have the same variables in the left and right-hand sides. The second kind are permutative axioms like commutativity that cannot be oriented without loosing the termination property of the reduction relation. However such non-orientable equalities may sometimes be used for reduction anyway, because some of their instances can be oriented. For instance, considering the commutativity axiom $(x + y = y + x)$, an instance like $(x + f(x) = f(x) + x)$ may be oriented using a lexicographic path ordering. Based on this idea, ordered rewriting does not require to use equalities always in the same direction, but the decreasing property of rewriting with respect to a given ordering is always satisfied. Ordered rewriting, confluence and completion are studied in [4, 6, 36].

The class rewriting approach, first developed for dealing with permutative axioms like associativity and commutativity, consists in working on equivalence classes of terms and choosing an adequate rewrite relation that transforms an element of the equivalence class and may involve some built-in axioms in the matching process [20, 44, 33]. Several approaches are surveyed in [23]. Completion methods have been designed to handle the case of class rewrite system [44, 20, 23, 4]. First concerned by associative and commutative theories, the technique has been extended in [35] to build in the rewriting process theories including identity or idempotency axioms, Abelian group theory and commutative ring theory.

Class rewriting can be fruitfully combined with ordered rewriting, and this yields the notion of ordered class rewriting which is detailed in this paper. This extension leads to significant proofs in theorem provers like RRL [26] and SBREVE [1].

Rewriting with constraints emerged more recently as a unified way to cover the previous concepts by looking at ordering and equations as symbolic constraints on terms. But even further, it provides a framework to incorporate disequations, built-in data types and sort constraints. A first motivation for introducing constraints in completion processes arises when considering the problem of completion modulo a set of axioms A [5, 23]. A main drawback of this class of completion procedures is an inherent inefficiency, due to the computation of matchers and unifiers modulo A. A natural idea is to use constraints to record unification problems in the theory A and to avoid solving them immediately. Constraints are just checked for satisfiablity, which is in general much simpler than finding a complete set of solutions or a solved form, especially in equational theories. Originally a completion procedure with associative commutative equational constraints has been proposed in [28] and a general framework for deduction with constraints developed in [30]. Ordering and equality constraints were proposed for several deduction processes in first-order logic with equality. The same idea was used in implementations of ordered completion described in [36, 45], and completion modulo associativity, commutativity and identity [10, 24]. Completion with membership constraints is studied in [12]. Refutational completeness results for deduction systems based on constrained superposition have been obtained in [9, 40, 41].

This paper attempts to present the evolution from ordered rewriting and class rewriting to rewriting with constraints in a comprehensive way. So Section 2 briefly reminds the definitions and results related to ordered rewriting, Section 3 combines this concept with equivalence classes modulo a set of axioms and Section 4 shows how the more general notion of rewriting with constraints adequately generalizes the previous ones.

The reader may refer to [13] for the concepts of terms, substitution and rewrite systems. The notations used in this paper are consistent with [15]. In particular, $\mathcal{T}(\Sigma, \mathcal{X})$ denotes the set of terms built on the signature Σ involving sort symbols $\mathcal{S}$, function symbols $\mathcal{F}$ and variables $\mathcal{X}$, $SUBST$ the set of substitutions of $\mathcal{T}(\Sigma, \mathcal{X})$, $Var(t)$ denotes the set of variables of a term t, $t_{|\omega}$ the subterm of t at position ω, and $t[u]_\omega$ the term t that contains the subterm u at position ω.

2   Ordered rewriting

In ordered rewrite systems, the reduction ordering, used to prove that any term is decreasing in a rewrite step, is made explicit. A reduction ordering is a transitive, irreflexive, well-founded relation, closed under context and substitution. A simplification ordering is a reduction ordering that satisfies in addition that a term is greater than any of its subterms.

Definition 1 [6] An *ordered rewrite system* denoted $(E, >)$, is a set of equalities E together with a reduction ordering $>$.

The *ordered rewriting* relation is just rewriting with the following set of ordered instances: $E^> = \{\sigma(l) \to \sigma(r) \mid (l = r) \in E$ and σ such that $\sigma(l) > \sigma(r)\}$.

Definition 2 Given an ordered rewrite system $(E, >)$, the term t $(E, >)$-*rewrites* to t', denoted $t \to_{E,>} t'$, if there exist an equality $(l = r)$ of E, a position ω in t, a substitution σ, such that $t_{|\omega} = \sigma(l)$, $\sigma(l) > \sigma(r)$ and $t' = t[\sigma(r)]_\omega$.

Assuming that the reduction ordering $>$ can be extended to a total reduction ordering on ground terms (i.e. terms without variables), the Church-Rosser property of $(E, >)$ means that the relation $\overset{*}{\longleftrightarrow}_E$ on ground terms is included into the composition of relations $\overset{*}{\longrightarrow}_{E>} \circ \overset{*}{\longleftarrow}_{E>}$.

Unlike a standard completion procedure, ordered completion, also called unfailing completion, does not stop with a non-orientable equality and may terminate with a non-empty set of equalities. It can be used to saturate a set of equalities by computing *ordered critical pairs*, so that the resulting system has the Church-Rosser property, but provides in addition a refutationally complete equational theorem prover [4, 6]. However for associative-commutative theories, ordered completion often does not terminate. By combining techniques from ordered completion and completion in equivalence classes, a powerful completion process is obtained which also provides a refutationally complete theorem prover.

3   Ordered rewriting modulo a set of equalities

Let A be any set of axioms with decidable unification, matching and word problems and $\overset{*}{\longleftrightarrow}_A$ be the generated congruence relation on $\mathcal{T}(\Sigma, \mathcal{X})$. A reduction ordering $>$ is *A-compatible* if $\overset{*}{\longleftrightarrow}_A \circ > \circ \overset{*}{\longleftrightarrow}_A \subseteq >$. An ordering $>$ is *total on A-equivalence classes of ground terms* if for all ground terms s and t, either $s \overset{*}{\longleftrightarrow}_A t$, or $s > t$ or $t > s$. Such orderings have been described for associative-commutative axioms by [39, 46].

Definition 3 An *ordered class rewrite system* denoted $(E/A, >)$, is defined by a set of axioms A, a set of equalities E and a A-compatible reduction ordering $>$ total on A-equivalence classes of ground terms. A and E are assumed disjoint.

The class rewrite relation applies to a term if there exists a term in the same equivalence class modulo A that is reducible with $E^>$.

Definition 4 Given an ordered class rewrite system $(E/A, >)$, the term t $(E/A, >)$-*rewrites* to t', denoted $t \rightarrow_{E/A,>} t'$, if there exist an equality $(l = r) \in E$, a term u, a position ω in u and a substitution σ such that $t \xleftrightarrow{*}_A u[\sigma(l)]_\omega$, $\sigma(l) > \sigma(r)$ and $t' \xleftrightarrow{*}_A u[\sigma(r)]_\omega$.

By construction $\rightarrow_{E/A,>}$ is terminating. A term irreducible for $\rightarrow_{E/A,>}$ is said in (E/A)-normal form w.r.t. $>$. The $(E/A, >)$-normal form of a term t is denoted $t \downarrow_{E/A,>}$.

A-compatible reduction orderings do not exist when E is non-empty and A contains an axiom like idempotency $(x + x = x)$ where a lone variable occurs on one side and several times on the other. From an instance σ of an equality $(l = r) \in E$, a contradiction to well-foundedness of $>$ may be built, provided $\sigma(l) > \sigma(r)$:
$\sigma(l) \xleftrightarrow{*}_A \sigma(l) + \sigma(l) > \sigma(r) + \sigma(l) \xleftrightarrow{*}_A \sigma(r) + (\sigma(l) + \sigma(l)) > \sigma(r) + (\sigma(r) + \sigma(l)) \ldots$
Other axioms that prevent the existence of an A-compatible reduction ordering are equalities like $(x * 0 = 0)$ where a variable occurs on one side and not on the other. Then $0 \xleftrightarrow{*}_A \sigma(l) * 0 > \sigma(r) * 0 \xleftrightarrow{*}_A 0$ provides the contradiction. Indeed, if such axioms are present, they must be considered as ordered equalities.

The rewrite relation $\rightarrow_{E/A,>}$ is not completely satisfactory from an operational point of view: even if E is finite and $\xleftrightarrow{*}_A$ decidable, $\rightarrow_{E/A,>}$ may not be computable since equivalence classes modulo A may be infinite or not computable. For instance, the axiom $(-x = x)$ generates infinite equivalence classes. To avoid scrutiny through equivalence classes, the idea is to use a weaker relation on terms, called *ordered rewriting modulo A*, which incorporates A in the matching process, and uses the set $E^>$ of ordered instances of E.

Definition 5 Given an ordered class rewrite system $(E/A, >)$, the term t $(E, A, >)$-*rewrites* to t', denoted by $t \rightarrow_{E,A,>}^{(l=r),\omega,\sigma} t'$, if there exist an equality $(l = r)$ of E, a position ω in t, a substitution σ, such that $t_{|\omega} \xleftrightarrow{*}_A \sigma(l)$, $\sigma(l) > \sigma(r)$ and $t' = t[\sigma(r)]_\omega$.

Definition 6 The class rewrite system $(E/A, >)$ is *Church-Rosser* on a set of terms $\mathcal{T}$ if
$$\xleftrightarrow{*}_{E \cup A} \subseteq \xrightarrow{*}_{E/A,>} \circ \xleftrightarrow{*}_A \circ \xleftarrow{*}_{E/A,>} .$$

The ordered rewriting relation $(E, A, >)$ defined on $\mathcal{T}$ is:

Church-Rosser modulo A   if $\xleftrightarrow{*}_{E \cup A} \subseteq \xrightarrow{*}_{E,A,>} \circ \xleftrightarrow{*}_A \circ \xleftarrow{*}_{E,A,>}$

confluent modulo A   if $\xleftarrow{*}_{E,A,>} \circ \xrightarrow{*}_{E,A,>} \subseteq \xrightarrow{*}_{E,A,>} \circ \xleftrightarrow{*}_A \circ \xleftarrow{*}_{E,A,>}$

coherent modulo A   if $\xleftarrow{*}_{E,A,>} \circ \xleftrightarrow{*}_A \subseteq \xrightarrow{*}_{E,A,>} \circ \xleftrightarrow{*}_A \circ \xleftarrow{*}_{E,A,>}$

locally confluent modulo A if $\xleftarrow{}_{E,A,>} \circ \rightarrow_{E,>} \subseteq \xrightarrow{*}_{E,A,>} \circ \xleftrightarrow{*}_A \circ \xleftarrow{*}_{E,A,>}$

locally coherent modulo A if $\xleftarrow{}_{E,A,>} \circ \xleftrightarrow{}_A \subseteq \xrightarrow{*}_{E,A,>} \circ \xleftrightarrow{*}_A \circ \xleftarrow{*}_{E,A,>}$

The next theorem, adapted from [23], relates the different properties.

Theorem 1 *The following properties of an ordered class rewrite system $(E/A, >)$, are equivalent on $\mathcal{T}$:*
- *$(E, A, >)$ is Church-Rosser modulo A.*
- *$(E, A, >)$ is confluent modulo A and coherent modulo A.*

- $(E, A, >)$ is locally confluent and locally coherent modulo A.
- $\forall t, t',\ t \xleftrightarrow{*}_{E \cup A} t'$ iff $t \downarrow_{E,A,>} \xleftrightarrow{*}_A t' \downarrow_{E,A,>}$.

In order to check local coherence and confluence properties of the relation $(E, A, >)$ on the sets E and A, the usual notion of critical pairs extends to take into account A-unification and the reduction ordering.

Definition 7 Let $(g = d)$ and $(l = r)$ be two equalities in E with disjoint sets of variables. If there exists a position ω in g such that $g_{|\omega}$ is not a variable, $g_{|\omega}$ and l are A-unifiable with an A-unifier ψ in a complete set of A-unifiers, and if in addition $\psi(d) \not> \psi(g)$ and $\psi(r) \not> \psi(l)$, then $(\psi(g[r]_\omega) = \psi(d))$ is an *ordered critical pair modulo A* of $(l = r)$ into $(g = d)$.

Beyond critical pairs between equalities in E, for ensuring coherence, extended equalities are needed.

Definition 8 Let $(g = d)$ be an axiom in A and $(l = r)$ an equality in E with disjoint sets of variables. If there exists a position ω in g such that $g_{|\omega}$ is not a variable, $g_{|\omega}$ and l are A-unifiable with an A-unifier ψ in a complete set of A-unifiers, such that $\psi(r) \not> \psi(l)$, then $(g[l]_\omega = g[r]_\omega)$ is the *extended equality* of $(l = r)$ with respect to $(g = d)$.

For a set E of equalities, E^{ext} denotes the saturation of E under adjunction of extended equalities. In general these extended equalities have to be recursively extended. However in the special case of A being associativity and commutativity (AC) axioms, only a first level of extended equalities is needed. Moreover they can be systematically built: for each $(l = r) \in E$, such that the top symbol f in l is associative and commutative, the extended equality is $(f(l, z) = f(r, z))$ where z is a new variable (distinct from variables in l and r). From now on, an equality $(f(l, z) = f(r, z))$ implicitly denotes an extended equality of $(l = r)$ where the top symbol of l is an AC-operator f. For such l, it is sufficient to compute critical pairs at positions ω that are not imediately below another f. The rest of this section restricts to the case where $A = AC$ and describes a completion process for these specific axioms, in which the computation of extended equalities is incorporated in the rules.

Given the set OCM of rules for Ordered Completion Modulo given in Figure 1, a derivation is a sequence of sets of equalities $E_0 \longmapsto E_1 \longmapsto E_2 \longmapsto \ldots$ using the system OCM. The persistent set E_∞ is $\bigcup_{i \geq 0} \bigcap_{j > i} E_j$. A derivation is *fair* if any equality obtained from E_∞ by applying any rule **Deduce − Eq − Eq**, **Deduce − Ext − Eq**, **Deduce − Ext − Ext**, is included in $\bigcup_{i \geq 0} E_i$.

Theorem 2 Let E_0 be a set of equalities, and $>$ be a reduction ordering AC-compatible and total on AC-equivalence classes of ground terms. If $E_0 \longmapsto E_1 \longmapsto \ldots$ is a fair derivation, then $(E_\infty^{ext}, AC, >)$ is Church-Rosser modulo AC on ground terms.

The result expressed in Theorem 2 also holds even if E_∞ is an infinite set, as in the case of standard completion [21]. The proof [2, 8] is an extension to AC equivalence classes of terms, of the proof of ordered completion [4].

Deduce – Eq – Eq $\quad E \cup \{g = d,\ l = r\}$

$\Vdash\!\!\to$

$E \cup \{g = d,\ l = r,\ \psi(g[r]_\omega) = \psi(d)\}$

if $\psi(g_{|\omega}) \xleftrightarrow{\ *\ }_{AC} \psi(l),\ \psi(d) \not\succ \psi(g),\ \psi(r) \not\succ \psi(l)$

Deduce – Ext – Eq $\quad E \cup \{g = d,\ l = r\}$

$\Vdash\!\!\to$

$E \cup \{g = d,\ l = r,\ \psi(g[f(r, z)]_\omega) = \psi(d)\}$

if $\psi(g_{|\omega}) \xleftrightarrow{\ *\ }_{AC} \psi(f(l, z)),\ \psi(d) \not\succ \psi(g),\ \psi(r) \not\succ \psi(l)$

Deduce – Ext – Ext $\ E \cup \{g = d,\ l = r\}$

$\Vdash\!\!\to$

$E \cup \{g = d,\ l = r,\ \psi(f(d, z)) = \psi(f(r, z'))\}$

if $\psi(f(g, z)) \xleftrightarrow{\ *\ }_{AC} \psi(f(l, z')),\ \psi(d) \not\succ \psi(g),\ \psi(r) \not\succ \psi(l)$

Delete $\quad\quad\quad\quad E \cup \{p = q\}$

$\Vdash\!\!\to$

E

if $p \xleftrightarrow{\ *\ }_{AC} q$

Simplify $\quad\quad\quad E \cup \{p = q\}$

$\Vdash\!\!\to$

$E \cup \{p' = q\}$

if $p \to_{E,AC,>}^{(g=d),\sigma} p'$ and $p > \sigma(g)$ or $q > \sigma(d)$

Fig. 1. OCM: Ordered Completion Modulo AC

Ordered completion modulo AC can also be adapted to act as a refutational theorem prover. Let E be a set of equalities and $(t = t')$ an equational theorem to be proved in the theory described by E, with $t, t' \in \mathcal{T}(\Sigma, \mathcal{X})$. Assume that t_0 and t'_0 are the skolemized versions of respectively t and t', that are terms whose variables are now considered as a set $\mathcal{H}$ of new constants disjoint from $\mathcal{F}$. Let us introduce a set D of disequalities and more specifically the disequality $(t_0 \neq t'_0)$. The notion of ordered critical pairs between two equalities then extends to the notion of ordered superposition of an equality into a disequality, producing then a new disequality.

Definition 9 Let $(g \neq d)$ be a disequality in D and $(l = r)$ an equality in E with disjoint sets of variables. If there exists a position ω in g such that $g_{|\omega}$ is not a variable, $g_{|\omega}$ and l are AC-unifiable with an AC-unifier ψ in a complete set of AC-unifiers, and if in addition $\psi(d) \not\succ \psi(g)$ and $\psi(r) \not\succ \psi(l)$, then $(\psi(g[r]_\omega) \neq \psi(d))$ is an *ordered critical disequality modulo AC* of $(l = r)$ into $(g \neq d)$.

The previous set OCM is modified by adding a set of disequalities D which is not modified by the previous rules but is transformed by additional rules given in Figure 2.

Let $ROCM$ denote the whole set of rules. A derivation $(E_0, D_0) \Vdash\!\!\to (E_1, D_1) \Vdash\!\!\to \ldots$ with $ROCM$, is *fair* if any equality and disequality obtained from persisting equalities and disequalities (E_∞, D_∞) by applying any rule **Deduce−Eq−Eq, Deduce− Ext − Eq, Deduce − Ext − Ext, Deduce − Eq − DEq, Deduce − Ext − DEq**, is included in $\bigcup_i (E_i \cup D_i)$.

Deduce − Eq − DEq $(E \cup \{l = r\}, D \cup \{g \neq d\})$

$$\longmapsto$$

$$(E \cup \{l = r\}, D \cup \{g \neq d, \ \psi(g[r]_\omega) \neq \psi(d)\})$$

$$\text{if } \psi(g_{|\omega}) \stackrel{*}{\longleftrightarrow}_{AC} \psi(l), \psi(d) \not\succ \psi(g), \psi(r) \not\succ \psi(l)$$

Deduce − Ext − DEq $(E \cup \{l = r\}, D \cup \{g \neq d\})$

$$\longmapsto$$

$$(E \cup \{l = r\}, D \cup \{g \neq d, \ \psi(g[f(r, z)]_\omega) \neq \psi(d)\})$$

$$\text{if } \psi(g_{|\omega}) \stackrel{*}{\longleftrightarrow}_{AC} \psi(f(l, z)), \psi(d) \not\succ \psi(g), \psi(r) \not\succ \psi(l)$$

Fig. 2. Additional rules for Refutational Ordered Completion Modulo AC

Definition 10 A *refutation* is a fair derivation $(E_0, D_0) \longmapsto (E_1, D_1) \longmapsto \ldots$ for which $\bigcup_i D_i$ contains a disequality $(u \neq v)$ with u and v AC-unifiable.

Refutational completeness of $ROCM$ is expressed by the next result, which is a consequence of Theorem 1 in [7].

Theorem 3 *Let E be a set of equalities, and $>$ be a reduction ordering AC-compatible and total on AC-equivalence classes of ground terms. Then the equality $(t = t')$ is valid in $E \cup AC$ (i.e. $t \stackrel{*}{\longleftrightarrow}_{E \cup AC} t')$ iff $ROCM$ generates a refutation from $E_0 = E \cup \{t_0 \neq t_0'\}$, where $(t_0 \neq t_0')$ is the skolemized negation of $(t = t')$.*

The most impressive results in automated deduction based on rewrite methods have been obtained with ordered completion modulo AC. But theorem provers such as SBREVE and RRL also use powerful simplification mechanisms especially cancellation laws that considerably prune the search space of the theorem prover. In addition, in order to avoid useless computations, critical pair criteria are applied. All these refinements do contribute to the efficiency and realistic use of an equational prover. An illustration of the ordered completion modulo AC technique, is for instance the proof of Moufang's Identities in Alternative Rings. A first computer proof has been reported in 1990 by S.Anantharaman and J.Hsiang in [1] using the system SBREVE.

Example 1 Another example is the Ring Commutativity Problems.
An associative ring is defined by the following set of axioms $RING$:

$$
\begin{array}{ll}
x + y = y + x & (x * y) * y = x * (y * y) \\
(x + y) + z = x + (y + z) & x * (y + z) = (x * y) + (x * z) \\
x + 0 = x & (x + y) * z = (x * z) + (y * z) \\
x + i(x) = 0 & 0 * x = 0 \\
i(x + y) = i(x) + i(y) & x * 0 = 0 \\
i(0) = 0 & i(x) * y = i(x * y) \\
i(i(x)) = x & x * i(y) = i(x * y)
\end{array}
$$

In 1945 the mathematician Jacobson proved that the next theorem holds in associative rings:

$$(\forall x, \exists n > 1, x^n = x) \Rightarrow \forall x, y, (x * y = y * x)$$

Weaker versions of this theorem have been proved using rewrite techniques. These are instances for specific n of the theorem: $(\forall x, x^n = x) \Rightarrow \forall x, y, (x * y = y * x)$.

The case $n = 2$ has been solved rather easily, but the case $n = 3$ was given as a challenge problem in [52]. The first mechanical proof was done in 1981 by Veroff [50] using the Argonne National Laboratory theorem prover based on resolution and paramodulation. In 1984, Stickel produced a proof using rewrite techniques [49]. The proof was also made in RRL using a careful selection of critical pairs [27]. These proofs proceed by refutation, that is in addition to the $RING$ equalities and to the hypothesis $w * w * w = w$, the skolemized negation of the conclusion is added: $a * b \neq b * a$.

In addition RRL has been able to prove the commutativity of associative rings in which every element satisfies $w^n = w$ for a large class of even numbers $n < 2^{50000}$. For instance for $n = 6$, the system first generates the equality $w * w = w$ and thus reduces the problem to the previous case $n = 2$. In this exemple, the first interesting critical pair is between the extended equality of distibutivity and the equality $w^n = w$. Following [17], it can be computed that an equation of the form $v * w^n =_{AC}^? u * x * (y + z)$ has a set of minimal AC-solutions whose cardinal is $(6n + 8)2^n - 12$. Instead of computing this huge set of corresponding critical pairs, the idea is to consider the following constrained critical pair $(u * ((x * y) + (x * z)) = v * w \;\|\; v * w^n =_{AC}^? u * x * (y + z))$ and to go on the deduction process with the hope to add other constraints which further narrow the set of solutions.

Example 2 The idea to extend the technique of ordered completion modulo A to theories involving commutativity, associativity and identity axioms ($ACIdentity$ for short) emerges from the remark that it is in general easier to solve equations modulo $ACIdentity$ than modulo AC, in the sense that complete sets of unifiers have less elements. So for theories like commutative group, it is interesting to deal with the commutativity, associativity and identity axioms through the matching and unification processes. Unfortunately a termination problem arises since the rule $-(x + y) \rightarrow (-x) + (-y)$ leads to an infinite derivation for any term t: $(-t) \xleftarrow{*}_{ACIdentity} -(t + 0) \rightarrow (-t) + (-0) \rightarrow \ldots$. The idea is then to prevent this infinite chain by imposing the constraint that both x and y must be non-equivalent to 0 modulo $ACIdentity$ to apply the rule $-(x + y) \rightarrow (-x) + (-y)$. So when generated, the equality $(-(x + y) = (-x) + (-y))$ is split into:
a rewrite rule $-(x+y) \rightarrow (-x)+(-y) \;\|\; (x \neq_{ACIdentity}^? 0 \wedge y \neq_{ACIdentity}^? 0)$, and two equalities $-(x+y) = (-x)+(-y) \;\|\; (x =_{ACIdentity}^? 0)$ and $-(x+y) = (-x)+(-y) \;\|\; (y =_{ACIdentity}^? 0)$, further reduced to $-(y) = (-0) + (-y)$ and $-(x) = (-x) + (-0)$, then to trivial equalities. Further developments may be found in [10, 24] and other examples of theories are handled in [10]: commutative ring with unit, Boolean algebra, group or ring homomorphism, distributive lattice.

4 Rewriting with constraints

Following the tradition of logic programming [22] and higher-order logic [19], constraints have been introduced in automated theorem proving to improve inference systems and deduction in several aspects. Some advantages in using deduction with constraints are to make explicit every symbolic computation step, especially unification, orientation and typing ; to modularize deduction and in particular to design better controls by delaying complex problem solving ; to schematize (infinitely) many objects and to get more expressive power. These advantages may be better illustrated by a few examples where the concept of constraints is of interest and where the gain in expressive power is obvious.

Example 3 In these examples, constraints are equations $(t =^? t')$, disequations $(t \neq^? t')$, inequations: $(t >^? t')$ or membership constraints $(t \in^? s_0)$. In order to emphasize the fact that the predicates used in constraints are interpreted in a specific way and that we are looking for solutions, a question mark is put as exponent in constraints. Indexes specify instead in which interpretation constraints are solved. For instance $(t =^?_\emptyset t')$ is an equation on terms to solve in the empty theory, while $(t =^?_A t')$ is solved in the theory A. We can then express:

• A rule applying everywhere except in one point:
$(-(x + y) \rightarrow (-x) + (-y) \parallel (x \neq^?_{ACIdentity} 0 \wedge y \neq^?_{ACIdentity} 0))$.

• Ordered rewriting: $(x + y \rightarrow y + x \parallel x >^?_\emptyset y)$.

• Rewriting modulo AC where AC-equalities only occur below a variable position of the matched rewrite rule: $(x + y \rightarrow y \parallel x =^?_{AC} 0)$.

• A relation true on even natural numbers: when $A = \{s(s(x)) = x\}$, the formula $(P(x) \parallel x =^?_A 0)$ schematizes $\{P(0), P(s(s(0))), \ldots, P(s^{2n}(0)) \ldots\}$.

• A meta-rule $(f(g(\dot{x})) \rightarrow g(\dot{x}) \parallel \dot{x} \in^? G)$ with G being the regular set of terms $\{g^n(f(x)), n \geq 0\}$. This represents the infinite family $\{f(g^n(f(x))) \rightarrow g^n(f(x)), n \geq 0\}$, generated by the divergent completion of the one-rule system $f(g(f(x))) \rightarrow g(f(x))$.

• Some structure sharing: $(f(x, x, x, x) \parallel x =^?_\emptyset b)$ where b may be a big term.

• Order-sorted rewriting: $(f(x) \rightarrow a \parallel x \in^? s_0)$, where $\mathcal{S} = \{s_0, s_1\}$, with $s_0 \leq s_1$, $\mathcal{F} = \{a, f\}$, with $a :\mapsto s_0$, $f : s_0 \mapsto s_1$.

Let us now formalize the notions of constraints and constraint language, before defining rewriting with constraints.

4.1 Constraints

A constraint is a first-order formula built on a signature $\Sigma = (\mathcal{S}, \mathcal{F}, \mathcal{P})$ where $\mathcal{S}$ is a set of sort symbols, $\mathcal{F}$ a set of function symbols and $\mathcal{P}$ a set of predicate symbols. This signature is used to build elementary constraints. For instance here $\mathcal{P} = \{=, \neq, >, \in\}$ and elementary constraints are equations, disequations and inequations. Elementary constraints are then combined with usual first-order connectives and quantifiers.

The definition of symbolic constraint languages adopted in the context of theorem proving, is an instance of the definition given in [48, 30]. The main difference is that we restrict to one interpretation that is a term algebra instead of considering a class of interpretations, and to solutions that are substitutions instead of general assignments.

Definition 11 Let $\Sigma = (\mathcal{S}, \mathcal{F}, \mathcal{P})$ be a signature and $\mathcal{X}$ a set of variables. A *symbolic constraint language* $L_\mathcal{K}[\Sigma, \mathcal{X}]$ (or $L_\mathcal{K}$ for short) is given by :

– A set of *constraints* $C[\Sigma, \mathcal{X}]$ defined as the smallest set such that
  - $\mathbb{T}, \mathbb{F} \in C[\Sigma, \mathcal{X}]$,
  - $p^?(t_1, \ldots, t_m) \in C[\Sigma, \mathcal{X}]$ if $p \in \mathcal{P}$ and $t_1, \ldots, t_m \in \mathcal{T}(\mathcal{S}, \mathcal{F}, \mathcal{X})$,
  - $c \wedge c' \in C[\Sigma, \mathcal{X}]$ if $c, c' \in C[\Sigma, \mathcal{X}]$,
  - $(\exists x : c) \in C[\Sigma, \mathcal{X}]$ if $c \in C[\Sigma, \mathcal{X}]$.

  The set $\mathcal{V}ar(c)$ of free variables of the constraint c is defined as follows:
  - $\mathcal{V}ar(\mathbb{T}) = \mathcal{V}ar(\mathbb{F}) = \emptyset$,
  - $\mathcal{V}ar(p^?(t_1, \ldots, t_m)) = \bigcup_{i=1}^{m} \mathcal{V}ar(t_i)$,
  - $\mathcal{V}ar(c \wedge c') = \mathcal{V}ar(c) \cup \mathcal{V}ar(c')$,
  - $\mathcal{V}ar(\exists x : c) = \mathcal{V}ar(c) \setminus \{x\}$.

– An interpretation $\mathcal{K}$, which is a Σ-term algebra, and a solution mapping that associates to each constraint c the set of its symbolic solutions, denoted by $SS_{\mathcal{K}}(c)$, defined as follows:
  - $SS_{\mathcal{K}}(\mathbb{T}) = SUBST$, $SS_{\mathcal{K}}(\mathbb{F}) = \emptyset$,
  - $SS_{\mathcal{K}}(p^?(t_1, \ldots, t_m)) = \{\sigma \in SUBST \mid \mathcal{K} \models p(\sigma(t_1), \ldots, \sigma(t_m))\}$,
  - $SS_{\mathcal{K}}(c \wedge c') = SS_{\mathcal{K}}(c) \cap SS_{\mathcal{K}}(c')$,
  - $SS_{\mathcal{K}}(\exists x : c) = \{\sigma \in SUBST \mid \exists \phi \in SUBST, \ \sigma_{|\mathcal{X} \setminus \{x\}} = \phi_{|\mathcal{X} \setminus \{x\}}$ and $\phi \in SS_{\mathcal{K}}(c)\}$.

Two constraints c and c' are *equivalent* if $SS_{\mathcal{K}}(c) = SS_{\mathcal{K}}(c')$, which denoted $c \equiv_{\mathcal{K}} c'$.

With this definition, $SS_{\mathcal{K}}(t \neq^? t') = \{\sigma \in SUBST \mid \mathcal{K} \models \sigma(t) \neq \sigma(t')\}$ contains all σ such that *for all substitutions* μ, $\mu\sigma(t)$ and $\mu\sigma(t')$ are distinct elements of $\mathcal{K}$. If instead of considering disequality as an atomic constraint, we had introduced negation and a negated constraint $\neg(t =^? t')$, with $SS_{\mathcal{K}}(\neg(t =^? t')) = SUBST \setminus SS_{\mathcal{K}}(t =^? t')$, as for instance in [3], we would have obtained a different set, containing all σ such that *there exists a substitution* μ which maps $\sigma(t)$ and $\sigma(t')$ onto two different elements in $\mathcal{K}$.

Substitutions are partially ordered by subsumption ordering, as follows: A substitution ϕ is an $L_{\mathcal{K}}[\Sigma, \mathcal{X}]$-*instance* on $V \subseteq \mathcal{X}$ of a substitution σ, written $\sigma \leq_{\mathcal{K}}^{V} \phi$ (and read as σ more general with respect to $\mathcal{K}$ than ϕ on V), if there exists some substitution μ such that $\forall x \in V, \ \mathcal{K} \models \phi(x) = \mu(\sigma(x))$.

We take advantage of the fact that any instance of a symbolic solution is still a symbolic solution, to keep a set of symbolic solutions minimal with respect to instantiation.

Definition 12 A set of substitutions is a *complete set of solutions* of the $L_{\mathcal{K}}[\Sigma, \mathcal{X}]$-constraint c, denoted by $CSS_{\mathcal{K}}(c)$, if
(1) $\forall \sigma \in CSS_{\mathcal{K}}(c), \ \mathcal{D}om(\sigma) \cap \mathcal{V}\mathcal{R}an(\sigma) = \emptyset$,
(2) $CSS_{\mathcal{K}}(c) \subseteq SS_{\mathcal{K}}(c)$ (correctness).
(3) $\forall \phi \in SS_{\mathcal{K}}(c), \ \exists \sigma \in CSS_{\mathcal{K}}(c), \ \sigma \leq_{\mathcal{K}}^{\mathcal{V}ar(c)} \phi$ (completeness).

4.2 Constrained equalities and rewrite rules

Constrained formulas, especially equalities and rewrite rules, are built in full generality on an extended signature Σ' and a superset of variables $\mathcal{X}'$.

Definition 13 Let $\Sigma \subseteq \Sigma'$ and $\mathcal{X} \subseteq \mathcal{X}'$. A *constrained equality*, denoted $(l = r \parallel c)$, is given by two terms l and r in $\mathcal{T}(\Sigma', \mathcal{X}')$ and a constraint c in $L_{\mathcal{K}}[\Sigma, \mathcal{X}]$.

The constrained equality $(l = r \parallel c)$ schematizes the following set of equalities on $\mathcal{T}(\Sigma', \mathcal{X}')$: $\mathcal{S}(l = r \parallel c) = \{\sigma(l) = \sigma(r) \mid \sigma \in SS_{\mathcal{K}}(c)\}$.

If there exists an ordering such that all these instances may be used from left to right, they are better represented by constrained rules.

Definition 14 Let $\Sigma \subseteq \Sigma'$ and $\mathcal{X} \subseteq \mathcal{X}'$. A *constrained rewrite rule*, denoted $(l \rightarrow r \parallel c)$, is given by two ordered terms l, r in $\mathcal{T}(\Sigma', \mathcal{X}')$ and a constraint c in $L_{\mathcal{K}}[\Sigma, \mathcal{X}]$.

A constrained rewrite rule $(l \rightarrow r \parallel c)$ schematizes the following set of rewrite rules:
$\mathcal{S}(l \rightarrow r \parallel c) = \{\sigma(l) \rightarrow \sigma(r) \mid \sigma \in SS_{\mathcal{K}}(c)\}$.

4.3 Rewriting with constraints

Let us first give a very general definition of rewriting with constraints in which the matching theory may be different from the theory in which constraints are solved.

Definition 15 Given a set CR of constrained rewrite rules with constraints in $L_{\mathcal{K}}[\Sigma, \mathcal{X}]$ and a set A of axioms, a term t $(CR, A, L_{\mathcal{K}})$-*rewrites* to t', denoted $t \rightarrow_{CR, A, L_{\mathcal{K}}} t'$, if there exist a constrained rewrite rule $(l \rightarrow r \parallel c)$ of CR, a position ω in t, a substitution σ, such that $t_{|\omega} \overset{*}{\longleftrightarrow}_A \sigma(l)$, $\sigma \in SS_{\mathcal{K}}(c)$ and $t' = t[\sigma(r)]_\omega$.

With this definition, a constrained rewrite rule is applicable if there exists a substitution that matches the left-hand side and makes the constraint hold in the interpretation $\mathcal{K}$. In its full generality, this $(CR, A, L_{\mathcal{K}})$ rewrite relation allows the use of built-in constraint solvers in $\mathcal{K}$, but this leads to combination problems in the matching and unification processes underlying rewriting and superposition with constrained rewrite rules. These matching and unification problems must be solved in a conservative extension of $\mathcal{K}$ taking into account axioms in A and all equalities valid in $\mathcal{K}$. This problem is addressed in [32].

Definition 16 Let CR be a set of constrained rewrite rules. The relation $(CR, A, L_{\mathcal{K}})$ is Church-Rosser modulo A on a set of terms $\mathcal{T}$ if
$\overset{*}{\longleftrightarrow}_{CR, A, L_{\mathcal{K}}} \subseteq \overset{*}{\longrightarrow}_{CR, A, L_{\mathcal{K}}} \circ \overset{*}{\longleftrightarrow}_A \circ \overset{*}{\longleftarrow}_{CR, A, L_{\mathcal{K}}}$.

Example 4 Examples of ordered rewrite system given in [36] can actually be described by a constrained rewrite system. Assume given a reduction ordering $>$ total on ground terms and satisfying for all ground terms x, y, z:

$$(x * y) * z > x * (y * z)$$
$$x * y > y * x \qquad \text{if } x > y$$
$$x * (y * z) > y * (x * z) \text{ if } x > y$$

Then the following set CR is a constrained rewrite system, where $A = \emptyset$:

$$(x * y) * z \rightarrow x * (y * z) \parallel \mathbb{T}$$
$$x * y \rightarrow y * x \parallel x >_{\emptyset}^{?} y$$
$$x * (y * z) \rightarrow y * (x * z) \parallel x >_{\emptyset}^{?} y$$

If $>$ is the lexicographic path ordering and a, b, c are constants such that $c > b > a$:

$$b*(c*(b*a)) \to_{CR} b*(c*(a*b)) \to_{CR} b*(a*(c*b)) \to_{CR} a*(b*(c*b)) \to_{CR} a*(b*(b*c)).$$

This constrained rewrite system allows deciding the word problem for associativity and commutativity of $*$.

The notion of rewriting with constraints bears much similarity with conditional rewriting, especially with contextual rewriting. However, in conditional rewriting, occurrences of the same function symbol in conditions and in conclusion are usually interpreted in the same way. This is no more true for rewriting with constraints, where the symbols in constraints may be subject to special deduction rules. For instance, an equation $(f(s) =^?_\emptyset f(t))$ in a constraint may be decomposed into $(s =^?_\emptyset t)$. Such a transformation is in general not valid in the first-order theory which underlies the constrained formula. The difference between constrained and conditional rewriting also appears for instance in the following example of idempotent semigroups from [47] where a rewrite system for the theory of an idempotent associative symbol $*$ is given:

$$x * x \to x$$
$$x * y * z \to x * z \text{ if } (x =^?_{ACI} z) \wedge (x * y =^?_{ACI} z)$$

where ACI is the theory of the associative commutative idempotent symbol $*$. So the equations in the condition are solved modulo the theory ACI of $*$, while the rules are used with matching modulo associativity. Since the theory of $*$ is different in the constraints, due to the commutativity axiom, this system is typically a rewrite system with constraints. Actually this system does not fit into the classical frameworks for conditional term rewriting [25].

4.4 A constrained rewriting logic

Following [37], a general logic setting can be proposed to formalize constrained rewrite deduction. In the constrained rewriting logic sketched now, sentences are defined as constrained sequents of the form $(\langle t \rangle_A \to \langle t' \rangle_A \parallel c)$ where $t, t' \in \mathcal{T}(\Sigma, \mathcal{X})$, $\langle t \rangle_A$ denotes the A-equivalence class of t and $c \in L_{\mathcal{K}}$. The informal meaning of such sentences is that t' is derived from t if c holds in $\mathcal{K}$. A constrained rewrite theory is a set CR of constrained rewrite rules. Each rule $(l \to r \parallel c)$ has a finite set of variables $\mathcal{V}ar(l) \cup \mathcal{V}ar(r) \cup \mathcal{V}ar(c) = \{x_1, \ldots, x_n\}$ which are recorded in the notation $(l(x_1, \ldots, x_n) \to r(x_1, \ldots, x_n) \parallel c(x_1, \ldots, x_n))$. A theory CR entails the sequent $(\langle t \rangle_A \to \langle t' \rangle_A \parallel c)$, if it is obtained by the finite application of the deduction rules in Figure 3.

4.5 Constrained Completion

Without disregarding its expressive power, let us come back now to the original idea which was to take advantage of constraints in a theorem proving process. So from now on, let us restrict to cases that are useful in this context, i.e. where $\Sigma = \Sigma'$, $\mathcal{X} = \mathcal{X}'$ and $\mathcal{K} = \mathcal{T}(\Sigma, \mathcal{X})/\xleftrightarrow{*}_A$. In order to compare with ordered completion

Reflexivity

$$\vdash$$
$$\langle t \rangle_A \to \langle t \rangle_A \parallel \mathbb{T}$$
if $\langle t \rangle_A \in \mathcal{T}(\Sigma, \mathcal{X}) / \xleftrightarrow{*}_A$

Congruence $\langle t_1 \rangle_A \to \langle t'_1 \rangle_A \parallel c_1, \quad \ldots, \quad \langle t_n \rangle_A \to \langle t'_n \rangle_A \parallel c_n$
$$\vdash$$
$$\langle f(t_1, \ldots, t_n) \rangle_A \to \langle f(t'_1, \ldots, t'_n) \rangle_A \parallel c_1 \wedge \ldots \wedge c_n$$
if $c_1 \wedge \ldots \wedge c_n$ satisfiable and $f \in \mathcal{F}$

Replacement $\langle t_1 \rangle_A \to \langle t'_1 \rangle_A \parallel c_1 \quad \ldots \quad \langle t_n \rangle_A \to \langle t'_n \rangle_A \parallel c_n$
$$\vdash$$
$$\langle l(t_1, \ldots, t_n) \rangle_A \to \langle r(t'_1, \ldots, t'_n) \rangle_A \parallel c_1 \wedge \ldots \wedge c_n \wedge c(t_1, \ldots, t_n)$$
if $\begin{array}{l}(l(x_1, \ldots, x_n) \to r(x_1, \ldots, x_n) \parallel c(x_1, \ldots, x_n)) \in CR \\ \text{and and } c_1 \wedge \ldots \wedge c_n \wedge c(t_1, \ldots, t_n) \text{ satisfiable}\end{array}$

Transitivity $\langle t_1 \rangle_A \to \langle t_2 \rangle_A \parallel c_1, \quad \langle t_2 \rangle_A \to \langle t_3 \rangle_A \parallel c_2$
$$\vdash$$
$$\langle t_1 \rangle_A \to \langle t_3 \rangle_A \parallel c_1 \wedge c_2$$
if $c_1 \wedge c_2$ satisfiable

Fig. 3. CONSREW: Constrained rewrite deduction

modulo A, the constraint language $L_{\mathcal{K}}$ is specialized to conjunctions of equations and inequations. The equality predicate is interpreted in $\mathcal{K}$ by equality modulo A and the ordering predicate by an A-compatible reduction ordering total on A-equivalence classes of ground terms. Let $L_>$ denote this instance of $L_{\mathcal{K}}$. A variant of Definition 15 is necessary:

Definition 17 Let CE be a set of constrained equalities and $>$ an A-compatible reduction ordering on $\mathcal{T}(\Sigma, \mathcal{X})$, total on A-equivalence classes of ground terms. The relation $(CE, A, L_>)$ is defined on $\mathcal{T}(\Sigma, \mathcal{X})$ by : $t \to_{CE, A, >} t'$ if there exist a constrained rewrite rule $(l = r \parallel c) \in CE$, a position ω in t and a substitution σ such that $t_{|\omega} \xleftrightarrow{*}_A \sigma(l)$, $\sigma \in SS_{\mathcal{K}}(c \wedge (l >^?_A r))$, and $t' = t[\sigma(r)]_\omega$.

Constraints in $L_>$ are appropriate to express constrained critical pairs.

Definition 18 A *constrained critical pair* of $(g = d \parallel c')$ and $(l = r \parallel c)$ is the constrained equality $(g[r]_\omega = d \parallel c \wedge c' \wedge (g_{|\omega} =^?_A l) \wedge (g >^?_A d) \wedge (l >^?_A r))$ if $c \wedge c' \wedge (g_{|\omega} =^?_A l) \wedge (g >^?_A d) \wedge (l >^?_A r)$ is satisfiable.
A *constrained extended equality* of $(l = r \parallel c)$ w.r.t. $(g = d) \in A$ is $(g[l]_\omega = g[r]_\omega \parallel c \wedge (g_{|\omega} =^?_A l) \wedge (l >^?_A r))$ if $c \wedge (g_{|\omega} =^?_A l) \wedge (l >^?_A r)$ is satisfiable.

For a set CE of constrained equalities, CE^{ext} denotes the saturation of CE under adjunction of constrained extended equalities.

The difficulty that arises in trying to prove confluence is that the critical pairs lemma does not hold anymore in the context of constrained rewrite rules.

Example 5 Let us consider $A = \emptyset$, $\mathcal{F} = \{a, b, f, g\}$ and a simplification ordering $>$ induced by the precedence $f, g > a > b$ [14]. Let CE be the set of two constrained equalities: $(g(a) = b \parallel \mathbb{T})$ and $(f(x) = a \parallel x =_\emptyset^? g(y))$. There is no constrained critical pair, nevertheless there exists a peak $a \leftarrow_{CE,\emptyset,L_>} f(g(a)) \rightarrow_{CE,\emptyset,L_>} f(b)$ which is not convergent since neither a nor $f(b)$ is reducible.

In the previous example, the problem comes from the fact that there is a superposition in the constraint part which is not taken into account by the computation of constrained critical pairs. A first idea is to look for cases where superposition into constraints is useless. Using a hierarchical approach in which constraints are restricted to a subsignature is enough to recover the critical pair lemma. This is done with so-called built-in constraints in [32] for instance. When the initial set of equalities is unconstrained, the *basic superposition* deduction rule (an instance with $A = \emptyset$ of the rule **Deduce** $-$ **Eq** $-$ **Eq** given in Figure 5) is the basis of a saturation process in [41, 9].

Another alternative initially proposed in [30] is to use propagation. Constraints are weakened by partially solving them and propagating the instantiations in the equality. This is formalized by the rule **Propagate** given in Figure 4, where $\hat{\theta}$ is the equational form of the substitution θ.

$$\textbf{Propagate } CE \cup \{(g = d \parallel c)\}$$
$$\longmapsto$$
$$CE \cup \{(\theta(g) = \theta(d) \parallel \theta(c'))\}$$
$$\text{if } c \equiv_{\mathcal{K}} c' \wedge \hat{\theta}$$

Fig. 4. Propagation Rule

Example 6 Coming back to the example 5, the rule **Propagate** applies straightforwardly and yields the (unconstrained) equality $(f(g(y)) = a)$. Now **Deduce** $-$ **Eq** $-$ **Eq** applies and generates with $(g(a) = b)$ the critical pair $(f(b) = a)$. The ordered rewrite system given by $>$ and the equalities

$$g(a) = b \quad f(g(y)) = a \quad f(b) = a$$

is Church-Rosser and generates the same congruence as the initial set of constrained equalities.

As for ordered completion, more optimized rules may be given when A is composed of associativity and commutativity axioms, which we assume from now on in this section. Let us call CCM the set of rules for Constrained Completion Modulo given in Figure 5. The next result is a reformulation of Theorem 6.1 in [42].

Theorem 4 *Let E_0 be a set of equalities without constraints, $>$ an AC-compatible simplification ordering total on AC-equivalence classes of ground terms, and let CE be the closure of E_0 under CCM. Then $(CE^{ext}, AC, L_>)$ is Church-Rosser modulo AC on ground terms.*

Deduce – Eq – Eq

$CE \cup \{(g = d \parallel c), (l = r \parallel c')\}$

$\longmapsto$

$CE \cup \{ \begin{matrix} (g = d \parallel c), (l = r \parallel c'), \\ (g[r]_\omega = d \parallel c \wedge c' \wedge (g_{|\omega} =^?_{AC} l) \wedge (g >^?_{AC} d) \wedge (l >^?_{AC} r)) \end{matrix} \}$

if $c \wedge c' \wedge (g_{|\omega} =^?_{AC} l) \wedge (g >^?_{AC} d) \wedge (l >^?_{AC} r)$ satisfiable

Deduce – Ext – Eq

$CE \cup \{(g = d \parallel c), (l = r \parallel c')\}$

$\longmapsto$

$CE \cup \{ \begin{matrix} (g = d \parallel c), (l = r \parallel c'), \\ (g[f(r, z)]_\omega = d \parallel c \wedge c' \wedge (g_{|\omega} =^?_{AC} f(l, z)) \wedge (g >^?_{AC} d) \wedge (l >^?_{AC} r)) \end{matrix} \}$

if $c \wedge c' \wedge (g_{|\omega} =^?_{AC} f(l, z)) \wedge (g >^?_{AC} d) \wedge (l >^?_{AC} r)$ satisfiable

Deduce – Ext – Ext

$CE \cup \{(g = d \parallel c), (l = r \parallel c')\}$

$\longmapsto$

$CE \cup \{ \begin{matrix} (g = d \parallel c), (l = r \parallel c'), \\ (f(d, z) = f(r, z') \parallel c \wedge c' \wedge (f(g, z) =^?_{AC} f(l, z')) \wedge (g >^?_{AC} d) \wedge (l >^?_{AC} r)) \end{matrix} \}$

if $c \wedge c' \wedge (f(g, z) =^?_{AC} f(l, z')) \wedge (g >^?_{AC} d) \wedge (l >^?_{AC} r)$ satisfiable

Delete

$CE \cup \{p = q \parallel c\}$

$\longmapsto$

CE

if $p \xleftrightarrow{\ *\ }_{AC} q$

Simplify

$CE \cup \{p = q \parallel c\}$

$\longmapsto$

$CE \cup \{p' = q \parallel c\}$

if $p \rightarrow^{(g=d \parallel \mathbb{T}), \sigma}_{CE, AC, L>} p'$ and $p > \sigma(g)$ or $q > \sigma(d)$

Fig. 5. CCM: Constrained Completion Modulo AC

A refutationally complete theorem prover based on constrained paramodulation and using a different proof technique is proposed in [51].

An additional difficulty is to prove that completeness is preserved when simplification and deletion are incorporated into constrained completion. This is only true under some conditions, proposed for the empty theory in [41] and for associative and commutative theories in [51]. Indeed, a simple sufficient condition is to allow simplification only by unconstrained rewrite rules, as expressed in the condition of rule **Simplify** in Figure 5. A restricted form of simplification is applied in this process and the next section is devoted to a more powerful notion of simplification using constrained rewrite rules.

4.6 Constrained simplification

Defining a very general notion of simplification for constrained formulas is more complex than constrained deduction. This is because when simplifying, the starting formula is *replaced* by the simplified one and lost, while otherwise, when a deduction step is applied, a new formula is *added*. In the simplification process, it must be taken care of not loosing schematized instances of the initial formula. This is why the definition of simplification given below involves two parts. The first one deals with instances which are really simplified by an instance of the constrained rewrite rule. The second part deals with the non-simplifiable instances and records the failure in the constraint. To simplify a constrained formula $(F_1 \parallel c_1)$, where F_1 may be in particular a rewrite rule or an equality, using a constrained rewrite rule $(l \rightarrow r \parallel c)$, it is assumed that the two constrained formulas are variable disjoint. This condition can always be satisfied by renaming variables of the constrained rewrite rule. It is also assumed that $(l \rightarrow r \parallel c)$ satisfies $Var(c) \subseteq Var(l) \cup Var(r)$.

In order to discard some instances that are not simplified, negation must be introduced. To avoid inconsistency between the definitions of symbolic solutions for $(t \neq^? t')$ and $\neg(t =^? t')$, we restrict to the set $GSUBST$ of ground substitutions in $\mathcal{K} = \mathcal{T}(\Sigma)/\overset{*}{\longleftrightarrow}_A$. Then $SS_{\mathcal{K}}(t \neq^? t') = \{\sigma \in GSUBST \mid \mathcal{T}(\Sigma)/\overset{*}{\longleftrightarrow}_A \models \sigma(t) \neq \sigma(t')\}$ contains all σ such that of $\sigma(t)$ and $\sigma(t')$ are non A-equivalent ground terms. On the other hand, $SS_{\mathcal{K}}(\neg(t =^? t')) = GSUBST \backslash SS_{\mathcal{K}}(t =^? t') = SS_{\mathcal{K}}(t \neq^? t')$. We also define $c \vee c' = \neg(\neg c \wedge \neg c')$ and $\forall x : c = \neg(\exists x : \neg c)$.

Definition 19 A constrained formula $(F_1 \parallel c_1)$ *simplifies* to $(F_2 \parallel c_2)$, with the rest $(F_1 \parallel c_2')$, at the non-variable position ω of F_1, with the constrained rewrite rule $(l \rightarrow r \parallel c)$, if the constraint $c_2 = c_1 \wedge (c \wedge (l =^?_A F_{1|\omega}))$ is satisfiable. Then $F_2 = F_1[r]_\omega$ and $c_2' = (c_1 \wedge [\forall Var(c) \cup Var(l), \neg c \vee \neg (l =^?_A F_{1|\omega})])$.

The previous definition given for simplifying a constrained formula $(F \parallel c)$ takes into account all the schematized formulas. Some of these instances that are not reducible are recorded in the rest. It should be noted that solving constraints with negation is needed in this definition. This general form of simplification is used in [34].

Example 7 Let us consider the simplification of $(a * y = z \parallel y * z =^?_{AC} d * b)$ using $(a * b = b \parallel \mathbb{T})$ and the substitution $\sigma = \{y \mapsto b, z \mapsto d\}$. Then the simplification produces two new constrained equalities: $(b = z \parallel y =^?_{AC} b \wedge z =^?_{AC} d)$ and $(a * y = z \parallel (y * z =^?_{AC} d * b) \wedge ((y \neq^?_{AC} b) \vee (z \neq^?_{AC} d)))$.

Such a simplification relation rises a new problem of termination. Constrained simplification needs to check first that the list of constraints c_2 is satisfiable. Otherwise obviously termination problems arise. But this is not enough to ensure termination of the process, as shown in the next example. The growth of the constraints must be controlled too and this must be taken into account by a reduction strategy.

Example 8 Let us consider $A = \emptyset$, the constrained rewrite rule $(f(x) \rightarrow f(y) \parallel (x >^?_\emptyset y))$ and the equality $(f(a) = b \parallel \mathbb{T})$. This equality is simplified into: $(f(y) = b \parallel (x =^?_\emptyset a) \wedge (x >^?_\emptyset y))$ and $(f(a) = b \parallel \forall x, y, (x \neq^?_\emptyset a) \vee \neg(x >^?_\emptyset y))$. The first constrained equality $(f(y) = b \ \| \ (x =_{\emptyset}^{?} a) \wedge (x >_{\emptyset}^{?} y))$ can be simplified again; for instance, we obtain after n steps:

$$(f(y_n) = b \ \| \ a >_{\emptyset}^{?} y >_{\emptyset}^{?} \cdots >_{\emptyset}^{?} y_n).$$

In pratice, weaker forms of Definition 19 are used. If simplification is performed by matching l to a subterm of F_1 with a substitution σ, variables from the formula F_1 are not instantiated. Then we can define $F_2 = F_1[\sigma(r)]_\omega$, $c_2 = c_1 \wedge \sigma(c)$ and $c_2' = c_1 \wedge \forall Var(c) - Var(l)$, $\neg\sigma(c)$. In the case where the simplifying rule satisfies in addition $Var(c) \subseteq Var(l)$, we get $c_2 = c_1 \wedge \sigma(c)$ and $c_2' = c_1 \wedge \neg\sigma(c)$. Restricting further to the case where c is an inequality constraint $(u >^{?} v)$ and $Var(c) \subseteq Var(l)$, $c_2' = c_1 \wedge \neg\sigma(u >^{?} v)$. Assuming that $>$ is interpreted as a total ordering on terms, this negation can be transformed to a disjunction: $c_2' = c_1 \wedge (\sigma(v >_{\emptyset}^{?} u) \vee \sigma(u =_{\emptyset}^{?} v))$. This is the definition of simplification used in [45].

Example 9 Let us consider the equality $(0 + (x + y) = x + (y + 0) \ \| \ \mathbb{T})$. It is simplified by $(x + 0 \to 0 + x \ \| \ x >_{\emptyset}^{?} 0)$ into: $(0 + (x + y) = x + (0 + y) \ \| \ y >_{\emptyset}^{?} 0)$ and $(0 + (x + y) = x + (y + 0) \ \| \ 0 >_{\emptyset}^{?} y \vee y =_{\emptyset}^{?} 0)$.

5 Conclusion

We have described here an evolution of rewrite techniques devoted to theorem proving applications. We have shown how constraints help to describe deduction procedures in a very precise way, and as a consequence, to improve their efficiency. This was illustrated by the case of completion processes in associative and commutative theories for which the similarities between the OCM and CCM deduction systems are obvious. Several other examples have been developed and implemented in equational or first-order logic, using in particular the systems Datac [51] and Saturate [42]. The yet open important problems are to incorporate a powerful simplification mechanism and to study its interaction with constraint propagation. A special investigation effort has to be put on the design of strategies for managing deduction rules in an efficient way. We think that expressing all the deduction rules, both on constraints and on formulas, in a uniform formalism of transformation rules, as done in ELAN [31], is a helpful step towards this goal.

References

1. S. Anantharaman and J. Hsiang. An automated proof of the Moufang identities in alternative rings. *Journal of Automated Reasoning*, 6:79–109, 1990.
2. S. Anantharaman and J. Mzali. Unfailing completion modulo a set of equations. Research Report 470, LRI-Orsay (Fr.), 1989.
3. F. Baader and K. Schulz. Combination techniques and decision problems for disunification. volume 690 of *Lecture Notes in Computer Science*, pages 301–315. Springer-Verlag, June 1993.
4. L. Bachmair. *Canonical equational proofs*. Computer Science Logic, Progress in Theoretical Computer Science. Birkhäuser Verlag AG, 1991.

5. L. Bachmair and N. Dershowitz. Completion for rewriting modulo a congruence. *Theoretical Computer Science*, 67(2-3):173–202, October 1989.

6. L. Bachmair, N. Dershowitz, and D. Plaisted. Completion without failure. In H. Aït-Kaci and M. Nivat, editors, *Resolution of Equations in Algebraic Structures, Volume 2: Rewriting Techniques*, pages 1–30. Academic Press, 1989.

7. L. Bachmair and H. Ganzinger. Associative-Commutative superposition. Technical Report MPI-I-93-250, Max-Planck-Institut für Informatik, Saarbrücken, 1993.

8. L. Bachmair and H. Ganzinger. Buchberger's algorithm: A constraint-based completion procedure. In *Proceedings 1st International Conference on Constraints in Computational Logics*, Munich (Germany), sept. 1994.

9. L. Bachmair, H. Ganzinger, C. Lynch, and W. Snyder. Basic paramodulation and superposition. In *Proceedings 11th International Conference on Automated Deduction, Saratoga Springs (N.Y., USA)*, pages 462–476, 1992.

10. T. B. Baird, G. E. Peterson, and R. W. Wilkerson. Complete sets of reductions modulo associativity, commutativity and identity. In N. Dershowitz, editor, *Proceedings 3rd Conference on Rewriting Techniques and Applications, Chapel Hill (N.C., USA)*, volume 355 of *Lecture Notes in Computer Science*, pages 29–44. Springer-Verlag, April 1989.

11. H. P. Barendregt et al. Term graph rewriting. In *Proc. of PARLE'87*, volume 259 of *Lecture Notes in Computer Science*. Springer-Verlag, 1987.

12. H. Comon. Completion of rewrite systems with membership constraints. In W. Kuich, editor, *Proceedings of ICALP 92*, volume 623 of *Lecture Notes in Computer Science*. Springer-Verlag, 1992.

13. N. Dershowitz and J.-P. Jouannaud. *Handbook of Theoretical Computer Science*, volume B, chapter 6: Rewrite Systems, pages 244–320. Elsevier Science Publishers B. V. (North-Holland), 1990. Also as: Research report 478, LRI.

14. N. Dershowitz and J.-P. Jouannaud. Rewrite Systems. In J. van Leeuwen, editor, *Handbook of Theoretical Computer Science*, chapter 6, pages 244–320. Elsevier Science Publishers B. V. (North-Holland), 1990.

15. N. Dershowitz and J.-P. Jouannaud. Notations for rewriting. *Bulletin of European Association for Theoretical Computer Science*, 43:162–172, February 1991.

16. N. Dershowitz and M. Okada. A rationale for conditional equational programming. *Theoretical Computer Science*, 75:111–138, 1990.

17. E. Domenjoud. A technical note on AC-unification. the number of minimal unifiers of the equation $\alpha x_1 + \cdots + \alpha x_p \doteq_{AC} \beta y_1 + \cdots + \beta y_q$. *Journal of Automated Reasoning*, 8:39–44, 1992. Also as research report CRIN 89-R-2.

18. J. A. Goguen, C. Kirchner, and J. Meseguer. Concurrent term rewriting as a model of computation. In R. Keller and J. Fasel, editors, *Proceedings of Graph Reduction Workshop*, volume 279 of *Lecture Notes in Computer Science*, pages 53–93, Santa Fe (NM, USA), 1987. Springer-Verlag.

19. G. Huet. *Constrained Resolution: A Complete Method for Higher Order Logic*. PhD thesis, Case Western Reserve University, 1972.

20. G. Huet. Confluent reductions: Abstract properties and applications to term rewriting systems. *Journal of the ACM*, 27(4):797–821, October 1980. Preliminary version in 18th Symposium on Foundations of Computer Science, IEEE, 1977.

21. G. Huet. A complete proof of the Knuth-Bendix completion algorithm. In *JCSS 23*, pages 11–21, 1981.

22. J. Jaffar and J.-L. Lassez. Constraint logic programming. In *Proceedings of the 14th Annual ACM Symposium on Principles Of Programming Languages, Munich (Germany)*, pages 111–119, 1987.

23. J.-P. Jouannaud and H. Kirchner. Completion of a set of rules modulo a set of equations. *SIAM Journal of Computing*, 15(4):1155–1194, 1986. Preliminary version in Proceedings 11th ACM Symposium on Principles of Programming Languages, Salt Lake City (USA), 1984.

24. J.-P. Jouannaud and C. Marché. Completion modulo associativity, commutativity and identity (AC1). In A. Miola, editor, *Proceedings of DISCO'90*, volume 429 of *Lecture Notes in Computer Science*, pages 111–120. Springer-Verlag, April 1990.

25. S. Kaplan and J.-L. Rémy. Completion algorithms for conditional rewriting systems. In H. Aït-Kaci and M. Nivat, editors, *Resolution of Equations in Algebraic Structures, Volume 2: Rewriting Techniques*, pages 141–170. Academic Press, 1989.

26. D. Kapur and H. Zhang. RRL: A rewrite rule laboratory. In *Proceedings 9th International Conference on Automated Deduction, Argonne (Ill., USA)*, volume 310 of *Lecture Notes in Computer Science*, pages 768–769. Springer-Verlag, 1988.

27. D. Kapur and H. Zhang. A case study of the completion procedure: ring commutativity problems. In J.-L. Lassez and G. Plotkin, editors, *Computational Logic. Essays in honor of Alan Robinson*, chapter 10, pages 360–394. MIT Press, Cambridge (MA, USA), 1991.

28. C. Kirchner and H. Kirchner. Constrained equational reasoning. In *Proceedings of the ACM-SIGSAM 1989 International Symposium on Symbolic and Algebraic Computation, Portland (Oregon)*, pages 382–389. ACM Press, July 1989. Report CRIN 89-R-220.

29. C. Kirchner, H. Kirchner, and J. Meseguer. Operational semantics of OBJ-3. In *Proceedings of 15th International Colloquium on Automata, Languages and Programming*, volume 317 of *Lecture Notes in Computer Science*, pages 287–301. Springer-Verlag, 1988.

30. C. Kirchner, H. Kirchner, and M. Rusinowitch. Deduction with symbolic constraints. *Revue d'Intelligence Artificielle*, 4(3):9–52, 1990. Special issue on Automatic Deduction.

31. C. Kirchner, H. Kirchner, and M. Vittek. Implementing computational systems with constraints. In Paris Kanellakis, Jean-Louis Lassez, and Vijay Saraswat, editors, *Proceedings of the first Workshop on Principles and Practice of Constraint Programming*, Providence (R.I., USA), pages 166–175. Brown University, 1993.

32. H. Kirchner and C. Ringeissen. Constraint solving by narrowing in combined algebraic domains. In P. Van Hentenryck, editor, *Proceedings of the 11th International Conference on Logic Programming*, S. Margherita Ligure (Italy), pages 617–631, MIT Press, 1994.

33. D. S. Lankford and A. Ballantyne. Decision procedures for simple equational theories with permutative axioms: complete sets of permutative reductions. Technical report, Univ. of Texas at Austin, Dept. of Mathematics and Computer Science, 1977.

34. C. Lynch and W. Snyder. Redundancy criteria for constrained completion. In C. Kirchner, editor, *Proceedings 5th Conference on Rewriting Techniques and Applications, Montreal (Canada)*, volume 690 of *Lecture Notes in Computer Science*, pages 2–16. Springer-Verlag, 1993.

35. C. Marché. *Réécriture modulo une théorie présentée par un système convergent et décidabilité du problème du mot dans certaines classes de théories équationnelles*. Thèse de Doctorat d'Université, Université de Paris-Sud, Orsay (France), October 1993.

36. U. Martin and T. Nipkow. Ordered rewriting and confluence. In M. E. Stickel, editor, *Proceedings 10th International Conference on Automated Deduction, Kaiserslautern (Germany)*, volume 449 of *Lecture Notes in Computer Science*. Springer-Verlag, 1990.

37. J. Meseguer. Conditional rewriting logic as a unified model of concurrency. *Theoretical Computer Science*, 96(1):73–155, 1992.

38. C. K. Mohan. Priority rewriting: Semantics, confluence, and conditionals. In N. Dershowitz, editor, *Proceedings 3rd Conference on Rewriting Techniques and Applications, Chapel Hill (N.C., USA)*, volume 355 of *Lecture Notes in Computer Science*, pages 278–291. Springer-Verlag, April 1989.

39. P. Narendran and M. Rusinowitch. Any ground associative-commutative theory has a finite canonical system. In R. V. Book, editor, *Proceedings 4th Conference on Rewriting Techniques and Applications, Como (Italy)*. Springer-Verlag, 1991.

40. R. Nieuwenhuis and A. Rubio. Basic superposition is complete. In B. Krieg-Brückner, editor, *Proceedings of ESOP'92*, volume 582 of *Lecture Notes in Computer Science*, pages 371–389. Springer-Verlag, 1992.

41. R. Nieuwenhuis and A. Rubio. Theorem proving with ordering constrained clauses. In D. Kapur, editor, *Proceedings of CADE-11*, volume 607 of *Lecture Notes in Computer Science*, pages 477–491. Springer-Verlag, 1992.

42. R. Nieuwenhuis and A. Rubio. AC-superposition with constraints: no AC-unifiers needed. In A. Bundy, editor, *Proceedings of CADE-12*, volume 814 of *Lecture Notes in Computer Science*, pages 545–559. Springer-Verlag, 1994.

43. J. Pedersen. *Confluence methods and the word problem in universal algebra*. PhD thesis, Emory University, 1984.

44. G. Peterson and M. E. Stickel. Complete sets of reductions for some equational theories. *Journal of the ACM*, 28:233–264, 1981.

45. G. E. Peterson. Complete sets of reductions with constraints. In M. E. Stickel, editor, *Proceedings 10th International Conference on Automated Deduction, Kaiserslautern (Germany)*, volume 449 of *Lecture Notes in Computer Science*, pages 381–395. Springer-Verlag, 1990.

46. A. Rubio and R. Nieuwenhuis. A precedence-based total ac-compatible ordering. In C. Kirchner, editor, *Proceedings 5th Conference on Rewriting Techniques and Applications, Montreal (Canada)*, volume 690 of *Lecture Notes in Computer Science*, pages 374–388. Springer-Verlag, 1993.

47. J. Siekmann and P. Szabó. A noetherian and confluent rewrite system for idempotent semigroups. *Semigroup Forum*, 25:83–110, 1982.

48. G. Smolka. *Logic Programming over Polymorphically Order-Sorted Types*. PhD thesis, FB Informatik, Universität Kaiserslautern, Germany, 1989.

49. M. E. Stickel. A case study of theorem proving by the Knuth-Bendix method: Discovering that $x^3 = x$ implies ring commutativity. In R. Shostak, editor, *Proceedings 7th International Conference on Automated Deduction, Napa Valley (Calif., USA)*, volume 170 of *Lecture Notes in Computer Science*, pages 248–258. Springer-Verlag, 1984.

50. R. L. Veroff. Canonicalization and demodulation. Internal Report ANL-81-6, Argonne National Laboratory, Argonne,IL, 1981.

51. L. Vigneron. Associative-commutative deduction with constraints. In A. Bundy, editor, *Proceedings of CADE-12*, volume 814 of *Lecture Notes in Computer Science*, pages 530–544. Springer-Verlag, 1994.

52. L. Wos. *Automated Reasoning: 33 basic research problems*. Prentice-Hall, Englewood Cliffs, NJ, 1988.

Graph Rewriting:
A Bibliographical Guide

Bruno Courcelle (+)
Université Bordeaux I
LaBRI (CNRS, URA 1304)

Abstract: Graph rewriting is not presently a unified theory. There are numerous notions of graph rewriting and this diversity reflects the diversity of motivations. We offer a classification of the main definitions. A selected and annotated bibliography reviews recent and accessible papers and books.

Note: This paper is not included in the present volume because it is written in French (the title is: "Réécriture de graphes: orientation bibliographique"). The reader can read it via WWW at the following address:

http://www.labri.u-bordeaux.fr/~courcell/ActSci.html

(+) Adresse postale : 351 Cours de la Libération, 33405 TALENCE Cedex, France;   Courrier électronique : **courcell@labri.u-bordeaux.fr**

Formal Languages & Word-Rewriting

Géraud Sénizergues

LaBRI
(the laboratory at Bordeaux for research in computing)
Université de Bordeaux I
**

1 INTRODUCTION

In this paper, we present results that link the theory of word-rewriting (also known as the theory of *semi-Thue* systems) to the theory of formal languages.

Thue systems were first defined by A. Thue in 1914 ([Thu14]). Since then, these systems have been the subject of much research with respect to decidability problems dealing with the relations $\xrightarrow[S]{*}, \xleftarrow[S]{*}$, produced by such systems. For examples, see the contributions of Y. Lafont and A. Prouté [LP94], G. Lallement [Lal94] as well as Y. Matiyasevich [Mat94] in this volume.

Formal language theory has, as its objects, the sets of words written over an alphabet X. This theory is concerned primarily with classifying these sets either according to the method of generating them (such methods as grammars, iterated morphisms, etc.) or according to the means of recognizing them (such means as automata, morphisms in algebraic structure, logical formulae, etc.).

A semi-Thue system obviously offers a way of generating words: we could define a language $L \subset X^*$ as the set of words derived from an axiom $u \in X^*$ modulo a semi-Thue system S. In consequence, studying the links between this way of defining a language and the conventional ways we just mentioned seems like a natural pre-occupation in language theory.

In fact, Maurice Nivat had already brought up this area of study in the '70s and had even pushed forward the first systematic work on this topic ([Ben69, Niv70, Niv71, CN71, Coc71, NB72, But73b, But73a, Coc75, Coc76, Ber77] [3]). Since that time, all sorts of researchers have contributed to this area, studying the links between semi-Thue systems and formal languages. ([AB92, BS86, Ben87, Boa80, BN84, BO85, Boo87, BJW82, BO93, Car91, Cau88, Cau89, Cau93,

---

** mailing address:LaBRI & UER Math-info, Université Bordeaux I
351, cours de la Libération
33405 Talence Cedex
France
e-mail:ges@labri.u-bordeaux.fr
fax: (+33) 56-84-66-69
[3] [Büc64, Gre67],and [McN67] take off from this idea; [McN67] is cited in [Niv70] as a guideline
[4] Even this list of works is far from exhaustive. [Jan88, BO93], for example, is also useful.

Cho79, Cho82, Jan88, Kie79, MNOZ93, McC93, MNO88, NOR86, Nar86, Nar90, O'D81, O'D83, Ott84, Ott87, OZ91, Ott92a, Ott92b, Sak79, Sén81, Sén85, Sén86, Sén87, Sén89, Sén90a, Sén90b, Zha92] [4])

In line with these antecedents, the theorems presented in this paper will take the following schematic form:

Characterization Theorem : Let L be a language. The following properties are equivalent:

(1) L is in the class $\mathcal{L}$.

(2) There exists a semi-Thue system S of the class $\mathcal{S}$ and a word f such that

$$L = [f] \underset{\overleftrightarrow{S}}{\xrightarrow{*}}$$

When we have only (1) $\Longrightarrow$ (2), we speak of a "theorem about *representation* of the languages of $\mathcal{L}$."

When we have only (2) $\Longrightarrow$ (1), we speak of a "theorem about the *structure* of congruence classes of the systems of $\mathcal{S}$".

These preliminaries provide a new means of investigating the properties of semi-Thue systems or of formal languages, as we can see from the initial work of [Búc64, Gre67, McN67]. After each characterization theorem, we will sytematically cite *applications* to word-rewriting or to formal languages.

2 PRELIMINARIES

2.1 Abstract reductions

Let E be some set and $\longrightarrow$ some binary relation over E .We shall call $\longrightarrow$ the *direct reduction*. We shall use the notations $\xrightarrow{i}$ for every integer $(i \geq 0)$, and $\xrightarrow{*}, \xrightarrow{+}$ in the usual way (see [Hue80]). The inverse relation , $\longrightarrow^{-1}$ will be denoted by $\longleftarrow$. By $\longleftrightarrow$, we denote the relation $\longrightarrow U \longleftarrow$. The three relations $\xrightarrow{*}, \xleftarrow{*}$ and $\xleftrightarrow{*}$ are respectively the reduction, derivation and the equivalence generated by $\longrightarrow$.

We shall use the notions of *confluent* reduction, *locally confluent* reduction, *Church-Rosser* reduction and *noetherian* reduction in their usual meaning ([Hue80] or [DJ91, §4, p.266-269]).

An element $e \in E$ is said *irreducible* modulo $(\longrightarrow)$ iff there exists no $e' \in E$ such that $e \longrightarrow e'$. By Irr($\longrightarrow$) we denote the set of all the elements of E which are irreducible modulo $(\longrightarrow)$.

An element $e \in E$ is said $\longrightarrow$-reducible iff, there exists some $e' \in E, e \longrightarrow e'$.

Given some subset A of E, we use the following notations:

$$< A > \xleftarrow{*} = \{e \in E \mid \exists a \in A, a \xleftarrow{*} e\}$$

$$[A] \overset{*}{\longleftrightarrow} = \{e \in E \mid \exists a \in A, a \overset{*}{\longleftrightarrow} e\}$$

The relation $\longrightarrow$ is said *partly confluent* over A if and only if :

$$< A > \overset{*}{\longleftarrow} = [A] \overset{*}{\longleftrightarrow}$$

(which is equivalent to: $\forall a \in A, \forall e \in E$, if $a \overset{*}{\longleftrightarrow} e$ then $\exists a' \in A$ such that $a' \overset{*}{\longleftarrow} e$)

2.2 Reductions over a free monoïd

Let us consider now the particular case where $E = X^*$, the free monoïd generated by some alphabet X. $\longrightarrow$ is said *l-decreasing* (resp. *strictly l-decreasing*) iff it reduces (resp. strictly reduces) the length, i.e.:

$$\forall f \in X^*, \forall g \in X^*, f \longrightarrow g \Longrightarrow \mid f \mid \geq \mid g \mid (resp. \mid f \mid > \mid g \mid).$$

We shall abreviate "strictly l-decreasing" by "strict".
A *valuation* over X^* is an homomorphism $\nu : (X^*, .) \longrightarrow (\mathbb{N}, +)$ such that, for every $x \in X, \nu(x) \neq 0$.
$\longrightarrow$ is said *v-decreasing* (resp. *strictly v-decreasing*) iff, there exists some valuation ν over X^*, such that $\longrightarrow$ reduces (resp. strictly reduces) the valuation ν, i.e.:

$$\forall f \in X^*, \forall g \in X^*, f \longrightarrow g \Longrightarrow \nu(f) \geq \nu(g)(resp. \nu(f) > \nu(g))$$

We shall abreviate "strictly v-decreasing" by "v-strict".

2.3 Controlled rewriting systems

The notion of *controlled rewriting system* over an alphabet X can be seen as generalising the notion of semi-Thue system over X: to every rule $u \longrightarrow v$ is associated some set of words $K(u, v)$ which is the set of left-contexts with which the given rule can be used: a word pus can be rewritten pvs only when $p \in K(u, v)$ [5].

In the particular case where for every rule $u \longrightarrow v$, $K(u, v)$ is the whole free monoïd X^* , one recovers the classical notion of semi-Thue system.

Let us give now formal definitions.

---

[5] hence we should call *left*-controlled rewriting systems such systems; for sake of brevity we have dropped the prefix "left"

A controlled rewriting system over the alphabet X is a subset S of $X^* \times X^* \times X^*$. Every element (l, u, v) of S is a *rule* of S. u is the *lefthand side* and v the *righthand side* of the rule (l, u, v). By LH(S) (resp. RH(S)) we denote the set of lefthand (resp. righthand) sides of rules of S. The direct reduction generated by S (which is denoted by $\xrightarrow{S}$) is defined by :

for every $f, g \in X^*, f \xrightarrow{S} g$ iff there exists $(l, u, v) \in S$ and $s \in X^*$ such that $f = lus$ and $g = lvs$.

The relations $\xrightarrow[S]{*}$ (*reduction generated by* S), $\xleftarrow[S]{*}$ (*derivation generated by* S) and $\xleftrightarrow[S]{*}$ (*equivalence generated by* S) are then fully defined from $\xrightarrow{S}$ by the general definitions given in §2.1. One can check that $\xleftrightarrow[S]{*}$ is the smallest right-congruence over $(X^*, .)$ which contains $\{(lu, lv) \mid (l, u, v) \in S\}$. $\xleftrightarrow[S]{*}$ is then called the *right-congruence generated by* S.

2.4 Classes of controlled rewriting systems

Let $\mathcal{C}_1, \mathcal{C}_2$ be two classes of languages. Let us denote by $\mathcal{C}_i(X)$ the set of languages over the alphabet X which belong to the class $\mathcal{C}_i$ (for $i \in \{1, 2\}$).

We call $\mathcal{C}_1 - \mathcal{C}_2$-*decomposition* over X every finite set

$$D = \{L_i \times V_i \times \{u_i\}\}_{i \in [1,n]}$$

such that,

$$\forall i \in [1, n], L_i \in \mathcal{C}_1(X), V_i \in \mathcal{C}_2(X), u_i \in X^*.$$

We call *component* of D every element $L_i \times V_i \times \{u_i\}$ of D.

With every decomposition D is associated a controlled rewriting system $\dot{D}$ as follows:

$$\dot{D} = \bigcup_{i=1}^{n} L_i \times V_i \times \{u_i\}$$

We say that some controlled rewriting system S belongs to the class $\mathcal{C}_1 - \mathcal{C}_2$ iff, there exists some $\mathcal{C}_1 - \mathcal{C}_2$-decomposition D such that $\dot{D} = S$. We shall also say that S is a $\mathcal{C}_1 - \mathcal{C}_2$ controlled rewriting system.

Let us mention below some classes of controlled rewriting systems which can be found in the litterature. Let us denote by Rec, Cf , Det, Rat, Fin respectively the classes of recursive, context-free, deterministic context-free, rational, finite languages and let us abreviate "controlled rewriting system" by "c-system".

The notion of Rec-Fin c-system was introduced in [But73a] in order to devise an equivalence algorithm for the so-called "simple" grammars , which, as in the case of "very-simple" grammars ([But73b]), would lean on the comparison of finitely generated congruences.

It was noticed in [Cho79] that the c-systems considered in [But73a] belong to the class Det-Fin. The notion of Rat-Fin c-system is studied in [Cho79, Cho82, Kie79], in connection with the notions of context-free or deterministic context-free language. The rational semi-Thue systems , studied in [O'D81, O'D83, Nar86] can be considered as particular cases of Rat-Rat c-systems. As well, the context-free semi-Thue systems, studied in [BJW82] are particular cases of Rat-Alg c-systems. A result of [BN84] shows that every Fin-Rat c-system defines a reduction which is a rational transduction (we state this in full details in §3.1). In the following, we call *finite* c-system every c-system in the class Rat-Fin. As well, we call *finite* decomposition, every Rat-Fin-decomposition.

2.5 Combinatorial properties of controlled rewriting systems

Let S be some c-system. S is said confluent, locally confluent, Church-Rosser, noetherian, strictly l-decreasing, l-decreasing, strictly v-decreasing, v-decreasing if and only if, the relation $\xrightarrow{S}$ fulfills that property. We use the notation $Irr(S)$ in place of $Irr(\xrightarrow{S})$ and we write that some word f is S-irreducible (resp. S-reducible) in place of $\xrightarrow{S}$-irreducible (resp. $\xrightarrow{S}$-reducible).

Let us now define some *combinatorial* properties which depend really on the c-system S itself (and not on the reduction $\xrightarrow{S}$ only).

Definition : Let us consider the following conditions on the rules of some c-system S :

C1 : for every $(r, u, v), (r', u', v') \in S$ and every $s' \in X^*$
$rv = r'u's'$ and $\mid r \mid \leq \mid r' \mid \Longrightarrow \mid s' \mid = 0$ and $\mid r \mid = \mid r' \mid$
C2 : for every $(r, u, v), (r', u', v') \in S$ and every $s' \in X^*$
$rv = r'u's'$ and $\mid r \mid > \mid r' \mid \Longrightarrow \mid s' \mid = 0$ or $\mid r'u' \mid \leq \mid r \mid$
C3 : for every $(r, u, v), (r', u', v') \in S$ and every $s \in X^*$
$rvs = r'u's'$ and $\mid r \mid < \mid r' \mid \Longrightarrow \mid rv \mid \leq \mid r' \mid$
S is said *left-basic* iff it fulfills C1 and C2
S is said *right-basic* iff it fulfills C1 and C3
S is said *basic* iff it fulfills C1, C2 and C3 (which is equivalent to say that S is both left- and right- basic).

Each condition $C_i (i \in [1, 3])$ can be seen as the prohibition of some superposition configuration for two rules $(r, u, v), (r', u', v')$ of S.

Condition C1 : C1 expresses the prohibition of the following configuration:
$rv = r'u's'$ where $\mid r \mid \leq \mid r' \mid$ and $\mid u' \mid < \mid v \mid$

schema 1:

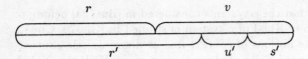

In other words, a righthand side of rule may not strictly embed any lefthand side of rule.

Condition C2 : C2 expresses the prohibition of the following configuration: $rv = r'u's'$ where $0 <| s' |$ and $| r' |<| r |<| r'u' |$

schema 2:

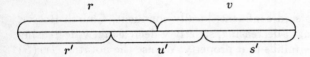

In other words, a righthand side of rule may not be "strictly overlapped on the left" by any lefthand side of rule.

Condition C3 : C3 expresses the prohibition of the following configuration: $rvs = r'u'$ where $| r |<| r' |<| rv |.$

schema 3:

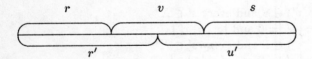

In other words, a righthand side of rule may not be "strictly overlapped on the right" by any lefthand side of rule.

These definitions were given in [Niv70, Coc71, But73b, Sak79] in the case of semi-Thue systems and were generalised to controlled systems in [But73a, Cho79]. This notion of *basic* system turns out to be a key notion for the study of the links between context-free langages and finitely generated congruences (or right-congruences generated by a finite c-system).

2.6 Finite & rational semi-Thue systems

A semi-Thue system over the alphabet X is (by definition) some subset T of $X^* \times X^*$. When the set T is finite , one says that T is a *finite* semi-Thue system.

A semi-Thue system T over X is said *rational* ([O'D81, O'D83]) iff it satisfies some equality :

$$T = \bigcup_{i=1}^{n} V_i \times \{u_i\}$$

where n is some integer, each V_i is some rational language over X and each u_i is some word over X. With every semi-Thue system T over X one can naturally associate a c-system $\overline{T}$ over X by:

$$\overline{T} = \{(l, u, v) \in X^* \times X^* \times X^* \mid (u, v) \in T\}$$

or, in other words $\overline{T} = X^* \times T$. It is clear that the direct reductions $\xrightarrow[\overline{T}]{}$ and $\xrightarrow[T]{}$ are equal (where $\xrightarrow[\overline{T}]{}$ is the relation defined in §2.3 and $\xrightarrow[T]{}$ is the reduction generated by T, in the usual meaning).

Hence, one of both systems $\overline{T}, T$ is confluent (resp. locally confluent, Church-Rosser, noetherian, strict, l-decreasing, v-strict, v-decreasing) iff the other fulfills the same property.

T will be said *left-basic* (resp. *right-basic, basic*) iff $\overline{T}$ is left-basic (resp. *right-basic, basic*) in the sense of definition 2.5 . This definition of the notion of basic semi-Thue system is equivalent to the definitions given in [Niv70] and [Ber77].

This definition of the notion of left-basic semi-Thue is equivalent, (up to some details) to the definition given in [Sak79].

A semi-Thue system S is said:

− *monadic* iff $\forall (u, v) \in S, 1 \leq |u|$ and $|v| \leq 1$
− *special* iff $\forall (u, v) \in S, 1 \leq |u|$ and $|v| = 0$

One can notice that every monadic or special semi-Thue system is basic.

2.7   General references

Some *general* surveys on semi-Thue systems (they do *not* focus exclusively on the links with formal languages) have been written successively in [Ber77, Boo87, Jan88, BO93].

In [BB91, §4, p. 95-100] and [MO89] one will find information on the links between semi-Thue systems , the so-called *context-free* groups and the *group languages*. We have left this subject out of this paper.

The language-theoretic notions used in this work are very classical and can be found in every treatise on the subject, for example [Aut87, Har78, HU79, KS86, Sal73].

3 RATIONAL LANGUAGES & WORD-REWRITING

3.1 Büchi systems

Büchi defined and studied in [Büc64, Büc90] what we shall call the *left-linear reduction* generated by a semi-Thue system S(he was seeing this kind of reductions as variants of the deduction relations generated by Post systems). The direct left-linear reduction generated by S, is denoted by $\xrightarrow{ll\ S}$ and is defined by:

for every $f, g \in X^*, f \xrightarrow{ll\ S} g$ iff there exist $(u, v) \in S$ and $s \in X^*$ such that $f = us$ and $g = vs$.

The left-linear reduction relation, denoted by $\xrightarrow{*}{}_{ll\ S}$, is then the reflexive and transitive closure of relation $\xrightarrow{ll\ S}$.

The *left-linear derivation* relation generated by S is the inverse of the left-linear reduction and will be denoted by $\xleftarrow{*}{}_{S\ ll}$. The *right-congruence* generated by S, denoted by $\xleftrightarrow{*}{}_{ll\ S}$, is the reflexive, symmetric and transitive closure of relation $\xrightarrow{ll\ S}$

Theorem 3.1 ([Büc64]) *Let* $L \in X^*$. *The following properties are equivalent*

(1) $L = < F >_{\xleftarrow{*}{}_{S\ ll}}$

for some finite set $F \subset X^*$ *and some finite semi-Thue system* $S \subset X^* \times X^*$
(2) $L = < F >_{\xleftarrow{*}{}_{S\ ll}}$

for some finite set $F \subset X^*$ *and some finite semi-Thue system* $S \subset X^* \times X^*$ *of the form* $S = \{(f_i p_i, f_i) | 1 \leq i \leq n\}$
(3) L *is rational*

Complement 3.2 ([Coc75]) *Let* $L \in X^*$. *The following properties are equivalent*

(3) L *is rational*
(4) $L = [F]_{\xrightarrow{*}{}_{ll\ S}}$

for some finite set $F \subset X^*$ *and some finite semi-Thue system* $S \subset X^* \times X^*$ *such that* $\xrightarrow{ll\ S}$ *is strictly decreasing and confluent.*

Theorem 3.1 is used in [Gre67] in order to show that any relation "computed" by some pushdown-automaton preserves rationality.

The following theorem brings more precisions about the structure of the relation $\underset{\Pi\,S}{\overset{*}{\longrightarrow}}$ itself.

Theorem 3.3 ([BN84, Cau88]) *Let S be some recognizable subset of $X^* \times X^*$.* *Then $\underset{\Pi\,S}{\overset{*}{\longrightarrow}}$ is a rational transduction.*

This theorem 3.3 is the key argument in the proof of the fact that the "center"of any context-free language is context-free too ([BN84]).

3.2 Special systems

We recall that a *special* semi-Thue system over X is any $S \subset X^+ \times \{\epsilon\}$. A subset P of X^* is said *unavoidable* in X^* iff the language $X^* - X^*.P.X^*$ is finite.Some ordering $\preceq$ over some set E is a *well* ordering iff, for every sequence $(e_i)_{0 \leq i}$ of elements of E, there exists a strictly increasing sequence of integers

$$i_1 < i_2 \ldots i_j < i_{j+1} < \ldots$$

such that

$$(e_{i_j})_{0 \leq j} \text{ is an increasing sequence with respect to } \preceq .$$

By $\alpha(S)$ we denote the set of letters appearing in the rules of system S.

Theorem 3.4 ([EHR83]) *Let S be a finite,special semi-Thue system over some finite alphabet X, let us suppose that $X = \alpha(S)$ and let $L = < \epsilon >$ $\underset{S}{\overset{*}{\longleftarrow}}$ .Then the following properties are equivalent*

(1) *L is rational*
(2) *$LH(S)$ is unavoidable in X^**
(3) $\underset{S}{\overset{*}{\longleftarrow}}$ *is a well ordering over X^**

An immediate corollary of theorem 3.4 is that rationality of a language of the form $< \epsilon >$ $\underset{S}{\overset{*}{\longleftarrow}}$, where S is finite, special, is decidable. (Let us recall that every such language is context-free but the general problem whether some context-free language is rational is undecidable). Theorem 3.4 is used in [Sén86] where it is shown that every rational language in the free *group* with finite basis X, has a syntactic congruence which either has finite index (which is always the case in the free *monoïd*) either is the equality relation.

Given a semi-Thue system S and a set of words W, by $\Delta_S^*(W)$ we denote the set of "descendants" of W modulo S i.e.:

$$\Delta_S^*(W) = \{v \in X^* | \exists w \in W, w \xrightarrow[S]{*} v\}$$

Theorem 3.5 ([BS86]) *Let S be a cancellation system , that is to say a finite semi-Thue system S such that $\forall(u,v) \in S, |u| = 2, |v| = 0$. Then*

(1) *for every rational set R, $\Delta_S^*(R)$ is rational*
(2) *a finite automaton recognizing $\Delta_S^*(R)$ can be built in time $O(n^3)$ from any finite automaton with size n recognizing R.*

The first result in this spirit was obtained in [Ben69];a first generalisation was given in [BO85] and theorem 3.5 improves on its complexity.

Remarks:

1. Point (1) of theorem 3.5 can be formulated as follows: the relation $\xrightarrow[S]{*}$ preserves rationality.

2. But relation $\xrightarrow[S]{*}$ is not a rational transduction in general:

   the languages $< R >_{\xleftarrow[S]{*}}$ with R rational and S cancellation system, are in general context-free but not rational

3. Conclusion (1) may fail as soon as R is merely assumed context-free (see part 6)

4. Conclusion (1) may fail as soon as S is merely assumed strictly decreasing (even when $\xrightarrow[S]{}$ is assumed confluent, see part 6)

Complement 3.6

(1) *If S is assumed to be a finite,basic,strict,semi-Thue system, conclusion (1) remains valid and complexity (2) becomes at most $O(n^4)$ ([Ben87])*
(2) *If S is assumed to be a finite,left-basic,strict,semi-Thue system, conclusion (1) remains valid ([Sak79])*
(3) *If S is assumed to be a finite,left-basic,strict, c-system, conclusion (1) remains valid ([Sén90b])*
(4) *If S is assumed to be a general semi-Thue system (maybe infinite, non-rational), which is basic, then conclusion (1) remains valid ([Sén81] in the general case, [BJW82] in the monadic case)[6]*

Theorem 3.5 allows one to prove that the family of rational subsets of the free group is closed under intersection and complement ([Ben69]). An application of theorem 3.5 to communication protocols is given in [BO85]. This theorem 3.5 is widely used in the proofs of the results exposed in part 4.

---

[6] but the properties "basic" and "monadic" though the first one generalises the second one, are essentially similar.

4 DETERMINISTIC CONTEXT-FREE LANGUAGES & WORD-REWRITING

4.1 Characterisations

The *deterministic context-free* languages are defined as the languages which can be recognized by some *deterministic* pushdown automaton ([GG66]).

Theorem 4.1 *Let $L \subset X^*$. The following properties are equivalent*

(1) *L is deterministic context-free*

(2) $L = [R]_{\underset{S}{\overset{*}{\longleftrightarrow}}}$

where R is some rational language over X^* and S is some strict,finite,basic,confluent, c-system

(3) $\#L\$ = [f]_{\underset{S}{\overset{*}{\longleftrightarrow}}} \bigcap (X + \# + \$)^*$

where f is some word in X^*, S is some v-strict,finite,left-basic, confluent semi-Thue system and $\#,\$$ are letters which do not belong to the alphabet X.

Proof(s):

(1) $\Longrightarrow$ (2): is shown in [Sén90a]
(2) $\Longrightarrow$ (3): is shown in [Sén90b]
(3) $\Longrightarrow$ (1): is shown in [Sak79]

A direct proof of (2) $\Longrightarrow$ (1) is given in [Cho79] and [Cho82].

Complement 4.2
- *All the structure theorems (in the sense defined in our introduction)* [7] *asserting conclusion (1), follow from theorem 4.1 and, more precisely, from part (2) $\Longrightarrow$ (1)*
- *Every deterministic context-free language fulfills formula (3) for some semi-Thue system S which is strict, finite and confluent ([MNO88]) (but it remains unknown whether S can be choosen simultaneously strict, finite, left-basic and confluent)*

4.2 The equivalence problem for deterministic pushdown automata

Let us recall the *equivalence problem* for deterministic pushdown automata is the following decision problem: given two deterministic pushdown automata A_1, A_2, is it true that the associated languages $L(A_1), L(A_2)$ are *equal*?

---

[7] excepted the tight result of [RS86]

Though a great deal of work has been devoted to this problem since the time it was raised ([GG66]), this problem remains open.We give below some applications of the results of the above section to this field of research.

Application 4.3

(1)([Sén89]) *The following problem is decidable*

    instance: $L_1 = [R]_{\underset{\xleftrightarrow{*}}{S}}$ *and* $L_2 = L(A)$

where S is some strict,rational,basic,confluent semi-Thue system and A is some general deterministic pushdown automaton.

question : $L_1 = L_2$?

(2)([Sén89] *Let C be a family of languages which is an* effective *cylinder[8]. If the equivalence problem is decidable for pairs of languages (L_1, L_2) both in this family, then the equivalence problem is decidable for pairs of languages (L_1, L_2) where L_1 belongs to C and L_2 is some general deterministic context-free language.*

(3)([Sén90b] *The following problems are Turing-equivalent* [9]

    (P1) *The equivalence problem for D.P.D.A.*

    (P2) *The problem "$[f]_{\underset{\xleftrightarrow{*}}{S_1}} = [f]_{\underset{\xleftrightarrow{*}}{S_2}}$?"*

    for S_1, S_2 strict,finite,left-basic,confluent semi-Thue systems

    (P3) *The problem "$<f>_{\underset{\xleftrightarrow{*}}{S}} = [f]_{\underset{\xleftrightarrow{*}}{S}}$?"*

    for S strict,finite,left-basic semi-Thue system.

Result (1) is obtained by means of a combination of theorem 4.1 with Valiant's theorem ([Val74],[Bee76])[10].

Result (2) is obtained directly from theorem 4.1 by means of a notion of syntactic right-congruence "with left contexts" associated to language L_1. This result solves (in some way)the problem raised in [OIH81]: "is it possible to find some *general* scheme extending any equivalence algorithm for some subclass $\mathcal{A}$ of D.P.D.A. to an equivalence algorithm for pairs of D.P.D.A. *one of which* is in the subclass?".

Result (3) is obtained from theorem 4.1,point (2), by a sequence of transformations of rewriting systems ([Sén90b, pages 318-340]).

Other results have been obtained by means of rewriting systems (and are neither corollaries nor extensions of theorem 4.1):

---

[8] we call here *effective* cylinder any family of languages which is *effectively* closed by intersection with rational sets and inverse homomorphism, see [Sén89] for a precise definition

[9] they are even "many-one" equivalent but the proof quoted above does not establish this explicitly

[10] this theorem states that the equivalence problem is *decidable* for the subclass of *finite-turn* D.P.D.A

- The equivalence problem is decidable for *parenthetic* grammars ([McN67]), *nest-sets*([Tak75]) and more generally for *NTS* grammars ([Boa80, Sén85]) and even for *pré*-NTS grammars ([AB92]). This class of grammars and of generalisations is further studied in [Zha92, McC93].
- The best known algorithm testing the equivalence for *simple* grammars is given in [Cau89], it uses some finite, v-strict and confluent semi-Thue system which generates the congruence "to generate the same language" over the words written in the alphabet of the grammar; a generalisation to *stateless* automata is given in [Cau93].

4.3 Decision problems for rewriting systems

Theorem 4.1 and some of its applications (particularly 4.3) raise naturally some decision problems about rewriting systems.

Theorem 4.4 *The confluence property is decidable for strict,finite,left-basic c-systems.*

This theorem was first shown by [O'D83] in the case of strict,rational, monadic semi-Thue systems and then generalised in [Sén90b] to the above case. Let us point out that this problem becomes undecidable for strict,rational semi-Thue systems ([O'D81, O'D83])(hence, a fortiori for strict, finite c-systems).

Theorem 4.5
(1) *Given S_1, S_2 strict,rational,confluent semi-Thue systems, one can decide whether $\xleftrightarrow[S_1]{*} = \xleftrightarrow[S_2]{*}$*

(2) *Given S_1, S_2 strict,finite,confluent,left-basic c-systems, one can decide whether $\xleftrightarrow[S_1]{*} \subseteq \xleftrightarrow[S_2]{*}$*

Point (1) is shown in [Nar86] and point (2) in [Sén90b].Let us point out that problem (1) becomes undecidable for strict,finite,confluent c-systems ([Sén90b]).

Theorem 4.6
(1) *The property " S is partly confluent on R "* [11] *where S is some strict, finite, basic semi-Thue system and $R \subseteq Irr(S)$ is rational, is decidable*

(2) *The property " S is confluent on $\Delta_S^*(R)$ " where S is a strict, finite, monadic semi-Thue system and R is a rational set, is decidable.*

Point (1) is shown in [Ott87] in the monadic case and for R reduced to a single word, and in [Sén90b] in the above case. The proofs are similar and lean essentially on Valiant's theorem ([Val74, Bee76], see footnote 10). Point (2) is shown in [Nar90]. Let us notice that (1) (resp.(2))becomes undecidable for semi-Thue systems S which are assumed strict, finite [Ott87, Sén90b] (resp. for semi-Thue systems S which are assumed l-decreasing, noetherian, finite [Car91]). The property to be "partly confluent" (as well as other analogous properties)is studied in more details in [OZ91, Ott92a, Ott92b, MNOZ93, Zha92].

---

[11] see the definition given in §2.1

5 CONTEXT-FREE LANGUAGES & WORD-REWRITING

We do not know any theorem characterising context-free languages in terms of word rewriting systems (in the sense defined in the introduction).One can nevertheless describe these languages by means of word rewriting systems and of *morphisms* of free-monoïds: it suffices to notice that context-free languages are the homomorphic images of deterministic context-free languages, and then to apply theorem 4.1. A tighter statement is the following

Theorem 5.1 ([But73b, Ber77]) *Let* $L \subseteq X^+$. *The following properties are equivalent*

(1) *L is context-free*

(2) $\exists Y \supseteq X, \exists F \subseteq Y^*, F$ *finite,* $\exists S$ *strict,finite,basic,confluent semi-Thue system,* $\exists \varphi : Y^* \longrightarrow X^*$, *strictly alphabetic morphism, such that*

$$L = \varphi([F]_{\underset{S}{\overset{*}{\longleftrightarrow}}})$$

Sketch of proof:

$(2) \Longrightarrow (1)$: follows from theorem 4.1

$(1) \Longrightarrow (2)$: L is generated by some context-free grammar in Greibach normal form. Hence L is the image by some strictly alphabetic morphism of some "very simple" language M. But every very simple language has the form $[F]_{\underset{S}{\overset{*}{\longleftrightarrow}}}$ where F, S are fulfilling the conditions of property (2) ([But73b]).

The family of all the context-free languages of the form $[f]_{\underset{S}{\overset{*}{\longleftrightarrow}}}$ with S strict , finite, confluent semi-Thue system, is a sub-family of the family of context-free languages which has no known characterisation in terms of grammars. A study of this family is presented in [Coc76].

Here are some examples of languages in this sub-family:

(1) Point (3) of theorem 4.1, enables one to generate a *deterministic* context-free example from every given D.P.D.A.

(2) The miror images of the examples of type (1) give examples which are *deterministic-miror* (but not necessarily deterministic)

(3) The union of some (suitably choosen) example of type (1) with some (suitably choosen) example of type (2) constructed on disjoint alphabets, gives an example which is *neither deterministic, nor deterministic-miror,* but remains *non-ambiguous.*

(4) It is possible to build ambiguous examples (i.e. *inherently ambiguous*). Such an example is given in [Sén87, p.301-308].This example leans on a theorem of [Ber86] and a theorem of [AFG86]; it consists essentially in "encoding" the Thue-Morse homomorphism ([Thu12, MH44]) into a strict,finite, confluent semi-Thue system.

Very few is known about the set of all pairs (f, S) such that $[f]_{\xleftrightarrow[S]{*}}$ is context-free (excepted the results exposed in part 4). The following theorem shows that it is not recursive.

Theorem 5.2 ([NOR86]) *Let Ω be some family of context-free languages which contains all the finite languages. Then*

(1) $\exists S$ *strict,finite,confluent semi-Thue system such that the question, given* $w \in X^*$

$$[w]_{\xleftrightarrow[S]{*}} \in \Omega?$$

is undecidable (even $\Sigma_1 - hard$)

(2) *The question , given some finite semi-Thue system S*

$$\forall w \in X^*, [w]_{\xleftrightarrow[S]{*}} \in \Omega?$$

is undecidable (even $\Pi_2 - hard$)

Let us notice that theorem 5.2 applies on the particular families:

$$\Omega_1 = \text{family of all rational languages}$$

and

$$\Omega_2 = \text{family of all deterministic context-free languages}$$

though these families can be described in terms of some families of finite semi-Thue systems or c-systems (see sections 3 et 4).

The statement obtained by choosing $\Omega = \Omega_1$ in theorem 5.2 solves negatively the question raised in [Coc71, p.72].

6 RECURSIVELY ENUMERABLE LANGUAGES & WORD-REWRITING

Theorem 6.1 ([O'D81, Ott84]) *Let $L \subset X^*$. The following properties are equivalent*

(1) L *is recursively enumerable*

(2) $\exists Y \supseteq X \cup \{\#, \bar{\#}, \$\}, \exists S$ *strict,finite,confluent semi-Thue system and* $\exists R \subseteq Y^*$ *rational such that*

$$\#\bar{\#}L\$ = [R] \underset{\overset{*}{\longleftrightarrow}}{S} \cap \#\#X^*\$ = \Delta_S^*(R) \cap \#\bar{\#}X^*\$$$

Theorem 6.2 ([BJW82]) *Let $L \subset X^*$. The following properties are equivalent*

(1) L *is recursively enumerable*

(2) $\exists Y \supseteq X, \exists S$ *finite,special,confluent semi-Thue system and* $\exists C \subseteq Y^*$ *context-free such that*

$$L = [C] \underset{\overset{*}{\longleftrightarrow}}{S} \cap X^* = \Delta_S^*(C) \cap X^*$$

These two theorems are somewhat "antithetic" to " Benois' theorem" (theorem 3.5). These theorems enable one to give "elegant" proofs (i.e. which do not consist in direct encodings of Turing machines or of instances of Post correspondence problem) of a great number of undecidability results about semi-Thue systems ([Ott84, Ott87, Sén90b]).

Let us give one application to formal language theory:

Application 6.3 ([Sén90b]) *The following problem is undecidable*

instance: Some word f and two semi-Thue systems S_1, S_2 assumed finite,strict and confluent.

question : $[f] \underset{\overset{*}{\longleftrightarrow}}{S_1} = [f] \underset{\overset{*}{\longleftrightarrow}}{S_2}$ *?*

This result is a negative answer to the question raised in [NB72, p.9]. Let us notice that the undecidability of this problem stems from the fact that here f is given in the instance (compare with theorem 4.5). Let us notice further that:

- if, in addition , it is assumed that S_1 or S_2 is basic, then the problem becomes decidable ([Sén89])
- if, in addition it is assumed that S_1 or S_2 is left-basic, then the problem becomes equivalent to the general equivalence problem for D.P.D.A. ([Sén90b],see section 4).

7 Acknowledgements

I thank L. Boasson for his comments on a first version of the paper.

References

[AB92]   J.M. Autebert and L. Boasson. The equivalence of pre-NTS grammars is decidable. *Math.Systems Theory 25*, pages 61–74, 1992.

[AFG86] J.M. Autebert, P. Flajolet, and J. Gabarro. Prefixes of infinite words and ambiguous context-free languages. *IPL 25 (4)*, 1986.

[Aut87] J.M. Autebert. *Langages algébriques*. Masson, 1987.

[BB91]   J. Berstel and L. Boasson. Context-free languages. In *Handbook of theoretical computer science, vol.B, Chapter 2*, pages 59–102. Elsevier, 1991.

[Bee76] C. Beeri. An improvement on Valiant's decision procedure for equivalence of deterministic finite-turn pushdown automata. *TCS 3*, pages 305–320, 1976.

[Ben69] M. Benois. Parties rationnelles du groupe libre. *C.R.Acad.Sci.série A*, pages 1188–1190, 1969.

[Ben87] M. Benois. Descendants of regular language in a class of rewriting systems:algorithm and complexity of an automata construction. *Proceedings RTA 87, LNCS 256*, pages 121–132, 1987.

[Ber77] J. Berstel. Congruences plus que parfaites et langages algébriques. *Séminaire d'informatique théorique de Paris6-7*, 1976-1977.

[Ber86] J. Berstel. Every iterated morphism yields a co-cfl. *IPL 22*, pages 7–9, 1986.

[BJW82] R.V. Book, M. Jantzen, and C. Wrathall. Monadic Thue systems. *TCS 19*, pages 231–251, 1982.

[BN84]   L. Boasson and M. Nivat. Centers of context-free languages. *LITP technical report no84-44*, 1984.

[BO85]   R.V. Book and F. Otto. Cancellation rules and extended word problems. *IPL 20*, pages 5–11, 1985.

[BO93]   R.V. Book and F. Otto. *String Rewriting Systems.Texts and monographs in Computer Science*. Springer-Verlag, 1993.

[Boa80] L. Boasson. Grammaires à non-terminaux séparés. In *Proceedings 7th ICALP*, pages 105–118. LNCS 85, 1980.

[Boo87] R.V. Book. Thue systems as rewriting systems. *J.Symbolic Computation.3*, pages 39–68, 1987.

[BS86]   M. Benois and J. Sakarovitch. On the complexity of some extended word problems defined by cancellation rules. *IPL 23*, pages 281–287, 1986.

[Büc64] J.R. Büchi. Regular canonical systems. *Archiv fur Math.Logik und Grundlagenforschung 6*, pages 91–111, 1964.

[Büc90] J.R. Büchi. Regular canonical systems. *the collected works of J.R. Buchi*, pages 317–337, 1990.

[But73a] P. Butzbach. Sur l'équivalence des grammaires simples. In *Actes des Premières journées d'Informatique Théorique,Bonascre*. ENSTA, 1973.

[But73b] P. Butzbach. Une famille de congruences de Thue pour lesquelles l'équivalence est décidable. In *Proceedings 1rst ICALP*, pages 3–12. LNCS, 1973.

[Car91]   A.C. Caron. Linear bounded automata and rewrite systems : influence of initial configurations on decision properties. In *Proceedings CAAP 91*, pages 74–89. LNCS ,Springer-Verlag, 1991.

[Cau88]   D. Caucal. Recritures suffixes de mots. *Internal report IRISA nr 413*, 1988.

[Cau89]   D. Caucal. A fast algorithm to decide on simple grammars equivalence. *L.N.C.S.,Vol.401*, pages 66–85, 1989.

[Cau93]   D. Caucal. A fast algorithm to decide on the equivalence of stateless dpda. *RAIRO Theoret.Infor.and App.*, pages 23–48, 1993.

[Cho79]   L. Chottin. Strict deterministic languages and controlled rewriting systems. In *Proceedings 6th ICALP*. LNCS Springer-Verlag, 1979.

[Cho82]   L. Chottin. Langages algébriques et systèmes de réécriture rationnels. *RAIRO Inform.Téor.16*, pages 1–20, 1982.

[CN71]   Y. Cochet and M. Nivat. Une généralisation des ensembles de Dyck. *Israel J. of Math. vol.9, n 3*, 1971.

[Coc71]   Y. Cochet. Sur l'algébricité des classes de certaines congruences définies sur le monoide libre. *Thèse de l'université de Rennes*, 1971.

[Coc75]   Y. Cochet. Congruences quasi-parfaites et langages rationnels. *Manuscrit non-publié*, 1975.

[Coc76]   Y. Cochet. Langages définis par des congruences. *Groupe d'étude d'Algèbre ,1ère année,no 16*, pages 1–7, 1975/76.

[DJ91]   N. Dershowitz and J.P. Jouannaud. Rewrite systems. In *Handbook of theoretical computer science, vol.B, Chapter 2*, pages 243–320. Elsevier, 1991.

[EHR83]   A. Ehrenfeucht, D. Haussler, and G. Rozenberg. On regularity of context-free languages. *T.C.S.27*, pages 311–322, 1983.

[GG66]   S. Ginsburg and S. Greibach. Deterministic context-free languages. *Information and Control 9*, pages 620–648, 1966.

[Gre67]   S. Greibach. A note on pushdown store automaton and regular systems. *Proc.Amer.Math.Soc.*, pages 263–268, 1967.

[Har78]   M.A. Harrison. *Introduction To Formal Language Theory*. Addison-Wesley, 1978.

[HU79]   J.E. Hopcroft and J.D. Ullman. *Introduction to Automata Theory,Languages, and Computation*. Addison-Wesley, 1979.

[Hue80]   G. Huet. Confluent reductions:abstract properties and applications to term rewriting systems. *JACM vol. 27 no 4*, pages 797–821, 1980.

[Jan88]   M. Jantzen. *Confluent String Rewriting (EATCS monograph)*. Springer-Verlag, 1988.

[Kie79]   F. Kierszenbaum. Les langages à opérateurs d'insertion. *Thèse de 3ième cycle , université Bordeaux I*, 1979.

[KS86]   W. Kuich and A. Salomaa. *Semirings,Automata,Languages (EATCS monograph)*. Springer-Verlag, 1986.

[Lal94]   G. Lallement. The word problem for Thue systems. In *Actes de l'école de printemps d'informatique théorique, Font-Romeu 93*. Springer-Verlag, 1994.

[LP94]   Y. Lafont and A. Prouté. Church-Rosser property and homology of monoids. In *Actes de l'école de printemps d'informatique théorique, Font-Romeu 93*. Springer-Verlag, 1994.

[Mat94]   Y. Matiyasevich. Word problem for Thue systems with a few relations. In *Actes de l'école de printemps d'informatique théorique, Font-Romeu 93*. Springer-Verlag, 1994.

[McC93]   R. McCloskey. Bounded context grammars and languages. *PHD*, 1993.

[McN67]   R. McNaughton. Parenthesis grammars. *JACM 14*, pages 490–500, 1967.

[MH44]   M. Morse and G.A. Hedlung. Unending chess,symbolic dynamics and a problem in semi-groups. *Duke Math. J.11*, pages 1–7, 1944.

[MNO88]   R. McNaughton, P. Narendran, and F. Otto. Church-Rosser Thue systems and formal languages. *JACM 35 (2)*, pages 324–344, 1988.

[MNOZ93]   K. Madlener, P. Narendran, F. Otto, and L. Zhang. On weakly confluent monadic string-rewriting systems. *T.C.S. 113*, pages 119–165, 1993.

[MO89]   K. Madlener and F. Otto. About the descriptive power of certain classes of finite string-rewriting systems. *T.C.S. 67*, pages 143–172, 1989.

[Nar86]   P. Narendran. On the equivalence problem for regular Thue systems. *TCS 44*, pages 237–245, 1986.

[Nar90]   P. Narendran. It is decidable whether a monadic Thue system is canonical over a regular set. *Math. Systems Theory 23*, pages 245–254, 1990.

[NB72]   M. Nivat and M. Benois. Congruences parfaites et quasi-parfaites. *Séminaire Dubreil,2ième année,no 7*, 1971/72.

[Niv70]   M. Nivat. On some families of languages related to the Dyck language. *2nd Annual Symposium on Theory of Computing*, 1970.

[Niv71]   M. Nivat. Congruences de Thue et t-langages. *Studia Scientiarum Mathematicarum Hungarica 6*, pages 243–249, 1971.

[NOR86]   P. Narendran, C. O'Dunlaing, and H. Rolletschek. Complexity of certain decision problems about congruential languages. *JCSS 30*, pages 343–358, 1986.

[O'D81]   C. O'Dunlaing. Finite and infinite regular Thue systems. *PHD University of California at Santa Barbara*, 1981.

[O'D83]   C. O'Dunlaing. Infinite regular thue systems. *TCS 2*, pages 171–192, 1983.

[OIH81]   M. Oyamaguchi, Y. Inagaki, and N. Honda. The equivalence problem for two dpda's one of which is a finite-turn or one-counter machine. *J. Comput. System Sci.23,nr 3*, pages 366–382, 1981.

[Ott84]   F. Otto. Some undecidability results for non-monadic Church-Rosser Thue systems. *TCS 33*, pages 261–278, 1984.

[Ott87]   F. Otto. On deciding the confluence of a finite string-rewriting system on a given congruence class. *JCSS 35*, pages 285–310, 1987.

[Ott92a]   F. Otto. Completing a finite special string-rewriting system on the congruence class of the empty word. *Applicable Algebra in Engeneering Comm.Comput. 2*, pages 257–274, 1992.

[Ott92b]   F. Otto. The problem of deciding confluence on a given congruence class is tractable for finite special string-rewriting systems. *Math. Systems Theory 25*, pages 241–251, 1992.

[OZ91]   F. Otto and L. Zhang. Decision problems for finite special string-rewriting systems that are confluent on some congruence class. *Acta Informatica 28*, pages 477–510, 1991.

[RS86]   F. Romian and J. Sakarovitch. One-sided Dyck reduction over two letters and deterministic context-free languages. In *Proceedings MFCS 86*, pages 554–563. Springer-Verlag, LNCS 233, 1986.

[Sak79]   J. Sakarovitch. Syntaxe des langages de Chomsky, essai sur le déterminisme. *Thèse de doctorat d'état de l'université Paris VII*, pages 1–175, 1979.

[Sal73]   A. Salomaa. *Formal Languages*. Academic Press, 1973.

[Sén81]   G. Sénizergues. Décidabilité de l'équivalence des grammaires NTS. *Thèse de 3ième cycle,université Paris 7*, pages 1–170, 1981.

[Sén85]   G. Sénizergues. The equivalence and inclusion problems for NTS languages. *J. Comput. System Sci. 31(3)*, pages 303–331, 1985.

[Sén86] G. Sénizergues. On the rational subsets of the free group. *LITP internal report nr 86-3, submitted to Acta Informatica*, pages 1–17, 1986.

[Sén87] G. Sénizergues. Sur la description des langages algébriques déterministes par des systèmes de réécriture confluents. *Thèse d'état,université Paris 7 et rapport LITP 88-39*, pages 1–330, 1987.

[Sén89] G. Sénizergues. Church-Rosser controlled rewriting systems and equivalence problems for deterministic context-free languages. *Information and Computation 81 (3)*, pages 265–279, 1989.

[Sén90a] G. Sénizergues. A characterisation of deterministic context-free languages by means of right-congruences. *TCS 70 (2)*, pages 213–232, 1990.

[Sén90b] G. Sénizergues. Some decision problems about controlled rewriting systems. *TCS 71*, pages 281–346, 1990.

[Tak75] M. Takahashi. Generalizations of regular sets and their application to a study of context-free languages. *Information and Control 27*, pages 1–35, 1975.

[Thu12] A. Thue. Uber die gegenseitiges lage gleicher teile gewisser zeichenreihen. *Skr.Vid.Kristiania,I Mat.Naturv.Klasse nr 8*, pages 1–67, 1912.

[Thu14] A. Thue. Probleme über veränderungen von zeichenreihen nach gegeben regeln. *Skr.Vid.Kristiania,I Mat.Naturv.Klasse nr 10*,, page 34 pp, 1914.

[Val74] L.G. Valiant. The equivalence problem for deterministic finite-turn push-down automata. *Information and Control 25*, pages 123–133, 1974.

[Zha92] L. Zhang. The pre-NTS property is undecidable for context-free grammars. *IPL 44*, pages 181–184, 1992.

Rewriting and Tree Automata*

Max Dauchet

LIFL , URA 369 CNRS
University of Lille I
59655 Villeneuve d'Ascq   France
dauchet@lifl.lifl.fr

Abstract. We summarize the main connections between rewriting, automata, and logical languages. We recall and illustrate from a rewriting point of view classical tree automata, Rabin and Büchi automata, which are associated with $(W)S1S$ and $(W)SkS$ logics. We introduce four recent classes of tree automata, closely linked to rewriting problems.

Introduction

The aim of this paper is to show that new classes of tree automata are closely related to rewrite systems and can be seen as an useful rewriting techniques for software engineering. This paper summarizes the main connections between rewriting and automata, but also emphasizes how the duality "logical languages, classes of automata" is a pregnant particularization of the general duality "specification - algorithm".

This duality is introduced and developed in the section 4; we study it in the section 5 for classical classes of automata (Büchi, Rabin automata), and in the section 6 for classes of automata closely linked to rewriting problems. Before we introduce well-known classical tree automata in the section 1 and Rabin automata (infinite tree automata) in the section 3.

From a rewriting point of view, we can consider that the outcome of the paper is the last section; we can't give any proof nor can we detail how works each kind of automata, but we try to motivate the reader for further reading, and we give at the head of each paragraph a crucial reference for more details. The other sections prepare for the section 6 and detail the processes and the motivations which lead to automata.

* This work was partly supported by PRC-GDR "Mathématiques et Informatique", by PRC project "Modèles logiques de la programmation", and by ESPRIT Basic Research Action 6317 ASMICS 2.

The section 2 is academic, it underlines a phenomena which is at the frontier of what automata forbid, and which leads to the undecidable. It contains the only formal proof of the paper, because this proof is an useful exercise to avoid misunderstandings. Furthermore, we use it in the section 6 to explain why Rabin's techniques are useless in the non linear case. The paragraph 4.2 is devoted to examples in a simple theory (Presburger arithmetic); it seems simplistic but it is paradigmatic, because the processes are much more intricate but the ideas are the same in other theories. Most of the examples are very simple and are intended for beginners.

We don't study the complexity aspects in this paper. Most of the problems are intractable in the *worst case*, but experimentations show that the complexity collapses often in practical cases. To get efficient algorithms, it is necessary to combine algorithms (as cleaning algorithms), fast heuristics, optimizations and sophisticated implementations. These aspects should be further explored [14].

We will assume the notions of (finite) automata on words, and the standard notions of rewrite systems and of universal algebra, such as signature, term, substitution, sort. The reader may refer to Thomas [18] for a survey of classical automata and connections with logics, and to Dershowitz and Jouannaud [11] for a survey of rewriting.

We usually denote $a(x)$ a function letter a of rank 1, $b(x,y)$ a function letter b of rank 2, x, y, z, or x_1, x_2, variable symbols... A term is *linear* if no variable occurs more than once. T_Σ (denoted $T(\Sigma, \varnothing)$ in [11]) is the set of ground terms over a ranked alphabet Σ. Automata work over ground terms.

☺☺ means *obvious;* ☺ *easy;* ☺ *medium, tedious;* ☹ *slightly difficult...*

⚠*be careful, hidden difficulty, important property;* ⚠ *open problem, further works.*

☺ 1. Usual tree automata

1.1 Definition
A *Bottom Up Tree Automaton* (BU *automaton*) over a finite ranked alphabet Σ is of the form M = (Q, R, F) with finite *state set* Q, *transition set* R, and a set F $\subseteq$ Q of *final states*. A *transition* is a ground rewrite rule of the form $f(q_1,...,q_n) \rightarrow q$, where f is a symbol of Σ of rank n, q, $q_1,...,$ q_n are states. (There are also ε - *rules* of the form $q \rightarrow q'$, but we can suppress them.)

A ground term t is *accepted* (or *recognized*) by M if and only if t -*$\rightarrow q$, for some final state q. The language L(M) *accepted* (or *recognized*) by M is the set of ground terms accepted. We often omit F and denote L(M, Q') the set of t such that t -*$\rightarrow q$, for some q of Q'. We see that M can be essentially identified with its set R of transitions, which is a special kind of ground rewrite system. A tree language is *recognizable* if and only if it is accepted by some automaton.

If we reverse the arrows, we define *Top Down Tree Automata (TD automata)* (final states become *initial states*). If we do not precise, we consider BU automata. Obviously, reverse the arrows does not modify the language which is recognized.

M is *deterministic* if there are not two rules with the same left-hand side.

A *run* of M on a term t is obtained by replacing each label of node of t by the state computed by rewriting (we assume that there is no ε - rule) (Figure 1).

1.2 Examples

1.2.1 Runs of BU automata can be seen as computations of (finitely valued) synthesized attributes; states are then the values of the attributes. TD automata are associated with inherited attributes.

Example: Evaluation of a Boolean expression. $\Sigma = \{T, F, \neg, \wedge, \vee\}$, $Q = \{\mathbb{T}, \mathbb{E}\}$,
$R = \{ T \to \mathbb{T}, F \to \mathbb{E}, \neg(\mathbb{T}) \to \mathbb{E}, \neg(\mathbb{E}) \to \mathbb{T}, \wedge(\mathbb{T}, \mathbb{T}) \to \mathbb{T}, \wedge(\mathbb{T}, \mathbb{E}) \to \mathbb{E}, \wedge(\mathbb{E}, \mathbb{T}) \to \mathbb{E}, \wedge(\mathbb{E}, \mathbb{E}) \to \mathbb{E}, \vee(\mathbb{T}, \mathbb{T}) \to \mathbb{T}, \vee(\mathbb{T}, \mathbb{E}) \to \mathbb{T}, \vee(\mathbb{E}, \mathbb{T}) \to \mathbb{T}, \vee(\mathbb{E}, \mathbb{E}) \to \mathbb{E}.$

In this example, the automaton is deterministic and *completely specified* (i.e. for any ground term, there is at least a run).

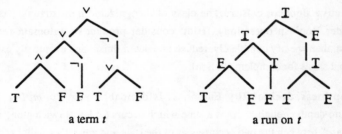

a term t a run on t

Figure 1. An example of run

1.2.2 Sort checking is a seminal class of examples. We can identify tree automata with signatures of order-sorted algebras (Comon [7]). Considering signatures as automata, algorithmic properties of automata can be used to get efficient manipulations for sort checking, compilation, interpretation, partial evaluation. States are identified with sorts *Stack, NonEmptyStack, Nat*. So, the following example (Dershowitz and Jouannaud [11]) can be seen as an automaton, the rules of which are:
$0 \to Nat$, $\sigma(Nat) \to Nat$, $\Lambda \to Stack$, $push(Nat, Stack) \to NonEmptyStack$, $top(NonEmptyStack) \to Nat$, $pop(NonEmptyStack) \to Stack$

The inclusion order on sorts corresponds with ε - rules. So, the rule *NonEmptyStack* $\to$ *Stack* is associated with *NonEmptyStack* $\subseteq$ *Stack*. Remark that ε - rules introduce non determinism (and multi-sorting), but non determinism can be reduced, i.e. there is an algorithm which associates an equivalent deterministic BU automaton with any BU automaton (see 1.3).

☺ 1.3 Basic properties

The following properties are well known. They are the basis of the classical tree automata theory. When we extend classes of tree automata, we try to keep the same kind of properties. Proofs of the properties bellow and constructions are straightforward generalisations of the word case.

1.3.1 Reduction properties

i/ Complete specification: We can effectively associate with any automaton an equivalent one which is completely specified. (Hint: add a "dead state").

ii/ Reduction of non determinism: We can effectively associate with any BU automaton an equivalent deterministic. (Hint: put together states which are reached by a same term).

iii/ Minimalization: There is an algorithm which associates with any BU automaton an equivalent deterministic BU automaton with as few states as possible (this *minimal automaton* is unique).

1.3.2 Effective Boolean closure The class of recognizable tree languages is effectively closed under Boolean operations. (Hint: consider product of automata for union and intersection, then specify completely, reduce non determinism and eventually exchange final and not-final states for complementation).

1.3.3 Emptiness decidability Emptiness is decidable, using *pumping*: if a term is accepted and depth enough, there is a state which occurs (at least) twice along a path; then, we can "erase" between the two occurrences of the state and we get a smaller accepted term.

⚠ ⚠ **1.3.4 Complexity properties** Algorithms used above are polynomial, except reduction of non determinism, which is intractable. Nevertheless, in practical cases, complexity often collapses (there are no many results in this area on average complexity).

1.3.5 Corollary Equivalence is decidable. It is a polynomial problem in the deterministic case.

1.3.6 Remark The class of recognizable tree languages is effectively closed under linear morphism and under inverse morphism (not necessarily linear). Obviously, it is not closed under non linear morphisms: the set of terms $b(t,t)$ is not recognizable (use pumping).

⚠ **1.3.7 Remark** Reduction of non determinism fails in the Top Down case (consider the automaton over $\{a,a', b(x,y)\}$ with states q,q',q'', initial state q'' and transitions rules $q'' \to b(q,q)$, $q'' \to b(q',q')$, $q \to a$ and $q' \to a'$). But as any recognizable tree language is accepted by a BU automaton, this result does not alter the properties of recognizable languages. In the same way, if we want completely specify a TD automaton, we must introduce final states.

1.4 Normal forms and recognizability

☺   Let $NF(R)$ be the set of normal forms for some rewrite system R. If R is left-linear, prove that $NF(R)$ is recognizable is an easy exercise. Note that generally a recognizable language is not a set of normal form for any rewrite system (example: $(aa)^*$).

☺ ☹ Kucherov & Tajin [15] and Vagvölgyi & Gilleron [19] recently proved that recognizability of $NF(R)$ is decidable.

2. Rewriting and the power of non linearity

We can consider any Turing machine as a word rewrite system. As a word rewrite system is a very particular case of linear rewrite system, we conclude that "linear rewrite systems are sufficient to compute anything" and it seems that the title of this section does not make sense. But we would like to illustrate here only the surprising gap between linear and non linear simple classes of rewriting. We first consider morphisms, which are particular rewrite systems.

More precisely, a morphism φ from T_Σ to T_Δ is an application such that $\varphi(a(t_1,...,t_n)) = \varphi(a)(\varphi(t_1),..., \varphi(t_n))$ for all $a \in \Sigma$ and $t_i \in T_\Sigma$. If $\Sigma \cap \Delta = \varnothing$, then $\varphi(t)$ is the normal form of t for the rewrite system defined by $a \to \varphi(a)$ for all $a \in \Sigma$.

2.1 Interleaving lemma

Let R and R' be recognizable sets of terms, φ and φ' be morphisms. Emptiness of $\varphi(R) \cap \varphi'(R')$ is undecidable.

    Proof: We will reduce Post Problem to our emptiness problem.

        Let f and f' word morphisms from A^* into B^*.

        $\text{Post}(f, f') \Leftrightarrow_{\text{def}} \exists\, m$; m non empty and $f(m) = f'(m)$.

        We associate φ, R, φ', R' with f, f' such that $\text{Post}(f, f') \Leftrightarrow \varphi(R) \cap \varphi'(R') = \varnothing$.

    As Post is undecidable (Post Problem), emptiness is undecidable.

    Construction:

        Assume $A = \{a_1,...,a_n\}$ and $B = \{b_1,...,b_m\}$. We define R over the ranked alphabet $A' \cup B' \cup \{\#, \gamma_1(x,y,z),...,\gamma_n(x,y,z)\}$ and R' over $B' \cup \{\#, \alpha(x), \gamma(x,y,z)\}$, with $A' = \{\alpha_1(x),...,\alpha_n(x)\}$, $B' = \{\beta_1(x),...,\beta_m(x)\}$. Using rational tree expressions in an obvious sense, and identifying $u + v$ with its interpretation $\{u, v\}$, we define

$$R = A'(\gamma_1(B'^*\#,B'^*\#,z)+...+\gamma_n(B'^*\#,B'^*\#,z))^*\#$$

and $$R' = (\gamma(B'^*\#,B'^*\#,z))^*\alpha(B'^*\#)$$

definition of φ : identity over B' and $\#$;

$\quad$ for $i = 1,..., n \quad \alpha_i(x) \rightarrow \gamma(f(a_i)\#, f'(a_i)\#, x)$;

$$\gamma_i(x,y,z) \rightarrow \gamma(x,y, \gamma(f(a_i)(x), f'(a_i)(y), z))$$

$\quad$ where $f(a_i)(x) = \beta_{i1}\beta_{i2}...\beta_{ip}(x)$ if $f(a_i) = b_{i1}b_{i2}...b_{ip}$

definition of φ' : identity over B' and $\#$;

$\quad$ for $i = 1,..., n \quad \alpha(x) \rightarrow \gamma(x, x, \#)$;

$$\gamma(x,y,z) \rightarrow \gamma(x,y, \gamma(x, y, z))$$

We left the end of the proof to the reader. Remark that for any term $t \in \varphi(R)$, the rightmost path of t is labelled with c (except its leave), and $t \in \varphi(R)$ implies equality on t of a subterm rooted at the second c (starting from the root) with a subterm of a subterm rooted at the third c, and so for the 4-th and the 5-th, for the 6-th and the 7-th, etc. Likewise $t \in \varphi'(R')$ implies equality of a subterm rooted at the first c with a subterm rooted at the second c, and so for the 3-rd and the 4-th, for the 5-th and the 6-th, etc. This interleaving of equality is the key of the undecidability.

☺ **2.2 Theorem** [10] *For any recursively enumerable set of terms* E, *there are three morphisms* φ, ψ *and* ϕ *and an alphabet* Σ *such that* $E = \phi(\psi^{-1}(\varphi(T_\Sigma)))$. *If* φ, ψ *and* ϕ *are linear, then* E *is recognizable.*

$\quad$ *Hint:* use techniques of lemma 2.1 to simulate any rewriting. (Furthermore, we can get $\phi = \psi = \varphi$).

3. Rabin automata

The subject on infinite trees was established by Rabin (1969) (refer to Rabin [17] and Thomas [18] illuminating papers). His works introduced intricate automaton constructions, opened new connections between automata theory and logic, and resulted in a tool which is fundamental for decision problems. Section 3 is devoted to Rabin automata for several reasons: these automata are a famous and powerful tool; they are directly or indirectly used in following sections to get decidability theories related to rewriting; the processes of generalisation are exemplary: designing a large class of automata preserving "good" decisions properties of the usual class.

3.1 Definition

A *Rabin automaton* over a finite ranked alphabet Σ is a top down tree automaton with *accepting pairs* $\{(L_1, U_1), \ldots, (L_n, U_n)\}$ of state sets L_i, U_i.

A Rabin automaton accepts infinite trees. Runs over infinite trees are defined in the same way as over finite trees.

For all run r over t and all path π on t, $\text{In}(r \mid \pi)$ denotes the set of states which occur infinitely often in π. A run r is *successful* if for all path π on t there exists i $(1 \leq i \leq n)$ with $\text{In}(r \mid \pi) \cap L_i = \varnothing$ and $\text{In}(r \mid \pi) \cap U_i \neq \varnothing$. A tree t is *accepted* (or *recognized*) if there is a successful run of the automaton on t.

3.2 Properties of the class of Rabin-recognizable languages

☺ i/ Any (usual) recognizable tree language is Rabin-recognizable.

> *Hint:* extend paths infinitely with a new symbol, extend runs infinitely with a new state q_ω and get the accepting pair $(Q, \{q_\omega\})$.

☺ ii/ Effective closure under union, product, linear morphism. (Do as in the usual case)

⚠ iii/ Effective closure under complementation.

☹ ☹ ☹ We can't use the straightforward procedure sketched in 1.3.2 because for infinite trees, we must use top-down computations, and as in the usual top down case, we can't reduce nondeterminism. Rabin gave a very difficult proof of effective closure under complementation, which is still the subject of many works.

☺ iv/ Decidability of emptiness.

We get decidability of equivalence as a corollary.

4. Logical specifications and automata

4.1 The relevance of automata

We only study word and tree automata here. In the graph case, many links between automata and specifications fail ([16], and Courcelle's paper in this book).

A main motivation of automata was the investigation of decision problems in mathematical logic. Büchi discovered that automata provide a normal form for certain monadic second-order theories. Rabin's tree theorem (which states that the monadic second-order theory of the infinite binary tree is decidable) turned out to be a powerful result to which a large number of decision problems related to software engineering could be reduced. Today, except applications to rewrite systems (section 6), major application areas of automata (on infinite sequences or infinite trees) are the connection with fixed point calculi, and the specification and verification of concurrent programs (most of the logical specification formalisms for concurrent programs, such as systems of program logic or temporal logic, are embeddable in the monadic theories studies by Büchi and Rabin).

In software engineering, we would like have high-level, ergonomic languages to specify problems, and efficient algorithms to compute. The duality "logical languages & classes of automata" satisfy this properties for restricted classes of problems:

Vocabulary of logic languages is basic: connectives, quantifiers, equality and ad hoc atomic formulas (plus terms and variables interpreted in specific domains).

On the other hand, automata are classes of algorithms that we can manipulate, compose and split up, compile, optimize, reduce...

Furthermore, the duality logical operators - algebraic operators (Fig. 2) makes easier modularity and reliability.

Formally, let F be a (non universal) specification language, more precisely a logical language; let A be a class of algorithms, more precisely a class of automata. For any formula $\phi(X_1,...,X_n)$, $L(\phi)$ denotes the set of instances $(a_1,...,a_n)$ which satisfy $\phi(a_1,...,a_n)$; $L(M)$ denotes the language accepted by an algorithm M. Here, we study some pairs (F, A) which are relevant in computer sciences and such that we can design an implementation algorithm which associates with any specification ϕ an (efficient) algorithm M such that $L(\phi) = L(M)$, and conversely a specification algorithm which associates some ϕ with any M (Figure 2). We say that F and A are *effectively equivalent*. We introduce classical pairs (*logical language, class of automata*) in the section 5 and pairs related to rewriting in the section 6.

Computation is incomplete for universal programming languages, because of non-termination. Ordered rewriting is a large frame for terminating computations, in which order makes the most of particularities of problems (see Dershowitz, Jouannaud, Kirchner's papers in this volume). Restriction to automata seems too much drastic, but in fact, the diversity of pregnant classes of automata and logics attests to the contrary.

Associating a class of automata with a class of problems presents two advantages. The first advantage is algorithmic; nevertheless, complexity in the worst case remains non elementary, and "People are beginning to realize that if something doesn't work *fast*, it doesn't really work at all" (Brachman [3]). Fortunately, complexity collapses often, ⚠ but efficient heuristics should be further explored. The second advantage is structural: finding a class of automata means fitting a structure with good algebraic and logical properties.

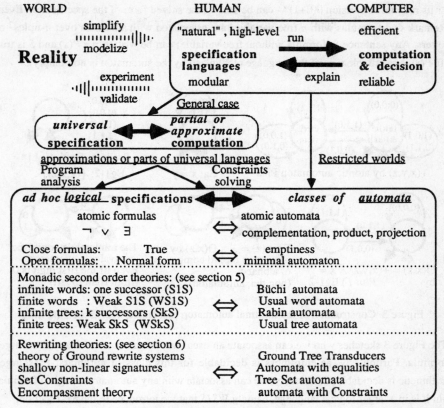

Figure 2. Rewriting and Automata

☺ ☺ 4.2 Informal example

Here, we give the idea of constructions by the mean of Presburger arithmetic simple formulas. *Presburger arithmetic* is the first order theory[1] of addition over non negative integers N: variables are interpreted in N, formulas are constructed from the atom $+(x,y,z)$, using logical connectives and quantifiers.

We associate an atomic usual word automaton Plus with +. The idea is to represent numbers in binary notations and to describe the process of digit by digit calculation of the sum (we read numbers from right to left).

The Figure 3 illustrates the automatic construction of an optimal checking algorithm, associated with the specification Even(z) " $\exists x : + (x, x, z)$". ⚠ The minimal automaton -

---

[1] First order means that only terms are quantified. In second order logics, quantifiers act on relations too; monadic means that these relations are unary and hence membership predicates. The theory is the set of true sentences.

or its rational expression $0(0+1)^*$ - can be seen as the solved form of the specification Even. Remark that formulas with n free variables are associated with automata over n-uples[2] of letters. Any sentence S (formula without free variable) can be written $\exists\, x\, P(x)$ and S is true iff $P(x)$ is satisfiable (i.e. iff the language recognized by the automaton is non-empty).

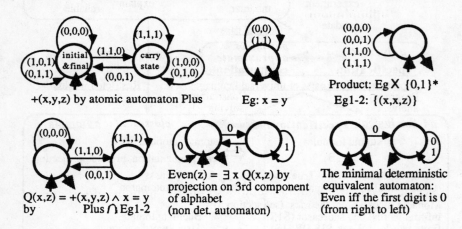

Figure 3. Construction of the minimal automaton associated with $\exists\, x : +\, (x, x, z)$

The Figure 3 sketches who we can associate an usual word automaton with any Presburger formula. Particularly, as emptiness is decidable for this class of automata, Presburger arithmetic is decidable. Conversely, we can associate with any automaton a logical formula, but it is in a larger logical language, namely *WS1S* that we introduce in the next section.

5. Classical Theories and Automata

5.1 The Sequential Calculus and Büchi automata

Here, we consider infinite sequences (ω-words) over some finite alphabet Σ. An ω-word α is represented by sets α_a (for $a \in \Sigma$); α_a is the set of positions on α which carry the letter a. For example, $\alpha = (ab)^\omega$ is represented by the set α_a of even integers and the set α_b of odd integers.

---

[2] We considere tuples of letters $(a_1,...,a_n)$ and tuples of words $(w_1,...,w_n)$, with $(w_1,...,w_n)\,(w'_1,...,w'_n)$ $=(ww'_1,...,ww'_n)$. If L is a set of tuples, its i-projection $\pi_i(L)$ is the set of $(w_1,...,w_{i-1},w_{i+1},...,w_n)$, for all $(w_1,...,w_n)$ in L. The i-cylindrification of L' is the set $\pi_i^{-1}(L')$ of $(w_1,...,w_{i-1},v,w_{i+1},...,w_n)$, for all words v and for all $(w_1,...,w_{i-1},w_{i+1},...,w_n)$ in L'. It is easy to associate an automaton which recognizes $\pi_i(L)$ (respectively $\pi_i^{-1}(L')$) with an automaton which recognizes L (respectively L').

5.1.1 The sequential Calculus

The *Sequential Calculus* $S1S_\Sigma$ is *the monadic Second-order logic of 1 Successor over* Σ. *Terms* are constructed from the constant 0 and the variables $x, y, \ldots$ (interpreted in $\mathbb{N}$) by application of "+1", *atomic formulas* are of the form $t = t'$, $t \in X$, $t \in \alpha_a$ (which means "t-th letter of α is a") where t, t' are terms and X is a set variable, and *formulas* are constructed from atomic formulas using logical connectives and the quantifiers $\exists, \forall$ acting on either kind of variables.

☺ ☺ **5.1.2 Example** The usual order $<$ over $\mathbb{N}$, $\cup$, the Max over subsets of $\mathbb{N}$, finiteness of sets, the usual $+$ bellow, are $S1S_\Sigma$ definable as follows:

$x < y$: $\forall X\, (x{+}1 \in X \wedge \forall z\, (z \in X \Rightarrow z{+}1 \in X) \Rightarrow y \in X)$

$\cup(X, Y)$: $x \in Z \Leftrightarrow (x \in X \vee x \in Y)$

$\mathrm{Max}(X)$: $x \in X \wedge \neg\, (\exists y \in X \wedge x < y)$; $\mathrm{Fin}(X)$: $\exists x\, (x = \mathrm{Max}(X))$

$\phi1(\alpha)$: $\forall x\, (x \in \alpha_a \Rightarrow \exists y\, (x < y \wedge y \in \alpha_b))$ specifies the set of ω-words over $\{a, b\}$ such that after any letter a there is eventually a letter b.

$\phi2(\alpha)$ specifies the set of ω-words over $\{a, b, c\}$ such that between any two succeeding occurrences of letter a there is an even number of letters b, c:

$\forall x\, \forall y\, (x \in \alpha_a \wedge y \in \alpha_a \wedge x < y \wedge \neg\, \exists z\, (x < z \wedge z < y \wedge z \in \alpha_a) \Rightarrow$
$\exists X\, (x \in X \wedge \forall z\, (z \in X \Leftrightarrow \neg\, z{+}1 \in X) \wedge \neg\, y \in X))$.

☺ **5.1.3 Example** $+(\alpha, \beta, \gamma)$:

$\exists m, Q, C\, (m = \mathrm{Max}(\alpha_0 \cup \alpha_1) = \mathrm{Max}(\beta_0 \cup \beta_1) = \mathrm{Max}(\gamma_0 \cup \gamma_1)$

$\wedge\, \neg\, \exists x\, (x \in Q \wedge x \in C) \wedge 0 \in Q \wedge m \in Q$

$\wedge\, \forall x\, (x \in Q \wedge x{+}1 \in Q \cap (\alpha_0 \cap \beta_0 \cap \gamma_0 \cup \alpha_1 \cap \beta_0 \cap \gamma_1 \cup \alpha_0 \cap \beta_1 \cap \gamma_1)$

$\vee\, (x \in Q \wedge x{+}1 \in C \cap (\alpha_1 \cap \beta_1 \cap \gamma_0) \vee (x \in C \wedge x{+}1 \in Q \cap (\alpha_0 \cap \beta_0 \cap \gamma_1)$

$\vee\, (x \in C \wedge x{+}1 \in C \cap (\alpha_1 \cap \beta_1 \cap \gamma_1 \cup \alpha_1 \cap \beta_0 \cap \gamma_0 \cup \alpha_0 \cap \beta_1 \cap \gamma_0))$

This formula specifies successful runs of length m of the automaton Plus (Q is associated with the final and initial state and C with the "carry" state).

5.1.4 An other notation: $S1S_\Sigma$ and $S1S$.

It is sometimes convenient to cancel the predicate symbols α_a and use free set variables α_k (k in an integer) in their place. The resulting formalism will be called $S1S$. $x \in \alpha_k$ says that the x-th letter of α has 1 in its k-th component.

5.1.5 Büchi automata

A *Büchi automaton* is defined as an usual word automaton, but is recognizes ω-words, and the classical set of final states plays the role of *infinitary* states. A run is *successful* if some state of the set F of infinitary states occurs infinitely often. An ω-word is *accepted* (or recognized) if there is a successful run of the automaton on this word.

5.1.6 Example Automata *B1* and *B2* of the Figure 4 recognize languages specified by formulas φ1, respectively φ2. Infinitary states are represented with a double circle.

Figure 4. Büchi automata *B1* and *B2*

5.1.7 Theorem [4], [18] *The monadic Second-order logic of 1 Successor and Büchi automata are effectively equivalent. Emptiness is decidable for Büchi automata, and then S1S is decidable.*

☺ *Hint:* Associate a formula with an automaton is easy, it is sufficient to specify the existence of a successful run . The example 5.1.3 illustrates the construction (here, specify infinitary acceptance condition instead of finite states).

⚠ ☹ ☹ Conversely, we proceed in two steps. first *S1S* is reduced to a simpler formalism. Secondly we associate an automaton by induction over simplified formulas. The crucial point is that it is not easy to treat ¬, because, as in the case of Rabin automata, we can't reduce non-determinism, and closure by complementation of Büchi automata is difficult to prove (but not so much as in the tree case).

5.2 The Weak S1S logic and classical word automata
Weak means that sets quantification refers to finite sets only, and so formulas are interpreted in finite words[3]. With minor modifications the above results also hold for finite words: the weak *S1S* logic (*WS1S* logic) and the class of usual word automata are effectively equivalent, and as emptiness is decidable, the theory *WS1S* is decidable.

Note that as we can reduce non determinism for usual automata, the equivalence is easier to prove, and was shown earlier.

Presburger arithmetic $(N,+)$ can be embedded in *WS1S*. We can extend the idea to the case where infinite binary expansions of real numbers are considered. Thus also the first-order theory of $(R,+)$ is decidable. Moreover, the fact that any *S1S*-definable set of ω-words contains an ultimately periodic sequence can be used to show that the first-order theories of $(R,+)$ and $(Q,+)$ coincide.

---

[3] Instead of this way, *WS1S* can be interpreted in *S1S*, because the example 5.1.2 shows the definability of finiteness in *S1S*.

5.3 The S2S logic and Rabin automata

For a transfer of the preceding results from words to binary trees, we consider two successor fonctions $succ_0$ and $succ_1$ over $\{0,1\}^*$ instead of the successor $+1$ ($succ_i(w) = wi$). So, a position x on an infinite binary tree is a Dewey indice. The language contains variables $x,y,...$ and $X,Y,...$ (ranging over elements, resp. subsets of $\{0,1\}^*$). *Terms* are obtained from the individual variables $x,y,...$ and the constant ε by application of $succ_0$, $succ_1$; we write $x0$ instead of $succ_0(x)$ etc. *Atomic formulas* are of the form $t = t'$, $t < t'$ ($<$ is the prefix order), $t \in X$, $t \in \tau_a$ (which means "position t of the tree τ carries letter a").

☺ **5.3.1 Examples** of *S2S*-formulas (using abbreviations such as $x \leq y$; $X \subseteq Y$, etc.):

Chain(X): $\forall x \forall y ((x \in X \wedge y \in X) \Rightarrow (x < y \vee x = y \vee x > y)$

Path(X):   Chain(X) $\wedge \neg \exists Y (X \subseteq Y \wedge X \neq Y \wedge$ Chain(Y))

Lexicographic ordering $x \langle y$: $x \leq y \vee \exists z (z0 \leq x \wedge z1 \leq y)$

$x \langle$-minimal in X: $x \in X \wedge \neg (\exists y \in X \wedge y < x)$

Fin(X): $\forall Y (Y \subseteq X \wedge Y \neq \varnothing \Rightarrow (\exists y$ "$y \langle$-minimal in Y" $\wedge \exists y$ "$y \langle$-maximal in Y"))

$\phi 3(\tau)$: the set of infinite binary trees τ over $\{a, b\}$ such that some path through τ carries infinitely many a :

$\exists Y$ (Path(Y) $\wedge \forall x (x \in Y \Rightarrow \exists y (y \in Y \wedge x < y \wedge y \in \tau_a)))$

$\phi 4(\tau)$ denotes the set $T_{\{a,b,c\}}$ of finite trees over $\{a, b, c\}$ (rank(a) = 0, rank(b) = 1, rank(c) = 2), using abbreviation $x \in \tau$ which means "$x \in \tau_a \vee x \in \tau_b \vee x \in \tau_c$":

$\forall X (((\text{Path}(X) \wedge \forall x (x \in X \Rightarrow x \in \tau)) \Rightarrow \text{Fin}(X))$

$\wedge \forall x (((x \in X \wedge x \in \tau_a \wedge x < y) \Rightarrow \neg y \in X) \wedge ((x \in X \wedge x0 \in \tau_b) \Rightarrow \neg x1 \in \tau))$

5.3.2 Theorem [17], [18] *The monadic Second-order logic of 2 Successor and Rabin automata are effectively equivalent. S2S is decidable.*

The proof is more interacted than in the word case but the process is the same, it uses properties of Rabin automata (section 3).

5.4 The WeakS2S logic and usual tree automata

The restriction to finite terms is an obvious transfer of the preceding results from words to trees.

Remark that we can obviously define the (Weak) *SkS* logic for any rank k.

6. Rewriting Theories and Automata

☹ **6.1** [9] **The theory of ground rewrite systems is decidable**

Huet and Lankford (1978) proved the decidability of termination of ground rewrite systems (g.r.s.), Huet and Oppen (1980) made the conjecture that confluence is decidable too. We proved this conjecture (1985), and so did Oyamaguchi (1987) independently. But in [9] we give a much more general result which we introduce here.

6.1.1 Definition of the ground rewrite system formulas *Variables* are interpreted in T_Σ (we built a first order logic), *atomic formulas* are of the form $t \text{ -}^*_R\!\!\to t'$, $t \text{ -}_R\!\!\to t'$, $t \text{ -}_{R||}\!\!\to t'^4$, $\text{Fin}_R(t)^5$ for any given ground rewrite system R . *Formulas* are constructed from atomic formulas using logical connectives and the quantifiers $\exists, \forall$.

☺ **6.1.2 Examples** of properties which are definable in this logic

  Equality $t = t'$ of terms: $t \text{ -}^*_\varnothing\!\!\to t'$

  Recognizable set constraints $t \in F$ (F recognizable):

    $t \text{ -}^*_M\!\!\to q$, where M is a bottom up automaton defined as a ground rewrite

    system (def 1.1), and q is the final state (we can assume that q is unique).

  Confluence of a ground rewrite system R:

    $\forall\ t, u, u'((t \text{ -}^*_R\!\!\to u \ \wedge t \text{ -}^*_R\!\!\to u') \Rightarrow \exists\ v\ (u \text{ -}^*_R\!\!\to v \wedge u' \text{ -}^*_R\!\!\to v))$

  Equivalence of ground rewrite systems R and S:

    $\forall\ t, t\ (t \text{ -}^*_R\!\!\to t' \Leftrightarrow\ t \text{ -}^*_S\!\!\to t')$

  Termination (Huet & Lankford) of R: $\forall\ t\ \text{Fin}_R(t)\ \wedge \neg\exists\ u\ (u \text{ -}^*_R\!\!\to u)$

6.1.3 Theorem [9] *The theory of ground rewrite systems is decidable*

  Roughly, the idea is the same as for Presburger arithmetic. We associate a tree automaton (that we call *ground tree transducers GTT*) with any ground rewrite relation $\text{-}^*_R\!\!\to$. Inductively, we associate with any formula an automaton of a class of tree automata (the class *RR*) which embeds the class *GTT* and get good closure properties.

6.1.4 Extension and application We uses only the fact that, for any rule of a g.r.s., the left-hand side and the right-hand side are recognizable tree languages. Hence theorem 6.1.3. is true if we consider "meta" rewrite rules of the form $L \to R$, which means "substitute any term of R to any term of L", where L and R are recogizable sets of terms. This extension can be used in program analysis [12], by approximation of any sorted rule by an associated meta rule.

  For example, the sorted (non-ground) rewrite rule
$x, z \in N^+$, $y \in N$: $\text{DIV}(\text{MUL}^6(x, y), \text{MUL}(x, z)) \to \text{DIV}(y, z)$ is approximated by the meta rule $\text{DIV}(\text{MUL}(N^+, N), \text{MUL}(N^+, N^+)) \to \text{DIV}(N, N^+)$. (We identify usual sorts and recognizable tree languages, as in example 1.2.2.)

---

[4] $t \text{ -}_R\!\!\to t'$ and $t \text{ -}_{R||}\!\!\to t'$ denote a rewriting step, respectively parallel steps (in an obvious sense).

[5] $\text{Fin}_R(t)$ means that $\{ u \mid t \text{ -}^*_R\!\!\to u\}$ is finite. This predicate is not crucial for most of the results.

[6] DIV is the divisibility relation and MUL the multiplication.

☺ **6.2** [13] **Solving systems of set constraints with negated relationships**

Set constraints give a natural formalism for many problems in program analysis and type inference. Recently, they have been studied and applied in amy paper including Heintze and Jaffar (LICS'90), Früwirth and Shapiro (LICS 91), Aiken and Wimmers (LICS'92), Uribe (ICAD'92), Gilleron, Tison and Tommasi (STACS'93), Bachmair, Ganzinger and Waldmann (LICS'93), Aiken, Kozen and Wimmers (technical report, 1993), Charatonik and Pacholski (to appear)).

6.2.1 Definition A *set expression* is either a variable, a constant, the special symbol $\top$ or $\bot$, or of the form $b(e_1,...,e_n)$ (for some fonction symbol b of rank n), $b_i^{-1}(e)$ (*projection on the i-th argument*), $\neg e$, $e \wedge e'$, where $e_1,...,e_n$, e, e' are set expressions. A *set constraint* is either a *positive* set constraint of the form $e \subseteq e'$ or a *negative* set constraint of the form $\neg (e \subseteq e')$, where e and e' are set expressions; a *system of set constraints* (*SSC*) is a conjunction of set constraints.

An *interpretation* I is a mapping from the set of variables into subsets of T_Σ . It is extended to any set expression by induction:

$I(\top) = T_\Sigma$; $I(\bot) = \varnothing$; $I(t) = \{t\}$; $I(b(e_1,...,e_n)) = b(I(e_1),..., I(e_n))$;

$I(b_i^{-1}(e)) = \{t_i \mid b(t_1,..., t_i,...,t_n) \in I(e)\}$, $I(\neg e) = T_\Sigma - I(e)$; $I(e \wedge e') = I(e) \cap I(e')$.

I is obviously extended to a mapping from *SSC* into {True, False}. An interpretation is *a solution* of a *SSC* σ if $I(\sigma)$ = True.

☺ **6.2.2 Example** Heintze's Thesis [14] summarizes many applications for functional languages, logic programming languages and imperative languages. For example, consider an imperative program statement $X := cons(Y, X)$. If μ is the program point just before this statement and ν is the program point just after this statement, then we introduce set variables $X\mu$, $X\nu$, $Y\mu$, $Y\nu$ to capture the values of X and Y at points μ and ν respectively, and we write the constraints

$X\nu \supseteq cons(Y\mu, X\mu)$

$Y\nu \supseteq Y\mu$.

The first constraint specifies that must contain all values of the form cons(v, v) such that is contained in ahd is contained in. The second specifies that must contain all values from. Note that these constraints apporximate the variable relationships contained in by ignoring dependencies between the values of X and Y.

Gilleron, Tison and Tommasi [13], and independently Aiken, Kozen and Wimmers [1] has been the first to prove the decidability of satisfiability of *SSC* including negative constraints7. They remark that in the word case, the general problem can be solved by Rabin automata. They introduce a new (intricate but powerful) class of tree automata, that they call *Tree Set Automata*, and then they follow the usual way.

---

[7] without projections. Charatonik and Pacholski give a new proof in a preprint.

☻ **6.2.3** [13] **Theorem** *Satisfiability of system of positive and negative set constraints (without projection) is decidable. Furthermore, if the set of solutions is not empty, we can exhibit a recognizable one (i.e. a product of recognizable tree languages).*

☺ ⚠ **6.3 Rabin automata and non linearity**

A large number of decision problems can be reduced[8] to Rabin's results. So, for any decision problem on rewriting or terms, we must try to use Rabin's techniques (as in 6.1) or extend them (as in 6.2). Nevertheless, the following result recalls that equality of subterms is not Rabin definable, and hence Rabin automata can't be used directly when we study sets of non linear terms (as we do in 6.3 and 6.4.).

For any words ξ, ξ' over $\{0,1\}$, the predicate $=_{(\xi, \xi')}(x, \tau)$ over a position x and a term τ, denotes the condition $\tau|_{x\xi'} = \tau|_{x\xi}$.

Limitation lemma *Predicates* $=_{(\xi, \xi')}(x, \tau)$ *are not Rabin definable.*

Sketch of proof: Else, tree language $\varphi(R)$ and $\varphi'(R')$ of the Interleaving lemma 2.1 should be Rabin definable, and then undecidability of emptiness of $\varphi(R) \cap \varphi'(R')$ refutes decidability of emptiness for Rabin automata.

6.4 [2] **Decidability in algebras with non-linear shallow signature**

Bogaert and Tison have introduced tree automata with equality and disequality tests between brothers which preserve the good closure properties, reducibility of non-determinism and decidability properties of usual tree automata. So, we can use sorts over non-linear shallow signatures as over usual one (which are shallow and linear). Remark that if we suppress the shallow condition, we can simulate the construction of the section 2 and obtain an undecidable emptiness problem.

6.4.1 Definition An *automaton with equality and disequality tests (ED automaton)* over a finite ranked alphabet Σ is of the form $M = (Q, R, F)$ with *finite state set* Q, *transition set* R, and a set $F \subseteq Q$ of *final states*. A transition is of the form $C: f(q_1,...,q_n) \to q$, where f is a symbol of Σ of rank n, q, $q_1,...,q_n$ are states and C is a set of *equalities constraints* $i = j$ ($1 \leq i < j \leq n$) and *disequalities constraints* $i \neq j$ ($1 \leq i < j \leq n$).

Let us define by induction the relation $\models^* = :$

For any constant a, $a \models^* = q$ iff $a \to q \in R$ (when $n=0$, there is no constraint).

　　(for $i = 1,...,n$, $t_i \models^* = q_i$)

If $\{$ and $C: f(q_1,...,q_n) \to q$ is a transition rule　　　　　　　then $f(t_1,...,t_n) \models^* = q$

　　and for any $i = j \in C$, $t_i = t_j$; for any $i \neq j \in C \Rightarrow t_i \neq t_j$)

t is *accepted (or recognized)* by M if and only if $t \models^* = q$, for some final state q.

---

[8] "reduced" means "easily reduced" (literally any decidable property can be reduced to any other one).

6.4.2 Examples If R does not contain any disequality constraint, it can be identified with a rewrite system (which is not ground (it is not linear)). For example, we associate the rewrite rule $b(q(x), q'(x), q'(y), q''(y)) \to q(b(x, x, y, y)$ with the transition rule $(1=2, 3=4)$: $b(q, q', q', q'') \to q$. Then we get $t \models^* q$ iff $t \text{-}^* \to q(t)$.

For example, the set of balanced trees over b (rank 2) and a (rank 0) is recognized by the transition rules $a \to q$ and $(1=2)$: $b(q, q) \to q$ (associated with the rewrite system $\{ a \to q(a); b(q(x), b(x)) \to q(b(x, x)) \}$

6.4.3 [2] Theorem *The class of ED automaton is effectively closed under Boolean operations and emptiness is decidable.*

☺ 6.5 [5] The theory of encompassment is decidable

Ground reducibility of a term t with respect to a rewrite system R is the property that all ground instances of t are reducible by R. This property is used in automatic proof by induction in equational theories, in proving properties of equational specifications, and in constraint solving in quotient algebras. Ground reducibility has been shown decidable in the general case by Plaisted, Kapur et al., Kounalis.

Ground reducibility is an example of *encompassment* property. A term s *encompasses* a term t if a subterm of s is an instance of t.. s (the usual notation is $s \rhd t$). We associate with any encompassment formula an automaton of the ad hoc new class of *Encompassment Automata*. Eventually, we prove that the theory of encompassment is decidable.

6.5.1 Definition of the encompassment formulas *Variables* are interpreted in T_Σ (we get a first order logic), *atomic formulas* are set constraints of the form $\text{encomp}_t (s)$[9], for any term t. *Formulas* are constructed from atomic formulas using logical connectives and the quantifiers $\exists, \forall$. We can also consider sort constraints $t \in R$ for any ED-recognizable sort R (i.e. tree language recognized by some ED automaton).

6.5.2 Examples

Ground reducibility of a rewrite system whose left-hand sides are $l_1, \dots, l_n$:
$$\forall s\ (\text{encomp}_t (s) \Rightarrow \text{encomp}_{l_1} (s) \vee \dots \vee \text{encomp}_{l_n}(s))$$
Let the signature ($a: A$; $a': A$; $b: A \to A$; $c: (A \vee B) \times (A \vee B) \to B$)
$$\forall s\ \ s \in B \wedge \text{encomp}_{c(x,x)}(s) \wedge \text{encomp}_{c(x,b(x))}(s) \Rightarrow \text{encomp}_{c(c(x,y),z)}(s)$$
is true.

6.5.3 [5] Theorem *The theory of encompassment (with non linear set constraints) is decidable.*

---

[9] We note $\text{encomp}_t (s)$ instead of $s \rhd t$ to explain that t is a constant and s is a variable.

⚠ ⚠ **6.5.4 Conclusion: pumping and cleaning** In this paper, for any class of languages, we reduce the decidability problem to the emptiness problem in the associated class of automata. In every case, emptiness decidability proof relies on a pumping property of the tree languages: if there is a tree in the language, then there should be a tree of bounded depth, where the bound only depends on the characteristics of the automaton. There is however an important drawback in these pumping techniques: the bound is usually huge and cannot be used for practical purposes. Moreover, when the language is empty, the naive algorithm derived from the pumping lemma consists in checking the membership of all trees of depth smaller than the bound. When the language is empty, that means that the bound is reached indeed. That is why Comon tried to design *cleaning algorithms* [7]. The idea is roughly to try to generate some tree , cutting the search branches for which we know in advance that there is no hope to find a tree in the language. We use this technique in the intricate case of encompassment constraints solving [6].

We did not study the complexity aspect in this paper. As we said, most of the problems are intractable in the *worst case*, but we think that implementing different kinds of tree automata efficiently is promising, because we saw that they are interesting tools in software engineering. To get efficient algorithms, it is necessary to combine theoretical studies (as cleaning algorithms), fast heuristic and sophisticated implementations.

References

[1] Aiken, A., D. Kozen, M. Vardi and E. L. Wimmers, The complexity of set constraints. *Technical Report 93-1352, Computer Science Department, Cornell University,* june 1993.

[2] Bogaert, B. and S. Tison, Equality and disequality constraints on direct subterms in tree automata. *Proceedings of STACS'92, Lecture Notes in Computer Science, Springer-Verlag,* volume 577, pp. 161-171, 1992.

[3] Brachman, R. J. What is Knowledge Representation, and where is it Going? *Future Tendencies in Computer Science, Control and Applied Mathematics, Lecture Notes in Computer Science, Springer-Verlag,* volume 653, pp. 189-203, 1992.

[4] Büchi, J.R. The monadic theory of ω1. *Decidable Theories II, Lecture Notes in Mathematics 328, Springer Verlag, Berlin,* pp. 1-127, 1973.

[5] Caron, A.-C., J.-L. Coquidé and M. Dauchet. Encompassment properties and automata with constraints. *Proceedings of 5th Conference on Rewriting Techniques and Applications, Montréal (Canada), Lecture Notes in Computer Science, Springer Verlag,* volume 690, pp. 328-342, june 1993.

[6] Caron, A.-C., H. Comon, J.-L. Coquidé, M. Dauchet, F. Jacquemard. Pumping, Cleaning and Symbolic Constraints Solving, *Proceedings of ICALP'94.*

[7]   Comon, H. Unification et disunification. Théorie et applications. *Ph. D. thesis. I.N.P. Grenoble,* 1988.

[8]   Comon, H. Equational formulas on order-sorted algebras. *Proceedings of ICALP'90, Lecture Notes in Computer Science, Springer-Verlag,* volume 443, pp. 674-688, 1990.

[9]   Dauchet, M. and S. Tison. The Theory of Ground Rewrite Systems is Decidable. *Proceedings of 5th IEEE Symposium on Logic in Computer Science* (Philadelphia, PA.), IEEE Computer Society Press, pp. 242-248, june 1990.

[10] Dauchet, M. and S. Tison. Structural complexity of classes of tree languages, *Tree Automata and Languages, Elsevier Sciences,* M. Nivat and A. Podelski ed., pp 327-353, 1992.

[11] Dershowitz, N. and J.-P. Jouannaud. Rewrite systems. *Handbook of Theoretical Computer Science,* volume B, pp. 243-309. North-Holland, 1990.

[12] Deruyver, A. VALERIAAN et EMMY: deux logiciels-laobratoires pour la réécriture, *Ph.D., University of Lille I,* 1990.

[13] Gilleron, R., S. Tison and M. Tommasi. Solving Systems of Set Constraints with Negated Subset Relationships. *Proceedings of 34th Symposium on Foundations of Computer Science* (Palo Alto, CA.), IEEE Computer Society Press, pp. 372-380, november 1993.

[14] Heintze, N. Set Based Program Analysis, *Ph. D.,* Carnegie Mellon University, 1992.

[15] Kucherov, G. and M. Tajin, Decidability of regularity and related properties of ground normal languages, *3rd International Workshop on Conditional Term Rewriting Systems, Lecture Notes in Computer Science, Springer-Verlag,* vol. 652, PP. 272-286, 1992.

[16] Litovsky, I., Y. Metivier and W. Zielonka. The power and limitations of local computations on graphs and networks. *Lecture Notes in Computer Science, Springer Verlag,* volume 657, pp. 333-343, 1993.

[17] Rabin, M.O. Decidable Theories, *Handbook of Mathematical Logic, North Holland Eds,* pp. 595-627, 1977.

[18] Thomas, W. Automata on Infinite Objects. *Handbook of Theoretical Computer Science,* volume B, pp. 135-192. North-Holland, 1990.

[19] Vagvölgyi, S. and R. Gilleron, For a rewriting system it is decidable whether the set of irreductible ground terms is recognizable, *Bulletin of EATCS,* 48, pp. 197-209, 1992.

On efficient reduction algorithms for some trace rewriting systems

Michael Bertol and Volker Diekert

Universität Stuttgart, Institut für Informatik
Breitwiesenstr. 20-22, D-70565 Stuttgart

Abstract. We consider some basic problems on the decidability and complexity of trace rewriting systems. The new contribution of this paper is an $\mathcal{O}(n \log(n))$ algorithm for some computing irreducible normal forms in the case of certain one-rule systems.

1 Introduction

Trace theory has been recognized as an important tool for investigations of concurrent processes. This dates back to the work of A. Mazurkiewicz, [16], who used traces as a suitable partial order semantics for elementary systems. Since then a systematic study of traces under various aspects has begun, see e.g. [1, 9, 12, 18].

The abstract model of a concurrent process is a finite, node-labelled, and acyclic graph, where arcs are between dependent actions. The semantics is that an execution has to respect the induced partial order, only. Using this model, program transformations and code-optimization can be described by rewriting rules. This is the main motivation to study rewriting systems over traces.

The theory of rewriting over free partially commutative monoids (trace rewriting) combines combinatorial aspects from string rewriting (modulo a congruence) and graph rewriting. This restriction of graph rewriting leads to feasible algorithms, but some interesting complexity questions are still open. For example, a challenging open problem is to improve the known quadratic time bound for the non-uniform complexity of finite and length-reducing systems.

We present an $\mathcal{O}(n \log(n))$ algorithm for computing irreducible normal forms in the case of certain one-rule systems. The best time bounds known before for these systems has been quadratic. It remains open whether this problem is solvable in linear time.

We assume the reader is familiar with the concept of Mazurkiewcz traces. However most facts are also explained below. So the paper is rather self-contained. For basic notions on rewriting systems see [2, 14] or any other chapter of the present lecture notes.

2 Notations

By Σ we denote a finite alphabet, $D \subseteq \Sigma \times \Sigma$ is a reflexive and symmetric dependence relation. The complement $I = \Sigma \times \Sigma \setminus D$ is called the independence relation and the quotient monoid $\mathbf{M} = \mathbf{M}(\Sigma, D) = \Sigma^*/\{ab = ba \mid (a, b) \in I\}$ is called the free partially commutative monoid. This monoid has been introduced in combinatorics by Cartier and Foata [3]. In computer science it is known as trace monoid, introduced by Mazurkiewicz [17]. Accordingly an element $t \in \mathbf{M}$ is a trace. We denote by $|t|$ the length of a trace t, by $|t|_a$ its a-length for some $a \in \Sigma$, and by $alph(t) = \{a \in \Sigma \mid |t|_a \geq 1\}$ its alphabet. It is convenient to extend the independence relation to a relation over $\mathbf{M}$. For $u, v \in \mathbf{M}$ we define $(u, v) \in I$, if we have $alph(u) \times alph(v) \subseteq I$. A trace, i.e., a congruence class, may be viewed as a dependence graph as follows.

Let $a_1 \cdots a_n \in \Sigma^*$ be a word, $a_i \in \Sigma$ for $1 \leq i \leq n$. Then the corresponding trace $[a_1 \cdots a_n] \in \mathbf{M}$ is given by the isomorphism class of a node-labeled acyclic graph $[V, E, \lambda]$ where the set of vertices is any n-point set, say $V = \{1, \ldots, n\}$ with the labeling $\lambda(i) = a_i$, and arcs are from i to j if both $i < j$ and $(a_i, a_j) \in D$. For a fixed dependence alphabet it is enough to draw the Hasse diagram. This means that all all redundant edges are canceled.

Example 1. Let the dependence alphabet (Σ, D) be $(\{a, b, c\}, \{\{a, b\}, \{b, c\}\}) = [a - b - c]$ and the trace $t = [acbacabca] = \{acbaacbac, acbaacbca, \ldots, cabcaabca\}$. Then the corresponding graph looks like

$$t = [acbacabca] \cong$$

It is convenient to distinguish between the notions of subtrace and factor. A *subtrace* s of t is a subgraph of the dependence graph of t such that all directed paths starting and ending in s are entirely contained in s. Every subtrace s of t is a factor, i.e., we can write $t = usv$, but this factorization is not unique, in general. The other way, if $t = usv$ then the traces u, s and v can be identified as subtraces of t. Of course, different subtraces may be equal as elements of $\mathbf{M}$. To be precise, if we speak of a subtrace $s \subseteq t$, we mean that we have identified the vertices belonging to s in the graph of t.

Example 2. In the graph of the trace in the example above we find two subgraphs that are subtraces of t that represents the trace $l = [acb]$. The occurrences are shaped by polygons. The dotted polygon is a subgraph which is no factor.

$$t = [acb][a][acb][ca] \cong$$

A dependence alphabet (Σ, D) (independence alphabet (Σ, I) resp.) will be viewed as an undirected graph where edges are between different dependent (independent resp.) letters. A trace is called *connected*, if the dependence graph t is connected or, equivalently, if $alph(t)$ induces a connected subgraph in (Σ, D).

Example 3. The trace t in the example above is connected since it contains a letter $b \in \Sigma$ and the induced subgraph of the dependence alphabet $[a - b - c]$ is also connected. The trace t' with $alph(t') = \{a, c\}$, i.e., $t' = [ac]$ is not connected since there is no path from a vertex marked with a to a c-marked. The induced graph of the dependence alphabet $(\{a, c\}, \emptyset) = [a \quad c]$ is disconnected, too.

3 Trace rewriting systems

In this section we give some overview of known results and open questions for trace rewriting systems. Most of the material from this section is from [11].

Definition 1 Trace-rewriting system. A trace-rewriting system is a (finite) set of rules $\mathcal{R} \subseteq \mathrm{M}(\Sigma, D) \times \mathrm{M}(\Sigma, D)$.

A trace-rewriting system $\mathcal{R}$ defines a reduction relation $\underset{\mathcal{R}}{\Longrightarrow}$ by $x \underset{\mathcal{R}}{\Longrightarrow} y$ if $x = ulv, y = urv$ for some $u, v \in \mathrm{M}$ and $l \to r \in \mathcal{R}$. The n-fold iteration of $\underset{\mathcal{R}}{\Longrightarrow}$ is denoted by $\underset{\mathcal{R}}{\overset{n}{\Longrightarrow}}$ for $n \in \mathbb{N}$. By $\underset{\mathcal{R}}{\overset{+}{\Longrightarrow}}$ ($\underset{\mathcal{R}}{\overset{*}{\Longrightarrow}}$ resp. , $\underset{\mathcal{R}}{\overset{*}{\Longleftrightarrow}}$ resp.) we denote the transitive (reflexive transitive resp., reflexive symmetric and transitive resp.) closure of $\underset{\mathcal{R}}{\Longrightarrow}$. The relation $\underset{\mathcal{R}}{\overset{*}{\Longleftrightarrow}}$ is a congruence and its quotient monoid is denoted by $\mathrm{M}/\mathcal{R}$.

A trace-rewriting system $\mathcal{R}$ is called:

− length-reducing, if $|l| > |r|$ for all $l \to r \in \mathcal{R}$
− Noetherian, if there is no infinite derivation chain $x_0 \underset{\mathcal{R}}{\Longrightarrow} x_1 \underset{\mathcal{R}}{\Longrightarrow} x_2 \cdots$
− confluent, if $\underset{\mathcal{R}}{\overset{*}{\Longleftrightarrow}} \subseteq \underset{\mathcal{R}}{\overset{*}{\Longrightarrow}} \circ \underset{\mathcal{R}}{\overset{*}{\Longleftarrow}}$
− locally confluent, if $\underset{\mathcal{R}}{\overset{}{\Longleftarrow}} \circ \underset{\mathcal{R}}{\Longrightarrow} \subseteq \underset{\mathcal{R}}{\overset{*}{\Longrightarrow}} \circ \underset{\mathcal{R}}{\overset{*}{\Longleftarrow}}$
− The set of irreducible traces is $Irr(\mathcal{R}) = \{t \in \mathrm{M} \mid \neg \exists s : t \underset{\mathcal{R}}{\Longrightarrow} s\}$.

It is well-known that confluence implies local confluence. If the system $\mathcal{R}$ is Noetherian, then confluence becomes equivalent to local confluence.

A classical result says that it is undecidable whether a finite semi-Thue system is Noetherian. More precisely, we can state:

Proposition 2. It is decidable whether a finite trace-rewriting system is Noetherian if and only if M is commutative, i.e. $\mathrm{M} = \Sigma^{\mathbb{N}}$.

Proof. If M is not commutative, we may use an encoding of semi-Thue systems over a two-letter alphabet. If M is commutative then the Noetherian property can be expressed by some Presburger formula.

The minimal number of rules which we need to have undecidability is not known. In fact, the following problem is open:

Problem 3. Given an one-rule system $\mathcal{R} = \{l \to r\}, l, r \in \mathbb{M}$. Is it decidable whether $\mathcal{R}$ is Noetherian?

For one-rule semi-Thue systems this is an outstanding open problem and for one-rule term rewriting systems the property of being Noetherian is undecidable [7]. Of course, a positive solution to Problem 3 would imply the semi-Thue case. However, due to the commutation rules it may happen that there is a negative answer in the trace case and a positive answer in the word case. This is similar to what happens for the decidability of the confluence of Noetherian systems.

Indeed, for finite Noetherian semi-Thue systems (local) confluence is decidable, since a finite system has finitely many *critical pairs*, only. For trace-rewriting systems a fully satisfactory notion of a critical pair is not available. Whatever definition we use, there must be finite Noetherian systems without any finite computable set of critical pairs. This is due to the following result of Narendran and Otto:

Proposition 4 [19]. There exists an alphabet (Σ, D) with exactly one pair of independent letters such that the confluence of finite length-reducing trace-rewriting systems is recursively undecidable.

Problem 5. Let (Σ, D) be a dependence alphabet such that confluence of finite Noetherian systems is decidable and let (Σ', D') be an induced subgraph of (Σ, D). Is the confluence of finite Noetherian systems decidable for (Σ', D')?

A positive solution of Problem 5 is not obvious, since the confluence of a system depends on the whole alphabet and not only on the letters occurring in the system.

Example 4. Let

$$(\Sigma, D) = \begin{bmatrix} a - b \\ | \quad | \\ d - c \end{bmatrix}, \quad (\Sigma', D') = [a - b - c]$$

and $\mathcal{R} = \{ab \to ba, bc \to cb\}$. We may view $\mathcal{R}$ as a system over $\mathbb{M} = \mathbb{M}(\Sigma, D)$ or over $\mathbb{M}' = \mathbb{M}(\Sigma', D')$. The system $\mathcal{R}$ is Noetherian in both cases. This can be seen by mapping it to $\{a, b\}^* \times \{b, c\}^*$. The system $\mathcal{R} \subseteq \mathbb{M} \times \mathbb{M}$ is confluent, since every trace reduces to an unique normal form in $c^* b^* a^*$. Viewing $\mathcal{R} \subseteq \mathbb{M}' \times \mathbb{M}'$ over the monoid $\mathbb{M}'$, the confluence disappears:

$$Irr(\mathcal{R}) \ni badc \xLeftarrow{\mathcal{R}} abdc \xRightarrow{\mathcal{R}} adcb \in Irr(\mathcal{R})$$

The minimal number of letters required to achieve the undecidability is not known. In particular, we do not know the answer for three letters.

Problem 6. Let $(\Sigma, D) = [a - b - c]$. Is it decidable whether a finite Noetherian system is confluent?

A more general problem is to find good (decidable) sufficient conditions for Noetherian systems such that confluence becomes decidable. Further details can be found in [9, Chapt.3].

4 A simple reduction algorithm

Let $\mathcal{R} \subseteq \mathbb{M} \times \mathbb{M}$ be a finite Noetherian trace rewriting system. Assume for the sake of simplicity that the system $\mathcal{R}$ is length-reducing and not part of the input. Then on input $t \in \mathbb{M}$ of length $n = |t|$ there are at most n reduction steps possible. We consider the time complexity of computing irreducible descendants $t \overset{*}{\underset{\mathcal{R}}{\Longrightarrow}} \hat{t} \in Irr(\mathcal{R})$. To be precise, we consider the non-uniform problem where the system $\mathcal{R}$ is fixed and we measure the complexity in the length of the input trace t.

> **FUNCTION** $reduce(t)$
> **begin**
> $v := 1$;
>   **while** $t \neq 1$ **do**
>   let $t = at'$ for some $a \in \Sigma, t' \in \mathbb{M}$;
> $v := va; t := t'$;
>   **if** $v = v'l$ for some $l \rightarrow r \in \mathcal{R}$ **then** $v := v'; t := rt$
>   **endwhile**
>   **return** v
> **end**

The complexity to evaluate the function $reduce$ is linear time, $\mathcal{O}(|t|)$; if $\mathbb{M}$ is free or commutative, then we have $reduce(t) \in Irr(\mathcal{R})$ for all $t \in \mathbb{M}$. Thus, if $\mathcal{R} \subseteq \mathbb{M} \times \mathbb{M}$ is a finite, confluent and length-reducing system over a free or commutative monoid $\mathbb{M}$ (i.e., $\mathbb{M} = \Sigma^*$ or $\mathbb{M} = \mathbb{N}^{\Sigma}$), then the word problem in the quotient monoid is solvable in linear time. For trace monoids in general no such positive result is known.

The basic problem is due to the fact that this procedure does not compute irreducible descendants, in general. In [10, 8] cones and blocks are introduced as some more general decidable and sufficient conditions such that irreducible descendants can be computed following the algorithmic scheme above.

In general we can use pattern matching to obtain a correct algorithm. The idea is that $Red(\mathcal{R}) = \mathbb{M} \setminus Irr(\mathcal{R})$ is a recognizable set. Hence, if $v \in Red(\mathcal{R})$, then this can be detected by some finite state control and we can also compute a factorization $v = v'lv''$ for some $l \rightarrow r \in \mathcal{R}$ via protocols. The reduction step is then to define $v := v'$ and $t := rv''t$. We obtain a correct algorithm, but its worst case behavior is now square time.

Proposition 7. *Let $\mathcal{R} \subseteq \mathbb{M} \times \mathbb{M}$ be a finite confluent and length reducing trace rewriting system. Then the word problem of the quotient monoid $\mathbb{M}/\mathcal{R}$ is solvable in square time.*

The most interesting problem in this area is therefore:

Problem 8. *Let $\mathcal{R} \subseteq \mathbb{M} \times \mathbb{M}$ be as in Prop. 3. What is the time complexity of solving the word problem of the monoid $\mathbb{M}/\mathcal{R}$?*

Of course, the problem above is equivalent to knowing the time complexity for computing irreducible descendants. More precisely, we can ask:

Problem 9. Let $\mathcal{R}$ be a finite length-reducing trace-rewriting system. Does there exist some linear time algorithm for computing irreducible descendants?

The representation of a trace as a tuple of words leads to efficient algorithms for factorizing and reducing traces. Since there is a couple of fast factorization algorithms (pattern matching algorithms) and reducing algorithms on free monoids Σ^*, we are done if we can synchronize our actions on each of the components. Therefore we use a well known embedding of a free commutative monoid $\mathbb{M}$ into a product of free monoids.

Lemma 10 Projection Lemma. Let $(\Sigma, D) = \bigcup_{A \in \mathcal{C}} (A, A \times A)$ be a dependence alphabet, which is covered by a set of cliques $\mathcal{C}$. For $A \in \mathcal{C}$ let $\pi_A : \mathbb{M}(\Sigma, D) \to A^*$ denote the canonical projection which is defined by erasing all letters from $\Sigma \setminus A$. Then the (in real time computable) homomorphism

$$
\begin{aligned}
\pi : \mathbb{M}(\Sigma, D) &\longrightarrow \prod_{A \in \mathcal{C}} A^* \\
t &\longmapsto (\pi_A(t))_{A \in \mathcal{C}}
\end{aligned}
$$

is injective.

The Projection Lemma has different independent sources. It can be found in [15, Lemma 2.5], [4], [5, Lemma 3.1], [6, Prop. 1.1]. A more categorial form is in [13, Thm. 2.1] and [9, Thm. 1.4.4]. Here we use it for transforming traces in a convenient data structure, i.e., representing traces as n-tuples of words. Note for that this structure depends on the dependence alphabet and the clique covering.

To find an occurrence of a left hand side of some rule, we have to find a synchronous pattern in each projection of the trace. Synchronous is equivalent to the second condition in the following characterization, which is an immediate consequence of the Projection Lemma.

Corollary 11. Let $l, t \in \mathbb{M}(\Sigma, D)$ be traces. Then the trace t contains the factor l, i.e., $t = u \cdot l \cdot v$, if and only if for all $A \in \mathcal{C}$

- there are factorizations $\pi_A(t) = u_A \pi_A(l) v_A$
- such that for all $c \in A \cap B$ the prefixes u_A and u_B have the same c-length, i.e., $|u_A|_c = |u_B|_c$.

5 On the complexity of reducing by one-rule system

In this section we consider the time complexity of computing irreducible descendants in the case of a fixed one-rule system $\mathcal{R} = \{l \to r\}$. We will assume that $\mathcal{R}$ is Noetherian. In fact we require for the complexity results that $\mathcal{R}$ is length-reducing. As in the other sections let (Σ, D) be the underlying dependence alphabet, and $(\Sigma_A)_{A \in \mathcal{C}}$ be a family of covering cliques, i.e., $(\Sigma, D) =$

$(\bigcup_{A \in C} \Sigma_A, \bigcup_{A \in C} \Sigma_A \times \Sigma_A)$. We denote by $\pi_A : \mathbb{M}(\Sigma, D) \to A^*$ the corresponding projections. We restrict ourself to the one-rule case, because this case is the most easy to explain. The general idea becomes clear already in the special case. In order to have a general solution we have to solve some additional technical problems. This will (hopefully) be done elsewhere and is not part of the present notes.

The first technical assumption is that we require $\pi_A(l) \neq 1$ for all $A \in C$; the second is that the left-hand side l is a connected trace. We prove that the time complexity of computing an irreducible descendant $t \stackrel{*}{\Longrightarrow}_R \hat{t} \in Irr(\mathcal{R})$ of an input trace with length $|t| = n$ is of order $\mathcal{O}(n \log n)$. This is a considerable improvement to the former known best time bound $\mathcal{O}(n^2)$.

Our algorithm is based on the notion of visible letters. If all letters of the right-hand side are visible, then we can even provide a linear algorithm. The well-known linear time algorithm in the free case then is a special case of our algorithm.

The basic data structure is the representation of a trace t as a tuple of words $(\pi_A)_{A \in C}$. Furthermore, we use pointers to identify the i-th a in $\pi_A(t)$ with the i-th a in $\pi_B(t)$ for $a \in A \cap B$. Obviously, this structure can be computed in linear time from t, if t is given e.g. as a sequence of letters.

Note that we are not able to compute the complete dependence graph of t in linear time. This is in general impossible since it contains $\Theta(|t|^2)$ edges. In some sense this is the main difficulty, since we will never be able to rely on the full information given by the dependence graph.

Lemma 12. *Let l be connected and $\pi_A(l) \neq 1$ for all $A \in C$. Assume that $ulv = u'lv'$ for some $u, u', v, v' \in \mathbb{M}(\Sigma, D)$. Then the following implications hold:*

1. *if $|u| = |u'|$ then $u = u'$,*
2. *if $|u| \leq |u'|$ then $|\pi_A(u)| \leq |\pi_A(u')|$ for all $A \in C$.*

Proof. Let t be the dependence graph of ulv and $u'lv'$. Identify the factors u and u' with a subtrace (prefix) of t. Assume that u' contains some vertex with label $a \in \Sigma$ such that this vertex is not in u. Then we have $|u|_a < |u'|_a$. Since l is connected, this implies $|u|_a < |u'|_a$ for all $a \in alph(l)$. Finally, since $\pi_A(l) \neq 1$, we obtain $|u|_a < |u'|_a$ for all $a \in \Sigma$.

Note that the assumption $\pi_A(l) \neq 1$ for all $A \in C$ is too strong. The lemma holds already, if l is connected and for every $a \in \Sigma$, there is some $b \in alph(l)$ such that $(a, b) \in D$.

The straightforward pattern matching algorithm yields the following lemma.

Lemma 13. *Let l be connected and $\pi_A(l) \neq 1$ for all $A \in C$. Let $t \in \mathbb{M}(\Sigma, D)$ be a trace, $|t| = n$, and $(u_i l v_i)_{1 \leq i \leq m}$ the family of all possible factorizations $t = u_i l v_i$, ordered by the length of u_i, i.e., $|u_{i-1}| < |u_i|$ for all $1 < i \leq m$. Then we have $m \in \mathcal{O}(n)$ and there is a linear time algorithm which computes on input t the sequence of locations $((|u_{i,A}|)_{A \in C})_{1 \leq i \leq m}$.*

Proof. The lemma is a direct consequence of lemma 12, which yields $m \in \mathcal{O}(n)$ and a pattern matching algorithm. This algorithm is explained below.

In the following we denote by a pattern a tuple of positions $(p_A)_{A \in \mathcal{C}}$ satisfying the following conditions.

– For every $A \in \mathcal{C}$, p_A is a position in $\pi_A(t)$ denoting the beginning of a local factor $\pi_A(l)$, i.e., we have $\pi_A(t) = u_A \pi_A(l) v_A$ with $p_A = |u_A| + 1$.
– Moreover we require, that a pattern marks only synchronized factors $\pi_A(l)$. This means, we require that $|u_A|_c = |u_B|_c$ for all $c \in A \cap B \cap alph(l)$.

Since we can instantaneously identify the occurrences of a letter c, i.e., a vertex in the dependence graph, by using counters; the second condition will be checked by looking at the factors $\pi_A(l)$. Note that a pattern does not necessarily locate a factor l of t. A pattern $(p_A)_{A \in \mathcal{C}}$ is called a global factor (or factor for short) if there is a factorization $t = ulv$ such that p_A yields to the factorization of the projections $\pi_A(t) = \pi_A(u)\pi_A(l)\pi_A(v)$.

We can now compute the sequence of patterns that are pointing to factors $((p_A^{(i)})_{A \in \mathcal{C}})_{1 \leq i \leq m}$ by scanning t from left to right. If we read a letter $a \in \Sigma$, we add it to all projections on A^* with $A \in \mathcal{C}$ where $a \in A$, and update the corresponding counters. We check in constant time if this completes some local factor $\pi_A(l)$. If so, we validate by using the counters whether this yields a pattern. Finally, to check whether or not this pattern points to the location of a factor we have to considder only the letters $c \in \Sigma \setminus alph(l)$. We need to know whether $|u_A|_c = |u_B|_c$ for all $c \in A \cap B$, $A, B \in \mathcal{C}$. During the reading of the input, we provid for each letter $a \in alph(l)$ the information, how many letters $c \in A \setminus alph(l)$ have been read before a for each $A \in \mathcal{C}$ with $a \in A$. These numbers must be equal for letters of $\pi_A(l)$ and $\pi_B(l)$ if $c \in (A \cap B) \setminus alph(l)$. To summarize, the sequence of factors is computable in linear time.

In the following we will encounter the problem how to maintain this information about the letters $c \in \Sigma \setminus alph(l)$ in a reduction step.

Definition 14. We say that two patterns $p = (p_A)_{A \in \mathcal{C}}$ and $q = (q_A)_{A \in \mathcal{C}}$ have an overlap, if there is some $A \in \mathcal{C}$ such that the positions p_A, q_A differ by a length less than $|\pi_A(l)|$.

This means, if p_A and q_A yield factorizations $u_A \pi_A(l) v_A$ and $u'_A \pi_A(l) v'_A$, then the two factors $\pi_A(l)$ have a non-trivial overlap in the string $\pi_A(l)$.

Our reduction algorithm starts with a linear time preprocessing, which computes on input t the internal representation $(\pi_A(t))_{A \in \mathcal{C}}$. Moreover, we compute the chain of all factors l in t by creating an ordered list of patterns $(p_i)_{1 \leq i \leq m}$ pointing to factors. Each p_i is a global factor, corresponding to a factorization $t = u_i l v_i$ such that $|u_{i-1}| < |u_i|$ for all $1 < i \leq m$. Clearly, t is irreducible if and only if $m = 0$, i.e., we terminate, if the chain of patterns is empty. Hence, we assume $m \geq 1$ and we perform a reduction step. We take any p_i, say the first p_1, and we replace each string $\pi_A(u_i)\pi_A(l)\pi_A(v_i)$ by the string $\pi_A(u_i)\pi_A(r)\pi_A(v_i)$. Note that this can be done in time $\mathcal{O}(|l|)$ by local modifications in our data structure. This yields a new trace $t' = u_i r_i v_i$. We have to reconstruct the list of factors. We may have destroyed some factors and some new factors may have been created. However, the destroyed factors are just those having an overlap with p_i. Thus there is a constant $k \leq \sum_{A \in \mathcal{C}} (|\pi_A(l)| - 1)$ such that all new factors are between p_{i-k-1} and p_{i+k+1} and they have an overlap with the position where the right-hand side r is inserted. The sequence $(p_1, \ldots, p_{i-k-1})$ remains at the beginning and $(p_{i+k+1}, \ldots, p_m)$ remains at the end of the list of factors.

Again in constant time, i.e., in time in order of $\mathcal{O}(|l|)$ we can create an ordered list of new patterns $(q_1, \ldots, q_s)$, $s \leq \sum_{A \in \mathcal{C}} (|\pi_A(l)| + |\pi_A(r)| - 1)$, which are candidates for new factors. Let q be an element of this list yielding the factorizations $u_A \pi_A(l) v_A$ for $A \in \mathcal{C}$. Then q represents a factorization, that means q points to the beginning of a factor, if and only if for all $A, B \in \mathcal{C}$, $c \in A \cap B$ we have $|u_A|_c = |u_B|_c$. This is given for $c \in alph(l)$ since by building the list $(q_i)_{1 \leq i \leq r}$, the patterns are synchronized. The question is whether or not a pattern is a factor.

Definition 15. A letter $c \in \Sigma$ is called visible (by l), if for all $A, B \in \mathcal{C}$ such that $c \in A \cap B$ there are $a \in A \cap alph(l)$ and $b \in B \cap alph(l)$, $C \in \mathcal{C}$ with $\{a, b, c\} \subseteq C$.

It is clear that all letters of $alph(l)$ are visible (simply take $a = b = c \in alph(l)$). The next lemma shows that visible letters do not prevent an element of the generated list from being a factor.

Lemma 16. *Let p be a pattern of a trace t yielding the factorizations $u_A \pi_A(l) v_A$ for $A \in \mathcal{C}$. Let $A, B \in \mathcal{C}$ and $c \in A \cap B$. If c is visible, then we have $|u_A|_c = |u_B|_c$.*

Proof. As noted above, this is true for $c \in alph(l)$. For $c \notin alph(l)$ assume $|u_A|_c < |u_B|_c$, $a \in A \cap alph(l)$, $b \in B \cap alph(l)$, $C \in \mathcal{C}$ with $\{a, b, c\} \subseteq C$. Since $|u_A|_c < |u_B|_c$ there are vertices x, y, z with labels a, b, c and arcs from x to z and z to y in the dependence graph of t. Looking at the projection $\pi_C(t) = u_C \pi_C(l) v_C$, the factor contains a scattered subword acb. This is impossible, since $c \notin alph(l)$.

The following theorem includes the case of one-rule semi-Thue systems or vector replacement systems. Thus, for one-rule systems the results known before are generalized.

Theorem 17. *Let $\mathcal{R} = \{l \to r\}$ be a length-reducing one-rule trace rewriting system such that l is connected and for each $A \in \mathcal{C}$ the projection is not empty, i.e., $\pi_A(l) \neq 1$. Assume that all letters $c \in alph(r)$ are visible by l. Then there is a linear time algorithm which computes an irreducible descendant $t \overset{*}{\Longrightarrow}_{\mathcal{R}} \hat{t} \in Irr(\mathcal{R})$ for any input trace $t \in \mathbb{M}(\Sigma, D)$.*

Note that the visibility condition is in particular fulfilled, if $alph(r) \subseteq alph(l)$ or if $\mathbb{M}(\Sigma, D)$ is a free monoid. We can also generalize to the case where $\mathbb{M}(\Sigma, D)$ is a direct product of free monoids, e.g., to the case $\mathbb{N}^{\Sigma}$.

Proof. Our reduction algorithm computes during the preprocessing of the input for each $A \in \mathcal{C}$ and $a \in A$ the c-length for each letter $c \in A$ at the time when a letter a is read. This number is stored with this letter. It is used to compute the ordered list of patterns representing factors $(p_i)_{1 \leq i \leq m}$. Later this information is needed for invisible letters. Assume we apply the rule to the i-th factor, i.e., we replace $t = u_i l v_i$ by $t' = u_i r v_i$ where $p_i = (p_A)_{A \in \mathcal{C}}$ corresponds to $(\pi_A(u_i)\pi_A(l)\pi_A(v_i))_{A \in \mathcal{C}}$. Then we have $\pi_A(t') = \pi_A(u_i)\pi_A(r)\pi_A(v_i)$. Since all letters of $alph(l) \cup alph(r)$ are visible, the c-length of an invisible letter w.r.t. a position in $\pi_A(u_i)$ or $\pi_A(v_i)$ remains unchanged. It is zero if $\pi_A(u_i) = 1$; otherwise we can simply copy the c-length of the last letter of $\pi_A(u_i)$. This is possible in constant time by our data structure. The result follows.

For the rest of this section we assume that $alph(r)$ contains an invisible letter c. In order to clarify the difficulty we consider an example.

Example 5. Let $(\Sigma, D) = \left[\begin{array}{c} c \\ a \text{—} d \text{—} e \text{—} b \end{array} \right]$ be the dependence alphabet and $l = [adeb]$. We have the cliques $A = \{a, c\}$, $B = \{b, e\}$, $C = \{b, c\}$, $D = \{a, d\}$ and $E = \{d, e\}$. The letter c is invisible by l, since there is no clique containing $\{a, b, c\}$. Consider two rewriting systems

$$\mathcal{R}_1 = \{l \to 1\} \text{ and } \mathcal{R}_2 = \{l \to c\}.$$

Let us study the different behavior for the reduction algorithm and the input trace $t = [ada^m adebb^m eb]$. We get the projections

$$t = \begin{pmatrix} aa^m a \\ ebb^m eb \\ bb^m b \\ ada^m ad \\ ddee \end{pmatrix} \cong \left[\begin{array}{c} a \qquad a^m \to a \qquad b \to b^m \qquad b \\ \searrow \nearrow \qquad \nearrow \qquad \searrow \nearrow \\ d \qquad d \to e \qquad e \end{array} \right]$$

There is exactly one factor l indicated by a box in each component.

$$t = \begin{pmatrix} aa^m \boxed{a} \\ eb \boxed{b^m eb} \\ \boxed{b} b^m b \\ ada^m \boxed{ad} \\ d \boxed{de} e \end{pmatrix} \cong \left[\begin{array}{c} a \qquad a^m \to a \qquad b \to b^m \qquad b \\ \searrow \nearrow \qquad \nearrow \qquad \searrow \nearrow \\ d \qquad d \to e \qquad e \end{array} \right]$$

Let $t \Rightarrow_{\mathcal{R}_1} t_1$ and $t \Rightarrow_{\mathcal{R}_2} t_2$. We have a new pattern in t_1 as well as in t_2 has a candidate for a factor.

$$t_1 = \begin{pmatrix} \boxed{a}\,\boxed{a^m} \\ \boxed{b^m}\,\boxed{eb} \\ \boxed{b^m}\,\boxed{b} \\ \boxed{ad}\,\boxed{a^m} \\ \boxed{de} \end{pmatrix} \cong \begin{bmatrix} & a & & & a^m \\ & & & d \rightarrow e & \\ & & b^m & & & b \end{bmatrix}$$

In t_1 the marked part is a factor. This can be checked in constant time, since we can use the old c-length.

$$t_2 = \begin{pmatrix} \boxed{a}\,\boxed{a^m\,c} \\ \boxed{b^m}\,\boxed{eb}\,\boxed{b^m} \\ \boxed{cb^m}\,\boxed{b} \\ \boxed{ad}\,\boxed{a^m} \\ \boxed{de} \end{pmatrix} \cong \begin{bmatrix} a & & a^m & & b^m & & b \\ & d & & c & & e & \end{bmatrix}$$

However the marked substrings in t_2 is not a factor. The c-length of the a is 0, whereas the c-length of all b is now 1. Updating the c-value of all $(m+1)$ letters b is certainly not the most efficient way to continue.

In order to achieve an $\mathcal{O}(n \cdot \log(n))$-algorithm we use a tree structure to represent each word $\pi_A(t)$ for $A \in \mathcal{C}$. In the following 2-3-trees would work, but we prefer AVL-trees as underlying data structure. Recall that an AVL-tree is a binary search tree. Each subtree represents a substring. With respect to the root of a subtree the left child represents a prefix and the right child the suffix. The idea is to provide each inner node with the information about the Parikh-image of the represented subtree (substring). To be more precise, let $A \in \mathcal{C}$ be a clique and $w \in A^*$. Let B be an AVL-tree representing w and x an inner node of B. Then x represents a factor w_x of $w = w_1 w_x w_2$. For each letter $c \in A$ we store the c-length $|w_x|_c$ in the node x. It is easy to see that insertion and deletion of letters is possible in logarithmic time such that the information about the Parikh-images can be maintained.

Let us return to our original problem. We have factorizations $u_A \pi_A(l) v_A$, $u_B \pi_B(l) v_B$ and for some invisible letter $c \in A \cap B$ we have to test whether $|u_A|_c = |u_B|_c$. Suppose $a \in A \cap alph(l)$, $b \in B \cap alph(l)$ such that a belongs to the factor $\pi_A(l)$ and b to $\pi_B(l)$ respectively. Since c is invisible, we have $c \notin alph(l)$. Let x_a be the inner node of the AVL-tree for $u_A \pi_A(l) v_A$ corresponding to a. Then the left child contains the information about the c-length $|u_A|_c$. This information is available in constant time. Likewise we obtain the information about $|u_B|_c$. Therefore we can check in constant time whether a position $(p_A)_{A \in \mathcal{C}}$ is a factor. This procedure allows to state our final result.

Theorem 18. *Let $\mathcal{R} = \{l \rightarrow r\}$ be a length-reducing one-rule trace rewriting system such that l is connected and for each $A \in \mathcal{C}$ the projection is not empty,* *i.e., $\pi_A(l) \neq 1$. Then there is an algorithm which computes an irreducible descendant $t \overset{*}{\Longrightarrow}_{\mathcal{R}} \hat{t} \in Irr(\mathcal{R})$ for any input trace $t \in \mathbb{M}(\Sigma, D)$ of length $|t| = n$ in time $\mathcal{O}(n \log(n))$.*

6 Conclusion and future work

The main result of this paper is the $\mathcal{O}(n \log(n))$ reduction algorithm for length-reducing one-rule systems. In a forthcoming work we will study multiple rule systems. We hope to find a general $\mathcal{O}(n \log(n))$ algorithm that manages multi-rule systems without any hypothesis of connectness. Whether or not a linear time algorithm is possible, remains unsolved. Such an algorithm exists for free or free-commutative monoids, but we do not think that linear time is impossible, in general. However this last remark is highly tentative.

References

1. I.J. Aalbersberg and G. Rozenberg. Theory of traces. *Theoret. Comput. Sci.*, 60:1–82, 1988.
2. R.V. Book and F. Otto. *String Rewriting Systems*. Texts and Monographs in Computer Science. Springer Verlag, New York, 1993.
3. P. Cartier and D. Foata. *Problèmes combinatoires de commutation et réarrangements*. Number 85 in Lecture Notes in Mathematics. Springer, Berlin-Heidelberg-New York, 1969.
4. M. Clerbout. *Commutations partielles et familles de langages*. Thése, Université de Lille (France), 1984.
5. M. Clerbout and M. Latteux. Partial commutations and faithful rational transductions. *Theoretical Computer Science*, 35:241–254, 1985.
6. R. Cori and D. Perrin. Automates et commutations partielles. *R.A.I.R.O. — Informatique Théorique et Applications*, 19:21–32, 1985.
7. Max Dauchet. Termination of rewriting is undecidable in the one-rule case. In M. Chytil et al., editors, *Proceedings of the 13th Symposium on Mathematical Foundations of Computer Science (MFCS'88), Carlsbad (CSSR) 1988*, number 324 in Lecture Notes in Computer Science, pages 262–288, Berlin-Heidelberg-New York, 1988. Springer.
8. V. Diekert. Combinatorial rewriting on traces. In C. Choffrut et al., editors, *Proceedings of the 7th Annual Symposium on Theoretical Aspects of Computer Science (STACS'90), Rouen (France) 1990*, number 415 in Lecture Notes in Computer Science, pages 138–151, Berlin-Heidelberg-New York, 1990. Springer.
9. V. Diekert. *Combinatorics on Traces*. Number 454 in Lecture Notes in Computer Science. Springer, Berlin-Heidelberg-New York, 1990.
10. V. Diekert. Word problems over traces which are solvable in linear time. *Theoret. Comput. Sci.*, 74:3–18, 1990.
11. V. Diekert. Rewriting, semi-commutations, and Möbius functions. In Z. Ésik, editor, *Proc. of the 9th Fundamentals of Computation Theory (FCT 93), Szeged (Hungary) 1993*, number 710 in Lecture Notes in Computer Science, pages 1–15, Berlin-Heidelberg-New York, 1993. Springer. Invited Lecture.

12. V. Diekert and G. Rozenberg, editors. *Book of Traces*. World Scientific, Singapore, to appear.
13. W. Fischer. Über erkennbare und rationale Mengen in freien partiell kommutativen Monoiden. Report FBI-HH-B-121/86, Fachbereich Informatik der Universität Hamburg, Hamburg, 1986. (Diplomarbeit 1985).
14. M. Jantzen. *Confluent String Rewriting*. EATCS Monographs on Theoretical Computer Science 14. Springer, Berlin-Heidelberg-New York, 1988.
15. R. Keller. Parallel program schemata and maximal parallelism I. Fundamental results. *Journal of the Association of Computing Machinery*, 20:514–537, 1973.
16. A. Mazurkiewicz. Concurrent program schemes and their interpretations. DAIMI Rep. PB 78, Aarhus University, Aarhus, 1977.
17. A. Mazurkiewicz. Concurrent program schemes and their interpretations. DAIMI Rep. PB 78, Aarhus University, Aarhus, 1977.
18. A. Mazurkiewicz. Trace theory. In W. Brauer, W. Reisig, and G. Rozenberg, editors, *Petri Nets, Applications and Relationship to other Models of Concurrency*, Lecture Notes in Computer Science 255, pages 279–324. Springer, Berlin-Heidelberg-New York, 1987.
19. P. Narendran and F. Otto. Preperfectness is undecidable for Thue systems containing only length-reducing rules and a single commutation rule. *Information Processing Letters*, 29:125–130, 1988.

Automatic Groups and String Rewriting

Robert H. Gilman

Department of Mathematics
Stevens Institute of Technology
Hoboken, NJ 07030 U. S. A.

1 · Introduction

In recent years developments in geometric topology have led to a remarkable interplay between group theory, geometry, and the theory of automata and formal languages. One of the best known result of this interplay has been the introduction of automatic groups. In this article we will consider this class of groups from the point of view of automata and language theory. We will see how work of Epstein, Holt and Rees [6] puts automatic groups naturally into the context of string rewriting.

We assume that the reader is familiar with the Knuth Bendix completion procedure for string rewriting [10], [12], [19, Chapter 2]. For a guide to the topological developments referred to above consult [5, Chapter 12] and [18].

Let G be a finitely generated group. In what follows we will distinguish between words in the generators and elements of the group. A *choice of generators* for G is a map $\pi : \Sigma \to G$ which extends to a surjective monoid homomorphism $\pi : \Sigma^* \to G$. Here Σ is a finite alphabet and Σ^* is the free monoid on Σ. We require that Σ be equipped with formal inverses and that π respect these inverses. More precisely $\Sigma = \{a, a^{-1}, b, b^{-1} \ldots\}$, and the involutory permutation $a \leftrightarrow a^{-1}, b \leftrightarrow b^{-1}, \cdots$ extends uniquely to an anti-automorphism $w \to w^{-1}$ of Σ^*. The homomorphism π satisfies $\pi(w^{-1}) = w^{-1}$.

2 String Rewriting with Infinite Sets of Rules

Suppose $G = \langle a, b, \ldots \mid w_1 = v_1, w_2 = v_2, \ldots \rangle$ is a finitely presented group, $\Sigma = \{a, a^{-1}, b, b^{-1}, \ldots\}$, and $<$ is a reduction ordering on Σ^* suitable for the Knuth-Bendix procedure. That is, $<$ is a well-ordering which respects multiplication.

Example 1. $\Sigma = \{a, a^{-1}, b, b^{-1}\}$, $G = \langle a, b \mid ab = ba \rangle$, and $<$ is the length plus lexicographic order with $a < b < b^{-1} < a^{-1}$.

Clearly the group G of Example 1 is isomorphic to $Z \times Z$, the direct product of the integers with itself. The KB procedure must fail to terminate in this example because there is no finite complete rewriting system for G with the given generators and reduction ordering. An infinite complete system is given in Table 1. It is easy to check these assertions. The infinite system is complete because the language of irreducible words, $\{a^i b^j, b^j a^{-i} \mid i, j \in Z, i \geq 0\}$, is a set of normal forms for elements of G. If there were a finite complete rewriting system, then each of its reductions would be a consequence of a finite number of the reductions in Table 1. Hence some finite subset of the reductions in this table would be a complete rewriting system.

$$aa^{-1} \rightarrow \epsilon \qquad a^{-1}a \rightarrow \epsilon$$
$$bb^{-1} \rightarrow \epsilon \qquad b^{-1}b \rightarrow \epsilon$$
$$ba \rightarrow ab \qquad b^{-1}a \rightarrow ab^{-1}$$
$$a^{-1}b \rightarrow ba^{-1} \qquad a^{-1}b^{-1} \rightarrow b^{-1}a^{-1}$$
$$ab^n a^{-1} \rightarrow b^n, n \geq 1 \quad ab^{-n}a^{-1} \rightarrow b^{-n}, n \geq 1$$

Table 1. An infinite complete rewriting system for Example 1.

But the system in Table 1 is reduced in the sense that the left hand side of every rewrite rule is irreducible with respect to all the other rules. It follows that any finite subsystem would have more irreducible words than the whole system. Thus finite subsystems cannot be complete.

In practice the KB procedure may generate a sequence of rewrite rules which looks like the start of an infinite system similar to the one in Table 1, and it is natural to try to extend the procedure to deal with this situation. Let us identify rewrite rules $w \rightarrow v$ with ordered pairs $(w, v) \in \Sigma^* \times \Sigma^*$. We might try to extend the KB procedure to systems of rewrite rules which are rational subsets of $\Sigma^* \times \Sigma^*$, but completeness is undecidable for these systems even if they are known to be terminating [1, Chapter III.1.3], [16]. The method we will use makes use of the smaller class of synchronized rational sets. As we mentioned above, it is taken from [6]. Other methods are discussed in [1] and a method using term rewriting has been implemented in [15].

Definition 1. A synchronized rational relation (or synchronized relation for short) on $\Sigma^* \times \Sigma^*$ is one accepted by a two-tape automaton in which both heads move synchronously. Equivalently it is a regular subset of $(\Sigma \times \Sigma)^* ((\Sigma^* \times \{\epsilon\}) \cup (\{\epsilon\} \times \Sigma^*))$.

The infinite rewriting system of Table 1 is a synchronized relation. For example $\{ab^n a^{-1} \rightarrow b^n \mid n \geq 1\} = (a, b)(b, b)^*(b, \epsilon)(a, \epsilon)$. See [5, Chapter 1] and [7] for a review of the properties of synchronized relations. Boolean operations on synchronized relations are computable in theory and in practice, and so are equality and composition. In addition n-ary synchronized relations are closed under existential and universal quantification, and the corresponding theory is decidable.

$$aa^{-1} \rightarrow \epsilon \qquad a^{-1}a \rightarrow \epsilon$$
$$bb^{-1} \rightarrow \epsilon \qquad b^{-1}b \rightarrow \epsilon$$
$$ba \rightarrow ab \qquad b^{-1}a \rightarrow ab^{-1}$$
$$a^{-1}b \rightarrow ba^{-1} \quad a^{-1}b^{-1} \rightarrow b^{-1}a^{-1}$$
$$aba^{-1} \rightarrow b \qquad ab^{-1}a^{-1} \rightarrow b^{-1}$$
$$ab^2 a^{-1} \rightarrow b^2 \quad ab^{-2}a^{-1} \rightarrow b^{-2}$$

Table 2. A finite incomplete rewriting system for Example 1.

We may imagine that we run the KB procedure on Example 1 for a finite amount of time and obtain the rules in Table 2. We will use this example to illustrate our extension of the KB procedure. The first step is to infer from a finite set of rewrite rules like those in Table 2 a valid infinite set in the form of a synchronous relation, and the second step is to verify that this infinite set is complete.

2.1 A Rule of Inference

To accomplish the first step mentioned above we make use of a construction based on the Cayley diagram Γ of G. First we note that words in Σ may be viewed as paths starting at the identity in Γ as in Figure 1. We will identify words with their corresponding paths. For any word $w \in \Sigma^*$ and integer $i \geq 0$, define $w(i)$ to be the prefix of w length $\min\{i, |w|\}$ where $|w|$ denotes the length of w.

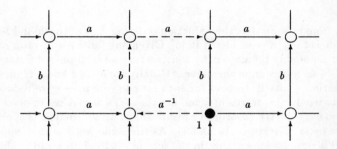

Fig. 1. The path $a^{-1}ba$ in the Cayley diagram for Example 1.

Definition 2. For $w, v \in \Sigma^*$ the word differences from w to v are the group elements $g_i = \pi(w(i)^{-1}v(i))$.

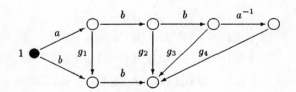

Fig. 2. Word differences from $abba^{-1}$ to bb

Figure 2 suggests a path consisting of a sequence of group elements $1, g_1, g_2, g_3, g_4$ joined by edges with labels $(a, b), (b, b), (b\epsilon), (a^{-1}, \epsilon)$.

Definition 3. The Cayley automaton $\Gamma_{g'}$ corresponding to a choice of generators $\pi : \Sigma \to G$ and a choice of $g' \in G$ is the automaton with vertices $g \in G$ and and an edge from g to h with label (a, b) whenever $\pi(a^{-1})g\pi(b) = h$ for $a, b \in \Sigma \cup \{\epsilon\}$. The initial vertex is 1 and the single terminal vertex is g'.

The vertices are the states of the automaton and the labeled edges indicate the transitions on a given input. In general $\Gamma_{g'}$ is infinite. It is straightforward to show that it accepts $\{(w, v) \mid \pi(w^{-1}v) = g'\}$.

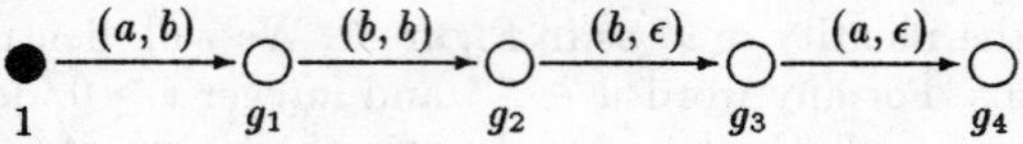

Fig. 3. The path in the Cayley automaton corresponding to the word differences in Figure 2.

Assume from now on that the reduction ordering $<$ is a length and lexicographic ordering; this is the case considered in [6]. Given any finite set of valid rewrite rules, we can infer a possibly infinite set by constructing a synchronized automaton which has part of Γ_1 as a homomorphic image. Usually we do not know G directly and so cannot construct Γ_1 itself. Instead for each rewrite rule $w \to v$ we reduce the words $w(i)^{-1}v(i)$ to irreducible words $u(i)$ and use the $u(i)$'s as vertices in place of the word differences $\pi(w(i)^{-1}v(i))$. In order to insure that our automaton is synchronous we will have two sets of vertices, V_0 and V_1. As the same word w may appear in both sets, we will denote its appearance in the second set by $\tilde{w}$ to avoid confusion. Edges with labels in $\Sigma \times \Sigma$ will connect pairs of vertices in V_0, and edges with labels in $\Sigma \times \{\epsilon\}$ will have their target vertices in V_1. There will be no other edges.

Definition 4. Let $\pi : \Sigma \to G$ be a choice of generators, $<$ a length and lexicographic reduction ordering on Σ^*, and $\mathcal{R}$ a finite reduced set of rewrite rules with respect to $<$. Suppose $a \in \Sigma \cup \{\epsilon\}$. The synchronous automaton A_a is constructed as follows. For each rule $w \to v \in \mathcal{R}$ with $w = a_1 \cdots a_n$ and $v = b_1 \cdots b_m$, reduce the words $w(i)^{-1}v(i)$ to irreducible words $u(i)$. Put $u(i)$ in V_0 if $i \leq m$ and in V_1 if $i > m$. Add an edge

$$\begin{cases} u(i-1) \overset{(a_i,b_i)}{\to} u(i) \text{ if } 0 < i \leq m \\ u(i-1) \overset{(a_i,\epsilon)}{\to} \tilde{u}(i) \text{ if } i = m+1 \\ \tilde{u}(i-1) \overset{(a_i,\epsilon)}{\to} \tilde{u}(i) \text{ if } m+1 < i \leq n. \end{cases}$$

The initial vertex of A_a is $\epsilon \in V_0$ and the terminal ones are $a \in V_0$ and $a \in V_1$.

Because of the choice of $<$ we know $m \leq n$ in the defintion above. It is clear that A_a accepts a synchronized relation. Figure 4 shows the part of A_ϵ from Example 1which accepts the infinite set of rewrite rules $ab^na^{-1} \to b^n, n \geq 1$.

In practice one runs the KB procedure until the set of word differences stabilizes and then constructs the transducers T_a. The proof of the following theorem is straightforward from the construction of the Cayley automaton.

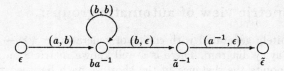

Fig. 4. Part of the automaton A_ϵ for Example 1. The edges shown are determined by the rewrite rule $ab^2a^{-1} \to b^2$ from Table 2.

Theorem 5. *There is a homomorphism from the automaton A_a to the Cayley automaton $\Gamma_{\pi(a)}$.*

Corollary 6. *If A_a accepts (w, v), then $\pi(wa) = \pi(v)$. In particular the rewrite rules accepted by the transducer A_ϵ are valid.*

2.2 Verifying confluence

Suppose $\mathcal{R}^+$ is the possibly infinite synchronous set of rewrite rules accepted by an automaton A_ϵ constructed as above. How do we verify that $\mathcal{R}^+$ is complete? Let ρ_a be the synchronous relation accepted by A_a. If L is the language of words irreducible with respect to $\mathcal{R}^+$, then $\mathcal{R}^+$ will be complete if and only if L projects bijectively to G. Since L is rational, we can use the decidability of synchronous relations to check that the following conditions hold.

1. The composition $\rho_a \circ \rho_{a^{-1}}$ is the identity on L;
2. For each relation $a_1 \ldots a_n = b_1 \ldots b_m$ in the finite presentation of G, $\rho_{a_1} \circ \ldots \circ \rho_{a_n} = \rho_{b_1} \circ \ldots \circ \rho_{b_m}$ on L.

If these conditions hold, then each ρ_a is a permutation of L, and the group generated by these permutations is isomorphic to G. It follows that L projects bijectively to G and the rewrite rules accepted by A_ϵ are complete. See [6] for the details. If the conditions do not hold, we can run the KB procedure longer and try again.

In this context it is natural to consider the class of groups G with generators $\pi : \Sigma \to G$ and a regular set $L \subset \Sigma$ such that L projects bijectively to G and for all $a \in \Sigma$ the relation $w \sim_a v$ if $w, v \in L$ and $\pi(wa) = \pi(v)$ is synchronized. This is the essentially the class of an automatic groups.

Definition 7. Let G be a finitely generated group with choice of generators $\pi : \Sigma \to G$. G is automatic if there is a regular set $L \subset \Sigma^*$ such that $\pi(L) = G$ and if for each $a \in \Sigma \cup \{\epsilon\}$ the binary relation $\sim_a$ defined by $w \sim_a v$ if $w, v \in L$ and $\pi(wa) = \pi(v)$ is a synchronized rational relation.

We required above that L project bijectively instead of merely surjectively as Definition 7 allows; but by [5, Theorem 2.5.1] if G is automatic, then we may take L to project bijectively (in which case $\sim_\epsilon$ is just the identity on L). We shall say that L is part of an automatic structure for G if the conditions of Definiton 7 hold.

3　The geometric view of automatic groups.

Suppose G is finitely generated with choice of generators $\pi : \Sigma \to G$ and Γ is the corresponding Cayley diagram. There is a well known metric d on Γ which assigns to each pair of points the distance of the shortest path between them. With this definition we can define the distance between w and v to be

$$D(w,v) = \max_i d\big(\pi(w(i)), \pi(v(i))\big).$$

$D(w,v)$ is essentially the maximum separation achieved by two particles starting from 1 at the same time and moving along the paths determined by w and v at unit speed. More precisely it is the maximum separation achieved at the vertices along the path. D is not a metric since it is possible for different words to determine the same path, but D is symmetric and satisfies the triangle inequality. One of the first results in the theory of automatic groups is the following geometric characterization [5, Theorem 2.3.5].

Theorem 8. *Suppose that G is a finitely generated group with choice of generators* $\pi : \Sigma \to G$. *G is automatic if and only if there is a language $L \subset \Sigma^*$ and constant K such that*

1. *L is rational;*
2. *$\pi(L) = G$;*
3. *For any $w, v \in L$ with $d(\pi(w), \pi(v)) \leq 1$, $D(w,v) \leq K$.*

Condition 3 is sometimes called the K fellow traveller property. If G satisfies the conditions of Theorem 8 with respect to one set of generators, then it does so with respect to any other set of generators although the value of K may change.

There are a number of interesting language theoretic problems arising from the theory of automatic groups. Perhaps the most intriguing one is that it is not known if condition 1 has any effect. That is, if we omit condition 1 in Definition 8, do we get any more groups? Let us call a group G *combable* if there exists a set $L \subset \Sigma^*$ for which G satisfies conditions 2 and 3. (The definition of combable in [5] is more restrictive.) It is known that H_3, the group of all integer matrices of the form

$$\begin{pmatrix} 1 & a & b \\ 0 & 1 & c \\ 0 & 0 & 1 \end{pmatrix}$$

is not automatic, but it is not known whether or not it is combable.

There is another measure of distance between paths, $D'(w,v)$, which is the maximum separation (at vertices) achieved by two particles starting from 1 at the same time and moving along the paths determined by w and v with each particle moving at variable but nonnegative speed in such a way as to minimize the maximum separation. A finitely generated group G which satisfies the conditions of Theorem 8 with D' in place of D is called *asynchronously automatic* [5, Chapter 7]. In the case of asynchronously automatic groups it is known that relaxing the condition that L be regular allows more groups. Specifically H_3 not asynchronously automatic [5, Theorem 8.2.8] and is not included if we allow L to be context free, but it is included if we allow L to range over the larger class of indexed languages [2].

4 Hyperbolic Groups

Hyperbolic group are an interesting class of groups introduced by Gromov [11]. Other references are [9] and [4].

Definition 9. Let G be finitely generated with choice of generators $\pi : \Sigma \rightarrow G$ and Cayley diagram Γ. A *geodesic* is a shortest path between two points in Γ, and a *geodesic triangle* is a triangle whose sides are geodesics. G is *hyperbolic* if there is a constant δ such that for every geodesic triangle each point on any side is a distance at most δ from some point on one of the other two sides.

The validity of the triangle condition above is independent of the choice of generators although the value of δ is not. All groups satisfying the small cancellation hypothesis $C'(1/6)$ or the hypotheses $C'(1/4)$ and $T(4)$ are hyperbolic [20] but it is easy to check that $Z \times Z$ is not.

Hyperbolic groups are a proper subclass of automatic groups. If $\pi : \Sigma \rightarrow G$ is any choice of generators for the hyperbolic group G, then the language L of all words $w \in \Sigma^*$ whose corresponding paths are geodesics is a regular set [11, §5] and is part of an automatic structure for G as in Definition 7 [5, Theorem 3.4.5]. In fact this condition characterizes hyperbolic groups. That is, G is hyperbolic if and only if its language of geodesics is rational and is part of an automatic structure for G [17].

Now we make a connection with string rewriting. A survey of groups with various kinds of length reducing confluent presentations is given in [13], and hyperbolic groups fill one gap in the table given there. They are precisely the groups which admit a length reducing presentation which is confluent on the identity [4, Chapter 4, §5]. It follows that a group which admits a length reducing rewriting system confluent at the identity with respect to one choice of generators does so with respect to any choice of generators. It does not seem easy to prove this result directly.

¿From the point of view of language theory a group is hyperbolic if and only if the language of words representing the identity (sometimes called the word problem of G) is generated by a context sensitive grammar in which productions are strictly length increasing and in which every nonterminal derives a terminal. These languages are included in the abstract family of growing context sensitive languages [3]. This AFL includes context free languages, and groups whose word problems are context free are known to be the groups with a free subgroup of finite index [14]. It would be interesting to characterize groups whose word problems are growing context sensitive.

References

1. B. Benninghofen, S. Kemmerich, M. M. Richter, *Systems of Reductions*, Lecture Notes in Computer Science **277**, Springer Verlag, Berlin 1987.
2. M. Bridson and R. Gilman, Formal language theory and the geometry of 3-manifolds, to appear.
3. G. Buntrock and K. Lorys, On growing context-sensitive languages, 19th ICALP, Lecture Notes in Computer Science **623**, Springer Verlag, Berlin 1992, 77-88.
4. M. Coornaert, T. Delzant, and A. Papadopoulos, *Géométrie et théorie des groupes*, Lecture Notes in Mathematics **1441**, Springer Verlag, Berlin 1990.

5. D. B. A. Epstein, J. W. Cannon, D. F. Holt, S. V. F. Levy, M. S. Paterson, and W. P. Thurston, *Word Processing in Groups*, Jones and Bartlett, Boston 1992.
6. D. B. A. Epstein, D. F. Holt, and S. Rees, The use of Knuth Bendix methods to solve the word problem in automatic groups, J. Symbolic Computation **12** 1991, 397-414.
7. C. Frougny and J. Sakarovitch, Synchronized rational relations of finite and infinite words, Theoretical Computer Science **108** 1993, 45–82.
8. S. M. Gersten and H. B. Short, Rational subgroups of biautomatic groups, Annals of Mathematics **134** 1991, 125-158.
9. E. Ghys and P. de la Harpe eds., *Sur les Groupes Hyperboliques d'apres Mikhael Gromov*, Birkhäuser, Boston 1990.
10. R. Gilman, Presentations of groups and monoids, J. Algebra **57** 1979, 544-554.
11. M. Gromov, Hyperbolic groups, in *Essays in Group Theory*, S. M. Gersten ed., MSRI Publ. **8**, Springer Verlag, New York 1987, 75-263.
12. M. Jantzen, *Confluent String Rewriting*, EATCS Monographs on Theoretical Computer Science **14**, Springer Verlag, Berlin 1988.
13. K. Madlener and F. Otto, Groups presented by certain classes of finite length-reducing string rewriting systems, Lecture Notes in Computer Science **256**, Springer Verlag, Berlin 1987, 133-144.
14. D. Muller and P. Schupp, Groups, the theory of ends and context-free languages, J. Computer and System Sciences **26** 1983, 295–310.
15. R. Needham, Term rewriting and the word problem for certain infinite presentations of groups, Dissertation, University of Michigan 1992.
16. C. O'Dunlaing, Infinite regular Thue systems, Theor. Comp. Sci. **25** 1983, 171-192.
17. P. Papasoglu, Geometric methods in group theory, Dissertation, Columbia Univ., 1993
18. G. P. Scott, The geometries of 3-manifolds, Bulletin of the London Mathematical Society, **15** 1983, 401-487.
19. C. Sims, *Computation with Finitely Presented Groups* Encyclopedia of Math. and Its Applications **48**, Cambridge Univ. Pr. 1994.
20. R. Strebel, Small cancellation groups, in *Sur les Groupes Hyperboliques d'apres Mikhael Gromov*, E. Ghys and P. de la Harpe eds., Birkhäuser, Boston 1990, 227–273.

A survey of symmetrized and complete group presentations

Philippe Le Chenadec
INRIA 78153 Le Chesnay Cedex France

We present two examples of rewriting techniques applied to groups, both emphasizing the geometrical content of rewriting. The first investigation recasts small cancellation theory in a rewriting perspective: it corresponds to a partial completion of a group presentation, here called symmetrization. The second one details, on some examples, families of complete presentations for concrete groups of geometric origin.

1 Rewriting in groups

The material developped below possesses common features with rewriting in other algebraic structures, e.g. the theory of standard bases for ideals in polynomial rings [8]. This analogy receives some meaning in the framework of universal algebra: when one succeeds in finding an interesting complete rewriting system associated to the defining equational axioms of a class of algebraic structures (groups, commutative rings, algebras over them...), this complete system may have interesting consequences for the investigation of complete presentations in this equational class. As well-known, such complete systems were first obtained for groups by Knuth [14], and later for other systems by Hullot [13]. Here two such investigations are briefly reported, see [15] for details about the material below, and [10] for a good introduction to rewriting. A formal framework for rewriting modulo some complete systems has recently been given by Claude Marché, see these proceedings and [19]. We try to emphasize the geometrical content of rewriting, which, according to the author's experience, is essential to gain deep insights.

Let Σ be a finite alphabet of *generators*. The set of generators inverses Σ^{-1} is a copy of Σ. For a a member of $\Sigma \cup \Sigma^{-1}$, a^{-1} denotes as usual its inverse. A *rule* is a pair of words (A, B) from $\mathcal{W} = (\Sigma \cup \Sigma^{-1})^*$, and will be written $A \to B$. For $A = a_1 \ldots a_n \in \mathcal{W}$, where $a_i \in \Sigma \cup \Sigma^{-1}$, $A^{-1} =_{def} a_n^{-1} \ldots a_1^{-1}$ denotes as usual its inverse. Given a set $\mathcal{R}$ of rules, a word C is $\mathcal{R}$-reducible if there exists a rule $A \to B$ in $\mathcal{R}$ such that A is a subword of C. The *reduction* of C under this rule replaces the occurrence of A in C by B.

If $AC \to B$ and $CD \to E$ are two rules such that C is distinct from the empty word, then the two reductions issued from the word ACD give a *critical pair* (AE, BD). Notice that an equation $A = B$ can be written $AB^{-1} = 1$, the word AB^{-1} is called a *relator*. The *completion procedure* takes as input a set of equations $\mathcal{E}$ over $\mathcal{W}$. These equations are oriented into rules and new equations are deduced by means of critical pairs between these rules. The completion procedure loops on these two steps. Although the question of termination is an important one, we assume throughout that all reductions are well-founded, i.e. there is no infinite chain $W_1 \rightarrow W_2 \cdots \rightarrow W_n \rightarrow \cdots$. Taking into account the group structure amounts to create, for a new rule $a_1 A a_2 \rightarrow B$, where a_1 and a_2 are in $\Sigma \cup \Sigma^{-1}$, three equations that will possibly create new rules: $(a_1 A, B a_2^{-1})$, $(A a_2, a_1^{-1} B)$ and $(a_2^{-1} A^{-1} a_1^{-1}, B^{-1})$. This claim can be made formal via the well-known Knuth-Bendix complete system for groups. The usual free cancellation rules $aa^{-1} \rightarrow 1$ and $a^{-1}a \rightarrow 1$, a in Σ, are always assumed to be present in a set of rules.

From standard arguments of rewriting theory, when the procedure returns a finite set $\mathcal{R}$ of rules, each word from $\mathcal{W}$ has a unique $\mathcal{R}$-*irreducible* form, called its *normal form*. Let us briefly mention two points of practical importance for this procedure: when a new rule is introduced, all rules must be kept in reduced form, i.e. both their left and right hand-sides should be irreducible with respect to the remaining rules. Lastly, the choice of a waiting equation selected to create a new rule should be performed on a first-in first-out basis. Under these elementary cautions, some light can be brought into the intricacies of rule configurations and regular patterns can be guessed in complete presentations. Further, a detailed proof of correctness of the completion can be carried out (reductions are supposed to be well-founded):

Theorem 1 *[12] Given a presentation $(\Sigma, \mathcal{E})$ of a group G, the completion procedure generates a confluent, possibly infinite, rewriting system $\mathcal{R}$ such that the presentation $(\Sigma, \mathcal{R})$ also defines the group G.*

From the well-known undecidability of the word problem for groups, we deduce the main difference between the computation of standard bases and group completion. While the former procedure always halts, the latter may loop indefinitely, and the resulting complete set may be non recursive. Consequently, we ask for interesting subclasses of groups that do possess finite completions. These classes are essentially the following ones: 1) abelian groups, 2) finite groups, 3) groups with "small" critical pairs, 4) groups from the mathematical practice: knot groups, surface groups, discrete groups of transformations in various geometries. See other talks by Gilman, Rey, Diekert, in this spring school for other classes of groups or monoids (automatic and polycyclic groups, see [7]). Reciprocally, is this technique complete? Recently, Squier [22] has exhibited several groups with decidable word problems that do not possess any finite complete rewriting system, whatever the chosen presentation (let us recall that the decidability of the word problem does not depend on a particular presentation), cf. the talks by Lafont. It is easy to see that the multiplication table of a group, which is a complete set of rules, is recursive iff its word problem is decidable. Thus, the class of groups having a finite completion is strictly included in the class of those possessing a recursive set of rules, while this last class is the one of groups having decidable word problems. Naturally, this points to the usefulness of infinite, but finitely described, complete presentations, such as ones for some Coxeter groups below. See the papers by Otto, Bauer, Book [2,3] for complexity results.

Besides a short account of symmetrization and its link with small cancellation, the reader will find the following classes of complete presentations:

- The fundamental groups of the orientable and non-orientable closed surfaces [24]. They initiated Dehn's study of small cancellation.
- The Coxeter groups, discrete transformation groups generated by reflections. The partial commutativity of some generators is a case of failure. This class possesses infinite sets of rules; a single parametrized rule describes the complete presentation.
- The Dyck groups, generated by rotations in the euclidean, spherical or hyperbolic geometry. They are the rotation subgroups of Coxeter groups. Length-increasing rules appear in some complete presentations, termination remains open in such cases.
- The symmetric groups S_n. Several complete systems exist, depending on the given generators. Generally these systems possess many rules (we found some of size $n!$, the size of S_n), but far from the upper bound (cf. infra): $2|\Sigma||G|$ for a finite group G with generator set Σ.

For a complete development of what follows, see [15,16,17], we give here no proofs. We conclude with two well-known classes of groups. The completion of abelian groups always halts and gives the usual cyclic decompositions (with the technical trick of adding new generators, one per "row operation"). This can be seen as a trivial application of standard bases, abelian groups being modules over the integers. For finite groups, the completion halts and the complete set has less than $2|\Sigma||G|$ rules. This bound is attained by presentations of the trivial group. Notice that this bound is on the size of the output, not on the length of the computation of the complete set. Also, it improves the quadratic one of the multiplication table. Finally, an alternative to rewriting techniques is provided by the Todd-Coxeter coset enumeration technique [6].

2 Symmetrization and small cancellation

Computing a complete set of rules can be expensive. The tools developed in small cancellation theory restricts such rewriting systems in three ways. First, we use only non length-increasing rules. Second, we do not require the set of rules to be complete. More precisely, we solve only critical pairs whose one associated rule is a free cancellation one, i.e. the left members to be superposed are of the form (wa, aa^{-1}) or $(a^{-1}a, aw)$, $a \in \Sigma \cup \Sigma^{-1}$. Third, we require confluence to hold only on relators, i.e. confluence over the unit element. Now, can we give sufficient conditions on a group presentation so that these restricted means will solve its word problem? The slightly different answers that have been proposed define classes of groups with a wide area of applications. Moreover, its history is interesting as an interaction between geometrical and syntactical methods.

This history begins with Dehn. A word is freely reduced if it does not contain adjacent pairs of inverse generators. From now on, relators and their cyclic permutations are supposed to be freely reduced. Dehn noticed that any relator of the group defined by the single equation $a_1...a_{2n}a_1^{-1}...a_{2n}^{-1} = 1$ contains a subword of length at least $2n + 1$ from the polygon of figure 1, to be read in clockwise or counterclockwise order. These groups are the fundamental groups

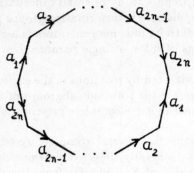

Fig. 1.

of the closed orientable surfaces. His method was purely geometrical, using an interpretation of this group in the hyperbolic plane. It was soon noticed that this method was in fact purely combinatorial. Schiek [20] gave two conditions on presentations such that the rewriting process, which both iteratively replaces all above subwords by their complement inverses and freely reduces, solves the word problem. This process is called Dehn's algorithm. For instance, with the group defined by $abca^{-1}b^{-1}c^{-1} = 1$, we have $\underline{bca^{-1}b^{-1}c^{-1}a} \to a^{-1}\underline{cc^{-1}}a \to \underline{a^{-1}a} \to 1$. From now on, defining relator means a freely reduced defining relator, its inverse, or a cyclic permutation of these words. These conditions are:

- non-existence of defining relators triples $(AUB^{-1}, BVC^{-1}, CWA^{-1})$ such that no two relators are inverses and the three words A, B and C are distinct from the empty word.
- All pairs of defining relators of the form (AU, AV), $U \neq V$ and A distinct from the empty word, are such that $|A| < \frac{1}{4}|AU|$ ($|X|$ word length of X).

Then, Greendlinger [11] proved that the second condition is sufficient if the coefficient 4 is replaced by 6. This second result was purely combinatorial, using a deep analysis of free cancellations. Thus, the geometric content of the original proof by Dehn had disappeared.

It was rediscovered by Lyndon [18,21], using *diagrams* over a given presentation. These diagrams encode the free cancellations. Let us illustrate them with an example. On the defining relators aab, $b^{-1}c^{-1}a$ and $ca^{-1}cc$, we have the following free reduction: $c(aab)c^{-1}c(b^{-1}c^{-1}a)c^{-1}(ca^{-1}cc) \to caac$. This is geometrically interpreted in figure 2: starting at vertex v, each region is followed clockwise once, we return to the original vertex v at the end as the given word $caac$ is equal to 1. Of course, this diagram is best interpreted as a local map in the Cayley graph [9,18]. In groups, every relator is obtained by free cancellation from a word of the form $\prod_i(T_iR_iT_i^{-1})$, where the R_i's are defining relators. This

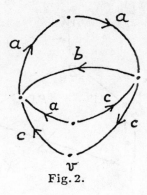

Fig. 2.

the analogue of the ideal generation by the sums $\sum_i (P_i Q_i)$ in polynomial rings. Therefore to each relator are associated freely reduced diagrams as above (i.e. no two successive edges with the same orientation are labeled by x and x^{-1}, and at any vertex there exists at most one edge with the label x), such that the boundary of the diagram is the relator itself. Small cancellation means that there is little free cancellation in this reduction, as more than half of a defining relator remains in the boundary of the reduced diagram. The previous conditions of Schiek and Greendlinger can then be stated in terms of diagrams whose labels are now words (vertices that belong to only two edges are removed, the two edges are merged and their label concatened). The common subwords, called pieces, that give superpositions are then interior edges. The connected regions of the diagrams correspond to defining relators, the degree of a vertex (resp. region) is the number of incident edges (resp. boundary edges). The above conditions become : 1) all interior vertices have degree at least 4, 2) all interior regions have degree at least 4 (resp. 6 for Greendlinger's condition). Notice that the second condition is in fact implied by those on word lengths. Lyndon proved, using Euler formula, that these conditions are sufficient to imply the correctness of Dehn's algorithm. The geometric argument was restored, but in a general framework.

Bücken [5] has investigated these basic small cancellation results under the critical pair approach. Using an implementation of the completion algorithm, we were able to find new geometrical conditions underlying his analysis of the small cancellation phenomenon. The first idea uses the localization principle of term rewriting systems: under well-founded reductions, if global confluence fails, there exists an unresolved critical pair that occurs in some word appearing in some reduction graph. This is just the negation of the well-known Newman lemma. We choose such a minimal word for a given relator W, non-confluent over 1, according to the graph of figure 3. It is easily seen that the pair (Z_1, Z_2) contains a critical pair. But here, we do not add a new rule as in the completion procedure. Instead, we look after conditions on diagrams that will imply a contradiction. Without entering in technical points beyond the scope of this survey, these conditions are: 1) The second Schiek condition, 2) Non-existence of reduced diagrams of the form shown in figure 4. The usual conditions can be

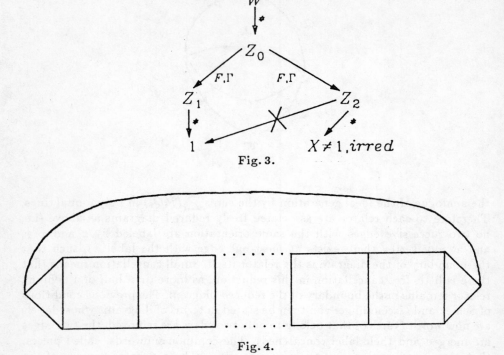

Fig. 3.

Fig. 4.

restored from this most general one. More precisely, there exist groups that fall under these new conditions without being small cancellation ones in the usual sense, for example the group U_1 defined by the equation $ABC = CBA$.

$$U_1 \begin{cases} CBA & \to & ABC & A^{-1}B^{-1}C^{-1} \to C^{-1}B^{-1}A^{-1} \\ BCA^{-1} & \to & A^{-1}CB & AC^{-1}B^{-1} & \to & B^{-1}C^{-1}A \\ B^{-1}A^{-1}C & \to CA^{-1}B^{-1} & C^{-1}AB & \to & BAC^{-1} \end{cases}$$

See below for its nœtherianity.

From this discussion, it appears that a better understanding of small cancellation involves the geometrical meaning of rewriting. Classes of groups falling under the scope of this theory include surface groups and knot groups. Finally we mention that this theory may be further extended in order to solve the conjugacy problem, and that small cancellation groups are automatic groups.

3 Surface Groups

Orientable surfaces. A defining presentation of a p-holed torus is

$$T_p = (A_1, \ldots, A_{2p} ; A_1 \cdots A_{2p} = A_{2p} \cdots A_1).$$

The pieces of the presentation are the generators and their inverses, so that when $p \geq 2$, the presentation has a word problem solved by Dehn's algorithm. The case $p=1$ defines the group $\mathbb{Z} \times \mathbb{Z}$. Its complete presentation expresses the commutativity between elements of $\mathcal{G}$. The following case $p = 2$ gives the system:

$$T_2 \begin{cases} DCBA & \to & ABCD & D^{-1}C^{-1}B^{-1}A^{-1} \to A^{-1}B^{-1}C^{-1}D^{-1} \\ BCDA^{-1} & \to & A^{-1}DCB & B^{-1}C^{-1}D^{-1}A \to AD^{-1}C^{-1}B^{-1} \\ B^{-1}A^{-1}DC & \to CDA^{-1}B^{-1} & BAD^{-1}C^{-1} & \to & C^{-1}D^{-1}AB \\ DA^{-1}B^{-1}C^{-1} \to C^{-1}B^{-1}A^{-1}D & D^{-1}ABC & \to & CBAD^{-1} \end{cases}$$

In the general case, the completion gives a system T_p of $4p$ rules composed of words of length $2p$:

$$T_p \begin{cases} A_{2k} \cdots A_{2p} A_1^{-1} \cdots A_{2k-1}^{-1} \to A_{2k-1}^{-1} \cdots A_1^{-1} A_{2p} \cdots A_{2k} \\ A_{2k} \cdots A_1 A_{2p}^{-1} \cdots A_{2k+1}^{-1} \to A_{2k+1}^{-1} \cdots A_{2p}^{-1} A_1 \cdots A_{2k} \\ A_{2k}^{-1} \cdots A_1^{-1} A_{2p} \cdots A_{2k+1} \to A_{2k+1} \cdots A_{2p} A_1^{-1} \cdots A_{2k}^{-1} \\ A_{2k}^{-1} \cdots A_{2p}^{-1} A_1 \cdots A_{2k-1} \to A_{2k-1} \cdots A_1 A_{2p}^{-1} \cdots A_{2k}^{-1} \end{cases} \quad k = 1, \ldots, p.$$

All rules have the form $\lambda \longrightarrow \overline{\lambda}$, where $\overline{\lambda}$ is the reverse word of λ. This fact is of practical importance for the speed-up of reductions. The proof that a system of rules defines a complete presentation requires three steps: termination, all rules are consequences of the definition and all critical pairs are resolved. Termination is proved with the lex. ordering such that:

$$A_{2p} > A_{2p}^{-1} > \cdots > A_2 > A_2^{-1} > A_1 > A_1^{-1} > \cdots > A_{2p-1} > A_{2p-1}^{-1}.$$

For each rule $\lambda \longrightarrow \rho$, the word $\lambda\rho^{-1}$ is a cyclic permutation of the defining relation or its inverse, i.e. the complete system equals the symmetrized one. Consequently, the induced relation refines Dehn's reduction algorithm in two ways: we have general confluence instead of confluence over the unit element and redexes are searched among $4p$ words of length $2p$ instead of $8p$ words of length $2p + 1$. For the third step, superpositions cannot occur on common subwords of length one. But pieces have length one, so that by the results of §2, all critical pairs are resolved (non-pieces critical pairs are resolved, cf. [17]).

Rewriting sets provide three algorithms, one for reducing a word to its normal form, and two others performing the two group operations on normal forms: multiplication and inversion. Let us mention a first insight in the computation of normal forms by giving an upper bound to the number of T_p-reductions. Book [3] has shown that a linear-time reduction algorithm exists for words rewriting systems with only length-reducing rules. For torus groups, we have even more.

Proposition 2 *Let T_p be a complete torus presentation as above. Then there exists a linear-time algorithm with no backtracking that computes the normal form of a word M with no more than $|M|/2p$ reductions.*

Let us detail the completion of the groups presented by the same defining relation as above, but on an odd number of generators: $(A_1, \ldots, A_{2p+1} ; A_1 \cdots A_{2p+1} =$

$A_{2p+1} \cdots A_1$). The group U_1 has a symmetrized set that is also complete (see the end of §2 for its small cancellation meaning).

$$U_1 \begin{cases} CBA & \to & ABC & A^{-1}B^{-1}C^{-1} \to C^{-1}B^{-1}A^{-1} \\ BCA^{-1} & \to & A^{-1}CB & AC^{-1}B^{-1} & \to & B^{-1}C^{-1}A \\ B^{-1}A^{-1}C & \to & CA^{-1}B^{-1} & C^{-1}AB & \to & BAC^{-1} \end{cases}$$

But its nœtherianity does not follow from a classical ordering. Here is a complete presentation U_p having $4p + 2$ rules, the words' common length is $2p + 1$.

$$U_p \begin{cases} A_{2k+1} \cdots A_1 A_{2p+1}^{-1} \cdots A_{2k+2}^{-1} \to A_{2k+2}^{-1} \cdots A_{2p+1}^{-1} A_1 \cdots A_{2k+1} \\ A_{2k+1}^{-1} \cdots A_{2p+1}^{-1} A_1 \cdots A_{2k} \to A_{2k} \cdots A_1 A_{2p+1}^{-1} \cdots A_{2k+1}^{-1} \\ A_{2k} \cdots A_{2p+1} A_1^{-1} \cdots A_{2k-1}^{-1} \to A_{2k-1}^{-1} \cdots A_1^{-1} A_{2p+1} \cdots A_{2k} \\ A_{2k}^{-1} \cdots A_1^{-1} A_{2p+1} \cdots A_{2k+1} \to A_{2k+1} \cdots A_{2p+1} A_1^{-1} \cdots A_{2k}^{-1} \end{cases} \quad k = 0, \ldots, p.$$

The nœtherianity of U_p follows from the fact that each member of $\mathcal{G}$ prefixes exactly one rule. All rules sides having the same length, we may restrict ourselves to reduction chains of words of the same length.

Lemma 3 *Let U and V be two words of the same length, and $b_1 \ldots b_{2p}$, $b_i \in \mathcal{G}$, be a left side prefix, then we never have $b_1 \ldots b_{2p} U \xrightarrow{*}_{U_p} b_{2p}^{-1} \ldots b_1^{-1} V$.*

Corollary 4 *Let U and V be two words of the same length, then one never has $\rho_i U \xrightarrow{*}_{U_p} \lambda_j V$, ρ_i (resp. λ_j) a right (resp. left) side of a rule.*

Thus the U_p-reductions must halt as a prefix may be reduced only once and length never increases. Geometrically, the two families of complete presentations possess a concise description by $4p$ and $4p+2$-gons (figures 5 and 6). The polygons

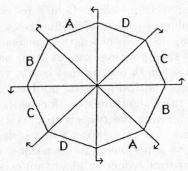

Fig. 5. T_2.

represent an elementary circuit in the Cayley diagram of the groups. The arrows show irreducible paths. All rules are embodied on these graphs.

Non-orientable surfaces. The non-orientable surface groups are defined by $(A_1, \ldots, A_p \; ; \; A_1^2 \cdots A_p^2 = 1)$. The general complete set of rules R_p depends on the parity of p. Let $n = \lfloor p/2 \rfloor$, $A_i = A_{i+p}$ if $i = 1 - p, \ldots, 0$ and $A_i = A_{i-p}$ if

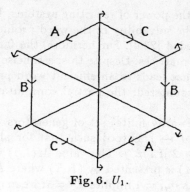

Fig. 6. U_1.

$i = p + 1, \ldots, 2p$. Note that $A_{k-n} = A_{k+n+1}$. Both cases split into two sets of rules:

$$p = 2n + 1 \begin{cases} \begin{cases} A_k^{-1} A_{k-1}^{-2} \cdots A_{k-n}^{-2} & \to & A_k A_{k+1}^2 \cdots A_{k+n}^2 \\ A_k^{-2} A_{k-1}^{-2} \cdots A_{k-n+1}^{-2} A_{k-n}^{-1} & \to & A_{k+1}^2 \cdots A_{k+n}^2 A_{k+n+1} \\ A_k^2 \cdots A_{k+n}^2 & \to & A_{k-1}^{-2} \cdots A_{k-n}^{-2} \\ A_k A_{k+1}^2 \cdots A_{k+n}^2 A_{k+n+1} & \to & A_k^{-1} A_{k-1}^{-2} \cdots A_{k-n+1}^{-2} A_{k-n}^{-1} \end{cases} \\ \begin{cases} A_k^{-2} \cdots A_{k-n+1}^{-2} A_{k-n} A_{k-n+1}^2 \cdots A_k^2 \\ \to A_{k+1}^2 \cdots A_{k+n}^2 A_{k+n+1} A_{k+n}^{-2} \cdots A_{k+1}^{-2} \\ A_k^{-1} A_{k-1}^{-2} \cdots A_{k-n+1}^{-2} A_{k-n}^{-1} A_{k-n+1}^2 \cdots A_k^2 A_{k+1} \\ \to A_k A_{k+1}^2 \cdots A_{k+n}^2 A_{k+n-1}^{-1} A_{k+n}^{-2} \cdots A_{k+2}^{-2} A_{k+1}^{-1} \end{cases} \end{cases}$$

$$p = 2n \begin{cases} \begin{cases} A_k^{-2} A_{k-1}^{-2} \cdots A_{k-n+1}^{-2} & \to & A_{k+1}^2 \cdots A_{k+n}^2 \\ A_k^{-1} A_{k-1}^{-2} \cdots A_{k-n+1}^{-2} A_{k-n}^{-1} & \to & A_k A_{k+1}^2 \cdots A_{k+n-1}^2 A_{k+n} \\ A_k^2 \cdots A_{k+n-1}^2 A_{k+n} & \to & A_{k-1}^{-2} \cdots A_{k-n+1}^{-2} A_{k-n}^{-1} \\ A_k A_{k+1}^2 \cdots A_{k+n}^2 & \to & A_k^{-1} A_{k-1}^{-2} \cdots A_{k-n+1}^{-2} \end{cases} \\ \begin{cases} A_k^{-2} \cdots A_{k-n+2}^{-2} A_{k-n+1} A_{k-n+2}^2 \cdots A_{k+1}^2 \\ \to A_{k+1}^2 \cdots A_{k+n}^2 A_{k+n+1} A_{k+n}^{-2} \cdots A_{k+2}^{-2} \\ A_k^{-1} A_{k-1}^{-2} \cdots A_{k-n+1}^{-2} A_{k-n} A_{k-n+1}^2 \cdots A_{k-1}^2 A_k \\ \to A_k A_{k+1}^2 \cdots A_{k+n-1}^2 A_{k+n} A_{k+n-1}^{-2} \cdots A_{k+1}^{-2} A_k^{-1} \end{cases} \end{cases}$$

For all these rules, k ranges from 1 to p.

Termination: lex. ordering with $A_1^{-1} > \cdots > A_p^{-1} > A_1 > \cdots > A_p$.

Every set has $6p$ rules. In both cases, the first four rules are symmetrized presentations, while the last two rules arise from critical pairs with the single-letters pieces of $\mathcal{G}$. For example, if $p = 4$, the two rules $A_3 A_4 A_4 A_1 A_1 \longrightarrow A_3^{-1} A_2^{-1} A_2^{-1}$ and $A_1 A_1 A_2 A_2 A_3 \longrightarrow A_4^{-1} A_4^{-1} A_3^{-1}$ superposed on the piece A_1 create the new rule $A_3^{-1} A_2^{-1} A_2^{-1} A_1 A_2 A_2 A_3 \longrightarrow A_3 A_4 A_4 A_1 A_4^{-1} A_4^{-1} A_3^{-1}$.

4 Coxeter Groups

Completion. The word problem for Coxeter groups has been proved decidable by Tits. The completion of these group presentations is among the most convincing examples of the power of rewriting systems. By elementary syntactical methods, it proves the solvability of the word problem whereas geometrical methods are usually needed [23,4]. Furthermore, the family is parametrized by $n \times n$ symmetric integer matrices. Despite this, a concise description of complete presentations is found that leads to an efficient word problem algorithm. However, a drawback is encountered: the partial commutativity of a presentation leads to a failure.

Let I be a (not necessarily finite) set of generators. A Coxeter matrix on I is a function $M : I \times I \mapsto \mathbb{N} \cup \{\infty\}$ such that for all i, j in I, $M(i, i) = 1$ and $M(i, j) = M(j, i) \geq 2$ if $i \neq j$. The value $M(i, j)$ will be denoted by m_{ij}. The Coxeter group $C(M)$ is presented by (I, E) where E is the set of equations $(ij)^{m_{ij}} = 1, m_{ij} \neq \infty$. As $m_{ii} = 1$ implies $i^{-1} = i$, we may represent the elements of $C(M)$ by words from the free monoid I^* on I.

Throughout this section, $[ij]^k$ will denote the product $ijij \ldots$ of k generators alternatively equal to i and j; α will denote $[ij]^{m_{ij}-1}$. The generators i and j will be denoted by $f(\alpha)$ and $s(\alpha)$ respectively, and $l(\alpha)$ is the last generator of α, equal to i (resp. j) when m_{ij} is even (resp. odd). To α is associated the word $\overline{\alpha} = [ji]^{m_{ij}-1}$. Finally, m_{ij} will be abbreviated as m_α. The same definitions stand for $\beta = [ij]^{m_{ij}}$ and $\gamma = [ij]^{m_{ij}-2}$.

A first solution to the word problem is given by a theorem of Tits (thm 1, p.93, Bourbaki [4]). Say I is finite with n generators. Generators are represented by linear transformations of a real vector space with basis $e_1, \ldots, e_n$:

$$s_i : e_j \longrightarrow e_j - 2(\cos \frac{\pi}{m_{ij}})e_i.$$

A word $w = i_1 \ldots i_k$ from I^* is equal to 1 in $C(M)$ iff $s_{i_1} \ldots s_{i_k}(\sum_{j=1}^n e_j) = \sum_{j=1}^n e_j$. This solution is not efficient. Another one was proposed by Tits based upon a reduction in I^* defined by the following rules:

$$\left\{ \begin{array}{ll} wiiw' \rightarrow ww', & i \in I, \ w, w' \in I^*, \\ w\beta w' \rightarrow w\overline{\beta}w', & w, w' \in I^*. \end{array} \right.$$

The confluence is proved via the previous linear representation. The reduction being non length-increasing, an enumeration of the words reduced from a given one halts, thereby solving the word problem. A completion based on any lexicographic ordering may be used to significantly improve this algorithm. We restrict ourselves to matrices with no entry equal to 2. The completion starts by symmetrizing the given presentation:

Lemma 5 *Given a Coxeter matrix M on the set I totally ordered by $>$, the completion generates the following two sets of rules:*

$$R_I = \{ i^{-1} \longrightarrow i, \ ii \longrightarrow 1 \mid i \in I \} \quad and \quad S_I = \{ \beta \longrightarrow \overline{\beta} \mid f(\beta) > s(\beta) \}.$$

From R_I we can restrict to words in I^*. Note that a word α is both a left side suffix (resp. prefix) and a right side prefix (resp. suffix) of a rule in S_I when $s(\alpha) > f(\alpha)$ (resp. $f(\alpha) > s(\alpha)$), and that both $\alpha\alpha$ and $\alpha\overline{\alpha}$ reduce to 1.

Theorem 6 *Let M be a Coxeter matrix on the set I totally ordered by $>$. If $m_{ij} \neq 2$, $i, j \in I$, the completion procedure generates the set of rules $R_I \cup T_I$, where T_I consists of all rules of the form:*

$$\alpha_1 \ldots \alpha_k l(\overline{\alpha_k}) \longrightarrow s(\alpha_1)\alpha_1 \ldots \alpha_k \tag{1}$$

with k a positive integer, and for all p such that $1 < p < k$:

$$f(\alpha_1) > s(\alpha_1), \; s(\alpha_p) > f(\alpha_p), \; f(\alpha_{p+1}) \neq l(\alpha_p), \; s(\alpha_{p+1}) = l(\overline{\alpha_p}). \tag{2}$$

Naturally, the importance of this theorem lies in its description of complete systems for many groups via what can be called a single metarule.

Examples. When we give a complete set of rules, we omit those from R_I.

$$G_1 \begin{cases} baba \rightarrow abab \\ bcbcb \rightarrow cbcbc \\ (ac)^3 \rightarrow (ca)^3 \\ (bc)^2(ab)^2 \rightarrow (cb)^2 caba \\ bab(ca)^3 \rightarrow (ab)^2(ca)^2 c \\ (bc)^2 aba(cb)^2 \rightarrow (cb)^2 caba(cb)^2 \end{cases} \qquad G_2 \begin{cases} abab \rightarrow baba \\ cbcbc \rightarrow bcbcb \\ (ac)^3 \rightarrow (ca)^3 \\ (ac)^2 a(bc)^2 b \rightarrow (ca)^3 (bc)^2 \end{cases}$$

Both sets G_1 and G_2 are complete and define the same group (for G_1, ordering $b > a > c$, for G_2 ordering $a > c > b$). Note that the number of rules depends on the ordering. The set of rules may be infinite: see G_3 defined by $dcd = cdc$, $dbdb = bdbd$ and $dada = adad$, whose completion creates infinitely many rules, e.g. $dcbdb(adabdb)^m d \longrightarrow cdcbdb(adabdb)^m$, $m \geq 0$. For reduction computations, it is noteworthy that all T-rules are in Post normal form: they are of the type $Va \longrightarrow bV$, with $V = \alpha_1 \ldots \alpha_m$. If M is a Coxeter matrix with infinite m_{ij}'s, the meta-rule T always gives the complete system, and the previous theorem remains valid for M with the convention that no component α exists for i and j. Here are two examples of commuting pairs of generators:

$$G_4 \begin{cases} ad \rightarrow da \quad bd \rightarrow db \\ ca \rightarrow ac \quad cd \rightarrow dc \\ cbc \rightarrow bcb \\ cbac \rightarrow bcba \\ cbabcb \rightarrow bcbabc \end{cases} \qquad G_5 \begin{cases} ca \rightarrow ac \\ cb \rightarrow bc \\ dad \rightarrow ada \\ dbd \rightarrow bdb \\ dcd \rightarrow cdc \end{cases}$$

With the *complete* system G_4, the T-rule $cbadc \longrightarrow bcbad$ is never created as its sides are confluent under the commutativity rules and the T-rule $cbac \longrightarrow bcba$. Given G_5, with S_I displayed, the completion procedure generates infinitely many rules $dxcd[yx]^m c \longrightarrow xdxcd[yx]^m$, $m \geq 0$, where $\{x, y\} = \{a, b\}$.

We now consider finite Coxeter groups first described by Coxeter [9]. The notation is taken from Bourbaki [4]. The finite Coxeter groups whose matrix entries are equal to 1,2,3,4 or 6 are called crystallographic groups.

$$H_4 \begin{cases} dcd \rightarrow cdc \\ cbc \rightarrow bcb \\ cbac \rightarrow bcba \\ babab \rightarrow ababa \\ cbabcb \rightarrow bcbabc \\ (c(ba)^2))^2 \rightarrow bc(ba)^2cbab \end{cases} \qquad H_3 \begin{cases} cbc \rightarrow bcb \\ cbac \rightarrow bcba \\ babab \rightarrow ababa \\ cbabcb \rightarrow bcbabc \\ (c(ba)^2)^2 \rightarrow bc(ba)^2cbab \end{cases} \qquad F_4 \begin{cases} bab \rightarrow aba \\ dcd \rightarrow cdc \\ cbcb \rightarrow bcbc \\ (cba)^2 \rightarrow bcbacb \end{cases}$$

The two groups H_3 and H_4 are not crystallographic. Nor are the dihedral groups $I_2(n)$, $n > 4$, except $I_2(6)$, whose critical pairs are resolved by symmetrization, their complete set being $R_I \cup S_I$. The other finite groups are crystallographic. Apart F_4 above and the families A_n, B_{n+1}, $n \geq 1$, below, we failed to complete the three isolated groups E_n, $n = 6, 7, 8$, and the family D_n, $n \geq 4$. The groups A_n are the symmetric groups, two complete presentations may be found in the last section. Despite commuting pairs of generators, observe that we have only T-rules. The Coxeter matrix of the group B_n is:

$$\begin{pmatrix} 1\,3 & & 2 \\ 3\,1 & & \\ & 1\,3\,2 & \\ 2 & 3\,1\,4 & \\ & 2\,4\,1 & \end{pmatrix}$$

The complete system includes the rules R_I, the commutativity rules and the following T-rules:

$$\begin{cases} a_i a_{i-1} \ldots a_{i-k} a_i \rightarrow a_{i-1} a_i a_{i-1} \ldots a_{i-k}, & n > i > k > 0, \\ (a_n a_{n-1} \ldots a_{n-k})^2 \rightarrow a_{n-1} a_n a_{n-1} \ldots a_{n-k} a_n a_{n-1} \ldots a_{n-k+1}, & n > k > 0. \end{cases}$$

The simplest reduction algorithm iterates the search of a left side and the substitution of right sides. We may improve it by using the uniform structure of the rules. A reasonable goal is a reduction algorithm without backward search in a word already scanned and reduced. Such an algorithm based on leftmost reductions does exist. As for orientable surfaces, not only is this algorithm linear in time, but it does not need any backtracking search as is the case in general.

5 Dyck Groups

Polyhedral groups. The polyhedral group (l, m, n) is defined by the presentation $(A, B, C \; ; \; A^l, B^m, C^n, ABC)$ [9]. We will also give complete systems for the following generalization, called Dyck groups:

$$(p_1, \ldots, p_n) = (A_1, \ldots, A_n \; ; \; A_1^{p_1}, \ldots, A_n^{p_n}, A_1 \cdots A_n), \quad n \geq 3.$$

Observe that these groups are subgroups of Coxeter groups (the "rotation" subgroups). The general complete system also requires $p_i \geq 3$, $i = 1, \ldots, n$. Let us first examine the case $n = 3$. This presentation is redundant, one among the generators can be eliminated. With this new presentation, we immediately observe that, whenever l, m and n are greater than 3, the group is a small cancellation one, as the only pieces are the generators and their inverses. Thus its word problem is solvable. For a study of Dyck and Coxeter groups from the small cancellation point of view, see [1]. The groups are infinite when $\frac{1}{l} + \frac{1}{m} + \frac{1}{n} \leq 1$. Finite ones are $(2, 2, n)$, $(2,3,3)$, $(2,3,4)$, $(2,3,5)$. The first one is the dihedral group $I_2(n)$ whose complete system is given in §4. The remaining finite groups are the rotation groups of the five platonic polyhedrons. As isolated finite groups they possess many complete presentations, for example:

$$(2,3,3) : Tetrahedron \begin{cases} C^{-1} \to CC & A \to C^{-1}B^{-1} \\ B^{-1} \to BB & A^{-1} \to BC \\ CBC \to BB & CCC \to 1 \\ CCBB \to BC & BBB \to 1 \\ CBBC \to BCCB & BCB \to CC \\ & BBCC \to CB \end{cases}$$

Termination: weight ordering with $\pi(B^{-1}) = 3, \pi(C^{-1}) = 3, \pi(B) = \pi(C) = 1$ and $C > B$.

$$(2,3,4) : \begin{matrix} Cube\ or \\ Octahedron \end{matrix} \begin{cases} A^{-1} \to A & \\ B^{-1} \to CA & CCC \to ACACA \\ C^{-1} \to ACACA & CACAC \to A \\ AA \to 1 & CACCAC \to ACCA \\ B \to A^{-1}C^{-1} & CCACCA \to ACCACC \end{cases}$$

Termination: weight ordering with $\pi(C^{-1}) = 5, \pi(A^{-1}) = \pi(C) = \pi(A) = 1$, $C^{-1} > A^{-1} > C > A$.

$$(2,3,5) : \begin{matrix} Icosahedron\ or \\ Dodecahedron \end{matrix} \begin{cases} A^{-1} \to A & (BABBA)^2 BA \to (ABABB)^2 AB \\ B^{-1} \to BB & BBABB \to ABABABA \\ C^{-1} \to AB & C \to B^{-1}C^{-1} \\ BABABAB \to ABBA & BBB \to 1 \\ BABABBABAB \to ABBABABBA & AA \to 1 \end{cases}$$

Termination: weight ordering with $\pi(B^{-1}) = 6, \pi(B) = 3, \pi(A^{-1}) = \pi(A) = 1$, and $A^{-1} > B^{-1} > A > B$.

The remaining groups are infinite and we assume that $l \leq m \leq n$. There are two distinct cases, either some generator has even order or not. The simpler case occurs when all parameters are odd: $l = 2p + 1, m = 2q + 1, n = 2r + 1$. The remaining cases have slight modifications of the exponents. A first set (1) results from the symmetrization process, and we have the critical pairs rules (2):

$$(1) \begin{cases} AB \to C^{-1} & A^{-1}C^{-1} \to B \\ BC \to A^{-1} & C^{-1}B^{-1} \to A \\ CA \to B^{-1} & B^{-1}A^{-1} \to C \\ A^{p+1} \to A^{-p} & A^{-(p+1)} \to A^p \\ B^{q+1} \to B^{-p} & B^{-(q+1)} \to B^p \\ C^{r+1} \to C^{-r} & C^{-(r+1)} \to C^r \end{cases} \qquad (2) \begin{cases} A^{-1}C^r \to BC^{-r} & A^{-p}B \to A^pC^{-1} \\ B^{-1}A^p \to CA^{-p} & B^{-q}C \to B^qA^{-1} \\ C^{-1}B^q \to AB^{-q} & C^{-r}A \to C^rB^{-1} \end{cases}$$

Termination: lex. ordering with $C^{-1} > B^{-1} > A^{-1} > C > B > A$.

Three cases remain, when one, two or three generators have even order. The set (1) is modified as the order of a generator becomes even, say A has order $2p$, the two corresponding rules become $A^{p+1} \rightarrow A^{-(p-1)}$ and $A^{-p} \rightarrow A^p$. Then, in the second set of rules, we have: $A^{-(p-1)}B \rightarrow A^p C^{-1}$ and $B^{-1}A^p \rightarrow CA^{-(p-1)}$. These modifications occur for every generator, whatever the order of the parity shift. We give four complete sets, omitting the rules symmetrizing the defining relation ABC:

$$(7,7,7) \begin{cases} A^4 \rightarrow A^{-3} \\ A^{-4} \rightarrow A^3 \\ B^4 \rightarrow B^{-3} \\ B^{-4} \rightarrow B^3 \\ C^4 \rightarrow C^{-3} \\ C^{-4} \rightarrow C^3 \\ A^{-1}C^3 \rightarrow BC^{-3} \\ A^{-3}B \rightarrow A^3 C^{-1} \\ B^{-1}A^3 \rightarrow CA^{-3} \\ B^{-3}C \rightarrow B^3 A^{-1} \\ C^{-1}B^3 \rightarrow AB^{-3} \\ C^{-3}A \rightarrow C^3 B^{-1} \end{cases} \qquad (7,8,9) \begin{cases} A^4 \rightarrow A^{-3} \\ A^{-4} \rightarrow A^3 \\ B^5 \rightarrow B^{-3} \\ B^{-4} \rightarrow B^4 \\ C^5 \rightarrow C^{-4} \\ C^{-5} \rightarrow C^4 \\ A^{-1}C^4 \rightarrow BC^{-4} \\ A^{-3}B \rightarrow A^3 C^{-1} \\ B^{-1}A^3 \rightarrow CA^{-3} \\ B^{-3}C \rightarrow B^4 A^{-1} \\ C^{-1}B^4 \rightarrow AB^{-3} \\ C^{-4}A \rightarrow C^4 B^{-1} \end{cases}$$

$$(7,8,8) \begin{cases} A^4 \rightarrow A^{-3} \\ A^{-4} \rightarrow A^3 \\ B^5 \rightarrow B^{-3} \\ B^{-4} \rightarrow B^4 \\ C^5 \rightarrow C^{-3} \\ C^{-4} \rightarrow C^4 \\ A^{-1}C^4 \rightarrow BC^{-3} \\ A^{-3}B \rightarrow A^3 C^{-1} \\ B^{-1}A^3 \rightarrow CA^{-3} \\ B^{-3}C \rightarrow B^4 A^{-1} \\ C^{-1}B^4 \rightarrow AB^{-3} \\ C^{-3}A \rightarrow C^4 B^{-1} \end{cases} \qquad (8,8,8) \begin{cases} A^5 \rightarrow A^{-3} \\ A^{-4} \rightarrow A^4 \\ B^5 \rightarrow B^{-3} \\ B^{-4} \rightarrow B^4 \\ C^5 \rightarrow C^{-3} \\ C^{-4} \rightarrow C^4 \\ A^{-1}C^4 \rightarrow BC^{-3} \\ A^{-3}B \rightarrow A^4 C^{-1} \\ B^{-1}A^4 \rightarrow CA^{-3} \\ B^{-3}C \rightarrow B^4 A^{-1} \\ C^{-1}B^4 \rightarrow AB^{-3} \\ C^{-3}A \rightarrow C^4 B^{-1} \end{cases}$$

At least one, and at most three rules in the even case are length increasing, and no classical ordering proves the nœtherianity. From hand computations, we conjecture that the reductions are well-founded. The irreducible forms of (l, m, n) are described by the finite automaton of figure 7, with the following conventions:

- A state labeled A (resp. B, C) recognizes the subwords A^i, $i = 1, \ldots, \lfloor \frac{l}{2} \rfloor$.
  A state labeled a (resp. b, c) recognizes the subwords A^{-i}, $i = 1, \ldots, \lfloor \frac{l-1}{2} \rfloor$.
- Simple arrows allow all transitions, whatever the subword recognized by the initial state of the arrow. Double arrows allow all transitions but the one whose initial state has recognized the maximal length subword (rules with left sides $B^{-3}C$). Triple arrows allow all transitions but the one whose final state recognizes the maximal subword (rules with left sides $B^{-1}A^3$).

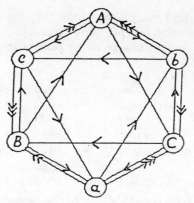

Fig. 7. Normal forms finite automaton.

We now describe complete systems for Dyck groups with at least four generators. Two cases occur according to the parity of the number of generators. As for Coxeter groups, we restrict ourselves to generators of order greater than 2.

Dyck groups with an odd number of generators. Let $G = \{A_1, \ldots, A_{2n+1}\}$ be the set of generators. The set $\mathcal{G}$ is ordered so that inverses are greater than generators. Let $\alpha_1 \ldots \alpha_{n+1}$ be any subword of length $n + 1$ in the word $W_G = A_1 \cdots A_{2n+1} A_1 \cdots A_n$. The word $\alpha_{n+2} \ldots \alpha_{2n+1}$ denotes its *complement*: suffix of length n, or prefix of length n if such a suffix does not exist. The complete system for $(2p_1 + 1, \ldots, 2p_{2n+1} + 1)$, $p_i > 0$, is:

$$
\begin{cases}
\alpha_1 \ldots \alpha_{n+1} & \longrightarrow & (\alpha_{n+2} \ldots \alpha_{2n+1})^{-1} \\
(\alpha_1 \ldots \alpha_{n+1})^{-1} & \longrightarrow & \alpha_{n+2} \ldots \alpha_{2n+1} \\
\alpha^{p_\alpha + 1} & \longrightarrow & \alpha^{-p_\alpha} \\
\alpha^{-(p_\alpha + 1)} & \longrightarrow & \alpha^{p_\alpha} \\
\alpha_{n+1}^{-1} \ldots \alpha_2^{-1} \alpha_1^{p_{\alpha_1}} & \longrightarrow & \alpha_{n+2} \ldots \alpha_{2n+1} \alpha_1^{-p_{\alpha_1}} \\
\alpha_1^{-p_{\alpha_1}} \alpha_2 \ldots \alpha_{n+1} & \longrightarrow & \alpha_1^{p_{\alpha_1}} (\alpha_{n+2} \ldots \alpha_{2n+1})^{-1}
\end{cases}
$$

For complete presentations with generators α of even order $2p_\alpha$, the third and fourth rules become $\alpha^{p_\alpha + 1} \longrightarrow \alpha^{-(p_\alpha - 1)}$ and $\alpha^{-p_\alpha} \longrightarrow \alpha^{p_\alpha}$ respectively. And the other pairs of exponents $(p_\alpha, -p_\alpha)$ become $(p_\alpha, -(p_\alpha - 1))$. The number of rules is $6|G|$. As for surface groups, the rules are simply described geometrically in the Cayley graph, by directing them away from a given vertex. We present $(5,5,5)$ in figure 8. For the other groups with an odd number $2n + 1$ of generators the number of polygons around the central vertex is $4n + 2$. The grey regions denote the defining relation $ABC = 1$. The Cayley graphs are planar, so that they are oriented according to the displayed arrow. The size of the other polygons depends on the order of the generator. Thick lines denote forbidden edges for paths in normal forms starting at the central vertex.

Dyck groups with an even number of generators. The number of rules is $10|G|$. Let $2n$ be the number of generators and define $W_G = A_1 \cdots A_{2n} A_1 \cdots A_n$.

The words $\alpha_1 \ldots \alpha_{n+1}$ and $\alpha_{n+2} \ldots \alpha_{2n}$ have the same definition as above. For the sake of clarity, the pairs (α_1, p_{α_1}) and $(\alpha_{n+1}, p_{\alpha_{n+1}})$ are replaced by (σ, s) and (ρ, r). We give the complete system for generators of odd exponent, $(2p_1 + 1, \ldots, 2p_{2n} + 1), p_i > 0$:

$$
\left\{
\begin{aligned}
\alpha_1 \ldots \alpha_{n+1} &\rightarrow (\alpha_{n+2} \ldots \alpha_{2n})^{-1} \\
(\alpha_1 \ldots \alpha_n)^{-1} &\rightarrow \alpha_{n+1} \ldots \alpha_{2n} \\
\alpha^{p_\alpha + 1} &\rightarrow \alpha^{-p_\alpha} \\
\alpha^{-(p_\alpha + 1)} &\rightarrow \alpha^{p_\alpha} \\
\alpha_1 \ldots \alpha_n \rho^{-r} &\rightarrow (\alpha_{n+2} \ldots \alpha_{2n})^{-1} \rho^r \\
\sigma^{-s} \alpha_2 \ldots \rho &\rightarrow \sigma^s (\alpha_{n+2} \ldots \alpha_{2n})^{-1} \\
\sigma^{-s} \alpha_2 \ldots \alpha_n \rho^{-r} &\rightarrow \sigma^s (\alpha_{n+2} \ldots \alpha_{2n})^{-1} \rho^r \\
(\alpha_{n+2} \ldots \alpha_{2n})^{-1} \rho^r (\alpha_2 \ldots \alpha_n)^{-1} \sigma^s &\rightarrow \alpha_1 \ldots \alpha_n \rho^{-(r-1)} \alpha_{n+2} \ldots \alpha_{2n} \sigma^{-s} \\
\alpha_1 \ldots \alpha_n \rho^{-(r-1)} \alpha_{n+2} \ldots \alpha_{2n} \alpha_1 &\rightarrow (\alpha_{n+2} \ldots \alpha_{2n})^{-1} \rho^r (\alpha_2 \ldots \alpha_n)^{-1} \\
\sigma^{-s} \alpha_2 \ldots \alpha_n \rho^{-(r-1)} \alpha_{n+2} \ldots \alpha_{2n} \alpha_1 &\rightarrow \sigma^s (\alpha_{n+2} \ldots \alpha_{2n})^{-1} \rho^r (\alpha_2 \ldots \alpha_n)^{-1}
\end{aligned}
\right.
$$

For generators with even order, the observations of the previous section remain valid, together with the convention that $-(p_\alpha - 1)$ becomes $-(p_\alpha - 2)$ for a generator α of order $2p_\alpha$. As in the previous section, we give a geometrical interpretation of the rules, here for $(5,5,5,5)$, see figure 9. When the number of

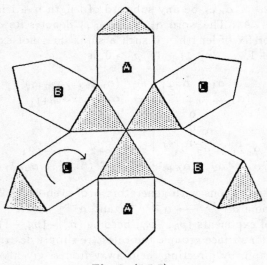

Fig. 8. $(5,5,5)$.

generators increases, so does the number of branches around the central vertex. And the number of edges in polygons varies according to the exponent of generators. Observe that the initial cycles surrounding the central vertex give two rules, the others only one. These figures give a concise construction of Cayley graphs. The critical pairs are computed by superposition on a *single* generator, as for Coxeter groups. The completion procedure stops since the remain-

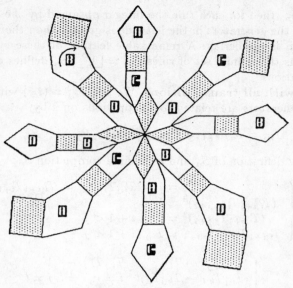

Fig. 9. (5,5,5,5).

ing superposition creates a subgraph appearing somewhere else in the graph. Lastly, recall that for presentations including generators with even order, we did not prove the termination of the system due to length-increasing rules, such as $A^{-2}BC^{-1}DA \longrightarrow A^3D^{-1}C^2B^{-1}$ in (6,5,5,5).

6 Symmetric Groups

We give two complete presentations of the symmetric group S_n. The first one has fewer generators and relations than the second one. Consequently, we obtain a bigger complete set for the last presentation ($O(n^4)$ against $O(n^2)$), but this last system allows us to work on shorter words and its left members are simpler. Again, the essential point is not the number of rules, but their regularity and the complexity of the underlying word problem algorithm.

Presentation with adjacent transpositions. The presentation S_n by adjacent transpositions is the following one:

$$S_n \left\{ \begin{array}{lll} R_i = (i\,i+1), & R_i^2 = 1 & i = 1, \ldots, n-1 \\ R_i R_j = R_j R_i & & i \leq j-2 \\ (R_i R_{i+1})^3 = 1 & & i \leq n-2. \end{array} \right.$$

The completion gives $n^2 - 2n + 2$ rules (cf. A_n of §4):

$$S_n \left\{ \begin{array}{lll} R_i^{-1} \rightarrow R_i, & R_i^2 \rightarrow 1 & i = 1, \ldots, n \\ R_i R_j \rightarrow R_j R_i & & j \leq i-2 \\ R_i R_{i-1} \ldots R_j R_i \rightarrow R_{i-1} R_i R_{i-1} \ldots R_j & j < i. \end{array} \right.$$

Let $1 = R_0$ *in* S_n, then for each rule the integer obtained by the concatenation of the indices of the generators in the left side is greater than the right side one. Thus the system is nœtherian. A remarkable feature of these systems is that $S_n \subset S_{n+1}$. Thus the infinite set of rules $S_\infty = \bigsqcup_{n=1}^{\infty} S_n$ defines a normal form for any permutation.

Presentation with all transpositions. We put $T_{i,j} = (i\ j)$ with $1 \leq i < j \leq n$. These new generators are related to the previous ones by:

$$T_{i,j} = R_i R_{i+1} \ldots R_{j-2} R_{j-1} R_{j-2} R_{j-3} \ldots R_i.$$

We give the new definition of S_n and a possible completion $\mathcal{S}_n$:

$$S_n \begin{cases} T_{i,j}^2 = 1 \qquad T_{i,j} T_{i,i+1} = T_{i,i+1} T_{i+1,j} \\ (T_{i,i+1} T_{i+1,i+2})^3 = 1 \\ (T_{i,i+1} T_{j,j+1})^2 = 1 \quad i+1 < j \\ T_{i,i+1} T_{i+1,j} T_{i,i+1} = T_{i,j} \quad i+1 < j. \end{cases}$$

$$\mathcal{S}_n \begin{cases} T_{i,j}^{-1} \rightarrow T_{i,j} \qquad T_{i,j} T_{i,j} \rightarrow 1 \\ T_{i,j} T_{k,l} \rightarrow T_{k,l} T_{i,j} \quad i \neq k, i \neq l, j \neq l \\ T_{i,j} T_{i,k} \rightarrow T_{i,k} T_{k,j} \quad i < k < j \\ T_{i,j} T_{k,j} \rightarrow T_{k,i} T_{i,j} \quad k < i < j \\ T_{i,j} T_{k,i} \rightarrow T_{k,i} T_{k,j} \quad k < i < j. \end{cases}$$

Termination: lex. ordering, with all the inverses greater than their corresponding generators and

$$T_{n-1,n} > T_{n-2,n} > \ldots > T_{1,n} > T_{n-2,n-1} > \ldots > T_{1,n-1} > \ldots > T_{1,2}.$$

The number of rules is $O(n^4)$, which is far from the upper bound of §1: $(n-1)(n-2)n!$. Once more, we have $T_n \subset T_{n+1}$. Thus $T_\infty = \bigsqcup_{n=1}^{\infty} T_n$ reduces an arbitrary length permutation to a normal form. This complete set is just *symmetrized*. The rules enumerate all the quasi-commutativity identities of transpositions, and these are sufficient to compute in S_n.

Acknowledgements. Thanks to Gérard Huet who suggested this research, supported it and helped us with some remarks and technical proofs of termination. Thanks also to the INRIA Algo project for his warm hospitality and to the participants of the Computational Group Theory seminar of May 1988 at Oberwolfach, who showed interest in these experimental results.

References

1. Appel K.I, Schupp P.E. Artin Groups and Infinite Coxeter Groups. *Inv. Math.*, **72** (1983), 201–220.
2. Bauer G., Otto F. Finite Complete Rewriting Systems and the Complexity of the Word Problem. *Acta Inf.* 21 (1984), 521–540.
3. Book R.V. Confluent and other types of Thue Systems. *J. of the ACM*, 29,1 (1982), 171–182.
4. Bourbaki N. *Groupes et algèbres de Lie*, Ch. 4,5 et 6. Hermann, Paris (1978).

5. Bücken H. Reduktionssysteme und Wortproblem. *Rhein.-Westf. Tech. Hochschule, Aachen, Inst. für Inf.*, Rep. 3 (1979).
6. Cannon J.J., Dimino L.A., Havas G., Watson J.M. Implementation and Analysis of the Todd-Coxeter Algorithm. *Math. Comp.* 27 (1973), 463–490.
7. Cannon J.W., Epstein D.B.A., Holt D.F., Paterson M.S., Thurston W.P. *Word Processing and Group Theory.* Unpublished research notes (1988).
8. Cox D., Little J., O'Shea D. *Ideals, Varieties and Algorithms.* Springer-Verlag (1992).
9. Coxeter H.S.M., Moser W.O.J. *Generators and Relations for Discrete Groups.* Springer-Verlag, 4th ed. (1980).
10. Dershowitz N., Jouannaud J.-P. Rewrite Systems. Ch. 6 of: *Handbook of Theoretical Computer Science, Vol. B*, J. van Leeuwen (ed.), Elsevier and MIT Press (1990), 243–320.
11. Greendlinger M. On Dehn's Algorithm for the Word Problem. *Comm. Pure Appl. Math.*, **13** (1960), 67–83.
12. Huet G. A Complete Proof of Correctness of the Knuth-Bendix Completion Algorithm. *J. Comp. Syst. Sci.* **23**,1 (1981), 11–21.
13. Hullot J.-M. Compilation de Formes Canoniques dans les Théories Equationnelles. Thèse, Univ. Paris-Sud (1980).
14. Knuth D.E., Bendix P. Simple Word Problems in Universal Algebras. in: *Computational Problems in Abstract Algebra*, Leech J. (ed.), Pergamon Press (1970), 263–297.
15. Le Chenadec P. *Canonical Forms in Finitely Presented Algebras and Application to Groups.* Lecture Notes in Theo. Comp. Sci., Pitman-Wiley, London (1986).
16. Le Chenadec P. A Catalogue of Complete Group Presentations. *J. of Symb. Comp.* **2** (1986), 363–381.
17. Le Chenadec P. Analysis of Dehn's Algorithm by Critical Pairs. *Theor. Comp. Sci.* **51** (1987), 27–52.
18. Lyndon R.C., Schupp P.E. *Combinatorial Group Theory.* Springer-Verlag (1977).
19. Marché C. Normalised Rewriting and Normal Completion. *Proc. LICS'94, IEEE Comp. Sci. Press (1994), 394–403.*
20. Schiek H. Ahnlichkeitsanalyse von Gruppenrelationen. *Acta Math.* **96** (1956), 157–252.
21. Schupp P.E. A Survey of Small Cancellation Theory. in: *Word Problems*, W.W. Boone, F.B. Cannonito, R.C. Lyndon (eds.), North-Holland (1973), 569–589.
22. Squier C.G. Word Problems and a Homological Finiteness Condition for Monoids. *J. Pure Appl. Algebra* **49** (1987), 201–217.
23. Tits J. Le Problème des Mots dans les Groupes de Coxeter. *Sympos. Math. Rome* 1967/68, Academic Press, London (1969), 175–185.
24. Zieschang H., Vogt E., Coldeway D.-H. *Surfaces and Planar Discontinuous Groups.* Lecture Notes in Math., 835, Springer-Verlag (1980).

Normalized Rewriting – Application to Ground Completion and Standard Bases

Claude Marché

Lab. de Recherche en Informatique, Bât. 490, Université Paris-Sud et CNRS URA 410, 91405 Orsay cedex, France, E-mail: marche@lri.lri.fr

1 Introduction

We define a new kind of rewriting which is a variant of the usual notion of rewriting modulo an equational theory. This rewrite relation allows us to rewrite modulo theories for which the previous notion was not applicable, including identity, idempotency, Abelian group theory and commutative ring theory. We obtain a new completion algorithm which contains as instances many completion-like algorithms, for example AC (associative-commutative) completion algorithm, constrained AC1-completion, Buchberger's algorithm for computing standard bases of polynomial ideals over a commutative ring.

We investigate then the particular case of completion of ground equations, and we prove by a uniform method the termination of the completion process for a interesting class of equational theories, generalising the result of Narendran and Rusinowitch [23] for ground equations modulo AC, and the result of Buchberger for polynomial ideals, which is the case of ground equations modulo the theory of commutative rings. We obtain also new decidability results on the word problem in ground theories modulo AC and identity, idempotency, nilpotency (new results to our knowledge), and the cases of ground theories modulo the theory of Abelian groups and commutative rings, which is already known in the case when the signature contains only constants, but is new for extended signatures.

2 Rewriting modulo a theory presented by a canonical system

S-normalized rewriting, for an equational theory S, is a variant of the usual notion of rewriting modulo S, which has several advantages but needs S to be presented by a canonical rewrite system (modulo AC if there are AC operators).

For the usual notions on rewriting we refer to the survey of Dershowitz and Jouannaud [7].

2.1 Definition of normalized rewriting — termination

Let S be a set of rules, canonical modulo AC, let us denote by $s\downarrow_S$ the normal form of a term s.

Definition 1. Let R be a set of rules, the *S-normalized* rewrite relation generated by R, denoted $s \xrightarrow[R/S]{} t$, is given by:

$$s \xrightarrow[l\to r/S]{p,\sigma} t \iff \begin{cases} s' = s \downarrow_S \\ s'|_p =_{AC} l\sigma \\ t = s'[r\sigma]_p \end{cases}$$

Example 1. Let S be the canonical rewrite system for AC1$(+,0)$, that is $\{x+0 \to x\}$. We have for example the reduction

$$-(a+b) \xrightarrow[\quad -(x+y)\to(-x)+(-y)/S \quad]{} (-a) + (-b)$$

but the following reduction is not valid

$$-(0+b) \xrightarrow[\quad -(x+y)\to(-x)+(-y)/S \quad]{} (-0) + (-b)$$

because the AC1-normal form of $-(0+b)$ is $(-b)$, which is not an instance of $-(x+y)$.

Termination of rewriting modulo a theory E (i.e. the usual notion) is rather difficult to check, because it needs a reduction ordering on terms compatible with E. On the contrary, termination of normalized rewriting needs only an ordering compatible with AC.

Let us assume now we have an AC-compatible reduction ordering $\succ$ such that each rule of S decreases w.r.t. $\succ$ that is $\xrightarrow[S]{} \subseteq \succ$. We have the following straightforward proposition.

Proposition 2 [21]. *Let R be a set of rules whose rules are decreasing w.r.t. $\succ$. Then the S-normalized rewriting by R terminates.*

2.2 Normalising pairs

We will give the completion algorithm adapted to normalized rewriting in the next section, but for that we need to define the notion of normalising pairs. This will allow us to give an orientation rule which will be general enough to contain as an instance many completion-like algorithms. For lack of space we just explain briefly where the notion of normalising pairs comes from, but the reader may look to [21] for more details.

Normalising pairs will allow in very general *orientation* rule in the completion process. Instead of building a unique rule from a given equation as in AC-completion, orientation in normalised completion will produce a set of rules and a set of equations: we will need to produce several rules at a time when using the symmetrisation technique, and we will need to keep some instances of the original equation as equations, as in AC1-constrained completion [10].

To define these normalising pairs, we need first to define a complexity measure on the algebra of equational proofs. Let $s \downarrow_p$ be the result of S-normalising s at position p (that is $s[(s|_p) \downarrow_S]_p$), and $c(s,p,t)$ be the multiset $\{s\}$ if $s|_p = s$ and $\{s \downarrow_p, t \downarrow_p\}$ otherwise. The complexity of a proof is the multiset of complexities of its

$$C(s \xleftrightarrow{\ \ } _{\text{AC}} t) = \langle \bot, \qquad\qquad \{s\}, \quad \bot, \bot \ \rangle$$

$$C(s \xleftrightarrow[l=r]{\sigma,p} t) = \langle \{s \downarrow_p, t \downarrow_p\}, \{s,t\}, \bot, \bot \ \rangle$$

$$C(s \xrightarrow[l \to r \downarrow_S]{\sigma} t) = \langle \{c(s,p,t)\}, \quad \{s\}, \quad l, \quad r\sigma \ \rangle$$

$$C(s \xrightarrow{\ \ } _s t) = \langle \bot, \qquad\qquad \{s\}, \quad \bot, \bot \ \rangle$$

Fig. 1. Elementary complexities of proofs

elementary sub-proofs, given on Figure 1. $\bot$ is a new minimal element, complexities are compared with the multiset extension of the lexicographic composition of $\succ_{mul}$ for the first two components, $\unrhd_{\text{AC}}$ for the third and $\succ$ for the fourth. $\unrhd_{\text{AC}}$ is the *encompassment* ordering, that is $s \unrhd_{\text{AC}} t$ if $s|_p =_{\text{AC}} t\sigma$.

Definition 3. A pair $(\Theta(u,v), \Psi(u,v))$, where $\Theta(u,v)$ is a set of equations and $\Psi(u,v)$ is a set of rules, is *S-normalising* (w.r.t. $\succ$) if

1. every elementary proof of the form $s \xleftrightarrow[u=v]{\sigma} t$ or $s \xrightarrow[u \to v]{\sigma} t$ such that u, v, σ are in normal form for S, $u \succ v$, there exists a proof with a lower complexity between s and t using equations in $\Theta(u,v)$, rules in $\Psi(u,v)$, S-steps and AC-steps;
2. for all rule $l \to r$ in $\Psi(u,v)$, $\Theta(l,r) \subseteq \Theta(u,v)$ and $\Psi(l,r) \subseteq \Psi(u,v)$.

We first give a definition of a S-normalising pair for an arbitrary S. Let us denote by $\mathcal{FP}os(s)$ the set of non-variable positions of a term s and $\text{CSU}_{\text{AC}}(s,t)$ a complete set of AC-unifiers of s and t.

Definition 4. Let $\Theta_{gen}(u,v)$ be the union of

$$\{u\theta[r\theta]_q = v\theta \mid q \in \mathcal{FP}os(u), l \to r \in S, \theta \in \text{CSU}_{\text{AC}}(u|_q, l) \ S\text{-irreducible}\}$$

and

$$\{l\theta[v\theta]_q = r\theta \mid q \in \mathcal{FP}os(l), q \neq \Lambda, l \to r \in S, \theta \in \text{CSU}_{\text{AC}}(u, l|_q) \ S\text{-irreducible}\}$$

and let $\Psi_{gen}(u,v) = \{u \to v\}$.

Proposition 5. *The pair $(\Theta_{gen}(u,v), \Psi_{gen}(u,v))$ is S-normalising for any arbitrary theory S.*

Example 2. Let $S = \text{AC1} = \{z + 0 \to z\}$. Let us compute $\Theta_{gen}(-(x+y), (-x) + (-y))$: we have to unify $x + y$ and $z + 0$, leading to 4 unifiers

$$\begin{cases} x \mapsto v_1 \\ y \mapsto 0 \\ z \mapsto v_1 \end{cases} \begin{cases} x \mapsto 0 \\ y \mapsto v_1 \\ z \mapsto v_1 \end{cases} \begin{cases} x \mapsto v_1 \\ y \mapsto v_2 + 0 \\ z \mapsto v_1 + v_2 \end{cases} \begin{cases} x \mapsto v_1 + 0 \\ y \mapsto v_2 \\ z \mapsto v_1 + v_2 \end{cases}$$

The last two are S-reducible hence we throw them away.

$$\Theta_{gen}(-(x+y),(-x)+(-y)) = \begin{cases} (-x) = (-x) + (-0) \\ (-y) = (-0) + (-y) \end{cases}$$

We see on this example that we get exactly the set of *forbidden instances* of $-(x+y) = (-x) + (-y)$ in constrained AC1-completion [10].

2.3 Normalized completion

ORIENT
$$E \cup \{u = v\}; R \vdash E \cup \Theta(u,v); R \cup \Psi(u,v)$$
$$\text{if } u = u{\downarrow}_S, \ v = v{\downarrow}_S, \ u \succ v$$

DEDUCE
$$E; R \vdash E \cup \{u = v\}; R \text{ if } u = v \in \mathrm{CP}_T(R)$$

NORMALIZE
$$E \cup \{u = v\}; R \vdash E \cup \{u{\downarrow}_S = v{\downarrow}_S\}; R$$

DELETE
$$E \cup \{u = v\}; R \vdash E; R \text{ if } u =_{\mathrm{AC}} v$$

COMPOSE
$$E; R \cup \{u \to v\} \vdash E; R \cup \{u \to v'\} \text{ if } v \xrightarrow[R/S]{} v'$$

SIMPLIFY
$$E \cup \{u = v\}; R \vdash E \cup \{u' = v\}; R \text{ if } u \xrightarrow[R/S]{} u'$$

COLLAPSE
$$E; R \cup \{u \to v\} \vdash E \cup \{u' = v\}; R \text{ if } \begin{cases} l \to r \in R \\ u \xrightarrow[l \to r/S]{\theta, p} u' \\ p \neq \Lambda \text{ or} \\ p = \Lambda \text{ and } \theta \text{ is not a renaming or} \\ p = \Lambda, \ \theta \text{ renaming and } u \succ r\theta \end{cases}$$

Fig. 2. Inference rules of generic S-normalized completion

Let us give now the completion algorithm corresponding to S-normalized rewriting. This algorithm is described by the set of inference rules of Figure 2. Orientation of an equation replace the given equation by its S-normalising pair, while deduction remains similar to the usual case ($\mathrm{CP}_T(R)$ denotes the set of critical pairs of R

modulo T), but a very important point is that unification can be done modulo any theory T between AC and $S \cup$ AC. This allows to choose a theory

1. not too "big" in order to keep unification decidable and finitary (for example we avoid ACD-unification);
2. not too "small" in order to have a small number of unifiers: if possible, we choose AC1 or ACI unification instead of AC-unification, because they generate much less solutions [16].

Definition 6. A S-normalized completion algorithm takes as input a set of equations E_0 and an AC-reduction ordering $\succ$, and produces a finite or infinite sequence $(E_n; R_n)$ where $R_0 = \emptyset$ and for all i, $E_i; R_i \vdash E_{i+1}; R_{i+1}$. Let

$$E_\infty = \bigcup_{n=0}^\infty \left(\bigcap_{i=n}^\infty E_i \right) , \ R_\infty = \bigcup_{n=0}^\infty \left(\bigcap_{i=n}^\infty R_i \right)$$

Completion *fails* if E_∞ is not empty, *succeeds* otherwise. Completion *diverges* if the derivation is infinite.

A derivation $E_0; R_0 \vdash E_1; R_1 \vdash \ldots$ is *fair* if every critical pairs between two persisting rules are computed, i.e.:

$$CP_T(R_\infty) \subset \bigcup_{i=0}^\infty E_i.$$

A completion strategy is *fair* if any derivations it produces is fair.

The proof of the following completeness theorem is by the *normalisation proof method* [2, 3].

Theorem 7. *If* (Θ, Ψ) *is* S-*normalising, if completion is fair and does not fail, then*

$$\forall s, t \ \ s =_{E_0 \cup \text{AC} \cup S} t \Longleftrightarrow \exists u, v \underset{R_\infty/S}{\overset{s}{\searrow}} \overset{*}{} \quad \overset{t}{\underset{R_\infty/S}{\nearrow}} \overset{*}{}$$

$$u \xrightarrow[S]{*} u{\downarrow}_S =_{\text{AC}} v{\downarrow}_S \xleftarrow[S]{*} v$$

2.4 Modularity

We show now that we can easily mix two theories if they don't share any symbol (i.e. are disjoint).

Theorem 8. *Let* S_1 *and* S_2 *be two disjoint canonical systems included in the same reduction ordering.*

(i) $S_1 \cup S_2$ *is canonical;*

(ii) if (Θ_1, Ψ_1) *is* S_1-*normalising and* (Θ_2, Ψ_2) *is* S_2-*normalising then* $(\Theta_1 \cup \Theta_2, \Psi_1 \cup \Psi_2)$ *is* $S_1 \cup S_2$-*normalising;*

(iii) if for a set of rules R, $\xrightarrow[R/S_1]{*}$ *and* $\xrightarrow[R/S_2]{*}$ *are convergent then* $\xrightarrow[R/(S_1 \cup S_2)]{*}$ *is convergent.*

2.5 Examples

We show now that it is interesting in some cases to give another form of normalising pair, to gain in efficiency. In particular, we will show that the algorithm for computing standard bases of polynomial ideals over $\mathbb{Z}$ is an instance of CR-normalized completion for a well-chosen CR-normalising pair.

2.6 Some shallow theories

Theory S	canonical system	$\Theta_S(u, v)$
$AC1(+, 0)$	$x + 0 \to x$	$\{u\theta = v\theta \mid \theta = x \mapsto 0, x + w \trianglelefteq u\}$
$ACI(+)$	$x + x \to x$	$\{u\sigma = v\sigma \mid \sigma = mgu_{AC}(l_1, l_2), l1 + l2 \trianglelefteq u\}$
$AC1I(+, 0)$	$x + x \to x,\ x + 0 \to x$	$\Theta_{AC1}(u, v) \cup \Theta_{ACI}(u, v)$
$AC0(., 0)$	$x.0 \to 0$	$\{u\theta = v\theta \mid \theta = x \mapsto 0, x.w \trianglelefteq u\}$
$ACN(+, 0)$	$x + x \to 0$	$\{u\sigma = v\sigma \mid \sigma = mgu_{AC}(l_1, l_2), l1 + l2 \trianglelefteq u\}$

Fig. 3. Set Θ_S for some shallow theories S

For theories S=AC1, ACI, AC1I, AC0, ACN, let $\Psi_S(u, v) = \{u \to v\}$ and Θ_S given in figure 3.

Proposition 9. *The pair defined above is S-normalising.*

Example 3. Figure 4 shows the completion of boolean rings theory modulo nilpotence of addition with identity 0, and idempotence of multiplication with identity 1.

2.7 Normalized completion modulo the theory of Abelian groups

$$S = AG \begin{cases} x + 0 \to x \\ x + (-x) \to 0 \\ -0 \to 0 \\ -(-x) \to x \\ -(x + y) \to (-x) + (-y) \end{cases}$$

We give now an optimized AG-normalising pair which assumes that the ordering $\succ$ is the *rpo* with a precedence of the form $\cdots > - > + > 0$, and such that $+$ has the multiset status.

Definition 10. For an equation $u = v$ of the form $n_1 u_1 + \cdots + n_k u_k = m_1 t_1 + \cdots + m_l t_l$, with $\forall j \geq 2,\ u_1 \succ u_j$ and $\forall j,\ u_1 \succ t_j$, let

$$s = n_1 u_1$$
$$t = -n_2 u_2 - \cdots - n_k u_k + m_1 t_1 + \cdots + m_l t_l$$

Source	Script of completion
operators	Orienting the equation x+-(x) = 0
+,. : AC	into
0,1 : constant	{[1] x+-(x) -> 0} (1 rules)
- : 1	with critical equations
x,y,z : variable	{...} (3 equations)
	Orienting the equation 0 = -(0)
theory AC1N(+,0)	into
AC1I(.,1)	{[2] -(0) -> 0} (1 rules)
	with critical equations
axioms	{}
x+-(x) = 0;	Orienting the equation x.(y+z) = (x.y)+(x.z)
x.(y+z) = (x.y)+(x.z);	into
	{[3] x.(y+z) -> (x.y)+(x.z)} (1 rules)
order rpo 1>.>->+>0	with critical equations
	{...} (33 equations)
end	Orienting the equation x.0 = 0
	into
	{[4] x.0 -> 0} (1 rules)
	with critical equations
	{...} (7 equations)
	Orienting the equation x = -(-(x))
	into
	{[5] -(-(x)) -> x} (1 rules)
	with critical equations
	{}
	Orienting the equation y+-(x+y) = -(x)
	into
	{[6] y+-(x+y) -> -(x)} (1 rules)
	with critical equations
	{...} (28 equations)
	Orienting the equation x = -(x)
	into
	{[7] -(x) -> x} (1 rules)
	with critical equations
	{}
	Result:
	{[4] x.0 -> 0,
	[7] -(x) -> x,
	[3] x.(y+z) -> (x.y)+(x.z)} (3 rules)
	Number of calls to AC matching : 4615
	Number of successful calls : 500 (10%)
	Number of calls to AC unification : 21
	Number of critical pairs generated : 117
	User time : 4.970 s
	System time : 0.250 s

Fig. 4. Completion of Boolean rings modulo $ACN(+, 0)$ and $AC1I(., 1)$

and

$$\Psi_{AG}(u,v) = \begin{cases} n_1 u_1 \to -n_2 u_2 - \cdots - n_k u_k + m_1 t_1 + \cdots + m_l t_l \\ -u_1 \to (n_1 - 1)u_1 + n_2 u_2 + \cdots + n_k u_k - m_1 t_1 + \cdots - m_l t_l \end{cases}$$

$$\Theta_{AG}(u,v) = \Theta_{AC1}(s,t) \cup \Sigma_1(s,t) \cup \Sigma_2(s,t)$$

where

$$\Sigma_1(s,t) = CP_{AC}(s \to t, x + (-x) \to 0)$$

$$\Sigma_2(s,t) = \{s\sigma = t\sigma | \sigma = x \mapsto 0 \text{ or } -y \text{ or } y + z \text{ if } -x \in u\}$$

Proposition 11. *The pair (Θ_{AG}, Ψ_{AG}) is AG-normalising.*

We can remark that this AG-normalising pair is a generalization to the non-ground case of the symmetrization method of Le Chenadec [19].

Example 4. Figure 5 shows the completion of boolean rings theory modulo Abelian groups theory $AG(+, 0, -)$ and idempotency $AC1I(., 1)$.

Example 5. Figure 6 compares completion of commutative rings modulo AC, AC1 and AG. Efficiency of AG-normalized completion is obvious.

2.8 Completion modulo the theory of commutative rings

$$S = CR \begin{cases} x + 0 \to x & \qquad x * (y + z) \to (x * y) + (x * z) \\ x + (-x) \to 0 & \qquad x * 1 \to x \\ -0 \to 0 & \qquad x * 0 \to 0 \\ -(-x) \to x & \qquad x * (-y) \to -(x * y) \\ -(x + y) \to (-x) + (-y) \end{cases}$$

The ordering $\succ$ is the *extended-apo* [6, 21] with a precedence of the form $\cdots > * > - > + > 0$, such that $+$ and $*$ have multiset status.

Definition 12. Let $u = n_1 u_1 + \cdots + n_k u_k$ and $v = m_1 t_1 + \cdots + m_l t_l$, such that $\forall j \geq 2$, $u_1 \succ u_j$ and $\forall j$, $u_1 \succ t_j$, let

$$s = n_1 u_1$$

$$t = -n_2 u_2 - \cdots - n_k u_k + m_1 t_1 + \cdots + m_l t_l$$

$$\Sigma_1(u,v) = CP_{AC}(s \to t, x + (-x) \to 0)$$

$$\Sigma_2(u,v) = \{u\sigma = v\sigma | \sigma = x \mapsto 0 \text{ or } -y \text{ or } y + z \text{ if } -x \trianglelefteq u$$

$$\Sigma_3(u,v) = \{u\sigma = v\sigma | \sigma = x \mapsto y + z \text{ or } -y \text{ if } x * w \trianglelefteq u$$

$$\Theta_{CR}(u,v) = \Theta_{AC1}(s,t) \cup \Theta_{AC0}(s,t) \cup \Sigma_1(s,t) \cup \Sigma_2(s,t) \cup \Sigma_3(s,t)$$

$$\Psi_{CR}(u,v) = \{n_1 u_1 \to -n_2 u_2 - \cdots - n_k u_k + m_1 t_1 + \cdots + m_l t_l\}$$

$$\cup \{-u_1 \to (n_1 - 1)u_1 + n_2 u_2 + \cdots + n_k u_k - m_1 t_1 + \cdots - m_l t_l$$

$$n_1 x * u_1 \to -n_2 x * u_2 - \cdots - n_k x * u_k + m_1 x * t_1 + \cdots + m_l x * t_l$$

$$-x * u_1 \to (n_1 - 1)x * u_1 + n_2 x * u_2 + \cdots + n_k x * u_k$$

$$-m_1 x * t_1 \cdots - m_l x * t_l \quad \}$$

if $n_1 \geq 2$, where x is a new variable

Source	Script of completion

operators
  +,. : AC
  0,1 : constant
  -   : 1
  x,y,z : variable
 	
theory AG(+,0,-)
      AC1I(.,1)
 	
axioms
  x.(y+z) = (x.y)+(x.z);
 	
order rpo 1>.>->+>0
 	
end
	Orienting the equation x.(y+z) = (x.y)+(x.z)
	into
	{[1] x.(y+z) -> (x.y)+(x.z)} (1 rules)
	with critical equations
	{...} (29 equations)
	Orienting the equation x.y = (x.y)+(x.0)
	into
	{[2] x.0 -> 0} (1 rules)
	with critical equations
	{...} (32 equations)
	Orienting the equation 0 = (x.-(z))+(x.z)
	into
	{[3] x.-(z) -> -(x.z)} (1 rules)
	with critical equations
	{...} (32 equations)
	Orienting the equation -(x)+-(x) = 0
	into
	{[5] x+x -> 0,
	[4] -(x) -> -(0)+x} (2 rules)
	with critical equations
	{...} (7 equations)
	
	Result:
	{[4] -(x) -> x,
	[5] x+x -> 0,
	[2] x.0 -> 0,
	[1] x.(y+z) -> (x.y)+(x.z)} (4 rules)
	
	Number of calls to AC matching : 7512
	Number of successful calls : 635 (8%)
	Number of calls to AC unification : 23
	Number of critical pairs generated : 138
	User time : 8.770 s
	System time : 0.240 s

Fig. 5. Boolean rings theory modulo $AG(+, 0, -)$ and $AC1I(., 1)$

	modulo AC	modulo AC1	modulo AG
Computation time	53.69"	47.10"	2.88"
number of calls to AC unification	136	76	11
number of critical pairs	537	412	30
number of calls to AC matching	23925	21246	1229

Fig. 6. Commutative rings modulo AC, AC1 and AG

Proposition 13. *The pair* (Θ_{CR}, Ψ_{CR}) *is CR-normalising.*

We will see an example of CR-normalised completion in the next section.

3 Decidability of the E-ground word problem

Definition 14. For a given set of equations E, a E-*ground theory* is an equational theory presented by E and any set of ground equations. The E-*ground word problem* is the uniform word problem of E-ground theories.

Our aim is to give a decision procedure for the word problem of E-ground theories, for some interesting E, by building an E-normalized canonical system by completion. Hence, we now look to the problem of termination of S-normalized completion, if the equations given are ground. We prove this termination for various interesting S by an almost uniform method. This give then decidability results for the uniform word problem of S-ground theories, including some already known cases, such as the AC-ground case [23], AG-ground and CR-ground cases when they are only constants [19] which contains in particular the result of existence of standard bases of ideals of polynomials over $\mathbb{Z}$ [13, 11, 14].

3.1 General Results

We assume now that $\succ$ is total [23, 21]. Let F be the set of symbols which appear in S. Because of lack of space, we omit the proofs, they can be found in [21].

Definition 15. The *generator set* of a term u w.r.t. F is given by

$$\begin{cases} \gamma_F(u) = \{u\} \text{ if } \mathcal{H}ead(u) \notin F \\ \gamma_F(u) = \bigcup_{1 \le i \le n} \gamma_F(u_i) \text{ if } u = f(u_1, \ldots, u_n) \text{ with } f \in F \end{cases}$$

Let E be a set of equations and R be a set of rules. The *generator set* of E and R is given by:

$$\Gamma_F(u, v) = \gamma_F(u) \cup \gamma_F(v)$$

$$G_F(E, R) = \bigcup_{u=v \in E} \Gamma_F(u, v) \cup \bigcup_{u \to v \in R} \Gamma_F(u, v)$$

Theorem 16. *Let* $E; R \overset{*}{\vdash} E'; R'$ *be a sequence of inferences such that* $E'; R'$ *are no longer simplifyable, that is neither* NORMALIZE, DELETE, SIMPLIFY, COMPOSE *nor* COLLAPSE *can be applied. Then*

$$G_F(E, R) \succeq_{\text{mul}} G_F(E', R')$$

Definition 17. We say that the strategy *simplifies first* if the simplification rules (DELETE, NORMALIZE, SIMPLIFY, COMPOSE and COLLAPSE) have priority over ORIENT and DEDUCE.

Theorem 18. *If the strategy simplifies first, and completion diverges, then R_∞ is infinite, and contains infinitely many rules whose root symbol is in F.*

Now, for each of the following cases, in order to prove termination of completion, we suppose by contradiction that the completion diverges, we use the previous theorem to obtain infinitely many rules of a particular form, and then we apply a particular case Higman's lemma [9] which is the following.

Lemma 19. *If $\preceq$ is a well-quasi-ordering over a set $\mathcal{E}$, $\preceq_{mul}$ is a well-quasi-ordering over $\mathcal{M}(\mathcal{E})$. In particular, if F is a finite set and $M_1, M_2, \ldots$ is an infinite sequence of multisets of elements of F, there exist i and j such that $M_i \subseteq M_j$.*

3.2 Ground completion modulo AC1, ACI, AC1I, AC1N and AC0

If we specialize definition of normalising pairs to ground equations, in these cases, we obtain

$$\begin{cases} \Theta_S(u, v) = \emptyset \\ \Psi_S(u, v) = \{u \to v\} \end{cases}$$

To prove termination of completion, we assume by contradiction that the completion diverges, it can be easily seen that ORIENT and DEDUCE do not modify G_F, hence by theorem 18 we know then that there are infinitely many rules whose root symbol of the lefthand side is an AC symbol $+$. We have an infinite sequence of rules $l_1 = l_{1,1} + \cdots + l_{1,k_1} \to r_1, l_2 = l_{2,1} + \cdots + l_{2,k_2} \to r_2, \ldots$ in R_∞. Each $l_{i,j}$ belongs to $G_F(R_\infty)$, but this set is finite by theorem 16. We apply lemma 19 on multisets $M_1 = \{l_{1,1}, \ldots, l_{1,k_1}\}, M_2 = \{l_{2,1}, \ldots, l_{2,k_2}\}, \ldots$ hence there exist i and j such that $M_i \subseteq M_j$ (modulo AC), hence l_i is a subterm modulo AC of l_j, hence $l_j \to r_j$ is simplifyable, a contradiction.

Theorem 20. *Every AC1-ground theory (resp. ACI, AC1I, ACN, AC0) has a AC1-normalized (resp. ACI-, AC1I-, ACN-, AC0-) canonical system, and consequently has a decidable word problem.*

3.3 Ground completion modulo the theory of Abelian groups

For an AC-compatible total reduction ordering, we use the *rpo* with a total precedence such that $\cdots > - > + > 0$, with multiset status for $+$ and lexicographic status for the other symbols. In the ground case, $\Theta_{AG}(u, v)$ becomes empty.

We can remark now that we have obtained an algorithm similar to the completion with symmetrization of Le Chenadec [19]. In fact here this is slightly more general since we allow non constant symbols. The termination of completion (already shown by Le Chenadec) is analogous to the AC1 case, with $F = \{+, -, 0\}$.

Theorem 21. *Every AG-ground equational theory has an AG-normalized canonical system, hence its word problem is decidable.*

Example 6. Figure 7 gives benchmarks of completion of a finitely presented group $\langle a, b, c; -3a + 2b + 3c = 0, 2a + 2b - 2c = 0 \rangle$. The AG-normalized canonical system contains $a \to 4b + c$, $10b \to 0$ et $-b \to 9b$, this shows in particular that the group is isomorphic to $\mathbb{Z}/{10\mathbb{Z}} \times \mathbb{Z}$.

	modulo AC	modulo AC1	modulo AG
Computation time	4' 30"	3' 37"	1" 7
number of calls to AC unification	96	82	9
number of critical pairs	804	779	4
number of calls to AC matching	119823	117289	773

Fig. 7. Completion of a finitely generated Abelian group

3.4 Ground Completion modulo the theory of commutative rings

We need a total AC-compatible reduction ordering which orients the rules of the usual canonical system for commutative rings. It is not easy to define such an ordering, we assume here we have such an ordering, the reader may look to [21] for information.

In the normalising pair, the set Θ becomes empty in the ground case.

Example 7. $\Psi_{CR}(2(a * a) - 3(b * b * b), -a + 4b)$ contains the rules

$$\begin{cases} 2(a * a) \rightarrow -a + 3(b * b * b) + 4b \\ 2(a * a * z) \rightarrow -a * z + 3(b * b * b * z) + 4(b * z) \\ -(a * a) \rightarrow a * a + a - 3(b * b * b) - 4b \\ -(a * a * z) \rightarrow a * a * z + a * z - 3(b * b * b * z) - 4(b * z) \end{cases}$$

The completion algorithm obtained is similar to Buchberger's algorithm for computing standard bases of polynomial ideals over $\mathbb{Z}$ [11, 15]. This is also analogous to the technique of symmetrization of Le Chenadec.

The proof of termination of completion is similar to the one for Abelian groups, this generalize the proof of termination, known for the Buchberger's and the Le Chenadec's algorithms, to the general case where there are non constant symbols.

Theorem 22. *Every CR-ground theory has a CR-normalized canonical system, and consequently has a decidable word problem.*

Example 8. To illustrate how a standard basis is computed by the normalized completion algorithm, let us show how to compute a basis for the ideal $(2X^2Y - Y, 3XY^2 - X)$. The source file to give to our implementation and the result is shown figure 8, which corresponds to the basis $\{2X^2Y - Y, X^2Y^2 - X^2 + Y^2, 3Y^2 - 2X^2, 2X^3 - X\}$.

Of course, this method is less efficient than algorithms dedicated to standard bases computation, because we still use general AC unification and general AC matching, which costs much time.

Source	Script of completion
operators	Result:
+,* : AC	{[12] (x*Y*Y)+(x*Y*Y)+(x*Y*Y) -> (x*X*X)+(x*X*X),
0,1 : constant	[17] (X*X*X)+(X*X*X) -> X,
- : unary	[16] (x*X*X*X)+(x*X*X*X) -> x*X,
X,Y,Z : constant	[9] X*X*Y*Y -> (Y*Y)+(Y*Y)+-(X*X),
x,y,z : variable	[1] -(x*X*X*Y) -> -(x*Y)+(x*X*X*Y),
	[14] -(x*X*X*X) -> -(x*X)+(x*X*X*X),
theory CR(+,0,-,*,1)	[3] (x*X*X*Y)+(x*X*X*Y) -> x*Y,
	[13] (Y*Y)+(Y*Y)+(Y*Y) -> (X*X)+(X*X),
axioms	[2] -(X*X*Y) -> -(Y)+(X*X*Y),
(X*X*Y) + (X*X*Y) +	[15] -(X*X*X) -> -(X)+(X*X*X),
-(Y) = 0;	[4] (X*X*Y)+(X*X*Y) -> Y,
(X*Y*Y) + (X*Y*Y) +	[11] -(Y*Y) -> -(X*X)+-(X*X)+(Y*Y)+(Y*Y),
(X*Y*Y) + -(X) = 0;	[10] -(x*Y*Y) -> -(x*X*X)+-(x*X*X)+(x*Y*Y)+(x*Y*Y)}
	(13 rules)
order	
rpo Y>X>1>*>->0>+ ;	Number of calls to AC matching : 17369
+ mul, * mul	Number of successful calls : 581 (3%)
	Number of calls to AC unification : 184
end	Number of critical pairs generated : 119
	User time : 24.780 s
	System time : 0.470 s

Fig. 8. Computation of a standard basis

4 Undecidability results

We have obtained decidability results in the previous section. We recall now already known undecidability results (see figure 9).

1. Decidability of word problem of ground equational theories has been shown first in 1954 by Ackermann [1].
2. Decidability of word problem in AC-ground theories has been proved by Narendran and Rusinovitch in 1991 [23], and is known since 1963 by Emilicev [8] in the particular case of finitely presented commutative semi-groups.
3. Undecidability of word problem in A-ground theories is known since 1947 because it is a consequence of undecidability of word porblem in Thue systems, proved independently by Post and Markov [26, 22].
4. Undecidability of word problem of G-ground theories is a consequence of the undecidability of word problem in finitely presented groups, and is known since 1955 by Novikov and Boone [24, 4, 28].
5. Undecidability of word problem of ACD-ground theories has been proved by Marché in 1991 [20].
6. Decidability of word problem in AC1, ACI or ACI ground theories is a consequence of the existence of a normalized canonical system.

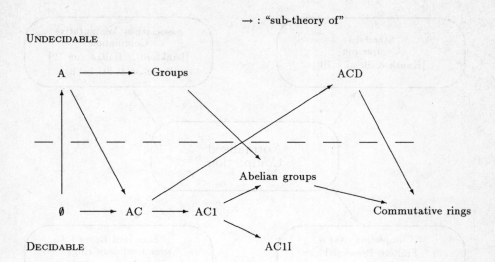

Fig. 9. Decidability of the E-ground word problem for some E

7. Decidability of word problem in AG-ground theories is known since 1966 [27] for the particular case of finitely presented Abelian groups, and a consequence of the existence of an AG-normalized canonical system in the general case.
8. Decidability of word problem in CR-ground theories is known since 1984 [12, 13] for the particular case of polynomial ideals, and a consequence of the existence of an CR-normalized canonical system in the general case.

5   Conclusion

The notion of S-normalized rewriting and S-normalized completion algorithm, whose completeness has been proved for an arbitrary S, allows us to unify in a single way a variety of completion-like algorithm, as shown on figure 10.

References

1. W. Ackermann. *Solvable Cases of the Decision Problem*. North-Holland, Amsterdam, 1954.
2. Leo Bachmair. *Proof Methods for Equational Theories*. PhD thesis, University of Illinois at Urbana-Champaign, 1987.
3. Leo Bachmair and Nachum Dershowitz. Completion for rewriting modulo a congruence. *Theoretical Computer Science*, 67(2&3):173–201, October 1989.
4. W. Boone. The word problem. *Annals of Math.*, 70:207–265, 1959.

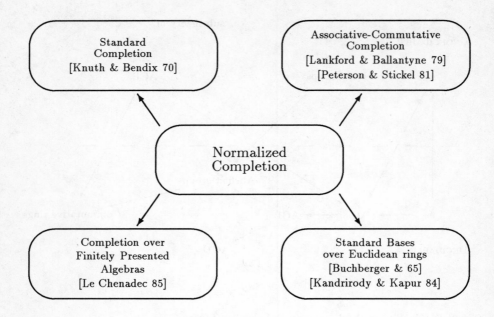

Fig. 10. Various instances of normalized completion

5. Bruno Buchberger. *An Algorithm for Finding a Basis for the Residue Class Ring of a Zero-Dimensional Ideal.* PhD thesis, University of Innsbruck, Austria, 1965. (in German).
6. Catherine Delor and Laurence Puel. Extension of the associative path ordering to a chain of associative-commutative symbols. In *Proc. 5th Rewriting Techniques and Applications, Montréal, LNCS 690,* 1993.
7. Nachum Dershowitz and Jean-Pierre Jouannaud. Rewrite systems. In J. van Leeuwen, editor, *Handbook of Theoretical Computer Science,* volume B, pages 243–309. North-Holland, 1990.
8. V. A. Emiličev. On algorithmic decidability of certain mass problems in the theory of commutative semigroups. *Sbirsk. Mat. Ž,* 4:788–798, 1963. In russian.
9. Graham Higman. Ordering by divisibility in abstract algebras. *Proceedings of the London Mathematical Society,* 2(3):326–336, September 1952.
10. Jean-Pierre Jouannaud and Claude Marché. Termination and completion modulo associativity, commutativity and identity. *Theoretical Computer Science,* 104:29–51, 1992.
11. Abdelilah Kandri-Rody and Deepak Kapur. An algorithm for computing the Gröbner basis of a polynomial ideal over an Euclidean ring. Technical Report 84CRD045, CRD, General Electric Company, Schenectady, New-York, December 1984.
12. Abdelilah Kandri-Rody and Deepak Kapur. Algorithms for computing gröbner bases of polynomial ideals over various Euclidian rings. In *Proc. Eurosam 84, Cambridge, England.* Springer-Verlag, 1984.

13. Abdelilah Kandri-Rody and Deepak Kapur. Computing the grobner basis of an ideal in polynomial rings over the integers. In V.E. Golden and M.A. Hussain, editors, *Proc. of the Thirds MACSYMA Users'Conference*, July 1984.

14. Abdelilah Kandri-Rody, Deepak Kapur, and Franz Winkler. Knuth-Bendix procedure and Buchberger algorithm — a synthesis. In *Proc. of the 20th Int. Symp. on Symbolic and Algebraic Computation, Portland, Oregon*, pages 55–67, 1989.

15. Deepak Kapur and Paliath Narendran. Constructing Gröbner bases for a polynomial ideal. Presented at the workshop *Combinatorial algorithms in algebraic structures* at Europaische Akademie, Otzenhause, 1985.

16. Claude Kirchner, editor. *Unification*. Academic Press, 1990.

17. Donald E. Knuth and Peter B. Bendix. Simple word problems in universal algebras. In J. Leech, editor, *Computational Problems in Abstract Algebra*, pages 263–297. Pergamon Press, 1970.

18. Dallas S. Lankford and A. M. Ballantyne. Decision procedures for simple equational theories with commutative-associative axioms: Complete sets of commutative-associative reductions. Research Report Memo ATP-39, Department of Mathematics and Computer Science, University of Texas, Austin, Texas, USA, August 1977.

19. Philippe Le Chenadec. *Canonical forms in finitely presented algebras*. Pitman, London, 1986.

20. Claude Marché. The word problem of ACD-ground theories is undecidable. *International Journal of Foundations of Computer Science*, 3(1):81–92, 1992.

21. Claude Marché. Réécriture modulo une théorie présentée par un système convergent et décidabilité des problèmes du mot dans certains classes de théories équationnelles. Thèse de Doctorat, Université de Paris-Sud, France, 1993.

22. A. A. Markov. On the impossibility of certain algorithms in the theory of associative systems. *Dokl. Akad. Nauk SSSR*, 55(7):587–590, 1947. In Russian, English translation in C.R. Acad. Sci. URSS, 55, 533-586.

23. Paliath Narendran and Michaël Rusinowitch. Any ground associative-commutative theory has a finite canonical system. In Ronald V. Book, editor, *Proc. 4th Rewriting Techniques and Applications, LNCS 488*, Como, Italy, April 1991. Springer-Verlag.

24. P. S. Novikov. On the algorithmic unsolvability of the word problem in group theory. *Trudy Mat. Inst. Steklov*, 44:1–143, 1955. in Russian.

25. Gerald E. Peterson and Mark E. Stickel. Complete sets of reductions for some equational theories. *Journal of the ACM*, 28(2):233–264, April 1981.

26. Emil L. Post. Recursive unsolvability of a problem of Thue. *Journal of Symbolic Logic*, 13:1–11, 1947.

27. D. A. Smith. A basis algorithm for finitely generated Abelian groups. *Maths. Algorithms*, I(1), 1966.

28. John Stillwell. The word problem and the isomorphism problem for groups. *Bulletin of the American Mathematical Society*, 6(1):33–56, January 1982.

Equational Reasoning with 2-dimensional Diagrams

Yves Lafont

Laboratoire de Mathématiques Discrètes, UPR 9016 du CNRS
163 avenue de Luminy - Case 930 - 13288 Marseille Cedex 9, France
Email: lafont@lmd.univ-mrs.fr

Abstract

The significance of the 2-dimensional calculus, which goes back to Penrose, has already been pointed out by Joyal and Street. Independently, Burroni has introduced a general notion of n-dimensional presentation and he has shown that the equational logic of terms is a special case of 2-dimensional calculus.

Here, we propose a combinatorial definition of 2-dimensional diagrams and a simple method for proving that certain monoidal categories are finitely 2-presentable. In particular, we consider Burroni's presentation of finite maps and we extend it to the case of finite relations.

This paper should serve as a reference for our future work on symbolic computation, including a theory of 2-dimensional rewriting and the design of software for interactive diagrammatic reasoning.

1 From terms to diagrams

Terms are one of the basic ingredients of logic. Consider for instance the theory of commutative rings, expressed by means of function symbols $+$, $\times$ (both of arity 2), $-$ (of arity 1), 0, 1 (both of arity 0) and variables. This theory is called *algebraic* because it consists of equations between terms. It is generated by the following axioms:

$$(x + y) + z = x + (y + z), \qquad 0 + x = x, \qquad x + y = y + x, \qquad (-x) + x = 0,$$

$$(x \times y) \times z = x \times (y \times z), \qquad 1 \times x = x, \qquad x \times y = y \times x,$$

$$x \times (y + z) = (x \times y) + (x \times z), \qquad x \times 0 = 0.$$

From those axioms, we derive theorems such as

$$-(-x) = x, \qquad (x + y) \times (x + (-y)) = (x \times x) + (-(y \times y)),$$

using the rules of *equational logic*, which are independent of the theory, and can be expressed as follows:

$$\frac{}{u = u} \qquad \frac{u = v \quad v = w}{u = w} \qquad \frac{u = v}{w[u/x] = w[v/x]} \qquad \frac{u = v}{u[w/x] = v[w/x]}$$

In these inference rules, u, v, w range over terms and $u[v/x]$ is the term u where all occurrences of the variable x have been replaced by v.

1.1 Lawvere's approach

Fix a set Σ of symbols with arities, and consider the following category $\mathbf{T}(\Sigma)$:

- The objects are natural numbers.
- A morphism $U : p \to q$ is given by a sequence $u_1, \ldots, u_q$ of terms built with symbols in Σ and variables in $\{x_1, \ldots, x_p\}$.
- The composition is defined by substitution. More precisely, if $U : p \to q$ and $V : q \to r$ are morphisms, then $V \circ U : p \to r$ is given by the sequence $w_1, \ldots, w_r$ where w_i is $v_i[u_1/x_1, \ldots, u_q/x_q]$. The identity on p is given by the sequence $x_1, \ldots, x_p$.

This $\mathbf{T}(\Sigma)$ is a *cartesian category* (or *category with finite products*, in the terminology of [Mac71]):

- The *cartesian product* of p by q is $p + q$. The *cartesian unit* (or *terminal object*) is 0.
- The *projections* $\pi_{p,q}^1 : p + q \to p$ and $\pi_{p,q}^2 : p + q \to q$ are given by the sequences $x_1, \ldots, x_p$ and $x_{p+1}, \ldots, x_{p+q}$.
- For any $U : r \to p$ and $V : r \to q$, there is a unique morphism $W = \langle U, V \rangle : r \to p + q$ such that $\pi_{p,q}^1 \circ W = U$ and $\pi_{p,q}^2 \circ W = V$:

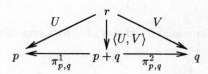

It is given by the sequence $u_1, \ldots, u_p, v_1, \ldots, v_q$. Similarly, for any object p, there is a unique morphism from p to 0, which is given by the empty sequence.

In fact, $\mathbf{T}(\Sigma)$ is the *free cartesian category* generated by Σ. Furthermore, if $\mathcal{E}$ is a set of equations on Σ, we can introduce the category $\mathbf{T}(\Sigma; \mathcal{E})$, whose objects are natural numbers and whose morphisms are sequences of terms modulo $\mathcal{E}$. This $\mathbf{T}(\Sigma; \mathcal{E})$ is also a cartesian category, and any model of $\mathcal{E}$ can be seen as a functor Φ from $\mathbf{T}(\Sigma; \mathcal{E})$ to the category of sets which preserves the cartesian structure. This functor is defined as follows:

- $\Phi(p) = M^p$ where M is the underlying set of the model.
- If $U : p \to q$ is given by the sequence $u_1, \ldots, u_q$, then $\Phi(U)$ is the map $f : M^p \to M^q$ which is defined by the formula $f(x_1, \ldots, x_p) = (u_1, \ldots, u_q)$ (interpreted in the model).

This is the basis of the *Categorical Logic* (see [Law63, Poi85]) which replaces the *syntactical* notions of terms, substitution, equational logic, ... by the *algebraic* notion of cartesian category.

1.2   Burroni's approach

The structure of cartesian category itself is rather sophisticated. Unlike composition, an operation such as $U, V \mapsto \langle U, V \rangle$ has no simple geometric interpretation. However, at the cost of adding a finite number of symbols and equations, cartesian categories can be replaced by strict monoidal categories, where all operations have an obvious geometric interpretation in dimension 2. This suggests an equational logic of planar diagrams, which is more low-level and also more general than the equational logic of terms. In fact, this kind of logic has already been used for a long time, for instance in theoretical physics (see [PeR86]).

Before giving a formal definition of these diagrams, we can already explain the representation of terms. Each function symbol of arity p is pictured as a cell with p inputs and one output:

In a first step, equations such as $x \times (y + z) = (x \times y) + (x \times z)$ and $x \times 0 = 0$ can be pictured as follows:

Next, variables are eliminated by means of three extra cells for sharing, discarding and swapping[1]:

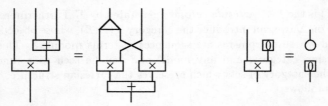

Now, our equations are pictured as follows:

No variable is needed because in each equation, the inputs of the left member correspond to the inputs of the right one, in the same order. Of course, this representation of terms is not unique and some extra equations will be needed, which do not appear at the level of terms. The precise correspondence between terms and diagrams has been established by Burroni (see [Bur93]). We shall return to this in section 5.

---

[1] Those cells are related to the so-called *structural rules* of Gentzen's sequent calculus: contraction, weakening and exchange.

2   2-dimensional syntax

We start with a finite set Σ of *symbols*, where a pair p, q of natural numbers is given for every $\alpha \in \Sigma$. We write $\alpha : p \to q$ and α is pictured as a cell with p inputs and q outputs:

$$
\begin{array}{c}
p \\
\cdots \\
\boxed{\alpha} \\
\cdots \\
q
\end{array}
$$

Here is a possible way of defining our planar diagrams:

– A *layer* a is given by a symbol $\alpha : p \to q$ and a pair i, j of natural numbers (the *context*). We write $a = i + \alpha + j : i + p + j \to i + q + j$.

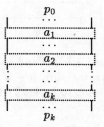

– A *diagram* u is given by a sequence of natural numbers $p_0, \ldots, p_k$ and a sequence of layers $a_1 : p_0 \to p_1$, $a_2 : p_1 \to p_2$, $\ldots$, $a_k : p_{k-1} \to p_k$. We write $u = a_k \circ \ldots \circ a_2 \circ a_1 : p_0 \to p_k$.

$$
\begin{array}{c}
p_0 \\
\cdots \\
a_1 \\
\cdots \\
a_2 \\
\cdots \\
a_k \\
p_k
\end{array}
$$

Now, assume that a diagram contains two consecutive layers $i + \alpha + j : i + p + j \to i + q + j$ and $i' + \alpha' + j' : i' + p' + j' \to i' + q' + j'$ such that $i + q \leq i'$, or equivalently $j \geq p' + j'$, and consider the diagram obtained by interchanging α with α':

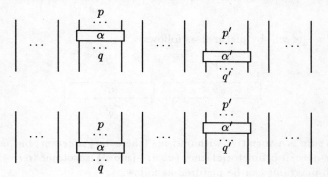

Note that, in this process, the context of α becomes $i, j - p' + q'$ and the one of α' becomes $i' - q + p, j'$. We call *syntactical isotopy* the equivalence relation generated by this transformation. Geometrically, two diagrams $u, v : p \to q$ are isotopic if it is possible to go from u to v by a continuous deformation. It is easy to see that equivalence classes are finite, so that isotopy is decidable. From now on, we shall always work modulo isotopy.

For any $u : p \to q$ and $v : q \to r$, the diagram $v \circ u : p \to r$ is defined by concatenation, and for any p, the diagram $\mathrm{id}_p : p \to p$ is defined by an empty sequence of layers:

Clearly, the composition is associative with unit id_p.

If $u : p \to q$ is a diagram and i, j are natural numbers, the diagram $i + u + j : i + p + j \to i + q + j$ is defined by extending the context:

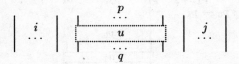

In particular we write $i + u$ for $i + u + 0$ and $u + j$ for $0 + u + j$. Now, if $u : p \to q$ and $u' : p' \to q'$ are diagrams, the sum $u + u' : p + p' \to q + q'$ is by definition $(q + u') \circ (u + p')$ which is isotopic to $(u + q') \circ (p + u')$:

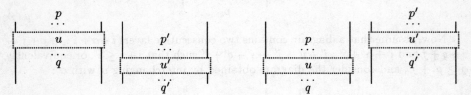

In practice, $u + u'$ will be pictured as follows:

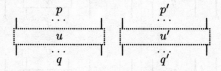

Clearly, this sum is associative with unit id_0 (the *empty diagram*) but not commutative. Furthermore, it is functorial since $(v \circ u) + (v' \circ u')$ is isotopic to $(v + v') \circ (u + u')$. Indeed, both diagrams can be pictured as follows:

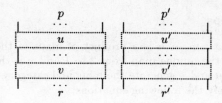

Therefore, we have defined a *strict monoidal category* $\mathbf{D}(\Sigma)$ whose objects are natural numbers and whose morphisms are (isotopy classes of) diagrams. In fact, it is not hard to see that $\mathbf{D}(\Sigma)$ is freely generated by Σ.

Now, let $\mathcal{E}$ be a set of pairs of diagrams $w, w' : p \to q$. Each pair will be called an *equation*. If a diagram is of the form $v \circ (i + w + j) \circ u$ where w is the left member of an equation, we can replace w by the right member w' of this equation:

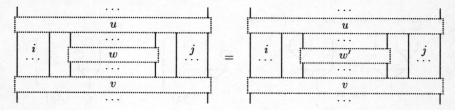

Again, it is easy to see that the equivalence generated by this transformation (and isotopy) is a congruence: it is compatible with composition and sum. The quotient of $\mathbf{D}(\Sigma)$ by this congruence is a strict monoidal category $\mathbf{D}(\Sigma; \mathcal{E})$. In the subsequent sections, we shall see examples of strict monoidal categories which can be presented in this way, with finite Σ and $\mathcal{E}$. Of course, $\mathbf{D}(\Sigma; \mathcal{E})$ satisfies a universal property: if C is a strict monoidal category with an object A and a morphism $\varphi_\alpha : A^p \to A^q$ for each $\alpha : p \to q$ in Σ, such that all equations in $\mathcal{E}$ are satisfied, then there is a unique strict monoidal functor $\Phi : \mathbf{D}(\Sigma; \mathcal{E}) \to C$ such that $\Phi(\alpha) = \varphi_\alpha$ for all $\alpha \in \Sigma$.

The most classical monoidal categories, for instance sets with cartesian product, or vector spaces with tensor product, are not strict. However, this is not a real problem since any monoidal category C is in fact equivalent to a strict one, whose objects are sequences of objects in C. Therefore we can forget about this bureaucratic distinction between strict and non-strict monoidal categories.

3 Presentation of the finite maps

Here we give the first example of a finitely presented monoidal category, which will play an essential role in the interpretation of algebraic theories. We consider the category $\mathbf{F}$ of finite maps:

- The objects are natural numbers.
- A morphism $\varphi : p \to q$ is a map from $\{1, \ldots, p\}$ to $\{1, \ldots, q\}$.

If $\varphi : p \to q$ and $\varphi' : p' \to q'$ are finite maps, then $\psi = \varphi + \varphi' : p + p' \to q + q'$ is defined by $\psi(i) = \varphi(i)$ for $i = 1, \ldots, p$ and $\psi(p + i) = q + \varphi'(i)$ for $i = 1, \ldots, p'$. This non-commutative addition defines a (strict) monoidal structure on $\mathbf{F}$. We shall write $\varphi + q$ for $\varphi + \mathrm{id}_q$ and $p + \psi$ for $\mathrm{id}_p + \psi$.

3.1 monotone maps

Any monotone map $\omega : m \to n$ is a product of maps of the form $i + \mu + j$ and $i + \eta + j$, where μ is the unique map from 2 to 1 and η is the unique map from 0 to 1. In other words, μ and η generate the monoidal category of monotone maps. These generators satisfy the following equations:

$$\mu \circ (\mu + 1) = \mu \circ (1 + \mu), \qquad \mu \circ (\eta + 1) = \mathrm{id}_1, \qquad \mu \circ (1 + \eta) = \mathrm{id}_1.$$

Let us introduce the following cells for μ and η:

The equations are pictured as follows:

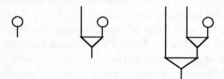

If two diagrams in $\mathbf{D}(\mu, \eta)$ are equivalent modulo (A_1), (A_2) and (A_3), they represent the same map. We shall now prove the converse.

Let α_n be the unique map from n to 1. It can be represented by a diagram a_n with $n + 1$ layers. For instance, here are a_0, a_1 and a_2:

Lemma 1. *(decomposition of a monotone map) Any monotone map $\omega : m \to n$ can be uniquely written as $\alpha_{p_1} + \ldots + \alpha_{p_n}$.*

This is obvious (p_i is the number of antecedents of i by ω), and this defines a canonical diagram $\hat{\omega}$ for every monotone map ω. In particular, this shows that μ and η generate the monotone maps. Here is a syntactical analogue of lemma 1:

Lemma 2. *Any diagram $u : m \to n$ in $\mathbf{D}(\mu, \eta)$ is equivalent to a diagram of the form $a_{p_1} + \ldots + a_{p_n}$ modulo (A_1), (A_2) and (A_3).*

Proof. By induction on the length of u. If u is id_n, then u is equivalent to $a_1 + \ldots + a_1$ by n applications of (A_3). Otherwise u is of the form $(i + \mu + j) \circ v$ or $(i + \eta + j) \circ v$. In the first case, we use the fact that $\mu \circ (a_p + a_q)$ is equivalent to a_{p+q} (generalized associativity) by p applications of (A_1) and one application of (A_2). The second case is obvious. $\qquad\square$

Using this lemma and the uniqueness of the decomposition in lemma 1, we see that any diagram representing a monotone map ω is equivalent to $\hat{\omega}$. Therefore, if two diagrams represent the same map, they are equivalent. In other words, the monoidal category of monotone maps is finitely presented by μ, η and the equations (A_1), (A_2), (A_3). The category of monotone maps is also called *simplicial category* because of its geometric interpretation (see [Mac71]).

3.2   permutations

It is well known that any permutation $\pi : n \to n$ is a product of transpositions $i + \tau + j$, where $\tau : 2 \to 2$ is defined by $\tau(1) = 2$ and $\tau(2) = 1$. In other words, τ generates the monoidal category of finite permutations.
This generator satisfies the following equation:

$$\tau \circ \tau = \mathrm{id}_2, \qquad (\tau + 1) \circ (1 + \tau) \circ (\tau + 1) = (1 + \tau) \circ (\tau + 1) \circ (1 + \tau).$$

Let us introduce the following cell for τ:

The equations can be pictured as follows:

(B_1) (B_2)

We shall now prove that we have indeed a 2-presentation of the permutations.

Let $\beta_n : n + 1 \to n + 1$ be the circular permutation mapping 1 to $n + 1$. It can be represented by a diagram b_n with n layers. For instance, here are b_0, b_1 and b_2:

Lemma 3. *(decomposition of a permutation) Any permutation $\pi : n + 1 \to n + 1$ can be uniquely written as $(\beta_p + q) \circ (1 + \pi')$ with $\pi' : n \to n$.*

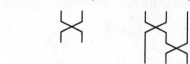

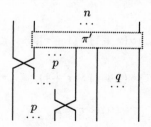

This is obvious (take $p = \pi(1) - 1$ and $q = n - p$). Applying this decomposition inductively, we get a canonical diagram $\hat{\pi}$ for every permutation $\pi : n \to n$ (if $n = 0$, take $\hat{\pi} = \mathrm{id}_0$). In particular, this shows that τ generates the finite permutations.

Lemma 4. *Any diagram $u : n+1 \to n+1$ in $\mathbf{D}(\tau)$ is equivalent to a diagram of the form $(b_p + q) \circ (1 + u')$ modulo (B_1) and (B_2).*

Proof. By induction on the length of u. If u is id_{n+1}, it is of the form $(b_0+n)\circ(1+\mathrm{id}_n)$. Otherwise u is of the form $(i + \tau + j) \circ v$ and by induction hypothesis, v is equivalent to $(b_p + q) \circ (1 + v')$. Now there are four cases (figure 1):

- If $i < p-1$, then u is equivalent to $(b_p + q) \circ (1 + u')$ where u' is $(i + \tau + (j-1)) \circ v'$.
- If $i = p - 1$, then u is equivalent to $(b_{p-1} + (q + 1)) \circ (1 + v')$.
- If $i = p$, then u is $(b_{p+1} + (q - 1)) \circ (1 + v')$.
- If $i > p$, then u is $(b_p + q) \circ (1 + u')$ where u' is $((i - 1) + \tau + j) \circ v'$.

We have used (B_2) in the first case and (B_1) in the second case. □

As in the case of monotone maps, we can therefore conclude that the monoidal category of finite permutations is finitely presented by τ and the equations $(B_1), (B_2)$. This 2-dimensional presentation can be compared with the traditional 1-dimensional presentation of the symmetric group S_n by means of $n - 1$ generators $\tau_0, \ldots, \tau_{n-2}$ and $n(n - 1)/2$ equations:

$$
\begin{aligned}
\tau_i^2 &= 1 && \text{for } i = 0, \ldots, n - 2, \\
\tau_i \tau_{i+1} \tau_i &= \tau_{i+1} \tau_i \tau_{i+1} && \text{for } i = 0, \ldots, n - 3, \\
\tau_i \tau_j &= \tau_j \tau_i && \text{for } i = 0, \ldots, n - 4 \text{ and } j = i + 2, \ldots, n - 2.
\end{aligned}
$$

Here, the generator τ_i represents the map $i + \tau + (n - i - 2)$. Therefore, the two first families of equations correspond to (B_1) and (B_2). The third one corresponds to isotopy. Of course, the 2-dimensional presentation is much more economical and deals with all S_n at the same time.

3.3 maps

Any map $\varphi : p \to q$ can be written as $\omega \circ \pi$ where ω is a monotone map and π is a permutation. Therefore μ, η and τ generate the monoidal category of finite maps. Of course, the above equations are satisfied, but there are some extra equations relating μ and η with τ:

$$
\tau \circ (\mu + 1) = (1 + \mu) \circ (\tau + 1) \circ (1 + \tau), \qquad \tau \circ (\eta + 1) = 1 + \eta,
$$

$$
\tau \circ (1 + \mu) = (\mu + 1) \circ (1 + \tau) \circ (\tau + 1), \qquad \tau \circ (1 + \eta) = \eta + 1,
$$

$$
\mu \circ \tau = \mu.
$$

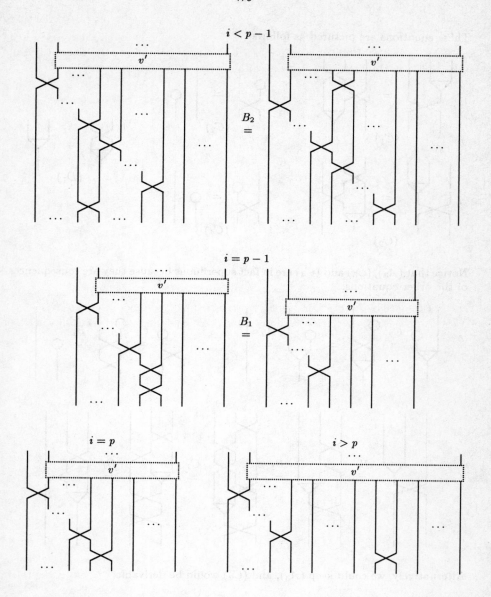

Fig. 1. Reducing a diagram of permutation to its canonical form (induction step)

These equations are pictured as follows:

(C_1) (C_2) (D_1) (C_3) (C_4)

Notice that (A_3), (C_3) and (C_4) are in fact superfluous because they are consequences of the other equations:

Alternatively, we could keep (A_3), and (C_2) would be derivable:

To show that we have a 2-presentation of the finite maps, we could start from the decomposition $\varphi = \omega \circ \pi$, as in [Bur93]. However, the permutation π is not uniquely determined by φ, the simplest counterexample being given by the equation (D_1). In fact, π is uniquely determined if we add the extra requirement that it does not permute any pair x, y such that $\varphi(x) = \varphi(y)$. Here, we shall avoid this complication by using a direct argument, without going through the 2-presentations of monotone maps and permutations.

Let $\eta_n = \eta + \ldots + \eta$ be the unique map from 0 to n. It can be represented by the following diagram h_n:

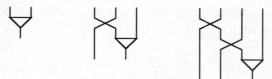

Lemma 5. *For any* $u : p \to q$ *in* $\mathbf{D}(\mu, \eta, \tau)$*, the diagram* $u \circ \eta_p$ *is equivalent to* η_q *modulo* (A_2) *and* (C_2).

This is easily proved by induction on the length of u. As a special case, since η_0 is the empty diagram id_0, we get the fact that any diagram $u : 0 \to n$ is equivalent to η_n.

Now, let $\gamma_n : n+2 \to n+1$ be the map defined by $\gamma_n(1) = n+1$ and $\gamma_n(i) = i-1$ for $i = 2, \ldots, n+2$. It can be represented by a diagram c_n with $n+1$ layers. For instance, here are c_0, c_1 and c_2:

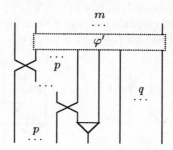

Lemma 6. *(decomposition of a map) Any map* $\varphi : m+1 \to n$ *can be uniquely written as* $(\gamma_p + q) \circ (1 + \varphi')$ *with* $\varphi' : m \to n$

This is obvious (take $p = \varphi(1)-1$ and $q = n-p-1$). Applying this decomposition inductively, we get a canonical diagram $\widehat{\varphi}$ for every map $\varphi : m \to n$ (if $m = 0$, take $\widehat{\varphi} = \eta_n$). In particular, this shows that μ, η and τ generate the finite maps.

Lemma 7. *Any diagram* $u : m+1 \to n$ *in* $\mathbf{D}(\mu, \eta, \tau)$ *is equivalent to a diagram of the form* $(c_p + q) \circ (1 + u')$ *modulo* (A_1)*,* (A_3)*,* (B_1)*,* (B_2)*,* (C_1)*,* (C_3)*,* (C_4) *and* (D_1).

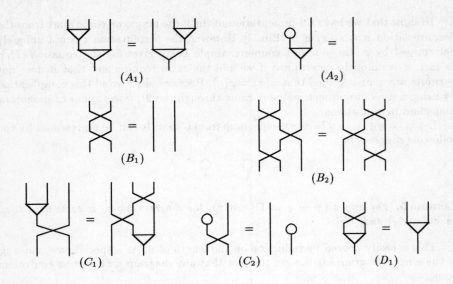

Fig. 2. 2-presentation of the finite maps

Proof. By induction on the length of u. If u is id_{m+1}, then u is equivalent to $(c_0 + n) \circ (1 + \eta + n)$ by (A_3):

$$\text{(diagram)} \quad \overset{m}{\underset{\cdots}{}}$$

Otherwise, u is of the form $(i + \tau + j) \circ v$, or $(i + \mu + j) \circ v$, or $(i + \eta + j) \circ v$, and by induction hypothesis, v is equivalent to $(c_p + q) \circ (1 + v')$. If $i > p$, then u is already in the required form (modulo isotopy). Otherwise, there are several cases to consider, as in the proof of lemma 4. We need (B_2), (C_3), (C_4), (C_1), (A_1) and the following equations

$$\text{(diagrams)}$$

which are derivable. $\qquad\square$

We conclude that $\mathbf{F}$ is finitely presented by μ, η, τ and the equations of figure 2. The dual $\mathbf{F}^{op}$ of $\mathbf{F}$ is the category $\mathbf{T}(\emptyset)$ of section 1, which is also the free cartesian category generated by a single object. The fact that $\mathbf{F}^{op}$ is finitely presentable is the first step towards the reduction of the cartesian structure to a monoidal one.

4 Presentation of the finite relations

We consider now the (strict) monoidal category of finite relations:

- The objects are natural numbers.
- A morphism $\rho : p \to q$ is a relation between $\{1, \ldots, p\}$ and $\{1, \ldots, q\}$.

Addition for relations is defined in the same way as for finite maps. Furthermore, we have a contravariant involution which maps a relation $\rho : p \to q$ to its dual $\rho^* : q \to p$. We shall draw upside down cells for μ^* and η^* (τ being its own dual):

Any relation $\rho : p \to q$ can be written as $\psi \circ \varphi^*$ where $\varphi : r \to p$, $\psi : r \to q$ are finite maps, and r is the cardinality of (the graph of) ρ. Therefore μ, η, μ^*, η^* and τ generate finite relations.

We have all equations for finite maps, those obtained by duality and some extra ones relating μ and η with μ^* and η^* (figure 3). To show that we have a 2-presentation of the finite relations, we follow the same method as for finite maps.

Lemma 8. *For any $u : p \to q$ in $\mathbf{D}(\mu, \eta, \mu^*, \eta^*, \tau)$, the diagram $u \circ \eta_p$ is equivalent to η_q modulo (A_2), (C_2), (E_2^*) and (E_3).*

In particular, any diagram $u : 0 \to n$ is equivalent to η_n. Now, let $\kappa : 2 \to 2$ be the relation consisting of the pairs $(1, 1)$, $(1, 2)$ and $(2, 1)$.

Lemma 9. *(decomposition of a relation) Any relation $\rho : m+1 \to n$ can be uniquely written as $(n + \eta^*) \circ ((n - 1) + \rho_n) \circ \cdots \circ (\rho_1 + (n - 1)) \circ (1 + \rho')$ with $\rho' : m \to n$ and where each $\rho_i : 2 \to 2$ is τ or κ.*

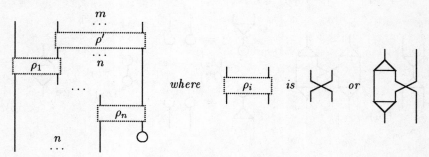

In this decomposition, ρ_i is κ when the pair $(1, i)$ belongs to (the graph of) ρ. Applying this decomposition inductively, we get a canonical diagram $\widehat{\rho}$ for every relation $\rho : m \to n$. In particular, this shows that μ, η, μ^*, η^* and τ generate finite relations.

Lemma 10. *Any diagram $u : m + 1 \to n$ in $\mathbf{D}(\mu, \eta, \mu^*, \eta^*, \tau)$ is equivalent to a diagram of the above form modulo the equations of figure 3.*

184

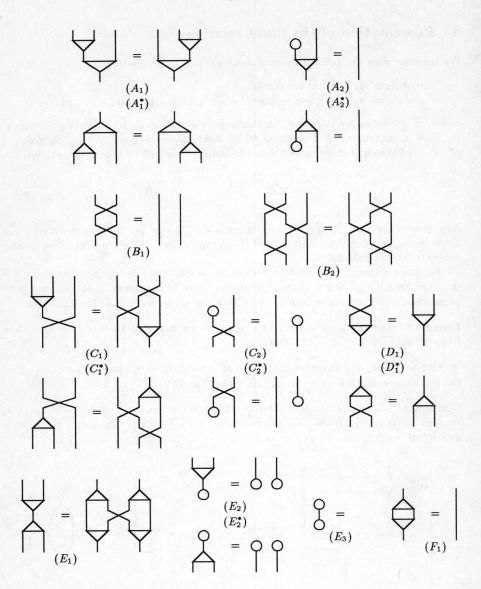

Fig. 3. 2-presentation of the finite relations

Proof. By induction on the length of u. If u is id_{m+1}, we use the derivable equations (A_3), (A_3^*) and (C_3^*). Otherwise, we proceed as in the proof of lemma 7, using (B_2), (C_3), (C_4), (C_1^*), (C_2^*) and eight other equations which are derivable. □

Using the same argument as for finite maps, we conclude that the monoidal category of finite relations is finitely presented by μ, η, μ^*, η^*, τ and the equations of figure 3. It is possible to show that, if we remove the equation (F_1) from the list of figure 3, we get a 2-presentation of the finite multirelations[2].

5 Algebraic theories

Here we consider a set Σ of symbols with arities, and a set $\mathcal{E}$ of equations on Σ.

5.1 syntax

Like any (strict) cartesian category, the category $\mathbf{T}(\Sigma)$ of section 1 has a (strict) monoidal structure:

- The monoidal product of p by q is $p + q$.
- If $U : p \to q$ and $U' : p' \to q'$ are morphisms, then $U+U' : p+p' \to q+q'$ is defined by the sequence $u_1, \ldots, u_q, v_1, \ldots, v_{q'}$ where v_i is $u_i'[x_{p+1}/x_1, \ldots, x_{p+p'}/x_{p'}]$.

In the special case where Σ is empty, we get the dual of the category of finite maps. Therefore, it is natural to consider three generators $\delta : 1 \to 2$, $\varepsilon : 0 \to 1$ and $\sigma : 2 \to 2$, respectively given by x_1, x_1, the empty sequence and x_2, x_1. They correspond to μ, η and τ by duality.

In the general case, an extra generator $\alpha : p \to 1$, given by the term $\alpha(x_1, \ldots, x_p)$, is needed for each symbol α of arity p. Beside the seven equations obtained by duality from the 2-presentation of the finite maps (figure 4), there are equations relating δ, ε and σ with each symbol of Σ:

$$\delta \circ \alpha = (\alpha + \alpha) \circ \delta_n, \qquad \varepsilon \circ \alpha = \varepsilon_n,$$

$$\sigma \circ (\alpha + 1) = (1 + \alpha) \circ \sigma_{n,1}, \qquad \sigma \circ (1 + \alpha) = (\alpha + 1) \circ \sigma_{1,n},$$

where $\delta_n : n \to 2n$, $\varepsilon_n : n \to 0$ and $\sigma_{p,q} : p + q \to p + q$ are respectively given by $x_1, \ldots, x_n, x_1, \ldots, x_n$, the empty sequence and $x_{p+1}, \ldots, x_{p+q}, x_1, \ldots, x_p$. Those equations are pictured in figure 5 for symbols of arity ≤ 2. Notice that (S_4) is in fact superfluous, since it is a consequence of (S_3) and (B_1). In the unary case, we have indeed the following derivation:

The other cases have been handled in 3.3.

---

[2] A multirelation between sets X and Y is a relation with multiplicities, *i.e.* a map from $X \times Y$ to $\mathbb{N}$.

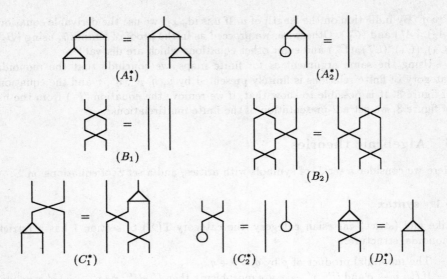

Fig. 4. Equations for δ, ε and σ

We shall say that a morphism $U : m \rightarrow n$ is *strongly linear* if the variables $x_1, \ldots, x_m$ appear exactly once and in order. Clearly, such a morphism is represented by a diagram built only with symbols of Σ, and this diagram is unique. Furthermore, we have the following decomposition:

Lemma 11. *Any morphism U in $\mathbf{T}(\Sigma)$ can be uniquely written as $W \circ V$ where V is (the dual of) a finite map and W is strongly linear.*

Now, let Γ be the alphabet consisting of δ, ε and σ.

Lemma 12. *Modulo (S_1), (S_2) and (S_3) for all $\alpha \in \Sigma$, any diagram u in $\mathbf{D}(\Gamma \cup \Sigma)$ is equivalent to a diagram of the form $w \circ v$ where v is in $\mathbf{D}(\Gamma)$ and w is in $\mathbf{D}(\Sigma)$.*

This is proved by induction on the length of u. Using those lemmas and the 2-presentation of the finite maps in section 3, we conclude that $\mathbf{T}(\Sigma)$ is finitely presented by $\Gamma \cup \Sigma$ and the equations of figures 4 and 5. Similarly, $\mathbf{T}(\Sigma; \mathcal{E})$ is a strict monoidal category which can be finitely presented by means of the same generators and equations as $\mathbf{T}(\Sigma)$, plus the equations of $\mathcal{E}$ expressed with diagrams. Therefore, if there are n functions symbols in Σ and m equations in $\mathcal{E}$, the 2-presentation has $n + 3$ generators and $m + 3n + 7$ equations.

5.2 semantics

In section 1, we have seen models of $\mathcal{E}$ as functors from $\mathbf{T}(\Sigma; \mathcal{E})$ to the category of sets which preserve the cartesian structure. Here, it would be more natural to

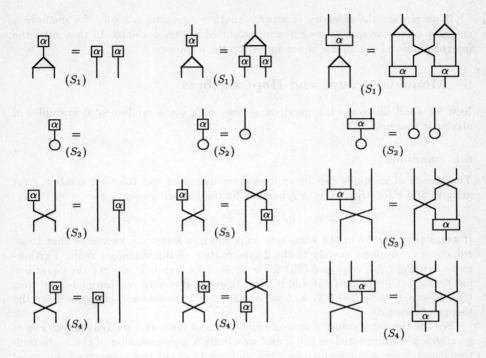

Fig. 5. Extra equations for symbols of arity 0, 1 and 2

consider functors preserving the monoidal structure. In fact, we shall see that the two notions coincide.

Let C be a cartesian category, for instance the category of sets. We can always assume that C is strict (see our remark at the end of section 2). Now, if A is an object of C, the *diagonal* $\delta = \langle \mathrm{id}_A, \mathrm{id}_A \rangle : A \to A \times A$, the *canonical morphism* $\varepsilon : A \to 1$ and the *symmetry* $\sigma = \langle \pi_{A,A}^2, \pi_{A,A}^1 \rangle : A \times A \to A \times A$ satisfy all the equations of figure 4. The converse holds:

Lemma 13. *If* $\delta : A \to A \times A$, $\varepsilon : A \to 1$ *and* $\sigma : A \times A \to A \times A$ *are three morphisms satisfying the 4 equations* (A_2^*), (A_3^*), (C_2^*) *and* (C_4^*), *then* δ *is the diagonal,* ε *is the canonical morphism and* σ *is the symmetry.*

Proof. Clearly, we have $\mathrm{id}_A \times \varepsilon = \pi_{A,A}^1$ and $\varepsilon \times \mathrm{id}_A = \pi_{A,A}^2$. Therefore, the 4 equations give $\pi_{A,A}^2 \circ \delta = \mathrm{id}_A$, $\pi_{A,A}^1 \circ \delta = \mathrm{id}_A$, $\pi_{A,A}^2 \circ \sigma = \pi_{A,A}^1$ and $\pi_{A,A}^1 \circ \sigma = \pi_{A,A}^2$. □

This means that, in the case of a cartesian category, there is no choice for interpreting the three generators δ, ε and σ. As a consequence, any functor from $\mathbf{T}(\Sigma; \mathcal{E})$ to C which preserves the monoidal structure also preserves the cartesian structure. In particular, a model of $\mathcal{E}$ can be seen as a monoidal functor from $\mathbf{T}(\Sigma; \mathcal{E})$ to the category of sets.

If we replace the category of sets by another monoidal category, for instance a category of vector spaces, we get a nonstandard notion of model. In that case, the interpretation of δ, ε and σ is not forced by the equations.

6 Monoids, groups and Hopf algebras

Now we shall illustrate the previous section with some fundamental examples of algebraic theories.

6.1 monoids

The theory of monoids can be expressed by means of two function symbols $\cdot$ (of arity 2) and e (of arity 0). It is generated by the following equations:

$$(x \cdot y) \cdot z = x \cdot (y \cdot z), \qquad e \cdot x = x, \qquad x \cdot e = x.$$

If we picture $\cdot$ and e in the same way as μ and η in section 3, we notice that those equations correspond exactly to the 2-presentation of the monotone maps. Furthermore, writing (S_1), (S_2) and (S_3) for both function symbols, we get the equations (E_1), (E_2), (C_1), (E_2^*), (E_3) and (C_2) of figure 3. But here, we have (A_3), so that (C_2) is superfluous (see 3.3) and we obtain the 2-presentation of figure 6 for the theory of monoids.

For the theory of commutative monoids, we add the commutativity axiom $x \cdot y = y \cdot x$ which is interpreted as (D_1), and we obtain a 2-presentation of the finite multirelations. This is not surprising, since an element of the free commutative monoid generated by a finite set $\{a_1, \ldots, a_k\}$ can be uniquely written as $\Sigma_{i=1}^{k} n_i a_i$ where the coefficients $n_1, \ldots, n_k$ are natural numbers. If furthermore, we add the idempotency axiom $x \cdot x = x$ which is interpreted as (F_1), we obtain a 2-presentation of the finite relations.

6.2 groups

For groups, we need another function symbol $^{-1}$ of arity 1, which will be pictured as follows:

Beside the axioms for monoids, we have the following equations:

$$x^{-1} \cdot x = e, \qquad x \cdot x^{-1} = e,$$

which are pictured as follows:

(G_1) $\qquad\qquad\qquad\qquad$ (G_2)

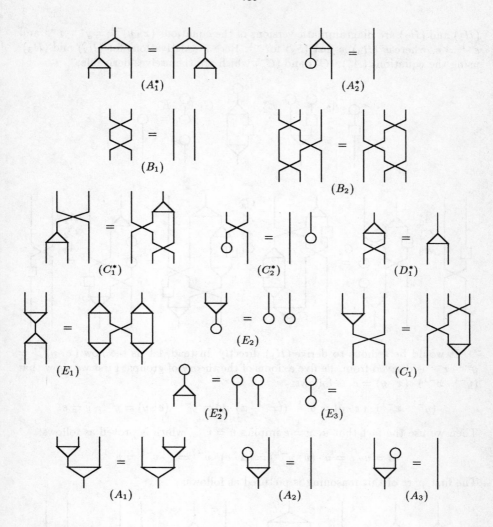

Fig. 6. Equations for monoids

Of course, we should add (S_1), (S_2) and (S_3) for $^{-1}$, but we shall see that in fact, all three are derivable. Consider indeed the three following equations:

(H_1) and (H_2) are diagrammatic versions of the equations $(x \cdot y)^{-1} = y^{-1} \cdot x^{-1}$ and $e^{-1} = e$, whereas (H_3) is just (S_3) for $^{-1}$. Here are derivations for (H_2) and (H_3), using the equations (A_3^*), (C_3^*) and (C_4^*) which are themselves derivable:

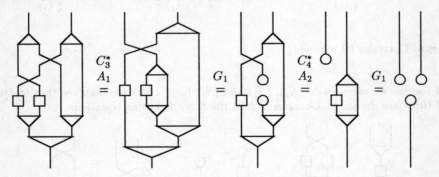

It would be tedious to derive (H_1) directly. Instead, let us see how $(x \cdot y)^{-1} = y^{-1} \cdot x^{-1}$ is derived from the five axioms of the theory of groups. First we show that $(y^{-1} \cdot x^{-1}) \cdot (x \cdot y) = e$ as follows:

$$(y^{-1} \cdot x^{-1}) \cdot (x \cdot y) = y^{-1} \cdot ((x^{-1} \cdot x) \cdot y) = y^{-1} \cdot (e \cdot y) = y^{-1} \cdot y = e.$$

Then we use the fact that $u \cdot v = e$ implies $u = v^{-1}$, which is proved as follows:

$$u = u \cdot e = u \cdot (v \cdot v^{-1}) = (u \cdot v) \cdot v^{-1} = e \cdot v^{-1} = v^{-1}.$$

The first part of this reasoning is pictured as follows:

For the second part, we assume that $u, v : 2 \to 1$ are arbitrary diagrams satisfying the three equations (1), (2) and (3) of figure 7. The equation (1) is just the diagrammatic version of $u \cdot v = e$ in the case of terms with two variables. If u and v are the diagrams

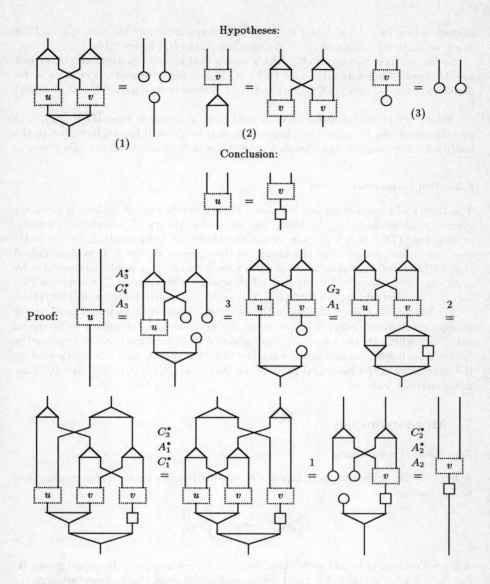

Fig. 7. Diagrammatic proof for $u \cdot v = e$ implies $u = v^{-1}$

corresponding to $y^{-1} \cdot x^{-1}$ and $x \cdot y$, all three hypotheses are satisfied, (2) and (3) being respectively (E_1) and (E_2). We conclude that (H_1) is derivable.

So far, we have not used (D_1^*), which means that all our equations can be turned upside down. Therefore, the dual (H_1^*) of (H_1) is also derivable, and from it we derive (S_1) for $^{-1}$, using (D_1^*), (H_3) and (B_1). Similarly we derive (H_2^*), that is (S_2) for $^{-1}$.

Alternatively, it is possible to show that (G_2) is derivable from (G_1), (S_1), (S_2) and the equations for monoids. This corresponds to the well-known fact that, in the traditional formulation, the equation $x \cdot x^{-1} = e$ is derivable from the other ones.

6.3 Hopf algebras

The theory of groups is almost self dual. There are two ways of making it perfectly symmetrical: adding (D_1), in which case we get the theory of commutative groups, or removing (D_1^*), in which case we get the theory of *Hopf algebras*. In the latter case, we do not get an algebraic theory in the sense of section 5. It is clear indeed that (D_1^*) is not derivable, because otherwise its dual (D_1) would be derivable by symmetry, and this would imply that all groups are commutative. The equation (S_1) for $^{-1}$ is not derivable either, but (H_1), (H_2), (H_3) and their duals are still derivable.

By lemma 13, a Hopf algebra in the category of sets with cartesian product (or in any cartesian category) is just a group. So we must look for models in monoidal categories which are not cartesian. Traditionally, Hopf algebras leave in a symmetric monoidal category, for instance a category of vector spaces, and σ is interpreted by the symmetry of the monoidal product. In that case (B_1), (B_2), (C_1) and (C_1^*) are automatically satisfied.

7 More examples

7.1 braids and knots

A braid is like a permutation, but where you distinguish between overcrossing and undercrossing:

A 2-presentation of braids is obtained from the 1-presentation of the braid group B_n just as a 2-presentation of permutations is obtained from the 1-presentation of the symmetric group S_n:

For knots, two extra generators are needed:

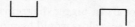

A diagram built with these two generators and those for braids represents a *tangle*.
A knot is a special kind of tangle. The extra equations for tangles are the following:

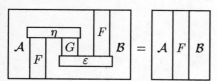

This 2-presentation is given in [FrY89], where several variants are also considered
such as oriented tangles, tangles up to regular isotopy and framed tangles. Algebraic
invariants for knots can be seen as models of those theories.

7.2   2-categorical reasoning

In all previous examples, we have considered monoidal categories generated by a
single object. In the case of a monoidal category generated by several objects, wires
in diagrams must be labeled or colored.

The next step consists in replacing monoidal categories by 2-categories. A strict
monoidal category is indeed a 2-category with a single 0-cell. The algebra group
of Santiago de Compostela has made an intensive use of 2-dimensional calculus in
the 2-category of categories with *Rodeja diagrams*, but a nice feature of Penrose
diagrams is the representation of 0-cells.

For instance, if $\mathcal{A}$ and $\mathcal{B}$ are categories, an *adjunction* between two functors
$F : \mathcal{A} \to \mathcal{B}$ and $G : \mathcal{B} \to \mathcal{A}$ consists of two natural transformations $\eta : \mathrm{Id}_{\mathcal{A}} \to GF$
and $\varepsilon : FG \to \mathrm{Id}_{\mathcal{B}}$ satisfying the following equations (see [Mac71]):

$$\varepsilon F \circ F\eta = \mathrm{id}_F, \qquad G\varepsilon \circ \eta G = \mathrm{id}_G.$$

Those equations can be pictured as follows:

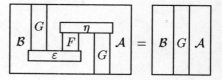

These diagrams are interpreted in the 2-category of categories. The wires has been thickened in order to be labeled by F or G, and each connected component of the background is labeled by $\mathcal{A}$ or $\mathcal{B}$. In bigger diagrams, the shape of the background may be quite complicated, and so, colors would be more suitable. The representation of 0-cells is not so nice in the other kinds of diagrams (figure 8).

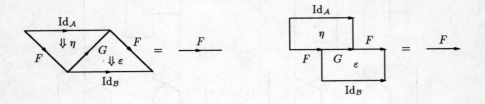

Fig. 8. Pasting diagrams and Rodeja diagrams for an adjunction

Conclusion

For many kinds of computations, the 2-dimensional calculus is very helpful, but drawing diagrams by hand becomes quickly tedious. We shall need computers for two purposes:

- manipulating diagrams without taking care of the details of the drawing, and with the assurance that our computations are correct (interactive reasoning),
- computing normal forms (automated reasoning).

In the second case, a theory of 2-dimensional rewriting is needed, with a generalization of the Knuth-Bendix completion. This approach is sketched in [Laf92].

References

[Bur93]   **A. Burroni**, *Higher Dimensional Word Problem*, Theoretical Computer Science 115, 1993, pp. 43–62.

[EW67]   **S. Eilenberg & J. B. Wright**, *Automata in general algebras*, Information and Control 115, 1967, pp. 452–470.

[FrY89]   **P.J. Freyd & D.N. Yetter**, *Braided Compact Closed Categories with Application to Low Dimensional Topology*, Advances in Mathematics 77, 1989, pp. 156–182.

[JoS91]   **A. Joyal & R. Street**, *The Geometry of Tensor Calculus*, Advances in Mathematics 88, 1991, pp. 55–112.

[Laf92]   **Y. Lafont**, *Penrose diagrams and 2-dimensional rewriting*, Applications of Categories in Computer Science (ed. M.P. Fourman, P.T. Johnstone & A.M. Pitts), LMSLNS 177, Cambridge University Press, 1992, pp. 191–201.

[Law63]   **F.L. Lawvere**, *Functorial Semantics of Algebraic Theories*, Proc. Nat. Acad. Sci. USA, 1963.

[Mac71]   **S. Mac Lane**, *Categories for the Working Mathematician*, GTM 5, Springer-Verlag, 1971.

[PeR86]   **R. Penrose & W. Rindler**, *Spinors and space-time, Vol. 1: Two-spinor calculus and relativistic fields*, Cambridge University Press, 1986.

[Poi85]   **A. Poigné**, *Algebra Categorically*, Category Theory and Computer Programming (ed. D. Pitt, S. Abramsky, A. Poigné & D. Rydeheard), LNCS 240, Springer-Verlag, 1985, pp. 76–102.

Affine geometry of collinearity and conditional term rewriting

Philippe Balbiani and Luis Fariñas del Cerro

Institut de recherche en informatique de Toulouse[a]

Abstract A geometrical figure is a relation on a finite set of points. Its properties can be expressed using equations between first order terms. A terminating and confluent conditional term rewriting system will prove some theorems of the affine geometry of collinearity. A narrowing-based unification algorithm will solve every system of geometrical equations in the language of affine geometry of collinearity.

1 Introduction

While the geometer draws, the algebraist calculates. On one hand, the geometer's activity consists in constructing geometrical figures with a ruler and a pair of compasses and in proving properties of these figures. It requires a lot of experience and know-how. Since Euclid, geometrical proofs are obtained from a set of axioms. They are nice and really explain the proved properties. On the other hand, the algebraist's activity is mainly concerned with symbolic manipulation of polynoms. Automated deduction methods built upon the algorithms of Buchberger [4] or Wu [19] operate on a polynomial translation of geometrical problems. They require the whole power of modern computers. The proofs elaborated by the algebraist are long. They cannot be used to lighten the proved geometrical property. Let us examine the geometer's position.

Hilbert [9] considers three distinct sets of beings: points, lines and planes and some relations we express saying: «to be on», «to lay between», «to be congruent with», etc. These relations are defined by axioms that Hilbert divides in five groups: axioms of incidence, axioms of order, axioms of congruence, one axiom of parallel and axioms of continuity. The axioms of incidence define the relations of collinearity and coplanarity we express saying «three points belong to the same line», «two lines are coplanar», etc. Our aim is to implement an automated deduction system for the theory defined by these axioms. We will presently concentrate our work on the automated deduction problem in the theory made of Hilbert's axioms of incidence.

The assets of algebra come from its use of symbolic expressions and mechanical rules of reasoning [5]. The use of figures in geometrical reasoning makes things tight for the geometer to find proofs that apply to several geometrical problems. Thus, abstract symbols should be used to formally represent geometrical figures as complex terms upon which the computation is made. We will be able to represent a figure by a term only if we adopt an equational approach to geometry where the geometrical beings are still points, lines and planes and where the relations between these beings are no longer expressed by relational symbols like « is on » or « passes through » but rather by function symbols l of arity three, the term $l(x,y,z)$ denoting a projection of a point z onto the line defined by two points x and y. Since the axioms of our geometry will be equational formulas saying under which conditions two terms can be identified, we easily imagine the benefit we will derive from this approach and the use of equational reasoning and rewriting techniques for the resolution of geometrical problems : analysis of figures where one has to prove that a given figure possesses such or such property and synthesis of figures where one has to construct a figure possessing such or such property. The equational axioms of our geometry will be such that the associated relation of reduction is terminating and confluent, these properties being essential for the proof that every term possesses exactly one normal form.

We will consider one class of geometrical beings : points. A line will be defined as the set of points collinear with two distinct given points. The incidence of a point z and a line defined by two points x and y will be expressed with the equation: $l(x,y,z)=z$. More generally, the equation $l(x,y,z)=t$ will signify that t is a projection of z onto the line xy. We give in section 3 an axiomatization of a first order theory E_l which language has one predicate symbol : equality, and one function symbol : l, of arity three. This axiomatization includes for example the formula $x{\neq}y \Rightarrow l(x,y,x)=x$ which says that if x and y are distinct points then x belongs to xy. The first order theory E_l is basically equivalent to a fragment of Hilbert's geometry of incidence we call E_L which language has the predicate symbol of equality and a ternary predicate L, the expression $L(x,y,z)$ meaning that x, y and z are collinear points. In section 4, we associate to E_l a positive/negative conditional term rewriting system (CTRS) we call R_l which is the first example ever produced of a positive/negative CTRS with some applications to the mechanization of reasoning in a first order theory like our affine geometry of collinearity.

This CTRS possesses the essential property that the associated reduction relation on terms is terminating and confluent, which becomes of fundamental importance for the use of our CTRS (i) in the mechanization of deduction in a constructive fragment of E_L and (ii) in the resolution of systems of equations in E_l. We associate in section 5 to each "constructive" sentence of E_L two terms t_1 and t_2 of the language of E_l and we prove that this sentence is a theorem of E_L if and only if the normal forms of t_1 and t_2 are equal. In section 6 we extend conditional narrowing (as Bockmayr [3], Kaplan [12] and Middeldorp and Hamoen [16] define it) to our positive/negative CTRS. We prove that, for a special class of sets of equations and disequations we call saturated sets, narrowing is complete for the unification problem in the algebra of the normal forms generated by R_l. We discuss in section 7 the ins and outs of the use of rewriting techniques for the mechanization of reasoning in geometrical first order theories like E_L.

2   Preliminaries

We assume the reader is familiar with the usual conventions and definitions of equational reasoning and term rewriting systems. The reader is invited to consult

Bachmair [2], Dershowitz and Jouannaud [6], Rusinowitch [18] or Snyder [18] for details. Let T be the set of first order terms defined with the function symbol l of arity three and an infinite set X of variables. Given a term s, $Var(s)$ denotes the set of variables occurring in s. A position is an element of $\mathbb{N}^*$, the monoid of finite sequences of positive integers. A term can be viewed as a finite prefix-closed set of positions. The subterm of t at position p is denoted t/p. The replacement by a term r in a term t at position p is written $t[r]_p$.

A substitution is any function $\sigma : X \to T$ such that $\sigma(x) \neq x$ for only finitely many x. Every substitution has a unique homomorphic extension $\sigma°$ on T such that, for every variable x, $\sigma°(x) = \sigma(x)$ and, for every term t_1, t_2, t_3, $\sigma°(l(t_1,t_2,t_3)) = l(\sigma°(t_1), \sigma°(t_2), \sigma°(t_3))$. The support or domain of a substitution σ is the set of variables $\{x: \sigma(x) \neq x\}$. The set of variables introduced by a substitution σ is the set of variables $\cup_{x \in D(\sigma)} Var(\sigma(x))$ where $D(\sigma)$ is the domain of σ. A substitution σ will sometimes be denoted by the set $\{\sigma(x)=x: x \in D(\sigma)\}$. Given a set W of "protected variables", a substitution ρ is a renaming substitution away from W if $\rho(x)$ is a variable for every x in $D(\rho), I(\rho) \cap W = \emptyset$ where $I(\rho)$ is the set of variables introduced by ρ and, for every x, y in $D(\rho)$, $\rho(x) = \rho(y)$ implies that $x = y$. The restriction of a substitution σ to a set V of variables is denoted $\sigma/_V$. The union of two substitutions σ and θ with disjoint domains, denoted by $\sigma \cup \theta$, is defined by: $\sigma \cup \theta(x) = \sigma(x)$ if $x \in D(\sigma)$, $\theta(x)$ if $x \in D(\theta)$, x otherwise. The composition of σ and θ is the substitution denoted by $\sigma \circ \theta$ such that, for every variable x, $\sigma \circ \theta(x) = \theta°(\sigma(x))$.

Let C be the equational theory generated by $\{l(x,y,z)=l(y,x,z)\}$. It defines a congruence relation $=_C$ for which each class is finite. The C-classe of a term t is equal to the set $\{t': t=_C t'\}$. Let V be a set of variables. Two substitutions σ and θ are equal over V (modulo C), $\sigma = \theta$ $[V]$ ($\sigma =_C \theta$ $[V]$), if, for every x in V, $\sigma(x) = \theta(x)$ ($\sigma(x) =_C \theta(x)$). A substitution σ is more general than a substitution θ over V (modulo C), $\sigma \leq \theta$ $[V]$ ($\sigma \leq_C \theta$ $[V]$), if there is a substitution η such that $\theta = \sigma \circ \eta$ $[V]$ ($\theta =_C \sigma \circ \eta$ $[V]$). A substitution σ is idempotent if $\sigma \circ \sigma = \sigma$. Idempotency is equivalent to the following property: $I(\sigma) \cap D(\sigma) = \emptyset$, where $I(\sigma)$ is the set of variables introduced by σ. If σ is an idempotent substitution then, for every term s and for every position p in s, $(s[(s/p)\sigma]_p)\sigma = s\sigma$. We will consider idempotent substitutions since any substitution σ is equivalent to an idempotent substitution: for every set of variables W containing $D(\sigma)$, there is an idempotent substitution σ' such that $D(\sigma) = D(\sigma')$, $\sigma \leq \sigma'$ $[W]$ and $\sigma' \leq \sigma$ $[W]$. For any term t, the term $t\sigma$ is called a substitution instance of t.

A substitution σ is called a matcher of two terms s and t modulo C if $s =_C t\sigma$. A substitution σ is called a unifying substitution or a unifier of two terms s and t modulo C if $s\sigma =_C t\sigma$. The set of unifiers modulo C of a system S of equations is denoted $U_C(S)$. Unification and matching problems modulo C are decidable and finitary. More precisely, for every system S of equations and for every set W of "protected variables", a finite set $CU_C(S)$ of substitutions σ such that $D(\sigma) \subseteq Var(S)$ and $I(\sigma) \cap (W \cup D(\sigma)) = \emptyset$ can be computed such that, for every unifier θ of S modulo C, there is a substitution σ in $CU_C(S)$ such that $\sigma \leq_C \theta$ $[Var(S)]$. $CU_C(S)$ is called a complete set of unifiers of S modulo C.

3 Affine geometry of collinearity: an equational presentation

We present in this section a first order theory E_l with equality and prove its equivalence with a fragment of Hilbert's incidence geometry we call E_L. The language of E_l is made of the equality predicate, a ternary function symbol l and an infinite set of variables X. The term $l(x,y,z)$ denotes some projection of the point z onto the line xy. It makes sense only if x and y denote distinct points. Let E_l be the first order theory with equality made of the following four axioms:

E_{l0} $l(x,y,z)=l(y,x,z)$

E_{l1} $x \neq y \Rightarrow l(x,y,x)=x$

E_{l2} $x \neq y \wedge z \neq t \wedge l(x,y,z)=z \wedge l(x,y,t)=t \Rightarrow l(x,y,l(z,t,u))=l(z,t,u)$

E_{l3} $y \neq z \wedge x \neq l(y,z,t) \wedge l(y,z,x)=x \Rightarrow l(x,l(y,z,t),u)=l(y,z,u)$

These four axioms express some basic properties of a projection function onto a line. E_{l2}, for example, says that if z and t belong to xy then every point on zt is on xy too. This corresponds to the fact that if a point belongs to a line then it is equal to its own projection onto the line.

Let E_L be the first order theory which language is made of the equality predicate, a ternary predicate symbol L and the infinite set of variables X. Its axiomatization contains the following three axioms:

E_{L0} $L(x,y,z) \Rightarrow L(y,x,z)$

E_{L1} $L(x,y,x)$

E_{L2} $x \neq y \wedge L(x,y,z) \wedge L(x,y,t) \Rightarrow L(y,z,t)$

The atom $L(x,y,z)$ means that the three points x, y and z are collinear. Let $[.]^*$ be the translation function between E_L and E_l defined by: $[L(x,y,z)]^* = (x \neq y \Rightarrow l(x,y,z)=z)$. Next theorem says that the translation of a theorem of E_l is a theorem of E_L. The first order theories E_l and E_L are basically equivalent.

theorem 3.1 Let F be a geometrical statement in the language of E_L. Let F^* be its translation into the language of E_l. Then F is a theorem of E_L if and only if F^* is a theorem of E_l.

proof. $\Rightarrow$. The proof is done by induction on the proof of F in E_L. If F is the axiom E_{L0} then F^* is the equational formula $(x \neq y \Rightarrow l(x,y,z)=z) \Rightarrow (y \neq x \Rightarrow l(y,x,z)=z)$ which is obviously a theorem of E_l. If F is the axiom E_{L1} then F^* is the equational formula $x \neq y \Rightarrow l(x,y,x)=x$ which is the axiom E_{l1}. If F is the axiom E_{L2}

then F^* is equivalent to the equational formula $x \neq y \wedge l(x,y,z)=z \wedge l(x,y,t)=t \Rightarrow (y \neq z \Rightarrow l(y,z,t)=t)$ which is a theorem of E_l since if $x \neq y$, $l(x,y,z)=z$, $l(x,y,t)=t$ and $y \neq z$ then $l(x,y,y)=y$ and $l(y,z,t)=l(y,l(x,y,z),t)=l(x,y,t)=t$.

$\Leftarrow$. Let M be a model of E_L and D be its domain. Let M^* be the interpretation of E_l which has the same domain as M and which is defined by: for every element x, y and z in D, if x and y are distinct and if the value of $L(x,y,z)$ is true in M then the value of $l(x,y,z)$ is z otherwise this value is any point belonging to the set $\{z' : z'$ belongs to D and the value of $L(x,y,z')$ is true in $M\}$. It is straightforward to see that M^* is a model of E_l. For any variable u and for any element a in D, $M[u=a]$ denotes the model assigning the value a to u. The same definition applies for $M^*[u=a]$ too. Let it be proved by induction on the complexity of F that, for every variable u and for every element a in D, if $M[u=a]$ is a model of F then $M^*[u=a]$ is a model of F^*.

first case: F is the atomic formula $L(x,y,z)$. If $M[u=a]$ is a model of F then either the interpretations of x and y in $M^*[u=a]$ are equal or the interpretations of $l(x,y,z)$ and z in $M^*[u=a]$ are equal. Therefore, $M^*[u=a]$ is a model of F^*.

second case: F is the atomic formula $\neg L(x,y,z)$. If $M[u=a]$ is a model of F then the interpretations of x and y in $M^*[u=a]$ are distinct and the interpretations of $l(x,y,z)$ and z in $M^*[u=a]$ are distinct. Therefore, $M^*[u=a]$ is a model of F^*.

third case: F is the formula $F_1 \wedge F_2$. If $M[u=a]$ is a model of F then $M[u=a]$ is a model of F_1 and $M[u=a]$ is a model of F_2. Thus, by induction hypothesis, $M^*[u=a]$ is a model of $F_1{}^*$, $M^*[u=a]$ is a model of $F_2{}^*$ and $M^*[u=a]$ is a model of F^*. The same argument applies if F is the formula $F_1 \vee F_2$.

fourth case: F is the formula $\forall u' F_1$. If $M[u=a]$ is a model of F then, for every element a' in D, $M[u=a][u'=a']$ is a model of F_1. Thus, by induction hypothesis, for every element a' in D, $M^*[u=a][u'=a']$ is a model of F^*. Therefore, $M^*[u=a]$ is a model of F^*. The same argument applies if F is the formula $\exists u' F_1$.

Thus, proving theorems in E_L is as difficult as proving theorems in E_l. We will show in section 5 how to use a positive/negative CTRS associated to E_l for the mechanization of reasoning in a constructive fragment of E_L.

4   A conditional term rewriting system for the affine geometry of collinearity

The conditional axioms of E_l can be obviously directed so that it becomes a reducing positive/negative CTRS we call R_l and which is made of the following three rules :

R_{l1} $x \neq y \Rightarrow l(x,y,x) \rightarrow x$

R_{12} $\quad x{\neq}y \land z{\neq}t \land l(x,y,z){=}z \land l(x,y,t){=}t \Rightarrow l(x,y,l(z,t,u)){\to}l(z,t,u)$

R_{13} $\quad y{\neq}z \land x{\neq}l(y,z,t) \land l(y,z,x){=}x \Rightarrow l(x,l(y,z,t),u){\to}l(y,z,u)$

Let C be the first order equational theory generated by $\{l(x,y,z){=}l(y,x,z)\}$. Unification and matching under C are finitary and constitute decidable classes of problems for which type conformal algorithms exist. A partial ordering $>$ on T is monotonic when: for every term u and for every position p in u, if $t > t'$ then $u[t]_p > u[t']_p$. It possesses the subterm property when: if t' is a proper subterm of t then $t > t'$. Let $>$ be the smallest monotonic ordering on T possessing the subterm property and such that:

(i) $\quad l(x,y,l(z,t,u)) > l(x,y,z)$
(ii) $\quad l(x,l(y,z,t),u) > l(y,z,x)$ and $l(x,l(y,z,t),u) > l(y,z,u)$
(iii) $\quad$ if $t > t'$ and $t'{=}_C t''$ then $t > t''$
(iv) $\quad$ if $t > t'$ and $t{=}_C t''$ then $t'' > t'$

proposition 4.1[b] $>$ is a well-founded ordering on T.

Let $\{u_i{=}v_i\}_i \land \{u_j{\neq}v_j\}_j \Rightarrow l{\to}r$ be a rule in R_l. Since, for every substitution σ, $l\sigma > u_i\sigma$, $v_i\sigma$, $u_j\sigma$, $v_j\sigma$, $r\sigma$, then the rules of R_l define a decidable and terminating relation $\to$ of reduction.

proposition 4.2 The rules of R_l define a decidable and terminating relation[c] $\to$ of reduction such that, for every term t and t', $t \to t'$ if and only if there are:

(i) $\quad$ a position p of t,
(ii) $\quad$ a substitution σ and
(iii) $\quad$ a variant $Q \Rightarrow l{\to}r$ of a rule such that
$\qquad$ (iv) $\quad t/p {=}_C l\sigma$,
$\qquad$ (v) $\quad t' {=} t[r\sigma]_p$ and
$\qquad$ (vi) $\quad Q\sigma{\downarrow}$,

that is to say: for every $u{=}v$ in Q, $u\sigma{\downarrow}v\sigma$ and, for every $u{\neq}v$ in Q, $u\sigma{\not\downarrow}v\sigma$, the relation $\downarrow$ being defined by $u{\downarrow}v$ if there are two terms w and w' such that $w{=}_C w'$, $u \to^* w$ and $v \to^* w'$.

In other respects, the proof that the reduction relation defined by the rules R_{11}, R_{12} and R_{13} and the equational theory generated by $C{=}\{l(x,y,z){=}l(y,x,z)\}$ is confluent has been done using CEC, the system to support modular order-sorted specifications with conditional equations designed by Ganzinger [7] [8].

proposition 4.3 The relation $\to$ is confluent.

A normal form is a term that cannot be reduced. Thus, for every term t, the normal forms of t are equal modulo C. For every term t, $NF(t)$ denotes the class modulo C of its normal forms. Let M be the interpretation of E_l defined by $\to$, that is to say : the domain of M is $\{NF(t): t \in T\}$ and the interpretation of l is

$l^M(NF(x),NF(y),NF(z))=NF(l(x,y,z))$. The confluence of $\rightarrow$ implies the correctness of this definition.

proposition 4.4 M is a minimal model of E_l.

This model is called the quasi-initial model of E_l.

5   Constructive theorems of the affine geometry of collinearity

Now, we use our term rewriting system for the proof of some theorems of the affine geometry of collinearity. Those theorems will be «constructive» according to the following definitions. A geometrical fact is one of the following two sentences:

(i) x is a point distinct from the points $x_1, ..., x_n$: $x{\neq}x_1 \wedge ... \wedge x{\neq}x_n$

(ii) x is a point collinear with y and z and distinct from the points $x_1, ..., x_n$:
$$L(y,z,x) \wedge x{\neq}x_1 \wedge ... \wedge x{\neq}x_n$$

Let $G = [F_1,...,F_k]$ be a finite sequence of geometrical facts. It is coherent whenever, for every $i=1,...,k$, if $F_i = $ «x is a point collinear with y and z and ...» then, for some $j=1,...,i-1$, F_j contains the disequation $y{\neq}z$. In geometrical facts of type *(i)*, x depends on $x_1, ..., x_n$. In geometrical facts of type *(ii)*, x depends on y, z, $x_1, ..., x_n$. A constructive geometrical proposition is a coherent finite sequence of geometrical facts in which no point depends directly or indirectly on itself. This notion of constructivity can be found in Hilbert [9] from a more general point of view. In our context, to any constructive geometrical proposition, we can constructively associate a figure of the affine geometry of collinearity. The proof of the following theorem is done by induction on the length of the constructive geometrical proposition.

theorem 5.1 Every constructive geometrical proposition is a consistent proposition of E_L satisfiable in the real plane.

example 5.2 The sequence: *(1)* x is a point, *(2)* y is a point distinct from x, *(3)* z is a point collinear with x and y and distinct from y, *(4)* t is a point collinear with x and y is a constructive geometrical proposition. It corresponds to the following figure.

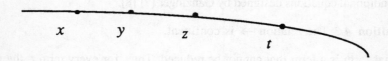

Let $G = [F_1,...,F_k]$ be a constructive geometrical proposition. Let F be an quantifier-free equational formula. Then $G*F$ is the equational formula defined by induction on the length of G in the following recursive way :

$[F_1,...,F_{k-1},$«x is a point distinct from the points $x_1, ..., x_n$»$]*F =$
$$[F_1,...,F_{k-1}]*(x{\neq}x_1 \wedge ... \wedge x{\neq}x_n \Rightarrow F)$$

$[F_1,...,F_{k-1},$«x is a point collinear with y and z and distinct from the points x_1, ..., x_n»$]*F = [F_1,...,F_{k-1}]*(x{\neq}x_1 \wedge ... \wedge x{\neq}x_n \Rightarrow F)\sigma$ where σ is the substitution: $x=l(y,z,x)$

$[]*F = F$

The equational formula associated to the constructive geometrical proposition of example 5.2 and to the equation $l(y,z,t)=t$ is: $x{\neq}y \wedge y{\neq}l(x,y,z) \Rightarrow l(y,l(x,y,z),l(x,y,t))=l(x,y,t)$. Next proposition will be used in the sequel to prove that our term rewriting system can be used to prove property of constructive geometrical figures.

proposition 5.3 Let F_i be the geometrical fact «x is a point collinear with y and z and distinct from the points $x_1, ..., x_n$» and D be a disjunction of equations containing the equation $y=z$. Then $F_i{}^* \Rightarrow D$ is logically equivalent in E_l to $(x{\neq}x_1 \wedge ... \wedge x{\neq}x_n \Rightarrow D)\sigma$ where σ is the substitution: $x=l(y,z,x)$.

Let $G = [F_1,...,F_k]$ be a constructive geometrical proposition. Let σ_i be the substitution and C_i be the conjunction of disequations associated to F_i, $i=1,...,k$, in the following way. If $F_i=$«x_i is a point distinct from the points $x_1, ..., x_n$» then σ_i is the empty substitution. If $F_i=$«x_i is a point collinear with y_i and z_i and distinct from the points $x_1, ..., x_n$» then σ_i is the substitution $\{x_i=l(y_i,z_i,x_i)\}$. In both case, C_i is $x_i{\neq}x_1 \wedge ... \wedge x_i{\neq}x_n$. Let $(y_{j1},z_{j1}), ..., (y_{jm},z_{jm})$ be the pairs of variables y and z appearing in the geometrical facts of type *(ii)* of G.

Let x, y and z be three distinct variables such that the disequation $x{\neq}y$ appears in one of the F_i. Since G is coherent, then, according to proposition 5.3, $F_1{}^* \wedge ... \wedge F_k{}^* \Rightarrow x=y \vee l(x,y,z)=z$ is logically equivalent to $(C_1 \wedge ... \wedge C_k \Rightarrow l(x,y,z)=z)\sigma_k o...o\sigma_1$. Let $G*(l(x,y,z)=z)$ be the equational formula associated to G and to the equation $l(x,y,z)=z$. According to the above discussion, $G*(l(x,y,z)=z)$ is logically equivalent to $C \Rightarrow t_1=t_2$ where $C=(C_1 \wedge ... \wedge C_k)\sigma_k o...o\sigma_1$, $t_1=l(x,y,z)\sigma_k o...o\sigma_1$ and $t_2=\sigma_k o...o\sigma_1(z)$. Next proposition is a direct consequence of proposition 5.3 and the above discussion.

proposition 5.4 $F_1 \wedge ... \wedge F_k \Rightarrow L(x,y,z)$ is a theorem of E_L if and only if $C \Rightarrow t_1=t_2$ is a theorem of E_l.

Moreover, the equational formula $C \Rightarrow t_1 = t_2$ is such that, for every subterm $l(u,v,w)$ in t_1 or t_2, the disequation $u \neq v$ is in C. This is important since the term $l(u,v,w)$ has a geometrical meaning only if u and v denote distinct points.

proposition 5.5 C contains all the disequations $u \neq v$ such that, for some term w, $l(u,v,w)$ is a subterm of t_1 or t_2.

Next proposition will be used in the proof of theorem 5.8. It implies that the set C of negative conditions is consistent in E_l.

proposition 5.6 C is true in M, the quasi-initial model of E_l.

Moreover, our term rewriting system can be directly used to show that $C \Rightarrow t_1 = t_2$ is a theorem of E_l. Next result is the key proposition for the proof of theorem 5.8.

proposition 5.7 If t_1 and t_2 have a same normal form with respect to the relation $\rightarrow$ then $C \Rightarrow t_1 = t_2$ is a theorem of E_l.

proof If t_1 and t_2 have a same normal form with respect to the relation $\rightarrow$ then, since t_1 is a term of the form $l(t_{11}, t_{12}, t_2)$, $t_1 \rightarrow^* t_2$. The proof can be done by induction on N, the number of rewrite steps needed to reduce t_1 to t_2.

If $N = 0$ then $t_1 =_C t_2$: a contradiction.

Now if $N > 0$ then t_1 can be rewritten into t_2 using R_{11} or R_{12} or can be rewritten into $l(t_{121}, t_{122}, t_2)$ using R_{13} - in the latter case, t_{12} is a term of the form $l(t_{121}, t_{122}, t_{123})$ such that $l(t_{121}, t_{122}, t_{11}) \downarrow t_{11}$.

If $l(t_{11}, t_{12}, t_2)$ can be rewritten into t_2 using R_{11} then $t_{11} =_C t_2$ or $t_{12} =_C t_2$ and, since C contains the disequation $t_{11} \neq t_{12}$, $C \Rightarrow t_1 = t_2$ is a theorem of E_l.

If $l(t_{11}, t_{12}, t_2)$ can be rewritten into t_2 using R_{12} then t_2 is a term of the form $l(t_{21}, t_{22}, t_{23})$ such that $l(t_{11}, t_{12}, t_{21}) \downarrow t_{21}$ and $l(t_{11}, t_{12}, t_{22}) \downarrow t_{22}$. By induction hypothesis, $C \Rightarrow l(t_{11}, t_{12}, t_{21}) = t_{21}$ and $C \Rightarrow l(t_{11}, t_{12}, t_{22}) = t_{22}$ are theorems of E_l. Consequently, since C contains the disequations $t_{11} \neq t_{12}$ and $t_{21} \neq t_{22}$, $C \Rightarrow t_1 = t_2$ is a theorem of E_l.

If $l(t_{11}, t_{12}, t_2)$ can be rewritten into $l(t_{121}, t_{122}, t_2)$ using R_{13} - that is to say: t_{12} is a term of the form $l(t_{121}, t_{122}, t_{123})$ such that $l(t_{121}, t_{122}, t_{11}) \downarrow t_{11}$ - then, by induction hypothesis, $C \Rightarrow l(t_{121}, t_{122}, t_{11}) = t_{11}$ and $C \Rightarrow l(t_{121}, t_{122}, t_2) = t_2$ are theorems of E_l. Consequently, since C contains the disequations $t_{11} \neq l(t_{121}, t_{122}, t_{123})$ and $t_{121} \neq t_{122}$, $C \Rightarrow t_1 = t_2$ is a theorem of E_l.

Now we can state the main theorem relating proofs in the theory E_L and rewrites with respect to the reduction relation $\rightarrow$.

theorem 5.8 $F_1 \wedge \ldots \wedge F_k \Rightarrow L(x,y,z)$ is a theorem of E_L if and only if t_1 and t_2 have a same normal form with respect to the relation $\rightarrow$.

Here are three examples that will demonstrate the basic points of our method.

end of example 5.2 Let it be proved that if the points x, y, z and t are such that (first hypothesis) x, y and z are collinear, x and y are distinct and y and z are distinct, and (second hypothesis) x, y and t are collinear then (conclusion) y, z and t are collinear.

The hypotheses and the conclusion can be expressed using the equations: $l(x,y,z)=z$, $l(x,y,t)=t$ and $l(y,z,t)=t$. In the hypothesis, x and y can be considered as parameters while z and t should be considered as variables verifying the equations $l(x,y,z)=z$ and $l(x,y,t)=t$. The constructive geometrical proposition associated to this problem is the following sequence of geometrical facts: x is a point, y is a point distinct from x, z is a point collinear with x and y and distinct from y, t is a point collinear with x and y.

What should be proved is that the terms $l(y,l(x,y,z),l(x,y,t))$ and $l(x,y,t)$ have a same normal form with respect to the relation $\rightarrow$. It holds:

the rule R_{13} rewrites the term $l(y,l(x,y,z),l(x,y,t))$ into the term $l(x,y,l(x,y,t))$ and the rule R_{12} rewrites the term $l(x,y,l(x,y,t))$ into the term $l(x,y,t)$

example 5.9 Let it be proved that if the points x, y, z, x', y' and z' are such that (first hypothesis) x, y and z' are collinear (second hypothesis) y, z and x' are collinear, (third hypothesis) z, x and y' are collinear and x' and y' are distinct, and (fourth hypothesis) x, y and z are collinear and pairwise distinct then (conclusion) x', y' are z' are collinear.

The hypotheses and the conclusion can be expressed using the equations: $l(x,y,z')=z'$, $l(y,z,x')=x'$, $l(z,x,y')=y'$, $l(x,y,z)=z$ and $l(x',y',z')=z'$. The constructive geometrical proposition associated to this problem is the following sequence of geometrical facts: x is a point, y is a point distinct from x, z is a point collinear with x and y and distinct from x and y, x' is a point collinear with y and z, y' is a point collinear with z and x and distinct from x', z' is a point collinear with x and y. These hypotheses correspond to the following figure. What should be proved is that the terms $l(l(y,l(x,y,z),x'),l(l(x,y,z),x,y'),l(x,y,z'))$ and $l(x,y,z')$ have a same normal form with respect to the relation $\rightarrow$. It holds:

the rule R_{13} rewrites in two steps the term $l(l(y,l(x,y,z),x'),l(l(x,y,z),x,y'),l(x,y,z'))$ into the term $l(l(x,y,x'),l(x,y,y'),l(x,y,z'))$ which is rewritten into $l(x,y,l(x,y,z'))$ using the rule R_{13}, and the rule R_{12} rewrites the term $l(x,y,l(x,y,z'))$ into the term $l(x,y,z')$

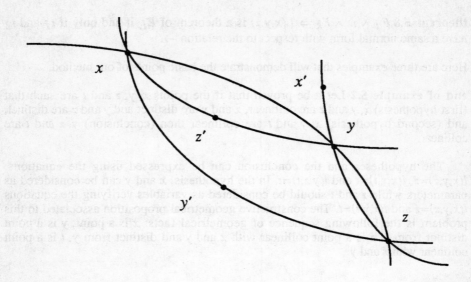

example 5.10 Let it be proved that if the points x, y, z, t and u are such that (first hypothesis) x, y and z are collinear and x and y are distinct, (second hypothesis) x, y and t are collinear and z and t are distinct, and (third hypothesis) z, t and u are collinear then (conclusion) x, y and u are collinear.

The hypotheses and the conclusion can be expressed using the equations: $l(x,y,z)=z$, $l(x,y,t)=t$, $l(z,t,u)=u$ and $l(x,y,u)=u$. These hypotheses correspond to the following figure.

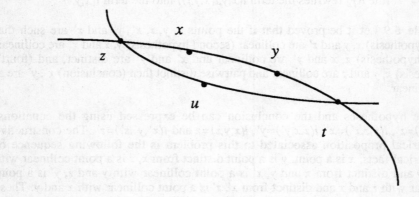

The constructive geometrical proposition associated to this problem is the following sequence of geometrical facts: x is a point, y is a point distinct from x, z is a point collinear with x and y, t is a point collinear with x and y and distinct from z, u is a point collinear with z and t. What should be proved is that the terms

$l(x,y,l(l(x,y,z),l(x,y,t),u))$ and $l(l(x,y,z),l(x,y,t),u)$ have a same normal form with respect to the relation $\rightarrow$. It holds:

the rule R_{12} rewrites the term $l(x,y,l(l(x,y,z),l(x,y,t),u))$ into the term
$$l(l(x,y,z),l(x,y,t),u)$$

6 Unification

We would like to solve equational problems in the algebra of the normal forms generated by the terminating and confluent reduction relation $\rightarrow$. This means that given any finite set of equations and disequations S, we would like to decide whether there is some substitution σ such that $S\sigma\downarrow$. Narrowing is a mechanism that can be used for this purpose. The narrowing approach to the problem of generating complete sets of unifiers has been successfully developed to an important class of equational theories [10] [14]. It has been extended to the conditional case by [3], [11], [12], [15] and [16]. We extend to our positive/negative CTRS the narrowing procedure and use it for the resolution of R_l-unification problem.

Let S be a finite set of equations and disequations. An idempotent substitution σ is an R_l-unifier of S if $S\sigma\downarrow$. A substitution σ is normalized with respect to R_l if, for every variable x in the domain of σ, $\sigma(x)$ is irreducible with respect to R_l. The main purpose of this section is to show that the narrowing procedure is complete for R_l-unification with respect to normalized substitution, that is to say: for every set S of equations and disequations and for every normalized R_l-unifier θ of S, the narrowing procedure computes an R_l-unifier σ of S such that $\sigma \leq_C \theta$ $[W]$. Let us remark that, for every normalized substitution σ, for every variant $Q \Rightarrow l \rightarrow r$ of a rule in R_l and for every term s, if a subterm in some non-variable position p of $s\sigma$ matches l modulo C via some substitution τ and if condition $Q\tau$ is satisfied then p is a non-variable position in s.

Let S be a set of equations and disequations. If the substitution σ is an R_l-unifier of S then either σ is a unifier of S^+ modulo C in the usual sense or S is narrowable according to the next definition. Let W be a set of "protected variables". The one step narrowing relation $\Rightarrow$ away from W is defined so that, for every set S and T of equations and disequations, $S \Rightarrow T$ $[W]$ if and only if there is an equation $s=t$ in S, a non-variable position p in s, a variant $Q \Rightarrow l \rightarrow r$ of a rule in R_l and a most general unifier σ of s/p and l modulo C away from W such that T is obtained from S replacing s/p by r, adding equations and disequations of Q and finally applying the substitution σ. The set T is called a surreduction of S away from W. Note here that an equation $s=t$ stands ambiguously for $s=t$ or $t=s$.

example 6.1 The set $S=\{l(x,y,z)=z\}$ has five surreductions:

(i) $S_1=\{x\neq y\}$ which uses R_{11} with substitution $\sigma_1=\{z=x\}$

(ii) $S_2=\{x\neq y\}$ which uses R_{11} with substitution $\sigma_2=\{z=y\}$

(iii) $S_3=\{l(x,y,z_1)=z_1,\ l(x,y,z_2)=z_2,\ x\neq y,\ z_1\neq z_2\}$ which uses R_{12} with substitution $\sigma_3=\{z=l(z_1,z_2,z_3)\}$

(iv) $S_4=\{l(y_1,y_2,z)=z,\ l(y_1,y_2,x)=x,\ x\neq l(y_1,y_2,y_3),\ y_1\neq y_2\}$ which uses R_{13} with substitution $\sigma_4=\{y=l(y_1,y_2,y_3)\}$

(v) $S_5=\{l(x_1,x_2,z)=z,\ l(x_1,x_2,y)=y,\ l(x_1,x_2,x_3)\neq y,\ x_1\neq x_2\}$ which uses R_{13} with substitution $\sigma_5=\{x=l(x_1,x_2,x_3)\}$

Next soundness result is that substitutions computed with the narrowing relation are R_l-unifiers.

theorem 6.2 *(soundness of narrowing)* Let S be a set of equations and disequations. For every narrowing sequence $S_0=S \Rightarrow_{\sigma 1} S_1 \Rightarrow_{\sigma 2} ... \Rightarrow_{\sigma n} S_n$ using variants $Q_1 \Rightarrow l_1 \rightarrow r_1$, $Q_2 \Rightarrow l_2 \rightarrow r_2$, ..., $Q_n \Rightarrow l_n \rightarrow r_n$ and substitutions $\sigma_1, \sigma_2, ..., \sigma_n$ and for every C-unifier μ of S_n, the substitution $\theta = \sigma_1 o \sigma_2 ... o \sigma_n o \mu$ is an R_l-unifier of S.

example 6.3 Let $S = \{l(x,y,z)=x,\ l(y,z,t)=y,\ x\neq y,\ y\neq z\}$. Using rule R_{11} and substitution $\{z=x\}$, $S_0=S \Rightarrow S_1=\{l(y,x,t)=y,\ x\neq y\}$. Using rule R_{11} and substitution $\{t=y\}$, $S_1 \Rightarrow S_2=\{x\neq y\}$. The substitution $\{z=x,\ t=y\}$ is a most general R_l-unifier of S.

From now on, S and T will denote finite sets of equations and disequations in the language of E_l. The expressions S^+ and S^- will respectively denote the set of equations and the set of disequations that appear in S. A set S is *consistent* if it is true in some model of E_l. For every set S and for every substitution σ, note that if $S\sigma\downarrow$ then $S\sigma$ is true in M and S is consistent. Any set S defines a sequence $(\rightarrow_{S,n})_{n\geq 0}$ of binary relations on T such that $\rightarrow_{S,0}=\emptyset$ and $t \rightarrow_{S,n+1} t'$ if either $t \rightarrow_{S,n} t'$ or there are :

(i) a position p of t
(ii) a substitution σ
(iii) a variant $Q \Rightarrow l \rightarrow r$ such that $t/p=C l\sigma$, $t'=t[r\sigma]_p$, for every $u=v$ in Q, $u\sigma\downarrow_{S,n} v\sigma$ and, for every $u\neq v$ in Q, there is $u'\neq v'$ in S such that $u\sigma\downarrow_{S,n} u'$ and $v\sigma\downarrow_{S,n} v'$

Let $\rightarrow_S = \cup_{n\geq 0} \rightarrow_{S,n}$. It can be proved that $\rightarrow_S$ is decidable and terminating. We study this new relation of reduction with respect to some set of equations and disequations because of its importance for the completeness proof of narrowing. This new relation possesses interesting properties that $\rightarrow$ does not satisfy. For example, the rewrite relation $\rightarrow$ is not stable under substitution: in general, $t \rightarrow t'$ does not imply $t\theta \rightarrow t'\theta$.

proposition 6.4 For every set S and for every substitution θ, $t \rightarrow_S t'$ implies that $t\theta \rightarrow_{S\theta} t'\theta$.

In other respects, rewrites with $\rightarrow_S$ or $\rightarrow$ are not related to each other. For example, if $S=\{x{\neq}x\}$ then $l(x,x,x) \rightarrow_S x$ but $l(x,x,x) \not\rightarrow x$. This is not the case if $S{\downarrow}$.

proposition 6.5 For every set S, if $S{\downarrow}$ then $\rightarrow_S \subseteq \rightarrow$.

Next proposition relates rewriting steps with respect to $\rightarrow_S$ and logical consequences of S in E_l.

proposition 6.6 For every set S, if $t{\downarrow}_S t'$ then $\vdash_{El} S \Rightarrow t = t'$.

The relation $\rightarrow$ was confluent (proposition 3.3). Is there some conditions on S such that the relation $\rightarrow_S$ is confluent too ?

proposition 6.7 For every consistent set S, $\rightarrow_S$ is confluent.

The function denoted by the symbol l is only partial, that is to say: the function is not properly defined when its two first arguments are equal. A set S is *saturated* if, for every of its subterms of the form $l(u,v,w)$, it contains an disequation $u'{\neq}v'$ such that $u{\downarrow}_S u'$ and $v{\downarrow}_S v'$. From a geometrical point of view non-saturated sets of equations and disequations are not interesting: the term $l(u,v,w)$ has a geometrical meaning only if u and v denote distinct points. It is always decidable to check whether a finite set of equations and disequations is saturated or not. Moreover, it is remarkable that saturation is preserved by unification modulo C.

proposition 6.8 For every saturated set S and for every mgu μ of S^+ modulo C, $S\mu$ is saturated.

The notion of a saturated set of equations and disequations is essential for the completeness proof of narrowing. We begin our study of saturated sets by next proposition which is the converse of proposition 6.5.

proposition 6.9 For every saturated set S and for every subterm w of S, if $w \rightarrow w'$ then $w \rightarrow_S w'$.

As a consequence, a saturated set S of disequations is consistent if and only if $S{\downarrow}$.

proposition 6.10 For every saturated set S of disequations, S is consistent if and only if $S{\downarrow}_S$ if and only if $S{\downarrow}$.

Next result states the completeness of narrowing, that is to say : if a normalized substitution θ R_l-unifies a saturated set S of equations and disequations then there is a narrowing sequence whose associated substitution is more general than θ.

theorem 6.11 (*completeness of narrowing*) For every saturated set S of equations and disequations, for every normalized R_l-unifier θ of S and for every set W of "protected variables" containing $Var(S)$ and $D(\theta)$, there exists a narrowing sequence $S_0=S \Rightarrow S_1 \Rightarrow ... \Rightarrow S_n$ away from W using substitutions $\sigma_1, \sigma_2, ..., \sigma_n$ and a most general unifier μ of S_n^+ modulo C such that $\sigma_1{\circ}\sigma_2...{\circ}\sigma_n{\circ}\mu \leq_C \theta \; [W]$ and $S_n^-\mu{\downarrow}$.

Let S be a saturated set of equations and disequations and W be a set of variables. A narrowing sequence $S_0=S \Rightarrow S_1 \Rightarrow ... \Rightarrow S_n$ away from W using substitutions σ_1, σ_2, ..., σ_n together with a most general unifier μ of S_n^+ modulo C such that $S_n^-\mu\downarrow$ will be denoted by $S \Rightarrow * S_n$ $[\theta,W]$ where $\theta=\sigma_1\circ\sigma_2...\circ\sigma_n\circ\mu$.

corollary 6.12 For every saturated set S of equations and disequations and for every set W of "protected variables" containing $Var(S)$, the set $CSU_{Rl}(S)$ $[W] = \{\theta/Var(S):$ $S \Rightarrow * S'$ $[\theta,W]\}$ is a complete set of R_l-unifiers of S away from W.

That is to say: for every normalized R_l-unifier σ of S, there is a substitution θ in $CSU_{Rl}(S)$ $[W]$ such that $\theta \leq_C \sigma$ $[Var(S)]$.

Now, we analyse what it means for a substitution to be an R_l-unifier. Since, for every set S, for every narrowing sequence $S_0=S \Rightarrow_{\sigma1} S_1 \Rightarrow_{\sigma2} ... \Rightarrow_{\sigma n} S_n$ starting from S and for every mgu μ of S_n^+ modulo C, $\vdash_{El} S_n^-\mu \Rightarrow S\sigma_1\circ\sigma_2...\circ\sigma_n\circ\mu$, then, given a saturated set S, narrowing computes two things :

(i)   an R_l-unifier $\sigma=\sigma_1\circ\sigma_2...\circ\sigma_n\circ\mu$ of S

(ii)   a finite set $S_n^-\mu$ of negative conditions such that $\vdash_{El} S_n^-\mu \Rightarrow S^+\sigma$ and $S_n^-\mu\downarrow$

The negative conditions $S_n^-\mu$ can be considered as *nondegenerate conditions* that the variables in $S^+\sigma$ have to satisfy. They should be such that $S_n^-\mu\downarrow$ since otherwise, according to proposition 6.10, $S_n^-\mu$ would not be consistent and $\vdash_{El} S_n^-\mu \Rightarrow S^+\sigma$ would be vacuously true.

example 6.13 The narrowing sequence:

$S_0=\{l(x,y,z)=z,\ x{\neq}y\} \Rightarrow_{\sigma1} S_1=\{l(x,y,z_1)=z_1,\ l(x,y,z_2)=z_2,\ x{\neq}y,\ z_1{\neq}z_2\}$
$S_1 \Rightarrow_{\sigma2} S_2=\{l(z_1,y,z_2)=z_2,\ z_1{\neq}y,\ z_1{\neq}z_2\}$
$S_2 \Rightarrow_{\sigma3} S_3=\{l(y_1,y_2,z_2)=z_2,\ l(y_1,y_2,z_1)=z_1,\ z_1{\neq}l(y_1,y_2,y_3),\ y_1{\neq}y_2,\ z_1{\neq}z_2\}$
$S_3 \Rightarrow_{\sigma4} S_4=\{l(y_1,z_2,z_1)=z_1,\ z_1{\neq}l(y_1,z_2,y_3),\ y_1{\neq}z_2,\ z_1{\neq}z_2\}$
$S_4 \Rightarrow_{\sigma5} S_5=\{z_1{\neq}l(z_1,z_2,y_3),\ z_1{\neq}z_2\}$

using rules $R_{12}, R_{11}, R_{13}, R_{11}$ and R_{11}, and substitutions $\sigma_1=\{z=l(z_1,z_2,z_3)\}$, $\sigma_2=\{x=z_1\}$, $\sigma_3=\{y=l(y_1,y_2,y_3)\}$, $\sigma_4=\{y_2=z_2\}$ and $\sigma_5=\{y_1=z_1\}$ proves that :

$$\vdash_{El} z_1{\neq}l(z_1,z_2,y_3) \wedge z_1{\neq}z_2 \Rightarrow l(z_1,l(z_1,z_2,y_3),l(z_1,z_2,z_3))=l(z_1,z_2,z_3)$$

7. Conclusion

The rewriting approach to geometrical reasoning we have presented reinstates geometry in its original form : direct reasoning upon figures instead of computing upon polynomial expressions. It is innovative for more than two reasons. Firstly, geometrical figures are considered as abstract terms in a first order language. This makes it easier for the geometer to find general proofs of constructive theorems (using some set of rewrite rules that simplify these terms). Secondly, the rewriting systems we have studied is the first example of a positive/negative CTRS with some applications for the mechanization of reasoning in some first order theory like our fragment of Hilbert's geometry of incidence.

Of course, this fragment is very small and contains no "difficult" theorems of elementary geometry like Desargues or Pappus theorems. Nevertheless, we believe this work can be easily extended to more "complex" geometrical theories like affine geometry with order or like projective geometry. The extension to projective geometry could be done in the following way [1]. The language of projective geometry is made of two types of geometrical beings : points (denoted by capital letters) and lines (denoted by lower case letters), together with an incidence relation such that two distinct points define exactly one line and two distinct lines intersect on exactly one point. This geometrical theory is equivalent to *(i)* the algebraic theory of ternary rings [1] and *(ii)* the first order theory with equality made of the following eight axioms [1]:

$$l(X,Y)=l(Y,X)$$
$$i(x,y)=i(y,x)$$
$$X \neq i(x,y) \wedge x \neq y \wedge p(X,x)=X \Rightarrow l(X,i(x,y))=x$$
$$X \neq p(Y,x) \wedge p(X,x)=X \Rightarrow l(X,p(Y,x))=x$$
$$x \neq l(X,Y) \wedge X \neq Y \wedge p(X,x)=X \Rightarrow i(x,l(X,Y))=X$$
$$X \neq Y \Rightarrow p(X,l(X,Y))=X$$
$$x \neq y \Rightarrow p(i(x,y),x)=i(x,y)$$
$$p(p(X,x),x)=p(X,x)$$

where $l(X,Y)$ denotes the line passing through the points X and Y, $i(x,y)$ denotes the intersection point of the lines x and y and $p(X,x)$ denotes a projection of the point X onto the line x. As a consequence, equation solving in ternary rings and unification in the geometrical theory axiomatized by the above formulas are equivalent classes of problems. The narrowing-based mechanism we have defined for the affine geometry of collinearity could thus be used as a geometrical tool for the resolution of algebraic equations in ternary systems.

Notes *(a)* Institut de recherche en informatique de Toulouse, 118 route de Narbonne, F-31062 Toulouse Cedex. Email: balbiani@irit.fr. *(b)* Its proof and the proof of other results can be found in Balbiani et al [1]. *(c)* Rewriting modulo commutativity is an easy generalization of standard rewriting.

Acknowledgements Vincent Dugat and Anne Lopez read a preliminary version of this paper and made suggestions that carried out many improvements to its content.

References

1.   P. Balbiani, V. Dugat, L. Fariñas del Cerro and A. Lopez. Eléments de géométrie mécanique. Hermès, Paris, France, 1994.

2. L. Bachmair. Canonical Equational Proofs. Birkhaüser, Boston, Massachusetts, 1991.

3. A. Bockmayr. Conditional rewriting and narrowing as a theoretical framework for logic-functional programming. Technical report 10/86, Institut für Informatik, Universität Karlsruhe, 1986.

4. B. Buchberger . Gröbner bases: an algorithmic method in polynomial ideal theory. In N. Bose editor : Recent Trends in Multidimensional Systems Theory. Reidel, Dordrecht, Netherlands, 1985.

5. J.-P. Colette. Histoire des mathématiques. Editions du renouveau pédagogique, Ottawa, Canada, 1979.

6. N. Dershowitz and J.-P. Jouannaud. Rewrite systems. In J. van Leeuwen, editor : Handbook of Theoretical Computer Science: Formal Models and Semantics. North-Holland, Amsterdam, Netherlands, p. 243-309, 1990.

7. H. Ganzinger. Ground term confluence in parametric conditional equational specifications. Proceedings of the Symposium on Theoretical Aspects of Computer Science. Springer-Verlag, LNCS 247, 1987.

8. H. Ganzinger. A completion procedure for conditional equations. In S. Kaplan and J.-P. Jouannaud, editors : Conditional Term Rewriting Systems, 1st International Workshop, Orsay, France, july 1987, Proceedings. Springer Verlag, LNCS 308, p. 62-83, 1988.

9. D. Hilbert. Les fondements de la géométrie. Dunod, Paris, France, 1971.

10. J.-M. Hullot. Canonical forms and unification. Proceedings of the Fifth Conference on Automated Deduction. Springer-Verlag, LNCS 87, p. 318-334, 1980.

11. H. Hußmann. Unification in conditional equational theories. In: EUROCAL, Linz, Austria, 1985, Proceedings. Springer-Verlag, LNCS 204, p. 543-553, 1985.

12. S. Kaplan. Simplifying conditional term rewriting systems: unification, termination and confluence. In : Journal of Symbolic Computation, volume 4, number 3, p. 295-334, 1987.

13. S. Kaplan. Positive/negative conditional rewriting. In S. Kaplan and J.-P. Jouannaud, editors : Conditional Term Rewriting Systems, 1st International Workshop, Orsay, France, july 1987, Proceedings. Springer Verlag, LNCS 308, p. 129-141, 1988.

14. C. Kirchner. Méthodes et outils de conception systématique d'algorithmes d'unification dans les théories équationnelles. Thèse d'état de l'université de Nancy, 1985.

15.   M. Martelli and U. Montanari. An efficient unification algorithm. In :
       ACM Transactions on Programming Languages and Systems, volume 4,
       number 2, pages 258-282, 1982.

16.   A. Middeldorp and E. Hamoen. Counterexamples to completeness
       results for basic narrowing. In H. Kirchner and G. Levi (editors): Algebraic
       and Logic Programming, Third International ALP Conference,
       Volterra, Italy, september 1992, Proceedings. Springer-Verlag,
       LNCS 632, p. 244-258, 1992.

17.   M. Rusinowitch. Démonstration automatique, techniques de réécriture.
       InterEditions, Paris, France, 1989.

18.   W. Snyder. A Proof Theory for General Unification. Birkhäuser,
       Boston, Massachusetts, 1991.

19.   W.-T. Wu. Basic Principles of Mechanical Theorem Proving in
       Geometries. Springer-Verlag, 1994.

Burnside Monoids
Word Problem and the Conjecture of Brzozowski

Jean-François Rey

IBP–LITP Université Paris VI
4, place Jussieu
75252 Paris Cedex 05
rey@litp.ibp.fr

1   Introduction

The aim of this lecture is to briefly present the results obtained by Alair Pereira do Lago [dL91]. His work brings to the fore the links which exist between the algebraic structure of Burnside monoids and a rewriting system which can be used to solve the word problem in these monoids.

If $n \geq 2$ and $m \geq 1$ are two integers and if A is a finite alphabet, we denote by $\mathcal{B}$ the quotient monoid of A^* by the congruence generated by $x^n = x^{n+m}$. The conjecture of Brzozowski [Brz80] asserts that the equivalence classes in A^* for this congruence are all rational sets. This problem has been initiated by Imre Simon as far back as 1970. In 1979, Janusz Brzozowski [Brz80] presents this problem, in the case $m = 1$, as one of the most difficult one in rational languages theory.

At that time, we knew that the monoid $\mathcal{B}$ was infinite, but the rationality of the equivalence classes was proved only for some peculiar cases [BCG71]. Imre Simon has shown up that the conjecture will be solved if we could prove that, for all $w \in \mathcal{B}$, the sets

$$\{u \in \mathcal{B} \mid w \leq_{\mathcal{J}} u\}$$

are finite, where $\leq_{\mathcal{J}}$ is the Green's preorder[1] which arises from the inclusion of principal ideals [How76, Pin84]. In this case, we say that the monoid $\mathcal{B}$ is *finite* $\mathcal{J}$–above, then the set

$$N_w = \{u \in \mathcal{B} \mid w \not\leq_{\mathcal{J}} u\}$$

is a cofinite ideal in $\mathcal{B}$ and the Rees quotient $\mathcal{B}/N_w$, which we get by equalling any element of N_w to 0 is a finite monoid which recognizes the class of w ; in other words, this class is recognizable by a finite automata.

The first signifiant advance in the resolution of the conjecture, which took place in 1990, is the work of Aldo de Luca and Stefano Varricchio [dLV90]. In the case $n \geq 5$ and $m = 1$, they have the idea of building a rewriting system solving the word problem in the monoid $\mathcal{B}$ to prove that, for all $w \in \mathcal{B}$, the Rees quotient $\mathcal{B}/N_w$ has only a finite number of $\mathcal{J}$–classes. From this, they deduce that $\mathcal{B}/N_w$ itself is finite since it verifies the hypotheses of Hotzel's lemma [Hot79]. This lemma says that, if a finitely generated semigroup has only a finite number of principal ideals and has

---

[1] $w \leq_{\mathcal{J}} u$ if and only if w belongs to the principal ideal $\mathcal{B}u\mathcal{B}$ generated by u.

only finite subgroups then the semigroup itself is finite. In their work, the hypothesis $m = 1$ is used to assert that subgroups are finite.

Concurrently, in a very different way, John McCammond [McC91] has proved the conjecture for $n \geq 6$ and any integer m. His proof based on automata surgery, is very difficult to follow (more than forty lemmas simultaneously proved by induction) and leaves in the dark numerous points. The advantage of his work lies in the results on the Burnside semigroups algebraic structure ; in particular, he proved that maximal subgroups of $\mathcal{B}$ are all cyclic of order m.

Alair Pereira do Lago goes back to the approach proposed by Aldo de Luca and Stefano Varricchio. On the one hand he proves the conjecture for $n \geq 4$ and any m, on the other hand he brings to the fore the tie which exists between his rewriting system and Green relations in Burnside monoid. Probably, his proof could be extended to the case $n = 3$ by means of accute results in combinatorics on words.

Since the session of the conference, the conjecture has been proved for $n = 3$ by V. S. Guba [Gu93a, Gu93b]. This new proof is an improvement of McCammond's work which has not yet been possibly extended to the proof done by Alair Pereira do Lago.

The methods used by Alair Pereira do Lago remain important since they bring to light new aspects of the algebraic structure of Burnside monoid, the interested reader could find a complete analysis of these methods in [Re92].

2   The rewriting system.

Let us recall that the word problem, in the case of Burnside monoid, is to decide whether two words w and w' in A^* are equivalent for the congruence $\sim_{n,m}$ generated by $x^n = x^{n+m}$.

For example, the two words $w' = (ab)^2(ba)^2b(ba)^2$ and $w = (ab)^2(ba)^2$ are equivalent for the congruence $\sim_{2,1}$ generated by $x^2 = x^3$:

$$
\begin{aligned}
(ab)^2(ba)^2b(ba)^2 &\sim_{2,1} (ab)^2(ba)^2b(ba)^3 \\
&= (ab)^2((ba)^2b)^2a \\
&\sim_{2,1} (ab)^3((ba)^2b)^2a \\
&= a((ba)^2b)^3a \\
&\sim_{2,1} a((ba)^2b)^2a \\
&= (ab)^3(ba)^3 \\
&\sim_{2,1} (ab)^2(ba)^2
\end{aligned}
$$

Hence, we can use the rewriting rule :

$$(ab)^2(ba)^2b(ba)^2 \longrightarrow (ab)^2(ba)^2.$$

With a closer look, we see that $(ab)^2(ba)^2$ is as the same time a prefix and a suffix of the word $(ab)^2(ba)^2b(ba)^2$, in this case we say that $(ab)^2(ba)^2$ is *a border* of the word $(ab)^2(ba)^2b(ba)^2$.

The analysis of critical pairs[2] of the rewriting system $\{x^{n+m} \longrightarrow x^n\}$ leads A. de Luca and S. Varricchio to look for a system where the rules will be of the form:

$$\sigma : l_\sigma = c_\sigma u^m \longrightarrow c_\sigma$$

and where c_σ is a border of l_σ; if that is the case l_σ could also be written as $l_\sigma = v^m c_\sigma$.

In what follows, we will denote by Ω the set of all rules having the above form. A rule in Ω is said to be *stable* if the period of c_σ is equal to the length of the word u.

In a rule σ, the word u that appears in the definition will be denoted by $\hat{\sigma}$. If σ is stable, the word $\hat{\sigma}$ is *primitive* word. In the same way the word v, which is a conjugate of u, is denoted by $\breve{\sigma}$.

We will see later that the concept of stability is essential to ensure that the rewriting system is confluent.

Now, let us state more precisely how the rules are built. In the process of eliminating critical pairs, we only need to consider overlaps at the ends of the rules.

Let u and v be two words in A^*. The longest suffix of u which is also a prefix of u is called the *overlap* of u by v. This word is also the longest prefix of v which is also a suffix of u.

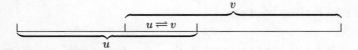

If τ and σ are two rules in Ω, we call *suffix of τ by σ* the word denoted by τ/σ and defined by the equation:

$$\tau/\sigma = \begin{cases} c_\sigma^{-1}(c_\tau \rightleftharpoons l_\sigma) & \text{if } |c_\tau \rightleftharpoons l_\sigma| > |c_\sigma| \text{ and } |\hat{\tau}| > |\hat{\sigma}|, \\ 1 & \text{otherwise.} \end{cases}$$

then we can use the rule:

$$l_\tau(\tau/\sigma)^{-1} \longrightarrow c_\tau(\tau/\sigma)^{-1}$$

in place of τ. This new rule is called the *right cut* of the rule τ by the rule σ.

---

[2] The reader can find in [De90] a description of the different tools used to solve word problem by means of rewriting systems.

In the same way, we define the *prefix of τ by σ* as the word denoted by $\sigma \backslash \tau$:

$$\sigma \backslash \tau = \begin{cases} (l_\sigma \rightleftharpoons c_\tau) c_\sigma^{-1} & \text{if } |l_\sigma \rightleftharpoons c_\tau| > |c_\sigma| \text{ and } |\hat{\tau}| > |\hat{\sigma}|, \\ 1 & \text{otherwise.} \end{cases}$$

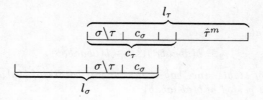

then we obtain the new rule :

$$(\sigma \backslash \tau)^{-1} l_\tau \longrightarrow (\sigma \backslash \tau)^{-1} c_\tau$$

which is called the *left cut* of τ by σ.

It is essential that the new rules built in this way are all stable, since only under this assumption we can prove the confluence of the rewriting system obtained by iterating the cutting process. The following example shows that it is not always possible to do so :

Example 2.1 *Let us assume $n = m = 2$ and $A = \{a, b\}$. If we take the following elements in Ω :*

$$\tau_0 = (abababa)^4 \longrightarrow (abababa)^2$$

$$\sigma_1 = (ab)^4 \longrightarrow (ab)^2$$

$$\sigma_2 = (ba)^4 \longrightarrow (ba)^2.$$

then we get the right cut of τ_0 by σ_1 :

$$
\overbrace{\underbrace{abab \mid aba \mid b}}^{l_{\sigma_1}}
$$
$$c\ sigma_1$$
$$\underbrace{abababa \mid abab \mid aba}_{c_{\tau_0}}$$

So we get :

$$\tau_1 = abab(abaabab)^3 \longrightarrow abab(abaabab)$$

since abab is the longest border of the word abab(abaabab), the shortest suffix period of abab(abaabab) is abaabab and the rule τ_1 is stable.

In the same way, we get the left cut of τ_1 by σ_2

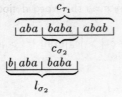

and we obtain the rule:

$$\tau_2 = b(abaabab)^3 \longrightarrow b(abaabab)$$

but the rule τ_2 is not stable since bab is the longest border of $b(abaabab)$ and aabab is the shortest suffix period of $b(abaabab)$.

If X is a subset of Ω, we call *closure* of X and we denote by $\mathcal{S}(X)$ the smallest subset of Ω which includes X and which is closed for left and right cuts.

We denote by $\mathrm{Irr}(X)$ the set of minimal elements of X, i.e. the rules in X which do not contain any other rule as a factor. It is easy to show that X, $\mathrm{Irr}(X)$ and $\mathcal{S}(X)$ are all equivalent in that these three sets of rules define the same congruence on A^*.

With this terminology, the building of the rewriting system could be seen as the building by induction of the following subsets of Ω :

$$(\pi_i)_{i \in \mathbf{N}} , (\pi_i')_{i \in \mathbf{N}} , (\Sigma_i)_{i \in \mathbf{N}} \text{ and } (\Sigma_i')_{i \in \mathbf{N}}$$

where $\pi_0 = \pi_0' = \Sigma_0 = \Sigma_0' = \emptyset$
and for $i > 0$

$$\pi_i = \left\{ x^{n+m} \longrightarrow x^n \mid x \in A^i \right\}$$
$$\pi_i' = \left\{ \tau \mid \tau \in \pi_i, \tau \text{ is stable and } \forall \sigma \in \Sigma_{\lfloor \frac{i-1}{m} \rfloor} , l_\sigma \text{ is not factor of } l_\tau \right\}$$
$$\Sigma_i' = \mathcal{S}(\pi_i' \cup \Sigma_{i-1})$$
$$\Sigma_i = \mathrm{Irr}(\Sigma_i')$$

We also define :

$$\pi = \bigcup_{i \in \mathbf{N}} \pi_i$$

$$\pi' = \bigcup_{i \in \mathbf{N}} \pi_i'$$

$$\Sigma = \bigcup_{i \in \mathbf{N}} \Sigma_i$$

$$\Sigma' = \bigcup_{i \in \mathbf{N}} \Sigma_i'$$

$$\Sigma'' = A^* \Sigma A^* \cap \Omega$$

The coherence of this construction relies on the following theorem :

Theorem 2.1 *The subsets π, π', Σ, Σ' and Σ'' are equivalent (i.e. they generate the same congruence).*

The proof is a very technical one and is based essentially on the previous work of Aldo de Luca and Stefano Varricchio [dLV90]. The delicate part is the proof of the equivalence of π and π'.

3   The completeness of Σ''

Let us denote by $\longrightarrow$ the rewriting relation on $A^* \times A^*$ generated by the system Σ'' and let us write $w \xrightarrow{\sigma} w'$ if the word w can be rewriten as w' in one step with the help of the rule σ. Clearly the relation $\longrightarrow$ is nœtherian since it reduces the length of words.

Moreover the stability of the system Σ'' implies that the relation $\longrightarrow$ is confluent:

Proposition 3.1 *If the system Σ'' is stable then the relation $\longrightarrow$ is locally confluent; more precisely, if $w \xrightarrow{\sigma} w_1$ and $w \xrightarrow{\tau} w_2$ and if $w_1 \neq w_2$, then there exists a word w_3 such that $w_1 \xrightarrow{\tau} w_3$ and $w_2 \xrightarrow{\sigma} w_3$.*

The stability of the system Σ'' becomes the key result we have to prove. This proof relies in fact on an accute analysis of the method by which the system Σ is generated:

Theorem 3.2 *If $n \geq 4$ then all the elements in Σ'' are stable.*
More precisely, for all $\tau \in \Sigma''$, we have:

$$(n-2)|\hat{\tau}| < |c_\tau|$$

and for all $\tau \in \Sigma'$, we have:

$$(n-2)|\hat{\tau}| < |c_\tau| \leq n|\hat{\tau}|.$$

The example 2.1 shows that the theorem is false if $n = m = 2$. More generally, it is false if $n = 2$ and $m \geq 2$. We do not know any counterexample in the case $n = 3$ or in the case $n = 2$ and $m = 1$. The work done by V. S. Guba [Gu93b] strengthens the conviction that this theorem is also true in the case $n = 3$.

In any case, for $n \geq 4$, the system $\{l_\sigma \longrightarrow c_\sigma | \sigma \in \Sigma\}$ is a complete one. If we denote by $\overline{w}$ the normal form of the word w for Σ, we deduce from the previous fact that:

- if w and w' are two words in A^* such that $w \sim_{n,m} w'$, then $\overline{w} = \overline{w'}$ and $\overline{w}$ is the shortest word in the equivalence class of w;
- a word is in normal form if and only if, for all $\sigma \in \Sigma$, l_σ is not a factor of the word w. In particular, if $\sigma \in \Sigma$ then any proper factor of l_σ is in normal form;
- there does not exist a proper subset of Σ which is equivalent to Σ, i.e. Σ is a minimal rewriting system.

4 The structure of Burnside monoids

The elements in $\mathcal{B}$ are the words of A^* which are in normal form. In order to avoid misunderstanding concatenation in A^* we will denote the law in $\mathcal{B}$ by $\cdot$. Hence,

$$\text{for all } w, w' \in \mathcal{B} \quad w \cdot w' = \overline{ww'}.$$

Let us recall that we denote by $\mathcal{R}$ the equivalence relation over $\mathcal{B}$ defined by

$$u \, \mathcal{R} \, v \text{ if and only if } u \in v\mathcal{B} \text{ and } v \in u\mathcal{B}.$$

Likewise, we define the equivalence relation $\mathcal{L}$ by

$$u \, \mathcal{L} \, v \text{ if and only if } u \in \mathcal{B}v \text{ and } v \in \mathcal{B}u.$$

The following proposition highlights the link which lies between the system Σ, the multiplication in $\mathcal{B}$ and the equivalence relation $\mathcal{R}$.

Proposition 4.1 *Let $u \in \mathcal{B}$ and $a \in A$. The following conditions are equivalent :*

1. *$ua \neq u \cdot a$;*
2. *There exist $\sigma \in \Sigma$ such that l_σ is suffix of ua.*

If they are satisfied, σ is unique and

$$u \, \mathcal{R} \, u \cdot a = xc_\sigma \text{ and } ua = xl_\sigma.$$

The main part of Alair Pereira do Lago's works is devoted to a close analysis of the $\mathcal{R}$–classes which goes beyond this lecture on rewriting methods.

One of the remarkable results over the $\mathcal{R}$–classes is the following:

Theorem 4.2 *Let w be the shortest word in its $\mathcal{R}$–class. Then there exists a bijection between this $\mathcal{R}$–class and the $\mathcal{R}$–class of the maximal suffix of the word w which is also a right part of a rule in Σ.*

Alair Pereira do Lago defines also the graph of the $\mathcal{R}$-classes. It is the oriented graph $G_\mathcal{R}$ whose edges are labelled by the letters of A and whose vertices are the $\mathcal{R}$-classes of $\mathcal{B}$. The edges are defined by :

$$R \xrightarrow{a} R' \text{ if and only if } a \in A, R \neq R' \text{ and there exists } u \in R \text{ such that } u \cdot a \in R'.$$

Likewise, the vertices of the oriented graph $G_\mathcal{L}$ are the $\mathcal{L}$-classes of $\mathcal{B}$ and its edges are :

$$L \xrightarrow{a} L' \text{ if and only if } a \in A, L \neq L' \text{ and there exists } u \in L \text{ such that } a \cdot u \in L'.$$

A precise characterization of reductions by the rewriting system Σ'' leads to the proof of the following theorem which is very important from the point of view of semigroups theorists, since it is a decisive step towards the proof of the decidability of the complexity of a semigroup [McC91].

Theorem 4.3 *The graphs $G_{\mathcal{R}}$ et $G_{\mathcal{L}}$ are trees.*

In order to prove the conjecture of Brzozowski (extended to any m) we have seen that we only need to show that $\mathcal{B}$ is finite $\mathcal{J}$–above. Since $\mathcal{B}$ is a torsion monoid, the relation $\mathcal{J}$ is nothing else but the relation $\mathcal{R}\,\mathcal{L}$ $(=\mathcal{L}\,\mathcal{R})$ and then the conjecture is deduced from the above theorem as soon as $n \geq 4$:

Theorem 4.4 *The $\mathcal{J}$-classes are finite and $\mathcal{B}$ is finite $\mathcal{J}$–above. In particular, if $w \in A^*$ then the equivalence class of the word w for the congruence $\sim_{n,m}$ is a rational set.*

To conclude, the links between combinatorics on words and the algebraic structure of Burnside monoids that have been brought to the fore by Alair Pereira do Lago should lead to a more accute knowledge of the algebraic structure of these monoids which crucially occur in global semigroup theory.

References

[BCG71] J. Brzozowski, K. Culik, and A. Gabrielian. Classification of non-counting events. *J. Comp. Syst. Sci.*, 5:41–53, 1971.

[Brz80] J. Brzozowski. Open problems about regular languages. In R. V. Book, editor, *Formal Language Theory, Perspectives and Open Problems*, pages 23–47. Academic Press, New York, 1980.

[De90] N. Dershowitz. Rewriting methods for word problems. In M. Ito, editor, *Words, Languages and Combinatorics* , pages 104–118, World Scientific, 1990.

[Gu93a] V. S. Guba. The word problem for the free semigroup satisfying $T^m = T^{m+n}$ with $m \geq 4$ or $m = 3$, $n = 1$. *Int. J. of Algebra and Computation*, Vol. 3, No. 2 (1993) 125–140.

[Gu93b] V. S. Guba. The word problem for the free semigroup satisfaying $T^m = T^{m+n}$ with $m \geq 3$. *Int. J. of Algebra and Computation*, Vol. 3, No. 3 (1993) 335–347.

[dL91] A. Pereira do Lago. Sobre os semigroupos de Burnside $x^n = x^{n+m}$. Master's thesis, Universidade de São Paulo, November 1991.

[dLV90] A. de Luca and S. Varrichio. On non-counting regular classes. In M. S. Patersen, editor, *Automata, Languages and Programming*, volume 443 of *Lecture Notes in Computer Science*, pages 74–87. Springer-Verlag, 1990.

[Hot79] E. Hotzel. On finiteness conditions in semigroups. *Journal of Algebra*, 60:352–370, 1979.

[How76] J. M. Howie. *An introduction to semigroup theory.* Academic Press, London, 1976.

[McC91] J. McCammond. The solution of the word problem for the relatively free semigroups satisfying $t^a = t^{a+b}$ with $a \geq 6$. *Int. J. of Algebra and Computation*, Vol. 1, No. 1 (1991) 1–32.

[Re92] J.-F. Rey. Semigroupes de Burnside et Conjecture de Brzozowski. Rapport technique I.B.P.–L.I.T.P. 92.57, Paris, juillet 1992.

[Pin84] J. E. Pin. *Variétés de langages formels.* études et recherches en informatique. Masson, 1984.

Lecture Notes in Computer Science

For information about Vols. 1–840
please contact your bookseller or Springer-Verlag

Vol. 841: I. Prívara, B. Rovan, P. Ružička (Eds.), Mathematical Foundations of Computer Science 1994. Proceedings, 1994. X, 628 pages. 1994.

Vol. 842: T. Kloks, Treewidth. IX, 209 pages. 1994.

Vol. 843: A. Szepietowski, Turing Machines with Sublogarithmic Space. VIII, 115 pages. 1994.

Vol. 844: M. Hermenegildo, J. Penjam (Eds.), Programming Language Implementation and Logic Programming. Proceedings, 1994. XII, 469 pages. 1994.

Vol. 845: J.-P. Jouannaud (Ed.), Constraints in Computational Logics. Proceedings, 1994. VIII, 367 pages. 1994.

Vol. 846: D. Shepherd, G. Blair, G. Coulson, N. Davies, F. Garcia (Eds.), Network and Operating System Support for Digital Audio and Video. Proceedings, 1993. VIII, 269 pages. 1994.

Vol. 847: A. L. Ralescu (Ed.) Fuzzy Logic in Artificial Intelligence. Proceedings, 1993. VII, 128 pages. 1994. (Subseries LNAI).

Vol. 848: A. R. Krommer, C. W. Ueberhuber, Numerical Integration on Advanced Computer Systems. XIII, 341 pages. 1994.

Vol. 849: R. W. Hartenstein, M. Z. Servít (Eds.), Field-Programmable Logic. Proceedings, 1994. XI, 434 pages. 1994.

Vol. 850: G. Levi, M. Rodríguez-Artalejo (Eds.), Algebraic and Logic Programming. Proceedings, 1994. VIII, 304 pages. 1994.

Vol. 851: H.-J. Kugler, A. Mullery, N. Niebert (Eds.), Towards a Pan-European Telecommunication Service Infrastructure. Proceedings, 1994. XIII, 582 pages. 1994.

Vol. 852: K. Echtle, D. Hammer, D. Powell (Eds.), Dependable Computing – EDCC-1. Proceedings, 1994. XVII, 618 pages. 1994.

Vol. 853: K. Bolding, L. Snyder (Eds.), Parallel Computer Routing and Communication. Proceedings, 1994. IX, 317 pages. 1994.

Vol. 854: B. Buchberger, J. Volkert (Eds.), Parallel Processing: CONPAR 94 – VAPP VI. Proceedings, 1994. XVI, 893 pages. 1994.

Vol. 855: J. van Leeuwen (Ed.), Algorithms – ESA '94. Proceedings, 1994. X, 510 pages. 1994.

Vol. 856: D. Karagiannis (Ed.), Database and Expert Systems Applications. Proceedings, 1994. XVII, 807 pages. 1994.

Vol. 857: G. Tel, P. Vitányi (Eds.), Distributed Algorithms. Proceedings, 1994. X, 370 pages. 1994.

Vol. 858: E. Bertino, S. Urban (Eds.), Object-Oriented Methodologies and Systems. Proceedings, 1994. X, 386 pages. 1994.

Vol. 859: T. F. Melham, J. Camilleri (Eds.), Higher Order Logic Theorem Proving and Its Applications. Proceedings, 1994. IX, 470 pages. 1994.

Vol. 860: W. L. Zagler, G. Busby, R. R. Wagner (Eds.), Computers for Handicapped Persons. Proceedings, 1994. XX, 625 pages. 1994.

Vol: 861: B. Nebel, L. Dreschler-Fischer (Eds.), KI-94: Advances in Artificial Intelligence. Proceedings, 1994. IX, 401 pages. 1994. (Subseries LNAI).

Vol. 862: R. C. Carrasco, J. Oncina (Eds.), Grammatical Inference and Applications. Proceedings, 1994. VIII, 290 pages. 1994. (Subseries LNAI).

Vol. 863: H. Langmaack, W.-P. de Roever, J. Vytopil (Eds.), Formal Techniques in Real-Time and Fault-Tolerant Systems. Proceedings, 1994. XIV, 787 pages. 1994.

Vol. 864: B. Le Charlier (Ed.), Static Analysis. Proceedings, 1994. XII, 465 pages. 1994.

Vol. 865: T. C. Fogarty (Ed.), Evolutionary Computing. Proceedings, 1994. XII, 332 pages. 1994.

Vol. 866: Y. Davidor, H.-P. Schwefel, R. Männer (Eds.), Parallel Problem Solving from Nature - PPSN III. Proceedings, 1994. XV, 642 pages. 1994.

Vol 867: L. Steels, G. Schreiber, W. Van de Velde (Eds.), A Future for Knowledge Acquisition. Proceedings, 1994. XII, 414 pages. 1994. (Subseries LNAI).

Vol. 868: R. Steinmetz (Ed.), Multimedia: Advanced Teleservices and High-Speed Communication Architectures. Proceedings, 1994. IX, 451 pages. 1994.

Vol. 869: Z. W. Raś, Zemankova (Eds.), Methodologies for Intelligent Systems. Proceedings, 1994. X, 613 pages. 1994. (Subseries LNAI).

Vol. 870: J. S. Greenfield, Distributed Programming Paradigms with Cryptography Applications. XI, 182 pages. 1994.

Vol. 871: J. P. Lee, G. G. Grinstein (Eds.), Database Issues for Data Visualization. Proceedings, 1993. XIV, 229 pages. 1994.

Vol. 872: S Arikawa, K. P. Jantke (Eds.), Algorithmic Learning Theory. Proceedings, 1994. XIV, 575 pages. 1994.

Vol. 873: M. Naftalin, T. Denvir, M. Bertran (Eds.), FME '94: Industrial Benefit of Formal Methods. Proceedings, 1994. XI, 723 pages. 1994.

Vol. 874: A. Borning (Ed.), Principles and Practice of Constraint Programming. Proceedings, 1994. IX, 361 pages. 1994.

Vol. 875: D. Gollmann (Ed.), Computer Security – ESORICS 94. Proceedings, 1994. XI, 469 pages. 1994.

Vol. 876: B. Blumenthal, J. Gornostaev, C. Unger (Eds.), Human-Computer Interaction. Proceedings, 1994. IX, 239 pages. 1994.

Vol. 877: L. M. Adleman, M.-D. Huang (Eds.), Algorithmic Number Theory. Proceedings, 1994. IX, 323 pages. 1994.

Vol. 878: T. Ishida; Parallel, Distributed and Multiagent Production Systems. XVII, 166 pages. 1994. (Subseries LNAI).

Vol. 879: J. Dongarra, J. Waśniewski (Eds.), Parallel Scientific Computing. Proceedings, 1994. XI, 566 pages. 1994.

Vol. 880: P. S. Thiagarajan (Ed.), Foundations of Software Technology and Theoretical Computer Science. Proceedings, 1994. XI, 451 pages. 1994.

Vol. 881: P. Loucopoulos (Ed.), Entity-Relationship Approach – ER'94. Proceedings, 1994. XIII, 579 pages. 1994.

Vol. 882: D. Hutchison, A. Danthine, H. Leopold, G. Coulson (Eds.), Multimedia Transport and Teleservices. Proceedings, 1994. XI, 380 pages. 1994.

Vol. 883: L. Fribourg, F. Turini (Eds.), Logic Program Synthesis and Transformation – Meta-Programming in Logic. Proceedings, 1994. IX, 451 pages. 1994.

Vol. 884: J. Nievergelt, T. Roos, H.-J. Schek, P. Widmayer (Eds.), IGIS '94: Geographic Information Systems. Proceedings, 1994. VIII, 292 pages. 19944.

Vol. 885: R. C. Veltkamp, Closed Objects Boundaries from Scattered Points. VIII, 144 pages. 1994.

Vol. 886: M. M. Veloso, Planning and Learning by Analogical Reasoning. XIII, 181 pages. 1994. (Subseries LNAI).

Vol. 887: M. Toussaint (Ed.), Ada in Europe. Proceedings, 1994. XII, 521 pages. 1994.

Vol. 888: S. A. Andersson (Ed.), Analysis of Dynamical and Cognitive Systems. Proceedings, 1993. VII, 260 pages. 1995.

Vol. 889: H. P. Lubich, Towards a CSCW Framework for Scientific Cooperation in Europe. X, 268 pages. 1995.

Vol. 890: M. J. Wooldridge, N. R. Jennings (Eds.), Intelligent Agents. Proceedings, 1994. VIII, 407 pages. 1995. (Subseries LNAI).

Vol. 891: C. Lewerentz, T. Lindner (Eds.), Formal Development of Reactive Systems. XI, 394 pages. 1995.

Vol. 892: K. Pingali, U. Banerjee, D. Gelernter, A. Nicolau, D. Padua (Eds.), Languages and Compilers for Parallel Computing. Proceedings, 1994. XI, 496 pages. 1995.

Vol. 893: G. Gottlob, M. Y. Vardi (Eds.), Database Theory – ICDT '95. Proceedings, 1995. XI, 454 pages. 1995.

Vol. 894: R. Tamassia, I. G. Tollis (Eds.), Graph Drawing. Proceedings, 1994. X, 471 pages. 1995.

Vol. 895: R. L. Ibrahim (Ed.), Software Engineering Education. Proceedings, 1995. XII, 449 pages. 1995.

Vol. 896: R. N. Taylor, J. Coutaz (Eds.), Software Engineering and Human-Computer Interaction. Proceedings, 1994. X, 281 pages. 1995.

Vol. 897: M. Fisher, R. Owens (Eds.), Executable Modal and Temporal Logics. Proceedings, 1993. VII, 180 pages. 1995. (Subseries LNAI).

Vol. 898: P. Steffens (Ed.), Machine Translation and the Lexicon. Proceedings, 1993. X, 251 pages. 1995. (Subseries LNAI).

Vol. 899: W. Banzhaf, F. H. Eeckman (Eds.), Evolution and Biocomputation. VII, 277 pages. 1995.

Vol. 900: E. W. Mayr, C. Puech (Eds.), STACS 95. Proceedings, 1995. XIII, 654 pages. 1995.

Vol. 901: R. Kumar, T. Kropf (Eds.), Theorem Provers in Circuit Design. Proceedings, 1994. VIII, 303 pages. 1995.

Vol. 902: M. Dezani-Ciancaglini, G. Plotkin (Eds.), Typed Lambda Calculi and Applications. Proceedings, 1995. VIII, 443 pages. 1995.

Vol. 903: E. W. Mayr, G. Schmidt, G. Tinhofer (Eds.), Graph-Theoretic Concepts in Computer Science. Proceedings, 1994. IX, 414 pages. 1995.

Vol. 904: P. Vitányi (Ed.), Computational Learning Theory. EuroCOLT'95. Proceedings, 1995. XVII, 415 pages. 1995. (Subseries LNAI).

Vol. 905: N. Ayache (Ed.), Computer Vision, Virtual Reality and Robotics in Medicine. Proceedings, 1995. XIV, 567 pages. 1995.

Vol. 906: E. Astesiano, G. Reggio, A. Tarlecki (Eds.), Recent Trends in Data Type Specification. Proceedings, 1995. VIII, 523 pages. 1995.

Vol. 907: T. Ito, A. Yonezawa (Eds.), Theory and Practice of Parallel Programming. Proceedings, 1995. VIII, 485 pages. 1995.

Vol. 908: J. R. Rao Extensions of the UNITY Methodology: Compositionality, Fairness and Probability in Parallelism. XI, 178 pages. 1995.

Vol. 909: H. Comon, J.-P. Jouannaud (Eds.), Term Rewriting. Proceedings, 1993. VIII, 221 pages. 1995.

Vol. 910: A. Podelski (Ed.), Constraint Programming: Basics and Trends. Proceedings, 1995. XI, 315 pages. 1995.

Vol. 911: R. Baeza-Yates, E. Goles, P. V. Poblete (Eds.), LATIN '95: Theoretical Informatics. Proceedings, 1995. IX, 525 pages. 1995.

Vol. 912: N. Lavrač, S. Wrobel (Eds.), Machine Learning: ECML – 95. Proceedings, 1995. XI, 370 pages. 1995. (Subseries LNAI).

Vol. 913: W. Schäfer (Ed.), Software Process Technology. Proceedings, 1995. IX, 261 pages. 1995.

Vol. 914: J. Hsiang (Ed.), Rewriting Techniques and Applications. Proceedings, 1995. XII, 473 pages. 1995.

Vol. 915: P. D. Mosses, M. Nielsen, M. I. Schwartzbach (Eds.), TAPSOFT '95: Theory and Practice of Software Development. Proceedings, 1995. XV, 810 pages. 1995.

Vol. 916: N. R. Adam, B. K. Bhargava, Y. Yesha (Eds.), Digital Libraries. Proceedings, 1994. XIII, 321 pages. 1995.

Vol. 917: J. Pieprzyk, R. Safavi-Naini (Eds.), Advances in Cryptology - ASIACRYPT '94. Proceedings, 1994. XII, 431 pages. 1995.

Vol. 918: P. Baumgartner, R. Hähnle, J. Posegga (Eds.), Theorem Proving with Analytic Tableaux and Related Methods. Proceedings, 1995. X, 352 pages. 1995. (Subseries LNAI).

Vol. 919: B. Hertzberger, G. Serazzi (Eds.), High-Performance Computing and Networking. Proceedings, 1995. XXIV, 957 pages. 1995.